commonsense
Baking

✦ ✦ ✦ ✦ ✦ ✦ ✦ ✦

commonsense
Baking
•••••••••

more than 300
easy everyday
recipes

MURDOCH BOOKS

CONTENTS

INTRODUCTION

There are two things you need to know about baking. One—it's a miracle that a pile of flour, some shortening and a good blast of heat can form the base for such a varied and scrumptious array of food. Two—the sum of these raw materials is temperamental, moody and difficult, and will drive you mad if your first attempts at baking are not as successful as you'd hoped.

If this does happen to you, try not to feel discouraged. As well as making sure our recipe methods are clear and informative, we've given a lot of thought to the some of the problems you might encounter along the way, and have put together a series of 'what went wrong?' and 'hints and tips' pages to help you with your next baking adventure.

There is nothing quite as comforting, or irresistible, as the delicious smells of home baking—the rewards of taking a tray of freshly cooked delights from the oven are many. Whoever first came up with the idea of combining these three essentially simple ingredients—butter, sugar and flour—to make batters and doughs, was onto a very good thing.

For centuries, people have been turning flour into food with the help of little more than water. Today, baking remains a pleasure and a passion for many of us who have fallen in love with this fascinating and age-old tradition.

In this book you will find classic recipes from granny's day alongside refreshing takes on all-time favourites and fabulous contemporary recipes, which are bound to be passed from one generation to another. Some recipes are purely indulgent—making the most of luscious ingredients such as cream and chocolate, fresh dates and burstingly ripe berries. The ingredients in others—oats, seeds, semolina, dried fruits and nuts—are healthy enough to make them ideal for wholesome snacks or nutritious lunch box additions. Some are so simple they'll be a cinch to make with the kids, while others may be a little more time-consuming, and take a bit more of your patience and concentration—but the impression they will leave on your guests will be well worth your efforts.

There should be something for all tastes in this book. But it could be difficult deciding between making your own breakfast croissants, or taking on the culinary adventure of turning out panettone or some pissaladiere. You can opt for the decadence of those delicious perennials—chocolate mud cake or black forest cake, or turn out a batch of comparatively understated yet no less scrumptious pistachio friands. Will you choose the lightness of a classic sponge for afternoon tea or the rich indulgence of a fig and raspberry cake, which could easily double as a dessert?

When it comes to filling the cookie barrel, there's a tantalising range from traditional melting moments to florentines and mouth-watering Viennese fingers. Sometimes only a slice will suffice—macadamia blondies or sticky toffee slice perhaps? And you'll no longer need to head to your nearest café if you have a sudden urge for Portuguese custard tarts, lemon meringue pie, baklava or tarte tatin—all your essential baking recipes are right here.

In short, baking is back. And the range and quality of kitchen equipment now available makes the once arduous tasks of beating, whipping and kneading a breeze. Buy the best quality ingredients you can afford, borrow baking pans and beaters if you need to, and make a beeline for the kitchen!

It really is worth taking the time to learn the art of baking, and once you've mastered it, you'll be so proud of yourself, you'll wonder why you didn't get started years ago.

GLOSSARY

Terms used in recipes for baking sometimes seem mysterious but once understood, help you cook with confidence. Knowing the function of common ingredients also helps you on your way.

Bake blind means to partially or totally cook a pastry case before filling it. This prevents the pastry going soggy. Pastry should be partially cooked when it is going to be filled with an uncooked mixture, or fully cooked for fresh fruit flans. The uncooked pastry is lined with baking paper or foil and, to prevent it rising, it is filled with dried beans, uncooked rice or special-purpose beads.

Baking powder is a leavener used to aerate cakes, bread and buns. It is a mixture of bicarbonate of soda (baking soda), cream of tartar (an acid) and usually cornflour.

Batter is an uncooked mixture of flour, liquid and sometimes a leavener such as baking powder.

Beat means to briskly combine ingredients, usually with electric beaters but sometimes with a wooden spoon, to introduce air into a mixture to make it smooth and light.

Bicarbonate of soda, or baking soda, is both a component of baking powder and a leavener in its own right, one that gets its leavening power with the aid of acid in yoghurt, sour cream, crème fraîche, molasses or buttermilk.

Biscuit base or crumb crust This is crushed bought biscuits combined with melted butter and sometimes spices. The mixture is pressed onto the base and/or sides of a cake or tart tin. It can be baked or unbaked.

Bread dough is a mixture of flour, liquid, leaven (yeast) and sometimes other flavouring and enriching ingredients.

Butter is produced when the fat content of milk (the sweet cream) is separated from the liquid (the buttermilk). The fat globules are churned until they combine and become solid, forming butter. Butter is the most commonly used fat for cake-making as it creams well and has an acceptable flavour. We specify unsalted butter (also known as sweet butter) for use in baking biscuits, slices, cakes and sweet pastries.

Buttermilk is traditionally the liquid that is left after cream is churned into butter. It has a tangy flavour. Because of its acidic content it is used as a raising agent.

Chocolate is made from components extracted from cocoa beans which grow in pods on the cacao tree. Couverture chocolate is considered the best.

Cinnamon is the dried aromatic bark from the laurel family of trees native to Asia. The paper-thin inner bark is rolled and dried to form quills or sticks. The sticks are used as a flavour infusion in syrups and poached fruits. Ground cinnamon adds flavour to cakes, puddings, biscuits and yeast breads.

Cinnamon sugar is used to decorate cakes, before or after baking, and to flavour buttered toast. Caster sugar and ground cinnamon are combined in a proportion of four sugar to one (or more, to taste) cinnamon.

Cloves are the strongly scented flower buds of the clove tree which are sun-dried until hard. They contain essential oils and are used whole or ground in baking. The flavour marries especially well with apple.

Cocoa is ground into a powder from the dry solids left when the cocoa butter (the fat) is removed. It is used extensively in baking. Cocoa is usually sifted in with the dry ingredients so it is distributed evenly. Sweetened cocoa powder is sold as drinking chocolate. Dutch cocoa, available from delicatessens, is considered to be the best flavoured cocoa for baking. It is rich, dark in colour and unsweetened.

Cookie is an American term for biscuit. It was originally a small dry flat cake that was twice baked so that it would be crisp and also so it would keep longer. Today, the terms 'cookie' and 'biscuit' cover a wide range of baked goods from crispy to chewy.

Copha, or white vegetable shortening, is made from purified coconut oil that is processed into a white solid. Copha is generally used in making uncooked confections and slices or bar cookies.

Corn syrup is a liquid form of sugar refined from corn. A variety of corn syrups are produced, from light, which is less sweet, to dark, which is a caramel colour and has flavour added. Corn syrup adds flavour to baked products.

Cornflour or cornstarch is a fine white powder made from maize or corn (gluten-free) or from wheat. It is used in small quantities in baking, such as in sponges and shortbread, to produce a lighter texture. It is also used to thicken sauces and fillings because it forms a gel when heated. Cornflour is usually mixed to a paste with a small amount of cold liquid before being added to the remaining liquid.

Cream is the fat globules that rise to the top of milk. The fat content determines the type of cream. Cream is used extensively in baking, either as part of the mixture or whipped to decorate. For successful whipping, cream must have a fat content of at least 30 per cent and if the fat content is higher than this, a lighter foam results when the cream is whipped.

Cream of tartar is a component of baking powder. It acts as a raising agent when combined with bicarbonate of soda. Sometimes it is used to help stabilise the beating of egg whites, as in meringue.

Cream together means to beat one or more ingredients, usually butter and sugar, until light and fluffy. Electric beaters or a whisk can be used. The creaming process dissolves the sugar.

Crème fraîche is a naturally soured cream with a nutty, slightly sour taste. It makes for an interesting flavour to accompany sweet desserts, especially tarts. It is available at delicatessens.

Dust means to cover lightly, usually referring to icing sugar or cocoa powder that is sifted over the top of a cake or pie for presentation.

Eggs In baking, eggs enrich and also add flavour, moisture, nutritive value and yellow colour. They have three main functional properties in cooking—coagulation, emulsification and foaming ability. To maintain freshness, eggs should be refrigerated. Bring them back to room temperature before using them in baking.

Egg whites increase in volume when whisked, due to the entrapment of air. There are four stages in the whisking of whites. The first is the large bubble stage where the foam is frothy and unstable. The soft peak stage is where the whites form a glossy mass and just hold shape (folded into creams and cake mixtures). The next stage is medium peaks where the foam is very white and glossy—the peaks are soft and the tip falls a little (used for soufflés, mousses and ice creams). The final stage is stiff peaks where the bubbles are very fine and the peaks hold their shape (as in meringue). To successfully whisk by hand or beat with electric beaters, make sure all utensils are clean and free of grease and that the bowl is deep enough to hold the volume of whisked whites. Egg whites also act as leaveners, adding volume and texture to soufflés, flourless cakes and sponge cakes. The whisked whites are folded into the mixture just before baking. When cooked, the air is trapped and the mixture expands and coagulates.

Essences and extracts are flavourings that enhance the taste of food. Vanilla extract is used extensively in the baking of cakes and biscuits. Almond extract is also used to boost chopped or ground almond flavour in cakes. An extract is a stronger, purer concentration.

Evaporated milk is canned milk with most of its water removed. Diluted, it can be used as milk. Undiluted, it can replace cream. It is used to enrich sauces and moisten food. With the addition of lemon juice, chilled evaporated milk will whip to form a stable foam.

Fat or shortening contributes flavour, colour and shortness (tenderness) to shortcrust pastries, cakes and biscuits, and flakiness to layered pastries such as flaky and puff. Lard, butter, margarine and half butter/half lard, are all suitable fats for baking. Shredded suet is used in traditional baked pie crusts including steak and kidney pie. Oils are sometimes used in one-bowl or quick-mix cake mixtures such as carrot cake, resulting in a heavier texture. A little oil or butter is added to bread dough to add flavour and tenderness. Fat can be creamed with sugar, rubbed into the dry ingredients, melted and mixed into the dry ingredients, or kneaded into bread doughs.

Flour provides the basic structure of bread, cakes, batters and pastry. The process of manufacturing the whole grain where the grain is converted into a variety of flours is called milling. Wheat flour is the most versatile of all the flours. Roller milling produces all white flours and most wholemeal flours. Some wholemeal flours are produced by stone milling. Other non-wheat cereals are milled and used in cooking, for example cornflour, cornmeal, potato flour, rice flour and rye flour. These are not termed high-quality flours because, unlike wheat flour, they lack the protein gluten (the strength, elasticity and structure) necessary for baking. However, they are useful for people who are intolerant to wheat products. Bread dough made with non- or low-gluten flour does not have the elasticity of dough made with wheat-based flour so the bread will be dense. Plain white flour, also called all-purpose flour, has a medium protein content of about 10 per cent. Most baked goods use this flour. Self-raising flour has the same protein qualities as plain flour but has baking powder added to it. Self-raising flour can be made by adding 2 teaspoons of baking powder to 150 g (5$\frac{1}{2}$ oz/1 cup) of plain flour and then sifting thoroughly several times. Wholemeal flours are coarsely milled or finely ground and can be used instead of plain white flour. If you do use wholemeal, the baked product will have a denser crumb and less volume. Bread flour is produced from hard wheat that has a higher protein (gluten) content, about 12 per cent, than all-purpose bleached or white flour. It is smoother in texture and is used to ensure that the dough is elastic and strong so that the bread has structure, strength and elasticity. It is available in supermarkets and health food stores. Sometimes it is called strong flour.

Frangipane is creamed butter and sugar with eggs, ground almonds and a liqueur. It is used to fill a pastry or tart case.

Galettes are small open fruit tarts. They have a thin pastry base topped with raw sliced or halved fruit that is sprinkled with sugar, then dotted with butter and baked. Galettes are usually made with puff pastry, either home-made or bought, cut into individual rounds or squares, topped with the fruit and sugar and baked. They can also be made with filo or shortcrust pastry.

Gelatine is extracted from collagen, the connective tissue present in the bones and cartilage of animals. Gelatine is a setting agent available in powdered form and as leaves. 3 teaspoons of gelatine powder is equivalent to 6 leaves, which will set 500 ml (17 fl oz/2 cups) of liquid to a light jelly. To dissolve gelatine leaves, soften them in a bowl of cold water for 5 minutes, then remove and squeeze well. Next, dissolve them in warm to hot liquid. To dissolve gelatine powder, sprinkle the powder over a small bowl of water. Sit the bowl in a larger bowl of hot water and leave to dissolve. Agar-agar is a substitute suitable for vegetarian people.

Ginger Native to Southeast Asia, ginger is the rhizome or root of the ginger plant. It is available fresh or dried (ground). Fresh ginger should be bought while plump and firm with a pale outer skin. The powder is used in baking to flavour cakes, biscuits, puddings and gingerbread. Crystallised fresh ginger is used in cakes, desserts and as decoration.

Glacé fruit is fruit that is preserved in sugar. The fruit, usually citrus or pineapple slices, or cherries, is cooked in a strong syrup solution until the fruit is impregnated by the sugar. Cherries are often coloured with various food dyes.

Glaze is a liquid such as milk, sugar syrup, melted butter, softened and sieved jam, beaten whole egg, egg yolk and water, or egg white that is brushed onto food, often before baking to give colour and shine.

Gluten, a protein found in wheat flour, is the muscular substance of great elasticity that strengthens the cellular structure of bread dough. Without the elasticity qualities of gluten, bread is flat and heavy. Gluten flour or powder is often added to bread dough to provide more protein and therefore improved volume, structure and texture. Non-wheat flours, notably rye, oat, barley and corn, lack gluten.

If volume is wanted, these flours require added gluten in the form of gluten flour or the addition of some wheat flour. Breads made without the addition of gluten are heavy and dense, as in German rye bread, corn breads and oatcakes. Gluten flour or powder is available at health food shops and some supermarkets.

Golden syrup is a by-product of sugar refining. It is a thick sticky syrup with a deep golden colour and distinctive flavour. It is used in the baking of gingerbread, tarts and some breads to give flavour and moisture. It can be substituted for treacle in baked goods.

Icing sugar Pure icing (confectioners') sugar is powdered white sugar used in the making of icings (frostings) including buttercreams, glacé and royal, and fondants, to decorate cakes. It should be sifted before use to remove lumps and to obtain a smooth finish. **Icing sugar mixture** is icing sugar to which a small amount of starch has been added to prevent lumping during storage. It is used in the making of icings such as buttercreams and glacé, but is not suitable for royal icing. It is also known as confectioners' sugar.

Jams are traditionally made from whole ripe fruit that has been cooked to a pulp with sugar until it gels or sets. Jam heated and strained through a sieve, then brushed over the top of baked goods like cakes makes an attractive finish. Small amounts of jam or marmalade blended into a cake mixture add extra flavour and moisture.

Knead This means to work a bread dough with your hands on a flat floured surface. The dough is rhythmically pushed, stretched and folded in order to develop the gluten in the flour. It takes about 10 minutes for the gluten to be fully developed.

Knock back After the first rising, bread dough is 'knocked back' or punched down. This allows all the bubbles of carbon dioxide to be expelled, thus preventing the gluten walls from overstretching and collapsing. The dough is then ready to be shaped and left to rise a second time.

Lard is purified fat from pork. It is sold in solid form in packets and can be refrigerated for weeks. It is traditionally used in pastry-making. Lard is a good shortening (tenderising) agent but lacks flavour and colour, so a blend of butter and lard will produce the most tender pastry with more flavour.

Leavened is a term describing baked products such as breads and cakes that contain a raising agent, usually yeast or baking powder, to increase the volume of the goods.

Malt extract is produced from grain, a process that converts grain starch to a sugar called maltose. The resulting powder or syrup is used widely in baking, brewing and distilling. It retains moisture, thus giving malted breads their distinctive flavour and moist texture. It also aids in the rising of the bread dough.

Maple syrup is a light brown syrup processed from the sap of the maple tree. It is often used as a topping for pancakes.

Marzipan is a mixture of almond paste (meal), egg white and icing sugar. It is mainly used by rolling out thinly to cover fruit cakes before they are finished with a layer of royal icing. Marzipan can be shaped, then tinted with food dyes to resemble fruits, and used to decorate cakes.

Meringue is stabilised egg-white foam and dissolved sugar crystals, brought about by whisking. The quantity of sugar required per egg white in order to form a stable meringue varies from 50 to 75 grams. There are three types of meringue. Swiss meringue produces an externally crisp and dry texture usually with a dry centre. It is suitable for piping, pie toppings and pavlovas. The standard proportion is 50 to 60 grams of sugar per egg white.

Soft and creamy in texture, Italian meringue is more stable than the Swiss and is used as a cake frosting, for Baked Alaska, and sometimes in ice creams and whipped cream (crème chantilly). The basic proportion is 50 to 60 grams of sugar per egg white—a sugar syrup is first made, then slowly poured onto the beaten white.

Meringue cuite (cooked) is a very firm dry meringue mostly used by pastry cooks in the making of meringue baskets and meringue decorations that can be stored for a length of time. About 75 grams of icing sugar per egg white is used for this.

Meringues need to be baked at a very low temperature, preferably in an electric oven, as they need to dry out and maintain their white colour.

Mixed peel is a mixture of chopped citrus fruit peel preserved in sugar and glucose syrup. It is mainly used in fruit cakes, mince pies and dried fruit puddings.

Mixed spice is a blend of ground spices, usually allspice, cinnamon, nutmeg, cloves and ginger. It adds a lightly spicy flavour to cooked fruit such as apples, and to cakes, fruit cakes, puddings and biscuits.

Nutmeg is the dried kernel or seed of the fruit of an evergreen tree native to Southeast Asia. The nutmeg kernel is grated whole or used in powder form to flavour cakes and desserts.

Nuts are formed after a tree or plant has flowered. They are the hardened and dried fruit encased in tough shells that have to be cracked to open (such as macadamias and chestnuts). However, the term 'nut' is also used to describe any seed or fruit with an edible kernel in a hard or brittle shell (almonds, walnuts and coconuts). Nuts are used extensively in baking. Because of their high fat content it is advisable to refrigerate nuts in an airtight container to prevent them turning rancid.

Oils are similar to fats but differ in their physical state. Oils are liquid at room temperature and fats are solid. Animal fats (i.e. saturated fats) that are used in baking include butter, cream, ghee, lard and suet. Vegetable oils (i.e. polyunsaturated and monounsaturated fats), include fruit oils (olive oil), nut oils (walnut, hazelnut), seed oils (sesame, sunflower), pulse oils (soybean) and cereal oils (corn). All are used in one form or the other for the baking of cakes, biscuits, desserts, puddings and breads. Oils enhance the flavour and moistness in baked products.

Organic ingredients have generally been produced without the use of pesticides, insecticides, herbicides, fungicides or artificial fertilisers.

Powdered milk is milk from which most of the moisture has been removed. The resulting milk powder can be stored in airtight tins or foil bags for up to a year. It is reconstituted to milk by adding water, or can be used in its powder form to enrich baked products, especially bread doughs. Powdered milks are made from both full-fat and non-fat (skim) milk.

Proving (also called the second rise) describes the process of the bread dough being knocked back, then shaped and left to rise on its baking tray until doubled in bulk, before baking.

Ribbon stage Eggs and sugar are beaten, either with an electric beater or hand whisk, until the sugar has dissolved and the egg becomes pale with small bubbles. The beater or whisk will leave a raised mark on top of the mixture when the ribbon stage is reached. The term is used when sponge cakes are being made. The result of the beating is a very light aerated cake.

Salt is used as a seasoning, preservative and flavour enhancer. Salt improves the balance of flavours in sweet baking goods. Iodised salt, often used as table salt, has a trace element of iodine added. Maldon salt, or sea salt, is produced in Essex in the UK and is made by extracting sea salt by natural means. Rock salt is mined from under the ground.

Suet is the fat that surrounds the kidneys of beef cattle. It is often used in dried fruit puddings. Fresh suet can be bought from a butcher. Dried, shredded suet can be found at supermarkets. Butter can be used instead.

Sugar is the common name for sucrose, the simplest form of carbohydrate. There are several types of sugar. The most widely used is white sugar (granulated, caster, cubed and icing sugar). It is usually manufactured from sugar cane or sugar beet and is used extensively in baking and general table use.

Coloured sugars, also manufactured from sugar cane, include brown sugar, often known as soft brown sugar, a golden brown refined sugar, which is used in baked goods. These sugars add colour and flavour and help create a moist texture. Brown sugar is also available as dark brown sugar. The colour in these sugars comes from the molasses content.

Raw sugar, coarse straw-coloured crystals, is also produced from sugar cane. It can be substituted for white sugar to add texture, but is difficult to dissolve. Demerara sugar, a coarse amber-coloured crystal, similar to raw sugar, is also used in baking, especially in crumble topping.

Treacle is a blend of concentrated refinery syrups and extract molasses. It is used in baking to give a distinctive colour and flavour. It also adds moistness and keeping qualities to a baked product. Golden syrup can be substituted in baking.

Vanilla is extracted from the pods of a climbing orchid plant native to South America. The pods or beans are dried and cured. For use in cooking, the pod is split open and infused with the food to allow for maximum flavour. Vanilla is also available as pure essence or extract, which has a more concentrated flavour and is widely used in cakes, biscuits and desserts.

Vanilla sugar is made by placing a whole vanilla pod or bean in a jar of caster sugar and leaving it to stand so the flavour can be absorbed into the sugar.

Yeast is a biological (naturally occurring) raising agent. Fresh yeast (compressed) needs to be blended with water to form a smooth cream, then added to any remaining liquid and left to foam before being added to the dry ingredients. Dried yeast, available in long-life sachets from supermarkets, can be added to liquid or mixed straight into the dry ingredients. For fermentation of the yeast to take place, it needs the right conditions of food (sugar), warmth (26–29°C) and moisture (liquid).

Zest or rind is the outside rind of any citrus fruit. The rind contains all the essential oils and therefore the flavour. Grated or shredded rind is used to flavour cakes, biscuits, syrups and doughs.

BASIC UTENSILS

Lattice cutters For topping pies and tarts, these simplify cutting a lattice pattern into rolled out pastry.

Rolling pins These should be big enough to roll out a full sheet of pastry. Good-quality rolling pins are made from hardwood with a close grain and smooth finish.

Flour sieves and dredgers These are ideal for incorporating air into flour or dusting flour onto work surfaces. They can also be used when decorating or dusting with icing sugar or cocoa.

Baking beads Reusable ceramic or metal beads used when blind baking pastry. Dried beans or uncooked rice can be used instead.

Wooden spoons These are useful for beating, mixing and stirring because they do not conduct heat or scratch non-stick surfaces. Choose spoons made from hard, close-grained wood.

Metal spoons Large metal spoons are best for folding in dry ingredients, or combining one mixture with another without losing too much air.

Piping bags and nozzles Piping bags of different sizes accommodate metal or plastic nozzles with various shaped openings.

Graters Graters with perforations of different sizes are designed for specific functions, from grating cheese to citrus zest. Nutmeg graters are small and concave.

Dough scrapers These are used to divide, separate and scrape dough on a work surface. They are used mainly for pastry and bread doughs.

Cutters These come in a various shapes and sizes, ranging from plain and fluted rounds to hearts and gingerbread people. Metal cutters have a better edge than plastic.

Cooling racks These footed metal grids enable air to circulate around baked food during cooling.

Citrus juicers These are available in glass, ceramic, plastic and wood, as well as electric.

LATTICE CUTTER

FLOUR SIEVES and DREDGERS (top)
BAKING BEADS (bottom)

DOUGH SCRAPER

ROLLING PINS

GRATERS

WOODEN SPOON (left)
and METAL SPOON (right)

PIPING BAGS AND NOZZLES

CUTTERS

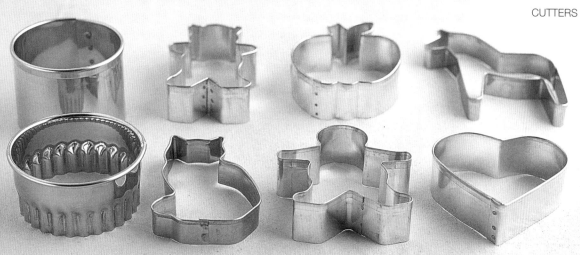

Oven thermometers These stand or hang in the oven. Always check the accuracy of the oven temperature when baking.

Whisks Whisks beat air into ingredients and remove any lumps.

Apple corers These have a blade that fits around an applecore and removes it without damaging the shape of the fruit.

Citrus zesters Zesters have a row of holes with sharp edges running across the top. They peel off the zest in thin shreds.

Metal skewers Long and thin with a sharp, pointed edge, these are useful for testing to see if a cake is cooked through.

Pastry brushes Made with nylon or natural bristles, these can be flat or round and are used for glazing.

Pastry wheels These are metal or plastic wheels used for cutting fluted edges on pastry.

Scales Essential for weighing ingredients, kitchen scales vary from balance scales to digital display.

Measuring cups and spoons All spoon and cup measures in this book are level. Dry ingredients should be levelled off.

Sifters A hand sifter is used to aerate lumpy flour.

Palette knives These are available in various sizes and degrees of flexibility. The blade is thin and flat with a rounded end and is useful for transferring biscuits and for spreading decorative icings.

Paring knives With a short blade, these are a handy all-purpose knife. They are perfect for cutting fruit.

Serrated knives These are best for slicing through bread and cakes neatly and evenly.

Spatulas These are useful for scraping a bowl clean.

Mixers These can be hand-held or table models. They make creaming mixtures, mixing batters and whisking whites easier.

Mixing bowls Stainless steel bowls are durable and are good conductors of heat and cold. Heatproof bowls are essential for slow heating over a water bath.

OVEN THERMOMETER

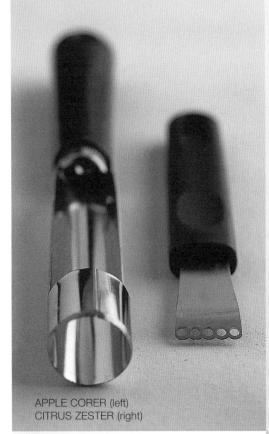

APPLE CORER (left)
CITRUS ZESTER (right)

SIFTER

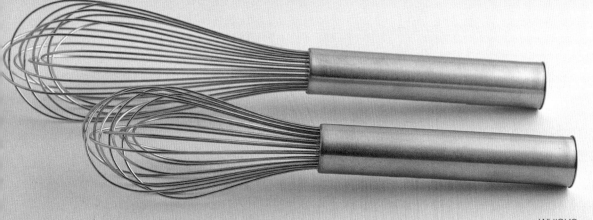

WHISKS

PASTRY BRUSHES and PASTRY WHEEL

METAL SKEWERS

SCALES

MEASURING CUPS and SPOONS

PALETTE KNIVES (top) and SPATULAS (bottom)

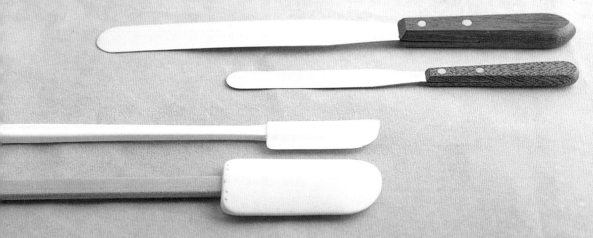

BREAD TINS

CAKE and SLAB TINS

ROUND TINS
1. Deep tins **2.** Shallow or sandwich tins **3.** Genoise tin
4. Fluted tart tins with removable base

1

2

3

4

BAKING TRAY, SLICE TINS and LOAF TINS
1. Non-stick loaf tin **2.** Loaf tin **3.** Swiss roll tin **4.** Baking or biscuit tray **5.** Bar tin **6.** Slice or brownie tin **7.** Loaf tin

1

2

3

4

5

6

7

SPECIALITY CAKE TINS

1. Angel food tin **2.** Deep fluted ring tin **3.** Round spring-form tins **4.** Nut-roll tin **5.** Charlotte tin **6.** Fluted baba tin **7.** Savarin tin **8.** Kugelhopf tin **9.** Tube tin

MUFFIN and SMALL CAKE TINS

1. Shallow patty tins **2.** Mini muffin tins **3.** Texas muffin tins **4.** Regular muffin tins **5.** Madeleine tins **6.** Friand tins

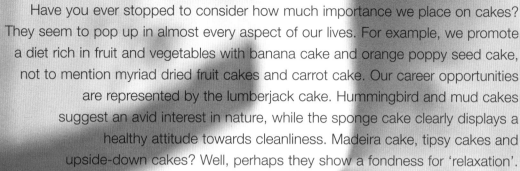

Have you ever stopped to consider how much importance we place on cakes? They seem to pop up in almost every aspect of our lives. For example, we promote a diet rich in fruit and vegetables with banana cake and orange poppy seed cake, not to mention myriad dried fruit cakes and carrot cake. Our career opportunities are represented by the lumberjack cake. Hummingbird and mud cakes suggest an avid interest in nature, while the sponge cake clearly displays a healthy attitude towards cleanliness. Madeira cake, tipsy cakes and upside-down cakes? Well, perhaps they show a fondness for 'relaxation'.

CAKES

PREPARING TINS

Preparation of cake tins varies according to the type of cake you are baking. For some cakes, greasing and flouring the tin is sufficient to prevent the batter sticking to the tin, and for the cake to easily turn out of the tin once cooked. Use melted, unsalted butter to grease tins, unless the recipe suggests otherwise.

Greasing tins Apply melted, unsalted butter or oil evenly using a pastry brush. Vegetable sprays can also be used.
Lining tins Greaseproof paper and non-stick baking paper are both good for lining cake tins. If you use greaseproof, it will need to be greased.
Dusting with flour Let the greased tin or paper dry off a little before dusting with plain (all-purpose) flour. Turn the tin to evenly coat the base and sides. Shake off any excess before spooning in the mixture.
Lining round tins Place the tin base on a square of baking paper, draw around it and cut out as marked. Cut a strip of baking paper the same length as the circumference of the tin and about 3 cm (1 1/4 in) deeper than the height. Fold down a cuff about 2 cm (3/4 in) deep on one edge of the strip. Cut the folded cuff diagonally at 2 cm (3/4 in) intervals. Grease the tin. Place the baking paper strip in the tin with the folded side on the base. The cut strip will act like pleats and sit on the base. Press the baking paper into the base and side. Place the round of baking paper on the base over the pleats.
Lining square tins Place the tin base on a square of baking paper, draw around the base, then cut out as marked. Cut a strip of baking paper the same length as the outside of the tin and about 1 cm (1/2 in) deeper than the height. Grease the base and sides of the tin. Place the square of baking paper in the base and the strip around the inside of the tin, pressing into the sides.

Lining swiss roll tins Place the tin base on a square of baking paper and draw around it. Measure the depth of the tin, add 2 cm (3/4 in), then measure that distance from the drawn line and cut at that distance all around. Crease the paper along the drawn lines, then cut a diagonal line from each outside corner to the nearest drawn corner. Grease the tin. Press the paper down into the base and sides of the tin.
Butter cakes and chocolate cakes For these cakes, you will need to line both the base and sides of the tin. Many bakers only line the base of the tin for butter cakes and this will work in most cases. However, if you have the time, it is better to line the sides as well to be sure the cake doesn't stick to the tin. Baba tins and kugelhopf tins need to be greased and lightly floured.
Sponge cakes For easy removal, the tins must be greased and the bases lined, then the whole tin dusted with flour.
Rich fruit cakes These cakes need to be cooked in tins which have the base and sides lined with a double thickness of paper but it is generally not necessary to grease the paper. Lining fruit cake tins is fully explained on pages 72–73.
To collar a cake tin Lightly grease a cake tin, then cut a strip of baking paper long enough to fit around the outside of the tin and tall enough to extend 5 cm (2 in) above the top. Fold down one cuff, about 2 cm (3/4 in) deep, along the length of the strip. Make diagonal cuts up to the fold line about 1 cm (1/2 in) apart. Fit the collar around the inside edge of the tin, with the cuts in the base, pressing the cuts out at right angles so they sit flat around the base. Cut a piece of paper to fit in the base, using the tin as a guide, and place in the tin over the cuts in the collar. A collar extends the height of a cake and gives extra protection. A single layer of baking paper is enough for a collar on an average-sized cake. Larger cakes and fruit cakes need two layers of paper for the collar and base.

HINTS AND TIPS

1 Before you start baking, read the recipe thoroughly and check you have the correct quantity of ingredients and the necessary equipment.

2 Bring chilled ingredients, such as butter and eggs, to room temperature.

3 Always use the shape and size of tin specified in each recipe, so as to ensure cooking times are accurate. Line the tin(s) as specified in the recipe, or grease or dust with flour.

4 Position a shelf in the centre of the oven, ensuring there is enough room above it to allow room for the cake to rise. Preheat the oven to the required temperature.

5 Always weigh and measure ingredients accurately, either with scales or cup measures (although cup measures are never as accurate as weighing the ingredients).

6 If melting ingredients in a saucepan, never allow the mixture to boil unless specified in the recipe.

7 Eggs or egg yolks should always be added to a creamed cake mixture one at a time, beating well after each addition.

8 If the creamed mixture looks like it may be starting to curdle, sift in a little of the flour alternately with each egg to prevent this occuring.

9 A raising agent should always be sifted into the bowl with the flour so that it is evenly dispersed.

10 When whisking egg whites, ensure the bowl and beaters (or whisk) are clean and dry before you start, or the egg whites won't whisk properly. The egg whites should always be at room temperature before whisking.

11 Dry ingredients should always be folded into a whisked egg and sugar mixture with a large metal spoon. Fold lightly and gently from the centre of the bowl outwards, turning the bowl a little with each fold. Fold whisked egg whites into the other ingredients (not the other way round), so as to retain as much aeration as possible.

12 Spoon thick cake batters into a tin. Gently pour thinner batters into a tin. If necessary, smooth the surface of the batter using a spatula to ensure even cooking and browning.

13 Never open the oven door during the first half of cooking time. After the halfway point, if you do need to open the door, open and close it gently.

14 If the cooked cake is stuck to the cake tin, run a palette knife gently between the cake and tin before unmoulding.

15 Allow the cake to cool a little before inverting it onto a wire rack to cool. So the wire rack does not mark the top of the cake, place another wire rack on the base of the cake and invert the cake onto the second rack so it is right side up.

16 If you intend to ice the cake, allow it to cool completely first. If you intend to drizzle it with hot syrup, however, do this while the cake is still hot.

BUTTER CAKES

If you follow our helpful hints you will have no trouble making a delicious butter cake which can be stored for a couple of days, wrapped tightly in plastic wrap.

EQUIPMENT

It is crucial to use the correct-sized tin. For this basic butter cake you will need a 20 cm (8 in) round tin. Lightly grease the base and side with melted unsalted butter or oil. Use a pastry brush to apply an even layer. Line the tin (see pages 22–23) with baking paper or greaseproof and brush the paper with melted unsalted butter or oil.

It is also essential to have a set of standard measuring cups and spoons and an accurate set of kitchen scales. You will also need a small and large mixing bowl, a metal spoon, a large sieve, a rubber spatula and an electric mixer. If the quantities are not too great, adequate results can be obtained using a hand-held electric beater or mixing by hand, but the mixing time increases considerably.

The butter, eggs and liquid should be at room temperature. The butter should be malleable, not melted or very soft.

OVEN

An accurate oven temperature is vital so invest in an oven thermometer. The recipes in this book have all been tested in a conventional (not fan-forced) oven.

BUTTER CAKE

To make one cake, you will need 185 g (6 oz/1$\frac{1}{2}$ cups) self-raising flour, 60 g (2 oz/$\frac{1}{2}$ cup) plain (all-purpose) flour, 185 g (6 oz) chopped unsalted butter, softened, 185 g (6 oz/$\frac{3}{4}$ cup) caster (superfine) sugar, 3 lightly beaten eggs, 1 teaspoon natural vanilla extract and 60 ml (2 fl oz/$\frac{1}{4}$ cup) milk. Preheat the oven to 180°C (375°F/Gas 4).

This cake is made using the creaming method, which is the most frequently used technique in cake-making. The first step is to sift the flours to aerate and separate the particles. Cream the butter and sugar in a small bowl by beating at speed until light and fluffy. The mixture will almost double in volume and should have no trace of the sugar granules. Scrape the side of the bowl with a spatula several times during the creaming process to make sure the butter and sugar are well incorporated. This initial creaming process can take up to 8 minutes.

With the beaters still running, gradually add the egg, a little at a time, beating thoroughly after each addition. Add the vanilla extract and beat well to combine.

Transfer the mixture to a large mixing bowl. Using a metal spoon, gently fold in the sifted flour and the milk. Stir until just combined and almost smooth. Take care with this final stage, mixing the ingredients lightly. Over-enthusiastic beating can produce a heavy, coarse-textured cake.

Next, gently spoon or pour the mixture into the tin, spread out evenly and smooth the surface. Check the oven temperature.

For best results when baking a cake, position an oven rack in the lower third of the oven so the top of the cake is in the middle of the oven.

Centre the cake tin on the oven rack and bake for 45 minutes. The cake is cooked when it begins to shrink from the side of the tin and is lightly golden. If gently pressed with a finger, it should spring back into shape. As a final check, insert a fine skewer in the centre—it should come out clean, without any moisture. Avoid opening the oven door until at least two-thirds of the way through baking.

A cake is fragile when removed from the oven, so leave in the tin for 10 minutes before turning out onto a wire rack to cool. If the cake is stuck to the tin, gently run a flat-bladed knife around the side to release it. Remove the paper lining immediately.

WHAT WENT WRONG?

BUTTER CAKES

Perfect The texture is light, moist and even, with a golden brown crust. When a skewer is inserted into the centre of the cake, it comes out clean. The cake springs back when pressed lightly with a fingertip.

Overcooked The top of the cake is very dark and the texture of the cake crumb quite dry. The cooking time may have been too long or the cooking temperature too high. It's also possible that the tin was the wrong size or that the cake was placed too high in the oven.

Undercooked and sunken The centre of the cake is sunken and when a skewer is inserted into the centre, it comes out sticky. The cake has a soggy, dense texture. The cooking time may have been too short or the oven temperature too low. Too little flour or too much butter may have been used in the recipe. The oven door may have been opened during the early stages of cooking.

APPLE TEACAKE

Preparation time **20 minutes +**
Total cooking time **1 hour**
Serves **8**

150 g (5¹/₂ oz) unsalted butter, chopped
200 g (7 oz/1 cup) caster (superfine) sugar
2 eggs, lightly beaten
1 teaspoon natural vanilla extract
185 g (6¹/₂ oz/1¹/₂ cups) self-raising flour, sifted
185 g (6¹/₂ oz/³/₄ cup) vanilla-flavoured yoghurt
1 apple (granny smith), peeled, cored and
  thinly sliced
1 teaspoon ground cinnamon

1 Preheat the oven to 180°C (350°F/Gas 4).
Grease a deep 20 cm (8 in) round cake tin
and line the base with baking paper.
2 Beat 130 g (4¹/₂ oz) of the butter and
185 g (6¹/₂ oz/³/₄ cup) of the sugar with
electric beaters until light and creamy.
3 Gradually add the egg, beating well after
each addition until combined. Add the
natural vanilla extract. Fold in the flour,
then the yoghurt and stir until smooth.
Spoon the mixture into the prepared tin
and smooth the surface.
4 Arrange the apple slices over the mixture
in a circular pattern starting in the centre.
Sprinkle with the cinnamon and remaining
sugar. Melt the remaining butter, then
drizzle over the top.
5 Bake for 1 hour, or until a skewer comes
out clean when inserted into the centre of
the cake. Leave in the tin for 30 minutes
before turning out onto a wire rack to cool.
If desired, combine a little extra cinnamon
and sugar and sprinkle over the apple.

CLASSIC SPONGE

Preparation time **20 minutes** +
Total cooking time **25 minutes**
Serves **8**

75 g (2³/4 oz) plain (all-purpose) flour
150 g (5¹/2 oz) self-raising flour
6 eggs
220 g (7³/4 oz) caster (superfine) sugar
2 tablespoons boiling water
160 g (5³/4 oz/¹/2 cup) strawberry jam
250 ml (9 fl oz/1 cup) pouring (whipping) cream
icing (confectioners') sugar, to dust

1 Preheat the oven to 180°C (350°F/Gas 4).
Grease two 22 cm (8¹/2 in) sandwich tins
or round cake tins and line the bases with
baking paper. Dust the tins with a little
flour, shaking off any excess.
2 Sift the flours together three times
onto a sheet of baking paper. Beat the
eggs in a large bowl using electric beaters
for 7 minutes, or until thick and pale.
Gradually add the sugar to the egg, beating
thoroughly after each addition. Using a
large metal spoon, quickly and gently fold
in the sifted flour and boiling water.
3 Spread the mixture evenly into the tins
and bake for 25 minutes, or until the
sponges are lightly golden and shrink
slightly from the sides of the tins. Leave
the sponges in their tins for 5 minutes
before turning out onto a wire rack to cool.
4 Spread jam over one of the sponges. Beat
the cream in a small bowl until stiff, then
spoon into a piping (icing) bag and pipe
rosettes over the jam. Place the other
sponge on top. Dust with icing sugar.
Notes The secret to making a perfect
sponge lies in the folding technique. A
beating action, or using a wooden spoon,
will cause loss of volume in the egg mixture
and result in a flat, heavy cake.

Unfilled sponges can be frozen for up
to 1 month—freeze in separate freezer
bags. Thaw at room temperature for about
20 minutes. Once a sponge is filled, it is
best served immediately.

DEVIL'S FOOD CAKE

Preparation time **20 minutes +**
Total cooking time **50 minutes**
Serves **8**

165 g (5³/₄ oz/1¹/₃ cups) plain (all-purpose)
   flour
85 g (3 oz/²/₃ cup) unsweetened cocoa powder
1 teaspoon bicarbonate of soda (baking soda)
250 g (9 oz/1 cup) sugar
250 ml (9 fl oz/1 cup) buttermilk
2 eggs, lightly beaten
125 g (4¹/₂ oz) unsalted butter, softened
125 ml (4 fl oz/¹/₂ cup) whipping cream
icing (confectioners') sugar, to dust
fresh raspberries and blueberries, to garnish

1 Preheat the oven to 180°C (350°F/Gas 4).
Grease a deep 20 cm (8 in) round cake tin
and line the base with baking paper.
2 Sift the flour, cocoa and bicarbonate of
soda (baking soda) into a large bowl. Add
the sugar to the sifted dry ingredients.

Combine the buttermilk, eggs and butter,
then pour onto the dry ingredients. Beat
using electric beaters on low speed for
3 minutes, or until just combined. Increase
the speed to high and beat for 3 minutes,
or until the mixture is free of lumps and
increased in volume.
3 Spoon the mixture into the prepared tin
and smooth the surface.
4 Bake for 40–50 minutes, or until a skewer
comes out clean when inserted into the
centre of the cake. Leave in the tin for
15 minutes before turning out onto a wire
rack to cool completely.
5 Whip the cream using electric beaters
until soft peaks form. Cut the cake in half
horizontally and fill with whipped cream.
Dust with icing sugar and garnish with
fresh raspberries and blueberries.
Note Unfilled, the cake will keep for
3 days in an airtight container. The filled
cake is best assembled and eaten on the
day of baking.

ANGEL FOOD CAKE WITH CHOCOLATE SAUCE

Preparation time **20 minutes +**
Total cooking time **50 minutes**
Serves **8**

125 g (4½ oz/1 cup) plain (all-purpose) flour
250 g (9 oz/1 cup) caster (superfine) sugar
10 egg whites, at room temperature
1 teaspoon cream of tartar
½ teaspoon natural vanilla extract

Chocolate sauce
250 g (9 oz) dark chocolate, chopped
185 ml (6 fl oz/¾ cup) pouring (whipping) cream
50 g (1¾ oz) unsalted butter, chopped

1 Preheat the oven to 180°C (350°F/Gas 4). Have an ungreased angel cake tin ready.
2 Sift the flour and 125 g (4½ oz/½ cup) of the sugar four times into a large bowl. Set aside.

3 Beat the egg whites, cream of tartar and ¼ teaspoon salt in a clean, large bowl with electric beaters until soft peaks form. Gradually add the remaining sugar and beat until thick and glossy.
4 Add the natural vanilla extract. Sift half the flour and sugar mixture over the meringue and gently fold into the mixture with a metal spoon. Repeat with the remaining flour and sugar.
5 Spoon into the cake tin and bake for 45 minutes, or until a skewer comes out clean when inserted into the centre of the cake. Gently loosen around the side of the cake with a spatula, then turn the cake out onto a wire rack to cool completely.
6 To make the sauce, heat the chocolate, cream and butter in a saucepan over low heat until the mixture is smooth. Drizzle over the cake and serve.
Note Ensure the tin is very clean and not greased or the cake will not rise and will slip down the side of the tin.

HUMMINGBIRD CAKE

Preparation time 30 minutes +
Total cooking time 1 hour
Serves 8–10

2 ripe bananas, mashed
130 g (4³/₄ oz/¹/₂ cup) drained and crushed
  tinned pineapple (see Note)
285 g (10¹/₄ oz/1¹/₄ cups) caster (superfine)
  sugar
210 g (7¹/₂ oz/1²/₃ cups) self-raising flour
2 teaspoons ground cinnamon
170 ml (5¹/₂ fl oz/²/₃ cup) oil
60 ml (2 fl oz/¹/₄ cup) pineapple juice
2 eggs

Icing (frosting)
60 g (2¹/₄ oz) unsalted butter, softened
125 g (4¹/₂ oz/¹/₂ cup) cream cheese, softened
185 g (6¹/₂ oz/1¹/₂ cups) icing (confectioners')
  sugar
1–2 teaspoons lemon juice

1 Preheat the oven to 180°C (350°F/Gas 4).
Lightly grease a 20 cm (8 in) square cake tin and line with baking paper.
2 Place the banana, pineapple and sugar in a large bowl. Add the sifted flour and cinnamon or mixed spice. Stir together with a wooden spoon until well combined.
3 Whisk together the oil, pineapple juice and eggs. Pour onto the banana mixture and stir until combined and the mixture is smooth.
4 Spoon into the tin and smooth the surface. Bake for 1 hour, or until a skewer inserted into the centre of the cake comes out clean. Leave in the tin for 15 minutes before turning out onto a wire rack to cool.
5 To make the icing, beat the butter and cream cheese using electric beaters until smooth. Gradually add the icing sugar alternately with the lemon juice. Beat until thick and creamy.
6 Spread the icing thickly over the top of the cooled cake.
Note If you are unable to buy crushed pineapple, use pineapple rings chopped very finely. Buy the fruit in natural juice and reserve the juice to use in the recipe.

BANANA CAKE

Preparation time **20 minutes +**
Total cooking time **1 hour**
Serves **8**

125 g (4 1/2 oz) unsalted butter, softened
115 g (4 oz/1/2 cup) caster (superfine)
    sugar
2 eggs, lightly beaten
1 teaspoon natural vanilla extract
4 very ripe bananas, mashed
1 teaspoon bicarbonate of soda (baking soda)
125 ml (4 fl oz/1/2 cup) milk
250 g (9 oz/2 cups) self-raising flour, sifted
1/2 teaspoon ground mixed (pumpkin pie) spice
15 g (1/2 oz/1/4 cup) flaked coconut, toasted

Butter frosting

125 g (4 1/2 oz) unsalted butter, softened
90 g (3 1/4 oz/3/4 cup) icing (confectioners')
    sugar
1 tablespoon lemon juice

1 Preheat the oven to 180°C (350°F/Gas 4).
Lightly grease a 20 cm (8 in) round cake tin and line the base with baking paper.
2 Cream the butter and sugar in a small bowl using electric beaters until light and creamy. Add the egg gradually, beating thoroughly after each addition. Add the vanilla and banana and beat until combined. Transfer to a large bowl.
3 Dissolve the bicarbonate of soda in the milk. Using a metal spoon, gently fold the sifted flour and mixed spice alternately with the milk into the banana mixture. Stir until all the ingredients are just combined and the mixture is smooth. Spoon into the prepared tin and smooth the surface.
4 Bake for 1 hour, or until a skewer inserted into the centre of the cake comes out clean. Leave the cake in the tin for 10 minutes before turning out onto a wire rack to cool completely.
5 To make the frosting, beat the butter, icing sugar and lemon juice using electric beaters until smooth and creamy. Spread over the cooled cake using a flat-bladed knife and sprinkle with the toasted coconut flakes.

PINEAPPLE UPSIDE-DOWN CAKE

Preparation time **20 minutes** +
Total cooking time **40 minutes**
Serves **6–8**

20 g (½ oz) unsalted butter, melted
2 tablespoons firmly packed soft brown sugar
440 g (1 lb) tinned pineapple rings in
   natural juice
90 g (3¼ oz) unsalted butter, extra, softened
125 g (4½ oz/½ cup) caster (superfine) sugar
2 eggs, lightly beaten
1 teaspoon natural vanilla extract
125 g (4½ oz/1 cup) self-raising flour

1 Preheat the oven to 180°C (350°F/Gas 4). Lightly grease a 20 cm (8 in) ring tin.

2 Pour the melted butter into the base of the tin and tip to evenly coat. Sprinkle with the brown sugar.

3 Drain the pineapple and reserve 80 ml (2½ fl oz/⅓ cup) of the juice. Cut the pineapple rings in half. Arrange on the base.

4 Beat the extra butter and the caster sugar using electric beaters until creamy. Add the egg gradually, beating well after each addition. Add the vanilla extract and beat until combined. Fold in the flour alternately with the reserved juice.

5 Spoon the mixture evenly over the pineapple and smooth the surface. Bake for 35–40 minutes, or until a skewer comes out clean when inserted into the centre of the cake. Leave in the tin for 10 minutes before turning out onto a wire rack to cool.

COCONUT SYRUP CAKE

Preparation time **10 minutes** +
Total cooking time **50 minutes**
Serves 12

200 g (7 oz) unsalted butter, softened
375 g (13 oz/1½ cups) caster (superfine) sugar
6 eggs
185 g (6½ oz/1½ cups) self-raising flour
270 g (9¾ oz/3 cups) desiccated coconut

Syrup
1 tablespoon lemon zest
375 g (13 oz/1½ cups) sugar

1 Preheat the oven to 180°C (350°F/Gas 4). Grease and flour a 2-litre (70 fl oz/8 cup) fluted baba tin or tube tin.

2 Shake off the excess flour. Beat the butter and sugar together with electric beaters for 5 minutes, or until pale and creamy. Add the eggs one at a time, beating well after each addition, until combined. Fold in the flour and coconut and mix well.

3 Spoon the mixture into the tin and bake for 45 minutes, or until a skewer comes out clean when inserted into the centre of the cake. Cool slightly in the tin, then turn out onto a wire rack.

4 To make the syrup, place the zest, sugar and 250 ml (9 fl oz/1 cup) of water in a small saucepan. Stir over medium heat until the sugar has dissolved. Allow to cool to room temperature.

5 Pierce the cake all over with a skewer, pour the syrup over the cake and leave for 2 hours to soak up the syrup. If desired, garnish with shaved coconut.

LAMINGTONS

Preparation time **50 minutes**
Total cooking time **1 hour**
Makes **16**

185 g (6½ oz/1½ cups) self-raising flour
40 g (1½ oz/⅓ cup) cornflour (cornstarch)
185 g (6½ oz) unsalted butter, softened
230 g (8½ oz/1 cup) caster (superfine) sugar
2 teaspoons natural vanilla extract
3 eggs, lightly beaten
125 ml (4 fl oz/½ cup) milk
185 ml (6 fl oz/¾ cup) thick (double/heavy)
   cream

Icing (frosting)
500 g (1 lb 2 oz) icing (confectioners') sugar
40 g (1½ oz/⅓ cup) cocoa powder
30 g (1 oz) unsalted butter, melted
170 ml (5½ fl oz/⅔ cup) milk
270 g (9½ oz/3 cups) desiccated coconut

1 Preheat the oven to 180°C (350°F/Gas 4).
Lightly grease a shallow 23 cm (9 in)
square cake tin and line with baking paper.
2 Sift the flour and cornflour into a bowl.
Add the butter, sugar, vanilla, egg and
milk. Using electric beaters, beat for 4
minutes, or until smooth. Pour into the tin.
3 Bake for 50–55 minutes, or until a skewer
inserted into the centre of the cake comes
out clean. Leave in the tin for 3 minutes
before turning out onto a wire rack to cool.
4 Using a serrated knife, trim the top of
the cake until flat. Trim the crusts from the
sides, then cut the cake in half horizontally.
5 Using electric beaters, beat the cream in
a bowl until stiff peaks form. Spread the
first layer of cake evenly with cream. Place
the remaining cake layer on top. Cut the
cake into 16 squares.
6 To make the icing, sift the icing sugar
and cocoa into a heatproof bowl and add
the butter and milk. Stand the bowl over a
saucepan of simmering water and stir until
the icing is smooth.
7 Place 90 g (3¼ oz/1 cup) of the coconut
on a sheet of baking paper. Using two
forks, roll a piece of cake in chocolate
icing, then hold the cake over a bowl and
allow the excess to drain. Roll the cake in
coconut, then place on a wire rack. Repeat.

MARBLE CAKE

Preparation time **20 minutes**
Total cooking time **1 hour**
Serves **6**

1 vanilla bean or 1 teaspoon natural vanilla
   extract
185 g (6½ oz) unsalted butter, chopped
230 g (8 oz/1 cup) caster (superfine) sugar
3 eggs
280 g (10 oz/2¼ cups) self-raising flour
185 ml (6 fl oz/¾ cup) milk
2 tablespoons unsweetened cocoa powder
1½ tablespoons warm milk, extra

1 Preheat the oven to 200°C (400°F/Gas 6).
Lightly grease a 25 x 11 x 7.5 cm (10 x
4¹/4 x 3 in) loaf (bar) tin and line the base
with baking paper.
2 If using the vanilla bean, split it down the
middle and scrape out the seeds. Put the
seeds (or vanilla extract) in a bowl with the
butter and sugar and, using electric beaters,
cream the mixture until pale and fluffy.
Add the eggs one at a time, beating well
after each addition. Sift the flour, then fold
it into the creamed mixture alternately
with the milk until combined. Divide the
mixture in half and put the second half
into another bowl.
3 Combine the cocoa powder and warm
milk in a small bowl and stir until smooth,
then add to one half of the cake mixture,
stirring to combine well.
4 Spoon the two mixtures into the
prepared tin in alternate spoonfuls. Using
a metal skewer, cut through the mixture
four times to create a marble effect.
5 Bake for 50–60 minutes, or until a skewer
inserted into the centre of the cake comes
out clean. Leave in the tin for 5 minutes
before turning out onto a wire rack to
cool completely.
Note This cake will keep, stored in an
airtight container, for 3–4 days. It is also
suitable to freeze.

ORANGE POPPY SEED CAKE

Preparation time **30 minutes** +
Total cooking time **1 hour**
Serves **8–10**

185 g (6½ oz/1½ cups) self-raising flour
35 g (1¼ oz/⅓ cup) ground almonds
40 g (1½ oz/¼ cup) poppy seeds
185 g (6½ oz) unsalted butter
145 g (5½ oz/⅔ cup) caster (superfine) sugar
80 g (2¾ oz/¼ cup) apricot jam or marmalade
2–3 teaspoons finely grated orange zest
80 ml (2½ fl oz/⅓ cup) orange juice
3 eggs, lightly beaten

Cream cheese icing (frosting)

100 g (3½ oz) unsalted butter, softened
100 g (3½ oz) cream cheese, softened
125 g (4½ oz/1 cup) icing (confectioners')
    sugar, sifted
1 teaspoon lemon juice or natural vanilla
    extract

1 Preheat the oven to 180°C (350°F/Gas 4). Lightly grease a deep 20 cm (8 in) round cake tin and line with baking paper.
2 Sift the flour into a bowl and add the almonds and poppy seeds. Make a well in the centre.
3 Place the butter, sugar, jam, orange zest and juice in a saucepan. Stir over low heat until the mixture is smooth. Add the butter mixture to the dry ingredients, stirring until smooth. Add the egg and whisk.
4 Pour into the tin and bake for 60 minutes, or until a skewer inserted into the centre of the cake comes out clean. Leave in the tin for 15 minutes before turning onto a wire rack to cool.
5 To make the icing, beat the butter and cream cheese using electric beaters until smooth. Add the icing sugar and lemon juice or vanilla extract and beat until thick. Spread the icing over the cake. Decorate with orange zest, if desired.

CARROT CAKE

Preparation time **40 minutes +**
Total cooking time **1 hour 30 minutes**
Serves **8–10**

125 g (4½ oz/1 cup) self-raising flour
125 g (4½ oz/1 cup) plain (all-purpose) flour
2 teaspoons ground cinnamon
1 teaspoon ground ginger
½ teaspoon freshly grated nutmeg
1 teaspoon bicarbonate of soda (baking soda)
250 ml (9 fl oz/1 cup) oil
185 g (6½ oz/1 cup) soft brown sugar
4 eggs
175 g (6 oz/½ cup) golden syrup
390 g (13¾ oz/2½ cups) grated carrot
60 g (2¼ oz/½ cup) chopped pecans
freshly grated nutmeg, extra, to sprinkle

Lemon icing (frosting)

175 g (6 oz) cream cheese, softened
60 g (2¼ oz) unsalted butter, softened
185 g (6½ oz/1½ cups) icing (confectioners')
   sugar
1 teaspoon natural vanilla extract
1–2 teaspoons lemon juice

1 Preheat the oven to 160°C (315°F/ Gas 2–3). Lightly grease a 23 cm (9 in) round cake tin and line the base and side with baking paper.

2 Sift the flours, cinnamon, ginger, nutmeg and bicarbonate of soda into a large bowl and make a well in the centre.

3 Whisk together the oil, sugar, eggs and golden syrup until combined. Add this mixture to the well in the flour and gradually stir until smooth. Stir in the grated carrot and nuts, then spoon into the tin and smooth the surface.

4 Bake for 1½ hours, or until a skewer inserted into the centre of the cake comes out clean. Leave the cake in the tin for at least 15 minutes before turning out onto a wire rack to cool completely.

5 To make the icing, beat the cream cheese and butter using electric beaters until smooth. Gradually add the icing sugar alternately with the vanilla and lemon juice, beating until light and creamy. Spread the icing evenly over the cake using a flat-bladed knife. Sprinkle with freshly grated nutmeg to serve.

CHOCOLATE CAKE

Preparation time **25 minutes** +
Total cooking time **50 minutes**
Serves **8–10**

125 g (4½ oz) unsalted butter, softened
115 g (4 oz/½ cup) caster (superfine) sugar
40 g (1½ oz/⅓ cup) icing (confectioners')
 sugar, sifted
2 eggs, lightly beaten
1 teaspoon natural vanilla extract
80 g (2¾ oz/¼ cup) blackberry jam
155 g (5½ oz/1¼ cups) self-raising flour
60 g (2¼ oz/½ cup) unsweetened
 cocoa powder
1 teaspoon bicarbonate of soda (baking soda)
250 ml (9 fl oz/1 cup) milk

Chocolate buttercream
50 g (1¾ oz) dark chocolate, finely chopped
25 g (1 oz) unsalted butter
3 teaspoons pouring (whipping) cream
30 g (1 oz/¼ cup) icing (confectioners') sugar

1 Preheat the oven to 180°C (350°F/Gas 4). Lightly grease a 20 cm (8 in) square cake tin and line with baking paper.

2 Cream the butter and sugars in a small mixing bowl using electric beaters until light and fluffy. Add the eggs gradually, beating thoroughly after each addition. Beat in the vanilla and jam. Transfer to a large bowl.

3 Using a metal spoon, gently fold in the combined sifted flour, cocoa powder and bicarbonate of soda alternately with the milk. Stir until the mixture is just combined and almost smooth.

4 Pour into the tin and smooth the surface. Bake for 45 minutes, or until a skewer inserted into the centre of the cake comes out clean. Leave in the tin for 15 minutes before turning out onto a wire rack to cool completely.

5 To make the buttercream, stir the ingredients in a small saucepan over low heat until smooth and glossy. Spread over the top of the cake evenly with a flat-bladed knife.

Note This cake (without icing) will keep, stored in an airtight container, for 3–4 days. It is also suitable to freeze.

BAKED CHEESECAKE

Preparation time **25 minutes** +
Total cooking time **1 hour**
Serves **10**

375 g (13 oz) plain sweet biscuits (cookies)
175 g (6 oz) unsalted butter, melted

Filling
500 g (1 lb 2 oz) cream cheese
200 g (7 oz) caster (superfine) sugar
4 eggs
300 ml (10½ fl oz) pouring (whipping) cream
2 tablespoons plain (all-purpose) flour
1 teaspoon ground cinnamon
¼ teaspoon freshly grated nutmeg
1 tablespoons lemon juice
2 teaspoon natural vanilla extract
freshly grated nutmeg, to dust
ground cinnamon, to dust

1 Preheat the oven to 180°C (350°F/Gas 4). Lightly grease a 23 cm (9 in) shallow spring-form cake tin.
2 Process the biscuits in a food processor until they are crushed into fine crumbs. Add the melted butter and process for another 10 seconds.
3 Press the mixture into the base and side of the prepared tin, then refrigerate for 1 hour.
4 Beat the cream cheese and sugar together, then add the eggs and cream and beat for about 4 minutes. Fold in the flour, cinnamon, nutmeg, lemon juice and vanilla. Pour the mixture into the chilled crust.
5 Bake for 1 hour without opening the oven door, or until the cheesecake is golden brown on top.
6 Turn off the heat and let the cake stand in the oven for 2 hours. Then open the oven door and let it stand for a further hour. Lastly, refrigerate overnight.
7 Sprinkle with nutmeg and cinnamon and then serve. Delicious with lashings of cream and some strawberries.

ZESTY OLIVE OIL CAKE

Preparation time **10 minutes**

Total cooking time **45 minutes**

Serves **8**

2 eggs

160 g (5¾ oz/⅔ cup) caster (superfine) sugar

2 teaspoons finely grated orange zest

2 teaspoons finely grated lemon zest

125 ml (4 fl oz/½ cup) olive oil

185 g (6½ oz/1½ cups) self-raising flour

60 ml (2 fl oz/¼ cup) milk

60 ml (2 fl oz/¼ cup) orange juice

1 Preheat the oven to 180°C (350°F/Gas 4). Grease a shallow 20 cm (8 in) round cake tin and line the base with baking paper.

2 Whisk the eggs and sugar in a large bowl using electric beaters until well combined. Add the orange and lemon zest, then stir in the olive oil.

3 Stir in the sifted flour alternately with the milk and orange juice. Stir the mixture gently for 30 seconds with a wooden spoon. Pour into the prepared tin.

4 Bake for 45 minutes, or until a skewer comes out clean when inserted into the centre of the cake. Leave to cool in the tin for 5 minutes before turning out onto a wire rack.

Note This cake can be dusted with icing sugar before serving, if desired.

CINNAMON, APPLE AND WALNUT CAKE

Preparation time **20 minutes**

Total cooking time **50 minutes**

Serves **10–12**

canola oil spray
250 g (9 oz/1²/₃ cups) stoneground
    self-raising flour
2 teaspoon ground cinnamon
½ teaspoon baking powder
55 g (2 oz/½ cup) ground almonds
55 g (2 oz/¼ cup) caster (superfine) sugar
2 apples, peeled, cored and diced
60 g (2¼ oz/½ cup) chopped walnuts
2 eggs
125 ml (4 fl oz/½ cup) buttermilk
140 g (5 oz/½ cup) unsweetened apple
    purée
2 tablespoons canola oil

1 Preheat the oven to 180°C (350°F/Gas 4). Spray a 23 cm (9 in) round cake tin with oil, then line the base with baking paper.
2 Sift the flour, cinnamon and baking powder into a large bowl, then return any husks to the bowl. Stir in the ground almonds and sucralose, then the diced apple and chopped walnuts.
3 Whisk together the eggs, buttermilk, apple purée and oil in a bowl. Add to the flour mixture, then stir until combined and smooth. Spoon into the prepared tin and smooth the surface.
4 Bake for 50 minutes, or until cooked when tested with a metal skewer. Leave in the tin for 15 minutes, then turn out onto a wire rack to cool. Cut into wedges to serve. Delicious served warm.
Note Will keep refrigerated for up to 1 week. Freeze for up to 1 month.

CHOCOLATE CHESTNUT ROULADE

Preparation time **30 minutes** +
Total cooking time **25 minutes**
Serves **6–8**

60 g (2¼ oz) dark chocolate, chopped
4 eggs
115 g (4 oz/½ cup) caster (superfine) sugar
100 g (3½ oz) tinned sweetened
   chestnut purée
60 g (2¼ oz/½ cup) self-raising flour, sifted
2 tablespoons hot water
unsweetened cocoa powder, to dust

Chestnut cream
150 g (5½ oz) tinned sweetened chestnut purée
300 ml (10½ fl oz) thick (double/heavy) cream
1 tablespoon dark rum

1 Preheat the oven to 180°C (350°F/Gas 4). Lightly grease a 25 x 30 cm (10 x 12 in) shallow Swiss roll tin (jelly roll tin) and line the base with baking paper.
2 Put the chocolate in a heatproof bowl. Sit the bowl over a saucepan of simmering water, stirring until the chocolate has melted. Take care that the base of the bowl doesn't touch the water. Allow to cool.

3 Whisk the eggs and sugar in a bowl for 5 minutes, or until pale and very thick. Beat in the chestnut purée and chocolate, then fold in the flour and water. Gently spread the mixture into the prepared tin and bake for 20 minutes, or until just cooked and springy to the touch (do not overcook or the cake will crack when it is rolled).
4 Put a tea towel (dish towel) on the work surface, cover with a sheet of baking paper and sprinkle the paper lightly with cocoa powder. Turn the cake out onto the paper, then carefully remove the baking paper from the base of the cake. Trim the edges to neaten. Using the tea towel as a guide, carefully roll the cake up from the long side, rolling the paper inside the roll. Put the rolled cake on a wire rack and leave to cool for 10 minutes, then carefully unroll the cake and cool completely.
5 To make the chestnut cream, combine the purée, cream and rum in a small bowl, then beat until just thick. Spread the cake with the chestnut cream, then carefully re-roll, using the paper to guide you. Place the roulade seam side down and dust the top lightly with cocoa powder.
Note This roulade is best eaten on the day it is made.

SWISS ROLL

Preparation time **25 minutes**
Total cooking time **12 minutes**
Serves **10**

90 g (3¼ oz/¾ cup) self-raising flour
3 eggs, lightly beaten
170 g (6 oz/¾ cup) caster (superfine) sugar
160 g (5¾ oz/½ cup) strawberry jam, beaten
icing (confectioners') sugar, to sprinkle

1 Preheat the oven to 190°C (375°F/Gas 5). Lightly grease a shallow 2 x 25 x 30 cm (³/4 x 10 x 12 in) Swiss roll tin (jelly roll tin) and line the base with baking paper, extending over the two long sides. Sift the flour three times onto baking paper.
2 Beat the eggs using electric beaters in a small bowl for 5 minutes, or until thick and pale. Add 115 g (4 oz/½ cup) of the sugar gradually, beating constantly until the mixture is pale and glossy. Transfer to a large bowl. Using a metal spoon, fold in the flour quickly and lightly. Spread into the tin and smooth the surface.
3 Bake for 10–12 minutes, or until lightly golden and springy to the touch.
4 Meanwhile, place a clean tea towel (dish towel) on a work surface, cover with baking paper and lightly sprinkle with the remaining caster sugar. When the cake is cooked, turn it out onto the sugar.
5 Using the tea towel as a guide, carefully roll the cake up from the short side, rolling the paper inside the roll. Put the rolled cake on a wire rack for 5 minutes, then carefully unroll and allow the cake to cool to room temperature. Spread with the jam and re-roll. Trim the ends with a knife. Sprinkle with icing sugar.

MADEIRA CAKE

Preparation time 20 minutes +
Total cooking time 1 hour
Serves 6

180 g (6 oz) unsalted butter, softened
185 g (6½ oz/¾ cup) caster (superfine) sugar
3 eggs, beaten
165 g (5¾ oz/1⅓ cups) self-raising flour
2 teaspoons finely grated lemon zest
1 teaspoon lemon juice
2 teaspoons caster (superfine) sugar, plus
    extra, to sprinkle
icing (confectioners') sugar, to dust
lemon zest, extra, to garnish

1 Preheat the oven to 160°C (315°F/ Gas 2–3). Grease and flour a deep 18 cm (7 in) round cake tin.

2 Beat the butter and sugar with electric beaters until pale and creamy. Add the eggs gradually, beating well after each addition. Fold in the flour, lemon zest and juice until combined.

3 Spoon into the prepared tin and level the surface. Sprinkle the extra caster sugar over the top.

4 Bake for 1 hour, or until a skewer comes out clean when inserted into the centre of the cake.

5 Allow to cool for 15 minutes in the tin before turning out onto a wire rack. To serve, dust with icing sugar and garnish with lemon zest.

Note This cake will keep for 4 days wrapped in foil.

LEMON CAKE WITH CRUNCHY TOPPING

Preparation time 25 minutes
Total cooking time 1 hour 20 minutes
Serves 8–10

250 g (9 oz) unsalted butter, softened
200 g (7 oz) caster (superfine) sugar
2 teaspoons finely grated lemon zest
4 eggs, lightly beaten
250 g (9 oz/2 cups) self-raising flour
1 teaspoon baking powder
2 tablespoons lemon juice

Crunchy topping
110 g (3³/4 oz/¹/2 cup) sugar
60 ml (2 fl oz/¹/4 cup) lemon juice

1 Preheat the oven to 170°C (325°F/Gas 3). Lightly grease a 22 cm (8¹/2 in) square cake tin and line the base with baking paper.
2 Cream the butter and sugar in a small bowl using electric beaters until the mixture is light and fluffy. Beat in the lemon zest, then gradually add the egg, beating thoroughly after each addition. Transfer the mixture to a large bowl.
3 Using a large metal spoon, fold in the combined sifted flour, baking powder and ¹/4 teaspoon salt, as well as the lemon juice. Stir until the mixture is just combined and almost smooth.
4 Spoon the mixture into the tin and smooth the surface. Bake for 1 hour 20 minutes, or until a skewer inserted into the centre of the cake comes out clean. Remove from the tin and turn out onto a wire rack.
5 To make the topping, mix together the sugar and lemon juice (do not dissolve the sugar), and quickly brush over the top of the warm cake. The juice will sink into the cake, and the sugar will form a crunchy topping. Allow to cool.

FLOURLESS CHOCOLATE CAKE

Preparation time **30 minutes** +
Total cooking time **1 hour**
Serves **10**

500 g (1 lb 2 oz) good-quality dark chocolate, chopped
6 eggs
2 tablespoons Frangelico or brandy
165 g (5³/4 oz/1 ½ cups) ground hazelnuts
250 ml (9 fl oz/1 cup) pouring (whipping) cream
icing (confectioners') sugar, to dust
thick (double/heavy) cream, to serve

1 Preheat the oven to 150°C (300°F/Gas 2). Grease a deep 20 cm (8 in) round cake tin and line the base with baking paper.
2 Place the chocolate in a heatproof bowl. Half fill a saucepan with water, boil, then remove from the heat and sit the bowl over the pan, making sure the base of the bowl doesn't touch the water. Stir occasionally until the chocolate melts.
3 Put the eggs in a large heatproof bowl and add the Frangelico. Put the bowl over a saucepan of barely simmering water, making sure the base of the bowl doesn't touch the water. Beat using electric beaters on high speed for 7 minutes, or until light and foamy. Remove from the heat.
4 Using a metal spoon, quickly and lightly fold the chocolate and ground nuts into the egg mixture until just combined. Fold in the whipped cream.
5 Pour the mixture into the prepared tin. Put the cake tin in a shallow roasting tin. Pour hot water into the roasting tin to come halfway up the side of the cake tin. Bake for 1 hour, or until just set.
6 Remove the cake tin from the oven and cool to room temperature. Cover with plastic wrap and refrigerate overnight.
7 Invert the cake onto a plate, remove the paper and dust with icing sugar. Cut into slices and serve with cream.

CHOCOLATE CHERRY CAKE

Preparation time **15 minutes**

Total cooking time **1 hour 10 minutes**

Serves **8**

200 g (7 oz) dark chocolate, chopped

250 g (9 oz) unsalted butter, chopped

230 g (8 oz/1 cup) firmly packed soft brown
   sugar

1 teaspoon natural vanilla extract

155 g (5½ oz/1¼ cups) self-raising flour

45 g (1½ oz/½ cup) desiccated coconut

2 eggs

180 g (6½ oz/1 cup) pitted sour cherries,
   drained

1 Preheat the oven to 160°C (315°F/
Gas 2–3). Grease a 23 cm (9 in) round cake
tin and line the base with baking paper.

2 Put the chocolate, butter, sugar and
vanilla in a heatproof bowl and melt over a
saucepan of simmering water, stirring
occasionally, until the chocolate has
melted—make sure the base of the bowl
doesn't touch the water. Sit the bowl in a
sink of cold water to cool.

3 Combine the flour and coconut in a food
processor. Add the chocolate mixture and
eggs and process in short bursts until just
combined. Add the cherries and process in
one longish burst to just chop.

4 Pour the mixture into the tin and bake
for 1 hour 10 minutes, or until a skewer
comes out clean when inserted into the
centre of the cake.

5 Leave in the tin for 15 minutes before
carefully turning out onto a wire rack
to cool. If desired, dust with icing sugar
and decorate with fresh cherries just
before serving.

Note This cake is best eaten on the day
it is made.

PLUM UPSIDE-DOWN CAKE

Preparation time **20 minutes +**
Total cooking time **50 minutes**
Serves **8**

450 g (1 lb) plums
30 g (1 oz/¼ cup) dark muscovado sugar
100 g (3½ oz) unsalted butter, softened
250 g (9 oz/1 heaped cup) caster (superfine)
  sugar
4 eggs, at room temperature
1 teaspoon natural vanilla extract
1 orange, zest grated
6 cardamom pods, seeds removed and
  crushed
150 g (5½ oz/1¼ cups) plain (all-purpose)
  flour
150 g (5½ oz/1½ cups) ground almonds
2 teaspoons baking powder
thick (double/heavy) cream, to serve

1 Preheat the oven to 180°C (350°F/Gas 4). Grease and line a 23 cm (9 in) spring-form cake tin.
2 Halve the plums, removing the stones. Sprinkle the muscovado sugar over the base of the prepared tin and arrange the plums, cut side down, over the sugar.
3 Cream the butter and caster sugar with electric beaters until light and fluffy. Add the eggs, one at a time, beating well after each addition. Add the vanilla, orange zest, crushed cardamom seeds, flour, ground almonds and baking powder. Spoon over the plums and smooth the surface with a spatula.
4 Bake for 50 minutes, or until a skewer comes out clean when inserted into the centre of the cake. Set aside to cool for 5 minutes before turning the cake out onto a plate. Serve with thick cream.

SOUR CHERRY CAKE

Preparation time **20 minutes**

Total cooking time **50 minutes**

Serves **8–10**

125 g (4½ oz) unsalted butter, softened

185 g (6½ oz/¾ cup) caster (superfine) sugar

2 eggs, lightly beaten

95 g (3¼ oz/1 cup) ground almonds

125 g (4½ oz/1 cup) self-raising flour

60 g (2¼ oz/½ cup) plain (all-purpose) flour

125 ml (4 fl oz/½ cup) milk

680 g (1 lb 8 oz) jar pitted morello cherries, well drained

1 Preheat the oven to 180°C (350°F/Gas 4). Grease and flour a 23 cm (9 in) fluted baba tin, shaking out the excess flour.

2 Beat the butter and sugar in a large bowl using electric beaters until pale but not creamy. Add the egg gradually, beating well after each addition. Take care not to overbeat.

3 Stir in the ground almonds, then fold in the sifted flours alternately with the milk. Gently fold in the cherries. Spoon the mixture into the prepared tin and smooth the surface.

4 Bake for 50 minutes, or until a skewer comes out clean when inserted into the centre of the cake. Leave to cool in the tin for 10 minutes before turning out onto a wire rack to cool. Dust with icing sugar before serving.

Note This cake is best eaten on the day it is made.

LUMBERJACK CAKE

Preparation time **30 minutes**
Total cooking time **1 hour 15 minutes**
Serves **8**

200 g (7 oz) fresh dates, stoned and chopped
1 teaspoon bicarbonate of soda (baking soda)
125 g (4½ oz) unsalted butter, softened
230 g (8½ oz/1 cup) caster (superfine) sugar
1 egg
1 teaspoon natural vanilla extract
2 granny smith apples, peeled, cored
  and grated
125 g (4½ oz/1 cup) plain (all-purpose) flour
60 g (2¼ oz/½ cup) self-raising flour
icing (confectioners') sugar (optional), to dust

Topping
75 g (2¾ oz) unsalted butter
95 g (3½ oz/½ cup) soft brown sugar
80 ml (2½ fl oz/½ cup) milk
60 g (2¼ oz/1 cup) shredded coconut

1 Preheat the oven to 180°C (350°F/Gas 4). Grease a 20 cm (8 in) spring-form cake tin and line the base with baking paper.
2 Put the dates in a small saucepan with 250 ml (9 fl oz/1 cup) water and bring to the boil. Stir in the bicarbonate of soda, then remove from the heat. Set aside until just warm.
3 Cream the butter and sugar in a small bowl using electric beaters until light and fluffy. Add the egg and vanilla and beat until well combined. Stir in the date mixture and the apple, then fold in the sifted flours until just combined and almost smooth.
4 Spoon into the tin and smooth the surface. Bake for 40 minutes, then remove from the oven.
5 To make the topping, combine the butter, sugar, milk and shredded coconut in a small saucepan. Stir over low heat until the butter has melted and the ingredients are well combined.
6 Spread the topping evenly over the cake using a spatula. Return the cake to the oven for 20–30 minutes, or until the topping is golden and lightly browned and a skewer inserted into the centre of the cake comes out clean.
7 Remove from the oven and leave the cake in the tin to cool completely, then turn out and place on a serving plate. Dust with icing sugar just before serving.

NEW YORK CHEESECAKE

Preparation time 1 hour +
Total cooking time 1 hour 50 minutes
Serves 10–12

60 g (2¼ oz/½ cup) self-raising flour
125 g (4½ oz/1 cup) plain (all-purpose) flour
55 g (2 oz/¼ cup) caster (superfine) sugar
1 teaspoon grated lemon zest
80 g (2¾ oz) unsalted butter, chopped
1 egg
375 ml (13 fl oz/1½ cups) pouring (whipping) cream, to serve

Filling
750 g (1 lb 10 oz/3 cups) cream cheese, softened
230 g (8½ oz/1 cup) caster (superfine) sugar
30 g (1 oz/¼ cup) plain (all-purpose) flour
2 teaspoons grated orange zest
2 teaspoons grated lemon zest
4 eggs
170 ml (5½ fl oz) pouring (whipping) cream

1 Preheat the oven to 210°C (415°F/ Gas 6–7). Lightly grease a 23 cm (9 in) spring-form cake tin.

2 To make the pastry, combine the flours, sugar, lemon zest and butter for 30 seconds in a food processor, until crumbly. Add the egg and process until the mixture comes together. Turn out onto floured surface and gather together into a ball. Refrigerate in plastic wrap for 20 minutes.

3 Roll the dough between two sheets of baking paper until large enough to fit the base and side of the tin. Ease into the tin and trim the edges. Cover the pastry with baking paper, then baking beads.

4 Bake for 10 minutes, then remove the baking paper and rice. Flatten the pastry lightly with the back of a spoon and bake for a further 5 minutes. Set aside to cool.

5 To make the filling, reduce the oven to 150°C (300°F/Gas 2). Beat the cream cheese, sugar, flour and orange and lemon zest until smooth. Add the eggs, one at a time, beating after each addition. Beat in the cream and pour over the pastry.

6 Bake for 1½ hours, or until almost set. Turn off the oven and leave to cool with the door ajar. When cool, refrigerate. Whip the cream, spoon over the cake and top with candied zest, if desired.

SAND CAKE

Preparation time **15 minutes**
Total cooking time **50 minutes**
Serves **8–10**

185 g (6½ oz) unsalted butter, softened
2 teaspoons natural vanilla extract
250 g (9 oz/1 cup) caster (superfine)
 sugar
3 eggs
185 g (6½ oz/1½ cups) self-raising flour
60 g (2¼ oz/⅓ cup) rice flour
80 ml (2½ fl oz/⅓ cup) milk

1 Preheat the oven to 180°C (350°F/Gas 4). Grease a 23 cm (9 in) square tin and line the base with baking paper.
2 Beat the butter, vanilla, sugar, eggs, flours and milk using electric beaters until combined, then beat at medium speed for 3 minutes, or until thick and creamy.
3 Pour the mixture into the tin and smooth the surface. Bake for 50 minutes, or until a skewer comes out clean when inserted into the centre of the cake. Leave for 10 minutes in the tin then turn out onto a wire rack to cool.

LEMON SEMOLINA CAKE

Preparation time **20 minutes** +
Total cooking time **40 minutes**
Serves **8–10**

6 eggs, separated
310 g (11 oz/1¼ cups) caster (superfine) sugar
2 teaspoons finely grated lemon zest
80 ml (2½ fl oz/⅓ cup) lemon juice
90 g (3¼ oz/¾ cup) semolina
95 g (3¼ oz/1 cup) ground almonds
2 tablespoons self-raising flour
thick (double/heavy) cream, to serve

1 Preheat the oven to 170°C (325°F/Gas 3). Grease a 24 cm (9½ in) spring-form cake tin and line the base with baking paper.
2 Place the egg yolks, 250 g (9 oz/1 cup) of the sugar, lemon zest and 2 tablespoons of the lemon juice in a bowl. Beat using electric beaters for 8 minutes, or until thick.
3 Beat the egg whites in a bowl using electric beaters until firm peaks form. Fold the whites into the egg yolk mixture alternately with the combined semolina, ground almonds and flour.
4 Pour into the tin and bake for 35 minutes, or until a skewer comes out clean when inserted into the centre of the cake. Leave for 5 minutes in the tin, then turn out onto a wire rack. Pierce a few holes in the cake with a skewer.
5 Place the remaining lemon juice and sugar in a saucepan with 125 ml (4 fl oz/½ cup) water. Stir over low heat until dissolved. Increase the heat and simmer for 3 minutes, or until thick. Pour the syrup over the cake. Serve with thick cream.

CHOCOLATE MUD CAKE

Preparation time 30 minutes +
Total cooking time 1 hour 55 minutes
Serves 8–10

250 g (9 oz) unsalted butter
250 g (9 oz) dark chocolate, broken
2 tablespoons instant coffee powder
150 g (5½ oz) self-raising flour
155 g (5½ oz/1¼ cups) plain (all-purpose) flour
60 g (2¼ oz/½ cup) unsweetened
   cocoa powder
½ teaspoon bicarbonate of soda (baking soda)
550 g (1 lb 4 oz/2½ cups) sugar
4 eggs
2 tablespoons oil
125 ml (4 fl oz/½ cup) buttermilk
chocolate, extra, to decorate

Glaze
250 g (9 oz) dark chocolate, chopped
125 ml (4 fl oz/½ cup) pouring (whipping)
   cream
145 g (5½ oz/⅔ cup) caster (superfine) sugar

1 Preheat the oven to 160°C (315°F/
Gas 2–3). Grease a deep 22 cm (8½ in)
round cake tin with melted butter or oil.
Line the base and side with baking paper,
extending at least 2 cm ($^3/4$ in) above
the rim.
2 Stir the butter, chocolate, coffee and
185 ml (6 fl oz/$^3/4$ cup) hot water in a
saucepan, over low heat, until melted
and smooth. Remove from the heat.
3 Sift the flours, cocoa and bicarbonate
of soda into a large bowl. Stir in the sugar
and make a well in the centre. Add the
combined eggs, oil and buttermilk and,
using a large metal spoon, slowly stir in
the dry ingredients, then the melted
chocolate mixture until combined.
4 Spoon the mixture into the tin and bake
for 1 hour 40 minutes, or until a skewer
inserted into the centre of the cake
comes out clean. Cool in the tin. When
completely cold, remove from the tin.
5 To make the glaze, stir all the ingredients
in a saucepan over low heat until melted.
Bring to the boil, reduce the heat and
simmer for 4–5 minutes. Remove from the
heat and cool slightly. Put a wire rack on
a baking tray and transfer the cake to the
rack. Pour the glaze over the cake, making
sure the sides are evenly covered. Decorate
with chocolate shavings.

CHOCOLATE AND ALMOND TORTE

Preparation time 25 minutes +
Total cooking time 1 hour 5 minutes
Serves 8

150 g (5½ oz) flaked or whole almonds
1 slice pandoro sweet cake or 1 small
   brioche (about 40 g/1½ oz)
300 g (10½ oz) dark chocolate
2 tablespoons brandy
150 g (5½ oz) unsalted butter, softened
150 g (5½ oz) caster (superfine) sugar
4 eggs
1 teaspoon natural vanilla extract (optional)
200 g (7 oz) mascarpone cheese
unsweetened cocoa powder, to dust
crème fraîche, to serve

1 Preheat the oven to 170°C (325°F/Gas 4). Grease a 23 cm (9 in) spring-form cake tin with butter.
2 Toast the almonds in the oven for 8–10 minutes until golden brown.

3 Put the almonds and pandoro in a food processor and process until the mixture resembles breadcrumbs. Tip some of the mixture into the prepared tin and shake it around so that it forms a coating on the bottom and side of the tin. Put the remaining nut mixture aside.
4 Gently melt the chocolate and brandy in a heatproof bowl set over a saucepan of simmering water, making sure that the bowl does not touch the water. Stir occasionally until the chocolate has melted. Cool slightly.
5 Cream the butter and sugar in the food processor or with a wooden spoon for a few minutes until light and pale. Add the melted chocolate, eggs, vanilla extract and mascarpone. Add the remaining nut mixture and mix well. Tip into the tin.
6 Bake for 50–60 minutes, or until just set. Leave to rest in the tin for about 15 minutes before taking out. Dust with a little cocoa when cool and serve with crème fraîche.

RHUBARB YOGHURT CAKE

Preparation time **20 minutes** +

Total cooking time **1 hour**

Serves **8**

150 g (5½ oz/1¼ cups) finely sliced rhubarb

310 g (11 oz/2½ cups) self-raising flour, sifted

250 g (9 oz/1 cup) caster (superfine) sugar

1 teaspoon natural vanilla extract

2 eggs, lightly beaten

125 g (4½ oz/½ cup) plain yoghurt

1 tablespoon rosewater

125 g (4½ oz) unsalted butter, melted

1 Preheat the oven to 180°C (350°F/Gas 4). Lightly grease a 23 cm (9 in) round cake tin and line the base with baking paper.

2 Combine the rhubarb, flour and sugar in a large bowl. Add the vanilla extract, egg, yoghurt, rosewater and melted butter, stirring until the mixture is just combined. Do not overmix.

3 Spoon the mixture into the cake tin and bake for 1 hour, or until a skewer comes out clean when inserted into the centre of the cake.

4 Leave in the tin for 15 minutes before turning out onto a wire rack. Serve with yoghurt or cream, if desired.

BLUEBERRY CRUMBLE CAKE

Preparation time **25 minutes** +
Total cooking time **55 minutes**
Serves **8–10**

125 g (4½ oz/1 cup) plain (all-purpose)
　flour
110 g (3¾ oz/¾ cup) wholemeal
　(whole-wheat) plain (all-purpose) flour
225 g (8 oz/1 cup) caster (superfine) sugar
2½ teaspoons baking powder
½ teaspoon ground cinnamon
150 g (5½ oz/1 cup) blueberries
1 egg, at room temperature
185 ml (6 fl oz/¾ cup) milk
80 ml (2½ fl oz/⅓ cup) oil
1 teaspoon natural vanilla extract
zest of 1 lemon, finely grated
thick (double/heavy) cream, to serve

Topping

60 g (2¼ oz/½ cup) pecans, chopped
55 g (2 oz/⅓ cup) soft brown sugar
30 g (1 oz/¼ cup) plain (all-purpose) flour
150 g (5½ oz/1 cup) blueberries
2 tablespoons oil

1 Preheat the oven to 190°C (375°F/Gas 5).
Grease a 20 cm (8 in) spring-form cake tin.
2 Sift the flours, sugar, baking powder
and cinnamon into a large bowl. Return
the husks collected in the sieve to the
bowl. Toss the blueberries through the
flour mixture.
3 Whisk together the egg, milk, oil,
vanilla extract and lemon zest. Pour onto
the dry ingredients and stir to combine.
Pour the mixture into the prepared tin.
4 To make the topping, combine the
pecans, brown sugar, flour and blueberries
in a bowl and sprinkle evenly over the
cake. Drizzle the oil over the topping.
5 Bake for 50–55 minutes, or until a skewer
comes out clean when inserted into the
centre of the cake. Serve the cake warm
with a dollop of thick cream.

ORANGE AND ALMOND CAKE

Preparation time **25 minutes** +
Total cooking time **3 hours**
Serves **6–8**

2 large navel oranges
6 eggs, separated
1 tablespoon orange blossom water or
   orange liqueur
250 g (9 oz/1 cup) caster (superfine) sugar
300 g (10½ oz/3 cups) ground almonds
1 teaspoon baking powder
3 navel oranges, peeled, pith and sinew
   removed, thinly sliced, to garnish

Orange syrup
500 ml (17 fl oz/2 cups) fresh orange juice,
   strained
185 g (6½ oz/¾ cup) caster (superfine) sugar
60 ml (2 fl oz/¼ cup) Sauternes

1 Grease and flour a 23 cm (9 in) spring-form cake tin, tipping out any excess flour.
2 Put the whole oranges into a saucepan full of water. Boil for 2 hours, topping up with water as needed. Remove the oranges, quarter them and process in a food processor until smooth. Cool thoroughly. Preheat the oven to 180°C (350°F/Gas 4).
3 Place the egg yolks, orange blossom water and caster (superfine) sugar in a large bowl and beat until smooth, then stir in the orange purée and mix well.
4 Whisk the egg whites in a dry bowl until firm peaks form. Add the ground almonds and baking powder to the orange mixture, stir well, then fold in the egg whites.
5 Pour into the cake tin and bake for 1 hour, or until firm—cover with foil if it begins to over-brown. Cool in the tin, then transfer to a serving plate.
6 To make the syrup, put the orange juice, sugar and Sauternes in a saucepan over medium heat and stir until the sugar is dissolved. Reduce the heat and simmer for 20 minutes, or until reduced by half and slightly syrupy, skimming off any scum.
7 Cut the cake into wedges, garnish with orange slices and drizzle with the syrup. Delicious served with cream.

PEAR AND ALMOND CAKE

Preparation time **25 minutes +**
Total cooking time **40 minutes**
Serves **12**

Almond pear topping

50 g (1³/₄ oz) unsalted butter, melted
2 tablespoons soft brown sugar
1 teaspoon ground nutmeg
425 g (15 oz) tinned pear halves, drained
    and halved
75 g (2¹/₂ oz/¹/₂ cup) finely chopped blanched
    almonds, lightly toasted

Cake batter

125 g (4¹/₂ oz) unsalted butter
115 g (4 oz/¹/₂ cup) caster (superfine)
    sugar
1 teaspoon natural vanilla extract
2 eggs
55 g (2 oz/¹/₂ cup) ground almonds
250 g (9 oz/2 cups) self-raising flour
1 teaspoon ground nutmeg
125 ml (4 fl oz/¹/₂ cup) milk

whipped cream, to serve

1 Preheat the oven to 180°C (350°F/Gas 4). Lightly grease and line the base of a 23 cm (9 in) tin with baking paper.
2 Combine the melted butter, brown sugar and nutmeg in a large mixing bowl. Evenly pour over the base of the tin. Arrange the pear quarters over and scatter the almonds over the pear slices.
3 Put the butter, caster sugar and vanilla into a mixing bowl and beat using electric beaters for 2–3 minutes, or until creamy. Add the eggs, one at a time, beating well between each addition. Stir in the ground almonds. Fold in the sifted flour and nutmeg in two to three batches, alternating with the milk.
4 Carefully spoon the batter into the prepared tin, on top of the pears, and smooth the surface.
5 Bake for 40 minutes, or until a skewer inserted in the centre comes out clean. Cool in the tin for 20 minutes, then remove and cool on a wire rack, pear side up. Carefully peel away the baking paper. Cut into wedges and serve warm with whipped cream.

YOGHURT CAKE WITH SYRUP

Preparation time 20 minutes +

Total cooking time 55 minutes

Serves 8–10

185 g (6¼ oz) unsalted butter, softened

250 g (9 oz/1 cup) caster (superfine) sugar

5 eggs, separated

250 g (9 oz/1 cup) Greek-style yoghurt

2 teaspoons grated lemon zest

½ teaspoon natural vanilla extract

280 g (10 oz/2¼ cups) plain (all-purpose) flour, sifted

2 teaspoons baking powder

½ teaspoon bicarbonate of soda (baking soda)

whipped cream, to serve

Syrup

250 g (9 oz/1 cup) caster (superfine) sugar

1 cinnamon stick

4 cm (1½ in) strip lemon zest

1 tablespoon lemon juice

1 Preheat the oven to 180°C (350°F/Gas 4). Lightly grease a 20 x 10 cm (8 x 4 in) loaf (bar) tin.

2 Place the butter and sugar in a large bowl and beat using electric beaters until light and creamy. Add the egg yolks gradually, beating well after each addition. Stir in the yoghurt, lemon zest and vanilla. Fold in the flour, baking powder and bicarbonate of soda (baking soda) with a metal spoon.

3 Whisk the egg whites in a clean, dry bowl until stiff, and fold into the mixture.

4 Spoon into the prepared tin and bake for 50 minutes, or until a skewer comes out clean when inserted into the centre of the cake. Cool in the tin for 10 minutes, then turn out onto a wire rack to cool.

4 Meanwhile, to make the syrup, place the sugar and cinnamon stick in a small saucepan with 185 ml (6 fl oz/³/4 cup) cold water. Stir over medium heat until the sugar is dissolved. Bring to the boil, add the lemon zest and juice, then reduce the heat and simmer for 5–6 minutes. Strain.

5 Pour the syrup over the cake and wait for most of it to be absorbed before serving. Cut into slices and serve warm with whipped cream.

FIG AND RASPBERRY CAKE

Preparation time **20 minutes** +
Total cooking time **30 minutes**
Serves **6**

185 g (6½ oz) unsalted butter
185 g (6½ oz /³/4 cup) caster (superfine) sugar
1 egg
1 egg yolk
335 g (11³/4 oz/2²/3 cups) plain (all-purpose)
   flour
1 teaspoon baking powder
4 figs, quartered
grated zest of 1 orange
200 g (7 oz/1²/3 cups) raspberries
2 tablespoons sugar

1 Preheat the oven to 180°C (350°F/Gas 4).
2 Cream the butter and sugar in a large bowl using electric beaters until light and pale. Add the egg and beat until combined. Sift the flour over the bowl and fold in with the baking powder and a pinch of salt. Chill for 15 minutes until firm enough to roll out.
3 Lightly grease a 23 cm (9 in) spring-form cake tin. Divide the dough in two and roll out one piece large enough to fit the base of the tin. Cover with the figs, orange zest and raspberries. Roll out the remaining dough and fit it over the filling. Lightly brush the dough with water and sprinkle with sugar.
4 Bake for 30 minutes, or until the top and bottom of the cake are cooked. Poke a skewer into the cake to see if it is ready—there should be no wet cake mixture clinging to the skewer. Serve with cream or mascarpone.
Note If fresh figs are not available, you can use the same amount of dried figs but you need to rehydrate them first. Simmer them in orange juice for 5 minutes until they are plumped up and soft.

LEMON AND HONEY RICOTTA CAKE

Preparation time **20 minutes +**
Total cooking time **1 hour**
Serves **10–12**

1 kg (2 lb 4 oz/4 cups) ricotta cheese
175 g (6 oz/½ cup) honey
1½ teaspoons natural vanilla extract
60 ml (2 fl oz/¼ cup) lemon juice
zest of 2 lemons, finely grated
½ teaspoon ground cinnamon
4 eggs, lightly beaten
35 g (1¼ oz/¼ cup) plain (all-purpose) flour
poached nectarines or peaches, to serve

1 Preheat the oven to 170°C (325°F/Gas 3).
Lightly grease and flour an 18 cm (7 in) spring-form cake tin.
2 Drain the ricotta if necessary, then process in a food processor until smooth. Add the honey, vanilla, lemon juice, zest, cinnamon and eggs and process until well combined. Add the flour and pulse until just combined and the mixture is smooth.
3 Spoon the mixture into the prepared tin and bake for 1 hour, or until light golden and still slightly soft in the middle.
4 Turn the oven off, open the door slightly and cool the cake in the oven. Put in the refrigerator to chill, then remove the cake from the tin. Serve at room temperature with poached fruit such as peaches or nectarines, if desired.

PASSIONFRUIT POLENTA CAKE

Preparation time **30 minutes** +
Total cooking time **45 minutes**
Serves **8–10**

6 eggs, at room temperature, separated
150 g (5½ oz/⅔ cup) caster (superfine) sugar
zest of 2 oranges, grated
125 ml (4 fl oz/½ cup) passionfruit pulp
2 teaspoons natural vanilla extract
150 g (5½ oz) toasted slivered almonds
150 g (5½ oz/1 cup) fine polenta
150 g (5½ oz/1¼ cups) self-raising flour
whipped cream, to serve

Syrup
zest and juice of 2 oranges
2 passionfruit
90 g (3¼ oz/¼ cup) orange blossom honey

Whisky butter sauce
90 g (3¼ oz/¼ cup) honey
60 ml (2 fl oz/¼ cup) whisky
50 g (1¾ oz) unsalted butter, cubed

1 Preheat the oven to 170°C (325°F/Gas 3). Grease a 24 cm (9½ in) spring-form cake tin.
2 Whisk the egg whites in a bowl until stiff peaks form. Beat the egg yolks and sugar in a separate bowl for 3–4 minutes, or until smooth. Add the orange zest, passionfruit pulp and vanilla and beat for 15 seconds.
3 Put the almonds in a food processor and process until ground. Add the polenta and flour and process until combined.
4 Using a metal spoon, fold a scoop of egg whites through the passionfruit mixture, then fold the passionfruit mixture through the remaining egg whites. Fold in the almond mixture and spoon into the tin. Bake for 30–35 minutes, or until a skewer inserted into the centre of the cake comes out clean. Set aside to cool for 15 minutes, then turn out onto a wire rack to cool.
5 To make the syrup, put the orange zest, orange juice, passionfruit pulp and honey in a saucepan. Bring to the boil over medium heat, then reduce the heat and simmer for 5 minutes.
6 Transfer the cake to a plate with a lip, and pierce several times with a fine metal skewer. Pour about one-quarter of the syrup over the top, then add the rest once absorbed. Set aside for 1 hour.
7 To make the whisky butter sauce, put the honey and whisky in a saucepan and bring to the boil. Simmer for 1 minute, then add the butter, one cube at a time. Serve the cake with lightly whipped cream and the whisky butter sauce.

RASPBERRY AND CARDAMOM CAKE WITH HONEY SYRUP

Preparation time **15 minutes** +

Total cooking time **50 minutes**

Serves **6–8**

125 g (4½ oz) unsalted butter, softened,
  cut into cubes
125 g (4½ oz/½ cup) caster (superfine)
  sugar
2 eggs
1 teaspoon natural vanilla extract
250 g (9 oz/2 cups) self-raising flour
2 teaspoons ground cardamom
125 ml (4 fl oz/½ cup) milk
150 g (5½ oz) raspberries, fresh or frozen
whipped cream, to serve

Honey syrup
175 g (6 oz/½ cup) honey
2 tablespoons caster (superfine) sugar
¼ teaspoon natural vanilla extract

1 Preheat the oven to 180°C (350°F/Gas 4). Grease a 20 cm (8 in) round cake tin and line the base with baking paper.

2 Using an electric mixer, beat the butter until soft. Add the caster sugar gradually and beat until the mixture is pale and creamy. Add the eggs and vanilla, and beat until the mixture is well combined.

3 Sift the flour and cardamom together. Using a large metal spoon, fold the flour into the creamed mixture alternately with the milk, starting with the flour and ending with flour. Do not overmix.

4 Lightly fold the raspberries into the mixture. Pour the batter into the prepared tin and gently smooth the surface.

5 Bake for 40–45 minutes, or until a skewer inserted into the centre comes out clean. Remove the cake from the oven and insert a thin metal skewer all over the cake.

6 To make the honey syrup, put 125 ml (4 fl oz/½ cup) of water, and the honey and sugar in a saucepan and stir over low heat until the sugar has dissolved. Remove the pan from the heat and add the vanilla.

7 Pour half of the honey syrup over the cake. Allow to stand for 10 minutes. Turn the cake out. Serve warm with whipped cream and the remaining honey syrup.

BLUEBERRY SHORTCAKE

Preparation time **20 minutes** +
Total cooking time **50 minutes**
Serves **8–10**

100 g (3½ oz/¾ cup) hazelnuts
280 g (10 oz/2¼ cups) self-raising flour
1½ teaspoons ground cinnamon
165 g (5¾ oz/¾ cup) demerara sugar
150 g (5½ oz) unsalted butter, chopped
2 eggs
160 g (5¾ oz/½ cup) blueberry jam
1 tablespoon demerara sugar, extra

1 Preheat the oven to 180°C (350°F/Gas 4). Grease a deep 20 cm (8 in) round cake tin and line the base with baking paper.
2 Spread the hazelnuts on a baking tray and bake for 5–10 minutes, or until lightly golden. Place in a tea towel (dish towel) and gently rub together to remove the skins, then roughly chop.
3 Mix the flour, cinnamon, sugar, butter and half the hazelnuts in a food processor in short bursts until finely chopped. Add the eggs and process until well combined.
4 Press half the mixture onto the base of the tin, then spread the jam evenly over the mixture.
5 Lightly knead the remaining hazelnuts into the remaining dough, then press evenly over the jam layer.
6 Sprinkle the extra sugar over the top and bake for 50 minutes, or until a skewer comes out clean when inserted into the centre of the cake. Leave in the tin for 15 minutes before carefully turning out onto a wire rack to cool. If desired, garnish with fresh blueberries and serve with thick cream.

PINEAPPLE PECAN CAKE

Preparation time **20 minutes** +
Total cooking time **1 hour**
Serves **8–10**

80 g (3 oz) unsalted butter, softened
250 g (9 oz/1 cup) sugar
2 eggs, lightly beaten
185 g (6½ oz/1½ cups) plain (all-purpose) flour
1¾ teaspoons baking powder
40 g (1½ oz/⅓ cup) finely chopped pecan
  nuts, toasted
180 g (6½ oz/¾ cup) finely chopped glacé
  pineapple
170 ml (5½ fl oz/⅔ cup) milk

1 Preheat the oven to 180°C (350°F/Gas 4).
Grease a 23 cm (9 in) round cake tin and
line the base with baking paper. Beat the
butter and sugar with electric beaters until
combined. Add the egg and beat until pale
and creamy.
2 Sift together the flour, baking powder
and ¼ teaspoon salt. Add to the butter
mixture with the pecans, pineapple and
milk, then beat on low for 1 minute, or
until almost smooth.
3 Spoon the mixture evenly into the
prepared tin and smooth the surface. Bake
for 1 hour, or until a skewer comes out
clean when inserted into the centre of the
cake. Leave in the tin for 10 minutes before
turning onto a wire rack to cool. If desired,
dust with icing sugar just before serving.
Note Glacé pineapple is available from
health food stores.

PANETTONE

Preparation time **30 minutes** +
Total cooking time **50 minutes**
Makes 1

90 g (3¼ oz/½ cup) mixed peel
80 g (2¾ oz/½ cup) sultanas (golden raisins)
1 teaspoon grated lemon zest
1 teaspoon grated orange zest
1 tablespoon brandy or rum
7 g (¼ oz) sachet dried yeast
220 ml (7½ fl oz) warm milk
60 g (2¼ oz/¼ cup) caster (superfine) sugar
400 g (14 oz/3¼ cups) white strong flour
2 eggs
1 teaspoon natural vanilla extract
150 g (5½ oz) unsalted butter, softened
20 g (½ oz) unsalted butter, melted, to glaze

1 Put the peel, sultanas and grated zest in a bowl. Add the alcohol, mix and set aside.
2 Put the yeast, warm milk and 1 teaspoon sugar in a bowl and leave in a warm place for 10–15 minutes. Sift 200 g (7 oz) flour and ½ teaspoon salt into a bowl, make a well in the centre and add the yeast mixture. Mix to a soft dough. Cover the bowl and leave to rise in a warm place for 45 minutes.
3 Add the eggs, remaining sugar and vanilla and mix. Add the butter and stir. Stir in the remaining flour and mix. Knead on a floured surface until smooth. Place in a greased bowl, cover with plastic wrap and leave in a warm place for 1½–2 hours.
4 Grease a 15 cm (6 in) round cake tin. Line the base and side with a double thickness of baking paper, ensuring the collar extends above the rim of the tin by 10 cm (4 in).
5 Knock back the dough and roll into a 30 x 20 cm (12 x 8 in) rectangle. Drain the fruit mixture and spread half the fruit over the surface of the dough. Fold over the short edges to cover the fruit. Roll again and repeat the process to incorporate all the fruit. Knead the dough for 2–3 minutes and shape into a ball. Place in the tin, brush with the butter, then slash a cross on the top with a sharp knife and leave to rise again in a warm place for 45 minutes.
6 Preheat the oven to 190°C (375°F/Gas 5). Bake for 50 minutes, or until golden brown and a skewer inserted into the centre comes out clean. Leave in the tin for 5 minutes, then transfer to a wire rack to cool.

CARAMEL PEACH CAKE

Preparation time 15 minutes +
Total cooking time 1 hour 25 minutes
Serves 10–12

250 g (9 oz) unsalted butter, softened
60 g (2¼ oz/⅓ cup) soft brown sugar
825 g (1 lb 13 oz) tinned peach halves in
    natural juice
250 g (9 oz/1 cup) caster (superfine) sugar
3 teaspoons finely grated lemon zest
3 eggs, lightly beaten
310 g (11 oz/2½ cups) self-raising flour, sifted
250 g (9 oz/1 cup) plain yoghurt

1 Preheat the oven to 180°C (350°F/Gas 4). Grease a deep 23 cm (9 in) round cake tin and line the base with baking paper.
2 Melt 50 g (1¾ oz) of the butter and pour on the base of the tin. Evenly sprinkle the brown sugar over the top.
3 Drain the peaches well, reserving about 1 tablespoon of the liquid. Arrange the peach halves, cut side up, over the sugar.
4 Beat the caster sugar, lemon zest and remaining butter using electric beaters for 5–6 minutes, or until pale and creamy. Add the egg gradually, beating well after each addition—the mixture may look curdled but once you add the flour, it will bring it back together. Using a metal spoon, fold in the flour alternately with the yoghurt (in two batches), then the reserved peach liquid. Spoon the mixture over the peaches and smooth the surface.
5 Bake for 1 hour 25 minutes, or until a skewer comes out clean when inserted into the centre of the cake. Cool in the tin for 30 minutes before turning out onto a large serving plate.

COCONUT CAKE WITH COCONUT FROSTING

Preparation time **15 minutes**

Total cooking time **40 minutes**

Serves **8**

340 g (11³/₄ oz) packet golden butter cake mix

2 eggs

60 g (2¹/₄ oz) unsalted butter, softened

250 ml (9 fl oz/1 cup) milk

120 g (4¹/₄ oz/1¹/₃ cups) desiccated coconut

250 g (9 oz/2 cups) icing (confectioners') sugar, sifted

1 egg white, lightly beaten

45 g (1¹/₂ oz/³/₄ cup) shredded coconut, toasted

1 Preheat the oven to 180°C (350°F/Gas 4). Grease a 20 cm (8 in) deep round cake tin and line the base with baking paper.

2 Beat the cake mix, whole eggs, butter and 170 ml (5¹/₂ fl oz/²/₃ cup) of the milk in a bowl with electric beaters on low speed for 1 minute, or until combined. Increase to medium speed and beat for 4 minutes. Fold in 30 g (1 oz/¹/₃ cup) of the desiccated coconut.

3 Spoon into the tin and bake for about 40 minutes, or until a skewer comes out clean when inserted into the centre of the cake. Leave in the tin for 5 minutes before turning out onto a wire rack to cool. Cut in half horizontally.

4 To make the coconut frosting, combine the icing sugar, egg white and remaining desiccated coconut in a small bowl. Mix to a paste, adding enough of the remaining milk to reach a spreadable consistency.

5 To assemble the cake, place the bottom layer on a plate and evenly spread with one third of the icing. Top with the other half of the cake.

6 Cover the top and side with the remaining icing using a flat-bladed knife, swirling to form a rough surface. Sprinkle with the shredded coconut.

FRUIT CAKES

With a little careful attention to the lining of the tin, you will be assured of that special feeling of fulfilment when lifting a freshly baked fruit cake out of the oven.

Fundamentals

Fruit cakes are generally made by the creaming method so it is recommended you read the detailed description of creaming butter and sugar on page 24.

Before you begin, read through your recipe, checking you have all the right equipment and ingredients at hand. Leave plenty of time as fruit cakes take a little longer to prepare than simple cakes and also take a few hours to cook.

Before you mix your cake, line the tin and make sure the oven rack is positioned so the cake will sit in the centre of the oven, then preheat the oven.

Lining the tin

Lightly grease the cake tin. Fruit cakes need a double layer of baking paper for the collar and base. Cut two circles of baking paper, using the base as a guide.

To make the collar, cut a double strip of baking paper long enough to fit around the outside of the tin and tall enough to extend 5 cm (2 in) above the top of the tin. Fold a 2 cm (3/4 in) deep cuff along the length of the strip, then make diagonal cuts up to the fold line about 1 cm (1/2 in) apart. Fit in the tin, with the cuts on the base, pressing them out at right angles so they sit flat around the base. Place the circles over the cuts.

Because of the long cooking time, fruit cakes require extra protection, both around the side and under the base. This is why we wrap layers of newspaper around the outside of the tin, and sit the tin on layers of newspaper in the oven. Because the oven temperature is low, this is quite safe.

Making the cake

Weigh all the ingredients in your recipe and complete preparations such as softening butter, sifting flour and spices, blanching nuts, tossing fruit in flour or marinating fruit, if required. Dates and prunes may have stones that need to be removed. Glacé fruit such as cherries, pineapple or ginger are better if cut into small pieces. If peel is large, cut or chop into smaller pieces.

Following the methods described in making a creamed butter cake, beat the butter and sugar with electric beaters until light and fluffy. Gradually add the eggs, beating thoroughly after each addition. Add any essences, rind, juice, jam, syrup or molasses as specified. Transfer to a large bowl and add the specified dried or glacé fruit. Mix with a large metal spoon until combined. Next, using a metal spoon, fold in the sifted dry ingredients. Alcohol, if specified, can also be added at this time. Stir until just combined and almost smooth. Spoon evenly into the tin, spread into the corners and smooth the top. Some fruit cakes are decorated at this stage by placing blanched almonds in a pattern on the top. Check that the oven temperature is correct. Wrap layers of newspaper around the tin, coming up as high as the collar, and secure with string or paper clips. Place a few layers of newspaper on the rack in the oven and place the tin on top. If the cake starts to brown before it is cooked, cover it loosely with foil.

When is it ready?

As ovens vary, check the cake 20 minutes before the specified time. If it is cooked, a skewer should come out clean when inserted into the centre. The cake should shrink from the side of the tin. Cool the cake completely in the tin, preferably overnight, before removing. Fruit cakes improve if kept for a few weeks wrapped in baking paper and foil, or kept in an airtight container, before decorating or cutting. Un-iced fruit cakes can be refrigerated for up to 3 months. They can be fed alcohol by inserting holes with a skewer and pouring in brandy or whisky.

WHAT WENT WRONG?

FRUIT CAKES

Perfect The crust is an even, deep golden brown. When a skewer is inserted into the centre of the cake, it comes out clean. The texture of the cake is moist and the fruit is evenly distributed.

Overcooked The oven temperature may have been too high or the cooking time too long. The mixture might have had too little fat or too much raising agent. Too much sugar may cause a dark crust. If the cake is colouring too quickly and the oven temperature is correct, then the top can be protected by covering with foil or a double layer of baking paper.

Undercooked and sunken The baking time may have been too short or the oven temperature too low. There might be too much fruit or too little raising agent. The cake may have been placed too low in the oven. The tin needs to be placed in the middle of the oven.

GOLDEN FRUIT CAKE

Preparation time **25 minutes**

Total cooking time **2 hours**

Serves 16–20

110 g (3³/₄ oz) chopped glacé pears
240 g (8³/₄ oz/1 cup) chopped glacé apricots
220 g (7³/₄ oz) chopped glacé pineapple
60 g (2¹/₄ oz) chopped mixed peel
95 g (3¹/₂ oz) chopped glacé orange slices
80 g (2³/₄ oz/¹/₂ cup) roughly chopped
    blanched almonds
185 g (6¹/₂ oz/1¹/₂ cups) plain (all-purpose) flour
60 g (2¹/₄ oz/¹/₂ cup) self-raising flour
250 g (9 oz) unsalted butter, softened
1 tablespoon finely grated orange zest
1 tablespoon finely grated lemon zest
230 g (8¹/₂ oz/1 cup) caster (superfine) sugar
4 eggs
60 ml (2 fl oz/¹/₄ cup) sweet sherry

1 Preheat the oven to 160°C (315°F/ Gas 2–3). Grease a deep 20 cm (8 in) square tin and line with baking paper.
2 Combine the fruits and almonds in a bowl and toss with 30 g (1 oz/¹/₄ cup) of the plain flour to help keep the fruits separate. Sift together the remaining flours.
3 Beat the butter and grated zest in a small bowl using electric beaters, gradually adding the sugar, until light and fluffy. Beat in the eggs, one at a time, beating thoroughly after each addition. Transfer the mixture to a large bowl, stir in the remaining flour alternately with the sherry, then fold in the fruit, nut and flour mixture.
4 Spread evenly into the tin and wrap paper around the outside of the tin. Sit the cake tin on layers of newspaper in the oven. Bake for about 1 hour 45 minutes– 2 hours, or until a skewer inserted into the centre of the cake comes out clean. Leave in the tin for 20 minutes before turning out onto a wire rack to cool.
Note Store in an airtight container for up to a month.

LIGHT FRUIT CAKE

Preparation time **30 minutes**

Total cooking time **2 hours**

Makes 1

185 g (6½ oz) unsalted butter, softened

115 g (4 oz/½ cup) caster (superfine) sugar

3 eggs

160 g (5½ oz/1 cup) sultanas (golden raisins)

100 g (3½ oz/⅔ cup) currants

60 g (2¼ oz/¼ cup) chopped glacé (candied) apricots

45 g (1½ oz/¼ cup) chopped glacé (candied) figs

240 g (7½ oz/1 cup) chopped glacé (candied) cherries, plus extra to decorate

80 g (2¾ oz/½ cup) macadamia nuts, coarsely chopped

185 g (6½ oz/1½ cups) plain (all-purpose) flour

60 g (2¼ oz/½ cup) self-raising flour

125 ml (4 fl oz/½ cup) milk

1 tablespoon sweet sherry

1 Preheat the oven to 160°C (315°F/ Gas 2–3). Grease and line a deep 20 cm (8 in) round or 18 cm (7 in) square cake tin.

2 Cream the butter and sugar in a bowl until just combined. Add the eggs, one at a time, beating well after each addition. Transfer the mixture to a bowl and stir in the fruit and nuts. Sift in half the flours and half the milk, stir to combine, then stir in the remaining flours and milk, and the sherry.

3 Spoon into the prepared tin and tap the tin on the bench to remove any air bubbles. Smooth the surface with wet fingers and decorate the top with nuts or cherries, or both.

4 Wrap the outside of the tin. Sit the tin on layers of newspaper in the oven and bake for 1¾–2 hours, or until a skewer inserted into the centre comes out clean. The top may need to be covered with a sheet of baking paper if it colours too much. Remove from the oven, remove the top baking paper and wrap the tin in a tea towel (dish towel) until cool. Remove the paper tin lining.

Note Store in an airtight container for up to 2 weeks.

BUTTERLESS RUM FRUIT CAKE

Preparation time **30 minutes**
Total cooking time **2 hours 25 minutes**
Serves **12–14**

310 g (11 oz/2½ cups) sultanas (golden raisins)
250 g (9 oz/2 cups) raisins
225 g (8 oz/1½ cups) currants
185 ml (6 fl oz/¾ cup) vegetable oil
125 ml (4 fl oz/½ cup) dark rum
125 ml (4 fl oz/½ cup) orange juice
230 g (8½ oz/1 cup) soft brown sugar
2 tablespoons treacle or golden syrup
½ teaspoon bicarbonate of soda (baking soda)
1 tablespoon grated orange zest
4 eggs, lightly beaten
185 g (6½ oz/1½ cups) plain (all-purpose) flour
60 g (2¼ oz/½ cup) self-raising flour
1 tablespoon mixed (pumpkin pie) spice
40 g (1½ oz/¼ cup) blanched whole almonds
80 g (2¾ oz/¼ cup) apricot jam, to glaze

1 Preheat the oven to 150°C (300°F/Gas 2). Grease a 20 cm (8 in) round cake tin.
2 Cut a double layer of baking paper into a strip long enough to fit around the outside of the tin and tall enough to come 5 cm (2 in) above the edge of the tin. Fold down a cuff about 2 cm (¾ in) deep along the length of the strip, along the folded edge. Make cuts along the cuff, cutting up to the fold line, about 1 cm (½ in) apart. Fit the strip around the inside of the tin, with the cuts on the base, pressing the cuts out at right angles so they sit flat around the base. Place the cake tin on a doubled piece of baking paper and draw around the edge. Cut out and sit the paper circles in the base of the tin.
3 Combine the dried fruit, oil, rum, orange juice, sugar and treacle in a large saucepan and stir over medium heat until the sugar has dissolved. Bring to the boil, reduce the heat and simmer, covered, over low heat for 10 minutes. Remove from the heat and stir in the bicarbonate of soda, then cool to room temperature. Stir in the zest, eggs, sifted flours and mixed spice.
4 Spread the mixture into the prepared tin and smooth the surface, then arrange the almonds over the top of the cake.
5 Bake for 2 hours 15 minutes, or until a skewer inserted into the centre of the cake comes out clean. Allow to cool in the tin.
6 Heat the jam in a saucepan over low heat for 3–4 minutes, or until runny. Brush the top of the cake with the jam.

FRUIT CAKE

Preparation time **40 minutes**
Total cooking time **3 hours 30 minutes**
Makes 1

250 g (9 oz) softened unsalted butter
230 g (8 oz/1 cup) soft brown sugar
2 teaspoons finely grated orange zest
2 teaspoons finely grated lemon zest
4 eggs
250 g (9 oz/2 cups) plain (all-purpose) flour
60 g (2¼ oz/½ cup) self-raising flour

Fruit mix

800 g (1 lb 12 oz) sultanas (golden raisins)
320 g (11¼ oz) raisins, chopped
185 g (6½ oz/1¼ cups) currants
155 g (5½ oz) glacé cherries, quartered
250 g (9 oz) pitted prunes, quartered
125 g (4½ oz) mixed peel
250 ml (9 fl oz/1 cup) brandy
55 g (2 oz/¼ cup) soft brown sugar
80 g (2¾ oz) sweet orange marmelade
1 tablespoon cocoa powder
½ tablespoon ground cinnamon
1 teaspoon ground ginger
1 teaspoon mixed spice

1 Preheat the oven to 150°C (300°F/Gas 2). Grease and line a 23 cm (9 in) round or square cake tin.

2 To make the fruit mince, combine all the ingredients in a bowl.

3 Beat the butter, soft brown sugar and orange and lemon zests in a bowl with electric beaters until just combined. Add the eggs, one at a time, beating well after each addition. Transfer to a bowl and stir in half of the soaked fruit mix alternately with the plain flour and the self-raising flour. Mix well.

4 Spread evenly into the tin and tap the tin on the bench to remove any air bubbles. Dip your fingers in water and level the surface. Decorate the top of the cake with whole blanched almonds, if desired.

5 Sit the cake on several layers of newspaper on the oven shelf and bake for 3¼–3½ hours, or until a skewer comes out clean.

6 Cover the top with baking paper, seal firmly with foil, then wrap the cake and tin in a clean tea towel (dish towel) and leave to cool.

PUMPKIN FRUITCAKE

Preparation time **25 minutes +**
Total cooking time **1 hour 40 minutes**
Serves **8–10**

250 g (9 oz) pumpkin, peeled and cut into
   small pieces
125 g (4½ oz) unsalted butter, softened
140 g (5 oz/¾ cup) soft brown sugar
2 tablespoons golden syrup or honey
2 eggs, lightly beaten
250 g (9 oz/2 cups) self-raising flour,
   sifted
200 g (7 oz/1 cup) mixed dried fruit
2 tablespoons chopped glacé ginger

1 Preheat the oven to 150°C (300°F/Gas 2). Grease a deep 20 cm (8 in) round cake tin and line the base and side with baking paper.

2 Steam the pumpkin for 10 minutes, or until cooked through. Mash with a potato masher or a fork until smooth. Measure 200 g (7 oz/¾ cup) and set aside until ready to use.

3 Beat the butter and sugar together with electric beaters until pale and creamy. Add the golden syrup and beat well. Gradually add the egg, beating well after each addition. Fold in the pumpkin until combined. Combine the flour, dried fruit and ginger, then fold into the butter mixture with a metal spoon until combined. Spoon the mixture into the prepared tin and smooth the surface.

4 Bake for 1 hour 40 minutes, or until a skewer comes out clean when inserted into the centre of the cake. Cool in the tin for 20 minutes before turning out onto a wire rack.

GINGER FRUIT LOAF

Preparation time **25 minutes +**
Total cooking time **1 hour 25 minutes**
Makes **1 loaf**

375 g (13 oz) mixed dried fruit
160 g (5¾ oz/1 cup) chopped pitted
   dried dates
75 g (2½ oz/⅓ cup) glacé ginger, chopped
60 g (2¼ oz) unsalted butter, chopped
185 g (6½ oz/1 cup) soft brown sugar
1 tablespoon golden or dark corn syrup
1 teaspoon natural vanilla extract
2 eggs, lightly beaten
185 g (6½ oz/1½ cups) plain (all-purpose) flour
1 teaspoon baking powder
2 teaspoons ground ginger
1 teaspoon ground nutmeg
20 blanched almonds

1 Put the mixed fruit, dates, glacé ginger, butter, brown sugar, golden syrup, vanilla extract and 310 ml (10¾ fl oz/1¾ cups) water in a saucepan. Bring slowly to the boil, then simmer over low heat for 5 minutes. Set aside to cool.

2 Preheat the oven to 160°C (315°F/ Gas 2–3). Grease the base and sides of a 25 x 11 cm (10 x 4¼ in) loaf (bar) tin and line the base with baking paper.

3 Stir the beaten eggs into the cooled fruit mixture. Sift together the flour, baking powder and spices. Stir the flour mixture into the fruit mixture and mix until smooth.

4 Spoon into the prepared tin and smooth the surface. Arrange the almonds over the surface.

5 Bake for 1 hour 20 minutes, or until a skewer inserted in the centre comes out clean. Cover with foil if the surface and almonds are browning too much. Leave to cool in the tin for 10 minutes, then turn out onto a wire rack to cool. Cut into thick slices to serve.

MUFFINS, FRIANDS & CUPCAKES

These little morsels are perfect for breakfast on the run, a mid-morning snack or a cosy afternoon tea. They are just enough to satisfy your cravings, without making you feel guilty and they won't spoil your appetite. It may take a little practice to master the art of perfect friand making or to achieve light-as-air muffins, but that is all part of the fun in learning the art of baking. Just remember one thing, the secret to making perfect muffins is a light hand when mixing the ingredients, so as not to over mix, otherwise the results will be tough and rubbery.

MUFFIN BASICS

Wonderfully simple, muffins can be plain, sweet or savoury. Master the basic muffin, then experiment with different flavour combinations and enjoy them for breakfast, snacks, lunch or dinner.

PERFECT MUFFINS

Follow these simple instructions to make twelve delicious muffins. You will need 310 g (11 oz/2$\frac{1}{2}$ cups) self-raising flour, 125 g (4$\frac{1}{2}$ oz/$\frac{1}{2}$ cup) caster (superfine) sugar, 375 ml (13 fl oz/1$\frac{1}{2}$ cups) milk, 2 lightly beaten eggs, 1 teaspoon natural vanilla extract and 150 g (5$\frac{1}{2}$ oz) unsalted butter that has been melted and cooled.

We used the regular (100 ml/3$\frac{1}{2}$ fl oz) size American-style non-stick tins but tins are also available in mini and Texan sizes. Even though most muffin tins have non-stick surfaces, it is worth greasing the holes, especially when making sweet muffins, as the sugar can make them very sticky.

Assemble your ingredients and utensils and preheat the oven to 200°C (400°F/ Gas 6). Sift the flour into a bowl to aerate the flour and ensure a light muffin. Add the sugar to the bowl and stir through the flour. Make a well in the centre.

In a jug, mix together the milk, eggs and natural vanilla extract. Pour the liquid into the well in the flour and add the cooled butter. Melted butter doesn't always combine well with other liquids so it is often added separately. Fold the mixture gently with a metal spoon until just combined. Be careful not to overbeat or the muffins will become tough and rubbery. The mixture should still be lumpy at this stage.

Divide the mixture evenly among the holes using two metal spoons—fill each hole to about three-quarters full. Always try to use the hole size indicated in the recipe because if you use a different size the cooking time changes.

COOKING

Bake the muffins for 20–25 minutes, or until they are risen, golden and come away slightly from the sides of the holes. Test them by pressing lightly with your fingertips—they are cooked when they feel firm, and spring back. Another test is to insert a skewer into the centre—if it comes out clean they are ready.

Most muffins should be left in the tin for a couple of minutes once out of the oven, but don't leave them too long or trapped steam will make the bases soggy.

Using a flat-bladed knife, loosen the muffins and transfer to a wire rack. They can be eaten warm or cool and can be decorated or iced.

SIMPLE VARIATIONS

The basic recipe can be adapted to add many flavours. You can use the same tin but the muffin holes will be quite full.

Banana Add an extra 60 g (2$\frac{1}{4}$ oz/$\frac{1}{4}$ cup) caster (superfine) sugar and $\frac{1}{2}$ teaspoon mixed spice to the flour and 240 g (8$\frac{1}{2}$ oz/ 1 cup) mashed ripe bananas to the butter. Use only 250 ml (9 fl oz/1 cup) milk. Proceed with the recipe.

Pecan Replace the caster (superfine) sugar with 140 g (5 oz/$\frac{3}{4}$ cup) soft brown sugar. Add 90 g (3$\frac{1}{4}$ oz/$\frac{3}{4}$ cup) chopped pecans with the flour. Mix to distribute, then proceed with the recipe.

STORAGE

Cold muffins can be frozen for 3 months. When required, thaw, wrap in foil, then reheat in a 180°C (350°F/Gas 4) oven for about 8 minutes, or until heated through.

WHAT WENT WRONG?

MUFFINS

Perfect The texture of the muffin is even with a nicely risen centre and good golden colouring. The muffin has started to come away from the side of the holes.

Undercooked The muffin is moist in the centre with insufficient peaking. The oven wasn't hot enough, or the cooking time may have been too short.

Poorly risen The texture is heavy and dense. This can be caused by insufficient raising agent or a missing ingredient.

Overflowing mixture Do not fill the muffin holes more than two-thirds full. This leaves room for the batter to rise.

More about muffins If you want freshly baked muffins for breakfast but don't have time in the morning, you can make a muffin mixture, then spoon it into the muffin tin and refrigerate overnight, ready for baking the next day. Uncooked mixture for the plainer muffins such as chocolate or blueberry, or those without fillings, can be frozen in paper-lined muffin tins for up to 1 month. When you want to cook them, remove from the freezer and bake in a 200°C (400°F/Gas 6) oven for 25–30 minutes, or until golden.

Too peaked The crust is too coloured and the muffin too peaked. This is caused by mixing too much or baking in an oven that is too hot.

BLUEBERRY MUFFINS

Preparation time **15 minutes**
Total cooking time **20 minutes**
Makes **12**

375 g (13 oz/3 cups) plain (all-purpose)
    flour
1 tablespoon baking powder
165 g (5¾ oz/¾ cup) soft brown sugar
125 g (4½ oz) unsalted butter, melted
2 eggs, lightly beaten
250 ml (9 fl oz/1 cup) milk
185 g (6½ oz/1¼ cups) fresh or thawed
    frozen blueberries

1 Preheat the oven to 210°C (415°F/
Gas 6–7). Grease or brush twelve 125 ml
(4 fl oz/½ cup) muffin holes with melted
butter or oil.
2 Sift the flour and baking powder into a
large bowl. Stir in the sugar and make a
well in the centre.
3 Add the combined melted butter, eggs
and milk all at once, and fold until just
combined. Do not overmix—the batter
should look quite lumpy.
4 Fold in the blueberries. Spoon the batter
into the prepared tin. Bake for 20 minutes,
or until golden brown. Cool on a wire rack.

CHOCOLATE CHIP MUFFINS

Preparation time **20 minutes**
Total cooking time **25 minutes**
Makes 12

310 g (11 oz/2½ cups) self-raising flour
265 g (9½ oz/1½ cups) chocolate chips
95 g (3½ oz/½ cup) soft brown sugar
375 ml (13 fl oz/1½ cups) milk
2 eggs, lightly beaten
1 teaspoon natural vanilla extract
150 g (5½ oz) unsalted butter, melted
  and cooled

1 Preheat the oven to 200°C (400°F/Gas 6).
Lightly grease a 12-hole standard muffin
tin, or line the muffin tin with paper cases.
2 Sift the flour into a large bowl. Add the
chocolate chips and sugar to the bowl and
stir through the flour. Make a well in
the centre.
3 Mix together the milk, egg and vanilla
extract. Pour the liquid into the well in the
flour and add the cooled butter. Gently
fold the mixture with a metal spoon until
just combined. Do not overmix—the batter
will still be slightly lumpy.
4 Divide the mixture evenly among the
holes—fill each hole to three-quarters
full. Bake the muffins for 20–25 minutes,
or until they are golden and a skewer
inserted into the centre of a muffin comes
out clean.
5 Leave the muffins in the tin for a few
minutes to cool. Gently loosen each
muffin with a flat-bladed knife before
turning out onto a wire rack. Serve warm
or at room temperature.

APPLE, BUTTERMILK, MAPLE SYRUP AND BRAN MUFFINS

Preparation time **20 minutes**

Total cooking time **25 minutes**

Makes **12 muffins**

70 g (2½ oz/1 cup) unprocessed bran
375 ml (13 fl oz/1½ cups) buttermilk
185 ml (6 fl oz/¾ cup) maple syrup
1 egg, lightly beaten
60 ml (2 fl oz/¼ cup) vegetable oil
1 cooking apple (such as granny smith),
   peeled, cored and chopped
70 g (2½ oz/½ cup) hazelnuts, toasted, peeled
   (see tip) and chopped
250 g (9 oz/2 cups) self-raising flour
1 teaspoon ground cinnamon

1 Preheat the oven to 180°C (350°F/Gas 4). Lightly grease a 12-hole standard muffin tin, or line the holes with paper cases.

2 Combine the bran and buttermilk in a bowl, stirring to mix well, then set aside for 5 minutes.

3 Add the maple syrup, egg, oil, apple and hazelnuts and stir to combine well. Sift the flour and cinnamon over the mixture, then gently fold in until just combined. Do not overmix—the batter will still be slightly lumpy.

4 Divide the mixture evenly between the muffin holes. Bake for 20–25 minutes, or until golden and a skewer inserted into the centre of a muffin comes out clean. Cool in the tin for 2 minutes before transferring to a wire rack.

Tip To toast the hazelnuts, put them in a single layer on a large baking tray. Toast in a 180°C (350°F/Gas 4) oven for about 2 minutes, turning after 1 minute (watch carefully as nuts burn quickly). Tip into a tea towel (dish towel) and rub the skins off.

ORANGE POPPY SEED MUFFINS

Preparation time **15 minutes**
Total cooking time **30 minutes**
Makes 12

310 g (11 oz/2½ cups) self-raising flour
40 g (1½ oz/¼ cup) poppy seeds
80 g (2¾ oz/⅓ cup) caster (superfine) sugar
125 g (4½ oz) unsalted butter
315 g (11¼ oz/1 cup) orange marmalade
250 ml (9 fl oz/1 cup) milk
2 eggs
1 tablespoon finely grated orange zest

1 Preheat the oven to 200°C (400°F/Gas 6). Lightly grease a 12-hole standard muffin tin, or line the muffin tin with paper cases.
2 Sift the flour into a bowl. Stir in the poppy seeds and sugar, and make a well in the centre.
3 Put the butter and 210 g (7½ oz/⅔ cup) of the marmalade in a small saucepan and stir over low heat until the butter has melted and the ingredients are combined.

4 Whisk together the milk, eggs and orange zest and pour into the well. Add the butter and marmalade. Fold with a metal spoon until just combined. Do not overmix—the batter will still be slightly lumpy.
5 Divide the mixture evenly among the holes—fill each hole to about three-quarters full. Bake for 20–25 minutes, or until golden and a skewer inserted into the centre of a muffin comes out clean.
6 Heat the remaining marmalade and push it through a fine sieve. Brush over the top of the warm muffins. Leave them to cool in the tin for a couple of minutes. Gently loosen each muffin with a flat-bladed knife before turning out onto a wire rack. Serve warm or at room temperature.
Notes A variation of this muffin can be made using lime marmalade and finely grated lemon zest.

Muffins are best eaten on the day they are made. If you want to store muffins for a couple of days, let them cool completely, then store them in an airtight container. Muffins are also suitable for freezing.

APRICOT AND ORANGE MUFFINS

Preparation time **15 minutes**
Total cooking time **25 minutes**
Makes **12**

140 g (5 oz/³/₄ cup) dried apricots, roughly chopped
zest of 1 orange, grated
125 ml (4 fl oz/½ cup) freshly squeezed orange juice
250 g (9 oz/2 cups) self-raising flour
175 g (6 oz/½ cup) honey
30 g (1 oz) unsalted butter, melted
185 ml (6 fl oz/³/₄ cup) skim milk
1 egg, lightly beaten

1 Preheat the oven to 180°C (350°F/Gas 4). Grease a 12-hole standard muffin tin, or line the holes with paper cases.
2 Combine the apricots, orange zest and juice in a small saucepan and cook over medium heat until just warmed through. Remove from the heat and cool.
3 Sift the flour into a large bowl and make a well in the centre. Combine the honey, butter, milk and egg in a bowl, stirring to mix well. Pour into the well, then add the apricot mixture and stir quickly until just combined. Do not overmix—the batter will still be slightly lumpy.
4 Divide the mixture evenly between the muffin holes. Bake for 20–25 minutes, or until golden and a skewer inserted into the centre of a muffin comes out clean.
5 Allow to cool in the tin for 2 minutes before transferring to a wire rack to cool completely.

OATMEAL AND RASPBERRY MUFFINS

Preparation time **20 minutes**
Total cooking time **25 minutes**
Makes **12 muffins**

125 g (4½ oz/1 cup) medium oatmeal
375 ml (13 fl oz/1½ cups) milk
250 g (9 oz/2 cups) plain (all-purpose) flour
1 tablespoon baking powder
115 g (4 oz/½ cup) soft brown sugar
1 egg, lightly beaten
90 g (3¼ oz/¼ cup) honey
60 g (2¼ oz) unsalted butter, melted
150 g (5½ oz/1¼ cups) raspberries

1 Preheat the oven to 190°C (375°F/Gas 5). Grease a 12-hole standard muffin tin, or line the holes with paper cases.

2 Put the oatmeal in a bowl, stir in the milk and set aside for 5 minutes. Sift the flour and baking powder into a large bowl, then stir in the sugar. Make a well in the centre.

3 Combine the egg, honey and butter in a large bowl and stir to mix well. Pour the egg mixture and oatmeal mixture into the well, then stir quickly until just combined. Do not overmix—the batter will still be slightly lumpy. Gently fold in the raspberries.

4 Divide the mixture evenly between the muffin holes. Bake for 20–25 minutes, or until the muffins are golden and a skewer inserted into the centre of a muffin comes out clean. Leave to cool in the tin for 5 minutes before transferring to a wire rack. Serve warm.

LEMON MERINGUE MUFFINS

Preparation time **20 minutes+**
Total cooking time **15 minutes**
Makes **12 regular muffins**

215 g (4 oz/1³/₄ cups) self-raising flour
185 g (6½ oz/³/₄ cup) caster (superfine) sugar
1 egg
1 egg yolk
170 ml (5½ fl oz/²/₃ cup) milk
½ teaspoon natural vanilla extract
90 g (3¼ oz) unsalted butter, melted
200 g (7 oz/²/₃ cup) ready-made lemon curd
2 egg whites
1 teaspoon caster (superfine) sugar, extra

1 Preheat the oven to 200°C (400°F/Gas 6). Grease 12 regular muffin holes.
2 Sift the flour into a bowl and stir in 60 g (2¼ oz/¼ cup) of the caster sugar. Make a well in the centre. Put a pinch of salt, the egg and egg yolk in a bowl and beat. Stir in the milk, vanilla and butter. Pour the egg mixture into the well. Fold until combined.
3 Divide the muffin mixture among the holes. Bake for 15 minutes. Leave the oven on. Cool in the tin for 10 minutes, then loosen with a knife but leave in the tin.
4 Hollow out the centre of each muffin with a melon baller. Fill a piping bag with the curd and fill the centre of each muffin.
5 Whisk the egg whites in a dry bowl until firm peaks form. Add a quarter of the remaining sugar at a time, beating after each addition until firm peaks form. Put a heaped tablespoon of meringue on top of each muffin and form peaks with the back of a spoon.
6 Sprinkle over a little caster sugar and bake for 5 minutes, or until golden. Cool in the tin for 10 minutes, then transfer to a wire rack. Serve warm or at room temperature.

STRAWBERRY CHEESECAKE MUFFINS

Preparation time 20 minutes

Total cooking time 15 minutes

Makes 6

250 g (9 oz/1^2/$_3$ cups) strawberries, hulled

125 g (4^1/$_2$ oz/^{1}/$_2$ cup) caster (superfine) sugar

85 g (3 oz/^{1}/$_3$ cup) cream cheese

1 tablespoon strawberry liqueur

175 g (6 oz/1^1/$_3$ cups) plain (all-purpose) flour

1 tablespoon baking powder

1 tablespoon butter, melted

1 teaspoon finely grated orange zest

1 egg

125 ml (4 fl oz/^{1}/$_2$ cup) milk

icing (confectioners') sugar, to dust

1 Preheat the oven to 180°C (350°F/Gas 4). Lightly grease six 125 ml (4 fl oz/^{1}/$_2$ cup) non-stick muffin holes with oil. Set aside six small strawberries.

2 Put half the sugar in a bowl with the cream cheese and mix together well. Put the remaining strawberries in a blender or food processor with the strawberry liqueur and remaining sugar, and blend until smooth. Strain through a fine sieve to remove the strawberry seeds.

3 Sift the flour and baking powder together in a large bowl and stir in the butter, orange zest and ^{1}/$_2$ teaspoon salt.

4 In a separate bowl, beat the egg and milk together, then add to the dry ingredients and mix well until combined.

5 Spoon half of the mixture into the base of the muffin holes, then add a strawberry and a teaspoon of the cheese mixture. Top with the remaining muffin mixture.

6 Bake for 15 minutes, or until cooked and golden. Remove from the tins and cool slightly. Place a muffin on each serving plate, dust with icing sugar and serve drizzled with the sauce.

HIGH-TOP CAPPUCCINO AND WHITE-CHOC MUFFINS

Preparation time **15 minutes**

Total cooking time **30 minutes**

Makes **8 regular muffins**

20 g (3/4 oz/1/4 cup) instant espresso
   coffee powder

1 tablespoon boiling water

310 g (11 oz/2½ cups) self-raising flour

115 g (4 oz/½ cup) caster (superfine) sugar

2 eggs, lightly beaten

375 ml (13 fl oz/1½ cups) buttermilk

1 teaspoon natural vanilla extract

150 g (5½ oz) butter, melted

100 g (3½ oz) white chocolate, chopped

30 g (1 oz) butter, extra

3 tablespoons brown sugar

1 Preheat the oven to 200°C (400°F/Gas 6). Cut eight lengths of baking paper and roll into 8 cm (3 in) high cylinders to fit into eight 125 ml (4 fl oz/½ cup) capacity ramekins. When in place in the ramekins, secure the cylinders with string and place all the ramekins onto a baking tray.

2 Dissolve the coffee in the boiling water and allow to cool. Sift the flour and sugar into a large bowl.

3 Combine the egg, buttermilk, vanilla extract, butter, white chocolate and the coffee mixture. Combine with the dry ingredients. Spoon the mixture into each cylinder.

4 Heat the extra butter and the brown sugar in a saucepan over medium heat and stir until the sugar dissolves. Spoon this mixture onto each muffin and gently swirl into the muffin using a skewer.

5 Bake for 25–30 minutes, or until golden and a skewer inserted into the centre of a muffin comes out clean.

STRAWBERRY AND PASSIONFRUIT MUFFINS

Preparation time **20 minutes**
Total cooking time **15 minutes**
Makes 12

215 g (7³/₄ oz/1³/₄ cups) self-raising flour
1 teaspoon baking powder
¹/₂ teaspoon bicarbonate of soda (baking soda)
55 g (2 oz/¹/₄ cup) caster (superfine) sugar
175 g (6 oz/1 cup) chopped strawberries
125 g (4¹/₂ oz) tinned (or fresh) passionfruit pulp
1 egg
185 ml (6 fl oz/³/₄ cup) milk
60 g (2¹/₄ oz) unsalted butter, melted
whipped cream, fresh strawberry halves
    and icing (confectioners') sugar,
    to serve (optional)

1 Preheat the oven to 210°C (415°F/ Gas 6–7). Lightly grease a 12-hole standard muffin tin, or line the muffin tin with paper cases.

2 Sift the flour, baking powder, bicarbonate of soda, sugar and a pinch of salt into a bowl. Add the strawberries and stir to combine. Make a well in the centre.
3 Add the passionfruit pulp and the combined egg and milk. Pour the melted butter into the flour mixture all at once and lightly stir with a fork until just combined. Do not overbeat—the batter will still be slightly lumpy.
4 Divide the mixture evenly among the holes—fill each hole to about three-quarters full. Bake for 10–15 minutes, or until golden and a skewer inserted into the centre of a muffin comes out clean. Leave the muffins in the tin for a couple of minutes to cool. Gently loosen each muffin with a flat-bladed knife before turning out onto a wire rack to cool.
5 Top the muffins with softened, sweetened cream cheese or whipped cream and fresh strawberry halves and sprinkle with icing sugar, if desired.

FRUIT AND OAT BRAN MUFFINS

Preparation time **20 minutes**

Total cooking time **25 minutes**

Makes **12**

225 g (8 oz/1½ cups) stoneground
  self-raising flour

1 teaspoon freshly grated nutmeg

½ teaspoon baking powder

150 g (5½ oz/1 cup) unprocessed oat bran

80 g (2¾ oz/⅓ cup) raw sugar

125 g (4½ oz/1 cup) fruit medley

1 egg

250 ml (9 fl oz/1 cup) low-fat milk

140 g (5 oz/½ cup) unsweetened apple purée

60 g (2¼ oz) light canola margarine, just
  melted

1 Preheat the oven to 180°C (350°F/Gas 4).
Lightly grease a 12-hole standard muffin tin.
2 Sift the flour, nutmeg and the baking
powder into a large bowl, then return any
husks to the bowl. Stir in the oat bran,
raw sugar and fruit medley, using your
fingertips to break up the fruit medley so
it doesn't clump together. Make a well in
the centre.
3 Whisk together the egg, milk, apple
purée and melted margarine and stir into
the flour mixture until just combined.
Do not overmix.
4 Spoon evenly into the muffin holes and
bake for 25 minutes, or until firm to the
touch and golden brown. Leave in the tin
for 5 minutes, then turn out onto a wire
rack to cool.
Note These muffins will keep refrigerated
for up to 5 days and frozen for up to
1 month.

EASY BERRY MUFFINS

Preparation time **10 minutes**

Total cooking time **25 minutes**

Makes **16**

250 g (9 oz/1 cup) plain yoghurt

100 g (3½ oz/1 cup) rolled (porridge) oats

60 ml (2 fl oz/¼ cup) oil

80 g (2¾ oz/⅓ cup) caster (superfine) sugar

1 egg

125 g (4½ oz/1 cup) self-raising flour, sifted

3 teaspoons baking powder

300 g (10½ oz/1⅓ cups) mixed frozen berries, thawed

1 Preheat the oven to 180°C (350°F/Gas 4). Place paper cases into 16 muffin holes.

2 Mix together the yoghurt, oats, oil, caster sugar and egg. Stir in the sifted flour and baking powder with the fruit.

3 Spoon the mixture into paper cases in the muffin tin and bake for 20–25 minutes or until golden brown and a skewer comes out clean when inserted into the centre.

Tip Muffins can be made with any number of delicious fruit-based combinations. Apple, sultanas (golden raisins) and cinnamon, or pear and date can make a tasty alternative.

HAM, CORN AND POLENTA MUFFINS

Preparation time **15 minutes** +
Total cooking time **20 minutes**
Makes **12**

110 g (3³/₄ oz/³/₄ cup) polenta
1 tablespoon sugar
210 g (7¹/₄ oz/1²/₃ cups) plain (all-purpose)
   flour
1 tablespoons baking powder
2 tablespoons oil
1 egg, lightly beaten
310 ml (11 fl oz/1¹/₄ cups) skim milk
125 g (4¹/₂ oz) tinned creamed corn
4 spring onions (scallions), thinly sliced
150 g (5¹/₂ oz) low-fat shaved ham, chopped
50 g (1³/₄ oz) low-fat cheddar cheese, grated

1 Preheat the oven to 200°C (400°F/Gas 6).
2 Sift the polenta, sugar, flour and baking powder into a bowl. Place the oil, egg and skim milk in a separate bowl, mix together well and pour into the dry ingredients.
3 Add the creamed corn, spring onions, ham and cheese, and stir together with a metal spoon until just combined. Do not overmix. The mixture should still be lumpy.
4 Spoon the mixture into twelve 125 ml (4 fl oz/¹/₂ cup) non-stick muffin holes. Bake for 20 minutes, or until risen and golden brown. Leave in the tin to cool for 5 minutes before turning out onto a wire rack to cool completely. Store in an airtight container.
Note Polenta is available at most supermarkets and health-food shops.

SPICY VEGETABLE MUFFINS

Preparation time **20 minutes**
Total cooking time **25 minutes**
Makes **12**

250 g (9 oz/2 cups) self-raising flour
3 teaspoons curry powder
80 g (2³/4 oz/¹/2 cup) grated carrot
60 g (2¹/4 oz) orange sweet potato, grated
125 g (4¹/2 oz/1 cup) grated cheddar cheese
90 g (3¹/4 oz) butter, melted
1 egg, lightly beaten
185 ml (6 fl oz/³/4 cup) milk

1 Preheat the oven to 180°C (350°F/Gas 4). Lightly grease a 12-hole standard muffin tin, or line the muffin tin with paper cases.
2 Sift the flour, curry powder and some salt and pepper into a bowl. Add the carrot, sweet potato and cheese and mix through with your fingertips until the ingredients are evenly combined. Make a well in the centre.
3 Combine the butter, egg and milk in large bowl and add to the flour mixture. Using a wooden spoon, stir until the ingredients are just combined. Take care not to overmix—the batter will still be slightly lumpy.
4 Divide the mixture evenly among the holes—fill each hole to about three-quarters full. Bake for 20–25 minutes, or until golden and a skewer inserted into the centre of a muffin comes out clean.
5 Allow to cool in the tin for a few minutes. Loosen each muffin with a flat-bladed knife before turning out onto a wire rack. Serve warm or at room temperature.

CORN AND CHIVE MUFFINS

Preparation time **15 minutes**
Total cooking time **20 minutes**
Makes **10 muffins**

canola oil, for greasing
300 g (10½ oz/2 cups) soy-free, gluten-free
  self-raising flour
2 teaspoons gluten-free baking powder
2 tablespoons soft brown sugar
100 g (3½ oz/½ cup) drained, tinned corn
  kernels
2 tablespoons finely chopped fresh chives
250 ml (9 fl oz/1 cup) rice milk
80 ml (2½ fl oz/⅓ cup) canola oil
2 eggs

1 Preheat the oven to 350°F (180°C/Gas 4). Lightly grease ten 80 ml (2½ fl oz/⅓ cup) muffin holes with canola oil.
2 Sift the flour and baking powder into a large bowl. Add the sugar. Stir in the pear and chives.
3 In a separate bowl, combine the rice milk, oil and egg. Add the milk mixture to the flour mixture. Mix until just combined.
4 Divide the batter among the prepared muffin holes. Bake for 18–20 minutes, or until a skewer inserted in the centre comes out clean. Leave in the tray for 5 minutes before turning out onto a wire rack to cool.
Note These muffins need to be eaten on the day they are made.

POLENTA, SEMI-DRIED TOMATO AND PECORINO MUFFINS

Preparation time **15 minutes**

Total cooking time **25 minutes**

Makes **12 muffins or 48 mini muffins**

155 g (5½ oz/1¼ cups) self-raising flour
110 g (3¾ oz/¾ cup) polenta (cornmeal)
60 g (2¼ oz/¾ cup) grated pecorino cheese
1 egg, lightly beaten
250 ml (9 fl oz/1 cup) milk
80 ml (2½ fl oz/⅓ cup) olive oil
40 g (1½ oz/¼ cup) chopped semi-dried
   (sun-blushed) tomatoes
15 g (½ oz/¼ cup) chopped basil

1 Preheat the oven to 180°C (350°F/Gas 4). Grease a 12-hole standard muffin tin or two 24-hole mini muffin tins, or line the holes with paper cases.

2 Sift the flour into a large bowl, then stir in the polenta and pecorino and season with freshly ground black pepper. Make a well in the centre.

3 Combine the egg, milk and oil in a bowl, then pour into the well. Add the tomatoes and basil and stir quickly until just combined. Do not overmix—the batter will still be slightly lumpy.

4 Divide the mixture evenly between the muffin holes. Bake for 20–25 minutes (or 10–12 minutes for mini muffins), or until the muffins are golden and come away from the sides of the tin.

5 Cool in the tin for 2 minutes before transferring to a wire rack. Serve warm or at room temperature.

FRIANDS AND CUPCAKES

These delightful little treats are just the thing to satisfy those afternoon sweet cravings. The only problem is that it can be almost impossible to stop at just one ...

Teatime gives us the chance to enjoy delicious baked goodies. Delicate little friands and cupcakes, washed down with a perfectly brewed cup of tea.

For the delightful custom of afternoon tea, we must thank Anna, wife of the seventh Duke of Bedford. In the 19th century, lunch was a very light meal, and dinner was not served until eight o'clock. Not happy with this arrangement, the Duchess of Bedford asked that tea and cakes be served mid-afternoon because, to quote herself, she had 'a sinking feeling'. She invited friends to join her and in no time at all this became a fashionable thing to do!

In an arguably more civilised age, the world stopped for a mid-morning snack— and perhaps even for an afternoon one as well. Home baking was a regular activity, deliciously warm aromas permeated the kitchen and cake tins were filled for another week. Now, it seems, we're all far too busy to enjoy even a half-hour's pause over a cup of tea or freshly brewed coffee. Let alone devote time to baking 'from scratch'. Before we completely relinquish the joys of snack-time though, it's good to remind ourselves that, in an increasingly frantic world, it makes sense to pause from life's demands and take time for an energizing drink and a nibble of some delectable morsel.

There's something deliciously therapeutic about getting into the kitchen to bake. The hardest part is determining what to whip up. Using these tempting recipes you'll be able to conjure fabulous home-baked treats suited to any occasion, from the poshest afternoon tea to casual, rustic sweet snacks suited to lunchboxes and mid-morning pick-me-ups.

This can be as intimate an affair as just you, a friend, a pot of coffee and a few muffins. There are plenty of larger-scale occasions too, when loading a prettily-set table with muffins, friands, cupcakes, and the like, is perfectly appropriate. Kitchen teas, baby showers, birthday celebrations, anniversaries and pre-Christmas get-togethers are also excellent opportunities to buff up silver teapots, dust off fine, bone china and pass around plates of sweet and savoury goodies.

Baking tips

For all baking, make sure the ingredients are fresh and not past their use-by date. For example, baking powder should be replaced every six months as it loses its effectiveness as a raising agent if stored for too long.

Proper storage of baking ingredients is also important. Flours should be stored in a cool, dry, dark cupboard. They can be kept for up to 3 months. Flours that contain a lot of oil, such as soy flour, should be kept refrigerated in hot weather to prevent them turning rancid.

Because oven temperatures vary a great deal, it is a good idea to invest in an oven thermometer so that you can check the oven temperature.

The time required to heat an oven to the correct temperature varies considerably from oven to oven but it takes at least 10 minutes. So, when baking, plan ahead and leave plenty of time for the oven to heat and be sure to wait until it has reached the specified temperature before placing the item in the oven.

WHAT WENT WRONG?

FRIANDS

Perfect The friand is nicely domed and has a moist, even texture and a good golden colour. The batter has shrunk from the side of the tin.

Undercooked The friand is a pale colour and has a wet, buttery texture. The oven was not hot enough. Cook friands in a preheated 210°C (415°F/ Gas 6–7) oven.

Overcooked The friand has a badly cracked top and the top and base are over-coloured. The friand is dark and crusty around the edges. Either the oven was too hot, or the cooking time was too long.

All about friands

Friands (pronounced free-onds) are small oval-shaped cakes baked in special-purpose oval tins called friand tins or barquette moulds. Sometimes the same mixture is baked in a rectangular tin and is then named Financier, meaning 'gold ingot', which the shape resembles. Both are very popular in cafés and come in a variety of flavours. The tins can be purchased from kitchen-ware shops. Traditional friands are made with almond meal.

Friands will keep well for up to three days in an airtight container.

To make berry friands, make the almond friand mixture (see page 100) and place a fresh or frozen raspberry or blueberry in the top of each friand before placing in the oven.

To make lemon friands, add 2 teaspoons grated lemon zest to the flour and sugar mixture in the almond friand recipe (see page 100) and follow the recipe.

ALMOND FRIANDS

Preparation time **10 minutes**
Total cooking time **20 minutes**
Makes 10

160 g (5¾ oz) unsalted butter
90 g (3¼ oz/1 cup) flaked almonds
40 g (1½ oz/⅓ cup) plain (all-purpose) flour
165 g (5¾ oz/1⅓ cups) icing (confectioners')
  sugar
5 egg whites
icing (confectioners') sugar, to dust

1 Preheat the oven to 210°C (415°F/ Gas 6–7). Grease ten 125 ml (4 fl oz/ ½ cup) friand tins.

2 Melt the butter in a small saucepan over medium heat. Cook for 3–4 minutes, or until the butter turns deep golden. Strain to remove any residue (the colour will deepen on standing). Remove from the heat and set aside to cool until just lukewarm.

3 Put the almonds in a food processor and process until finely ground. Transfer to a bowl and sift the flour and icing sugar into the same bowl.

4 Put the egg whites in a separate bowl and lightly whisk with a fork until just combined. Add the butter to the flour mixture along with the egg whites. Mix gently with a metal spoon until all the ingredients are well combined.

5 Spoon some mixture into each friand tin to fill to three-quarters. Put the tins on a baking tray and bake in the centre of the oven for 10 minutes, then reduce the heat to 180°C (350°F/Gas 4) and bake for a further 5 minutes, or until a skewer comes out clean when inserted in the centre of a friand.

6 Remove and leave to cool in the tins for 5 minutes before turning out onto a wire rack to cool completely. Dust with icing sugar before serving.

PISTACHIO FRIANDS

Preparation time **10 minutes**
Total cooking time **20 minutes**
Makes **10**

165 g (5¾ oz/1⅓ cups) icing (confectioners')
  sugar, plus extra for dusting
40 g (1½ oz/⅓ cup) plain (all-purpose) flour
125 g (4½ oz/1 cup) ground pistachio nuts
160 g (5¾ oz) unsalted butter, melted
5 egg whites, lightly beaten
½ teaspoon natural vanilla extract
55 g (2 oz/¼ cup) caster (superfine) sugar
35 g (1¼ oz/¼ cup) chopped pistachio nuts

1 Preheat the oven to 190°C (375°F/Gas 5).
Lightly grease ten 125 ml (4 fl oz/½ cup)
friand tins.
2 Sift the icing sugar and flour into a bowl.
Add the ground pistachios, butter, egg
whites and vanilla and stir with a metal
spoon until just combined.

3 Spoon the mixture into the prepared
tins and place on a baking tray.
4 Bake for 15–20 minutes, or until a
skewer inserted into the centre of a friand
comes out clean. Leave in the tins for
5 minutes, then turn out onto a wire rack
to cool.
5 Meanwhile, put the sugar and 60 ml
(2 fl oz/¼ cup) water in a small saucepan
and stir over low heat until the sugar has
dissolved. Increase the heat, then boil for
4 minutes, or until thick and syrupy.
Remove from the heat and stir in the
chopped pistachios.
6 Working quickly, spoon the mixture over
the tops of the friands. Dust with icing
sugar and serve.
Notes The friands will keep, stored in an
airtight container, for up to 4 days, or
frozen for up to 3 months.
  Friand tins can be purchased from
kitchenware shops.

CHOCOLATE HAZELNUT FRIANDS

Preparation time **20 minutes**
Total cooking time **35 minutes**
Makes 12

200 g (7 oz/1 1/2 cups) hazelnuts
185 g (6 1/2 oz) unsalted butter
6 egg whites
155 g (5 1/2 oz/1 1/4 cups) plain (all-purpose) flour
30 g (1 oz/1/4 cup) unsweetened cocoa powder
250 g (9 oz/2 cups) icing (confectioners') sugar
icing (confectioners') sugar, extra, to dust

1 Preheat the oven to 200°C (400°F/Gas 6). Grease twelve 125 ml (4 fl oz/1/2 cup) friand holes.
2 Spread the hazelnuts out on a baking tray and bake for 8–10 minutes, or until fragrant (take care not to burn). Put in a clean tea towel (dish towel) and rub vigorously to loosen the skins. Discard the skins. Cool, then process in a food processor until finely ground.
3 Place the butter in a small pan and melt over medium heat, then cook for 3–4 minutes, or until it turns a deep golden colour. Strain any dark solids and set aside to cool (the colour will become deeper on standing).
4 Lightly whisk the egg whites in a bowl until frothy but not firm. Sift the flour, cocoa powder and icing sugar into a large bowl and stir in the ground hazelnuts. Make a well in the centre, add the egg whites and butter and mix until combined.
5 Spoon the mixture into the friand holes until three-quarters filled. Bake for 20–25 minutes, or until a skewer inserted into the centre comes out clean. Leave in the tin for a few minutes, then cool on a wire rack. Dust with icing sugar, to serve.

RICE FLOUR AND MADEIRA FRIANDS

Preparation time 20 minutes
Total cooking time 30 minutes
Makes 18

250 g (9 oz) unsalted butter, softened
350 g (12 oz/1½ cups) caster (superfine) sugar
8 eggs
1 teaspoon finely grated orange zest
80 g (2¾ oz/¾ cup) ground almonds
300 g (10½ oz/1¾ cups) rice flour, sifted
60 ml (2 fl oz/¼ cup) madeira
80 g (2¾ oz/½ cup) chopped blanched
   almonds
icing (confectioners') sugar, to dust
whipped cream and berries, to serve

1 Preheat the oven to 170°C (325°F/Gas 3). Grease eighteen 125 ml (4 fl oz/½ cup) friand tins.

2 Cream the butter and sugar in a bowl using electric beaters until pale and fluffy. Add the eggs one at a time, beating well after each addition, then add the orange zest and continue to beat for 5 minutes.
3 Combine the ground almonds and rice flour and fold into the butter mixture, in three stages, alternately with the madeira, until just combined.
4 Spoon the mixture into the prepared tins and sprinkle over the almonds. Bake for 25–30 minutes, or until golden and a skewer inserted into the centre of a friand comes out clean.
5 Leave in the tins for 5 minutes, then turn out onto a wire rack to cool. Dust with icing sugar and serve with whipped cream and berries.
Note These friands will keep, stored in an airtight container, for up to 4 days, or frozen for up to 3 months.

VANILLA COCONUT CUPCAKES

Preparation time **20 minutes**

Total cooking time **20 minutes**

Makes **12**

150 g (5½ oz) unsalted butter, cut into cubes
115 g (4 oz/½ cup) caster (superfine) sugar
2 teaspoons natural vanilla extract
2 eggs
185 g (6½ oz/1½ cups) plain (all-purpose) flour
1 teaspoon baking powder
45 g (1½ oz/½ cup) desiccated coconut
125 ml (4 fl oz/½ cup) milk

Vanilla icing (frosting)

60 g (2¼ oz/1 cup) flaked coconut
20 g (¾ oz) unsalted butter, cut into cubes
2 teaspoons natural vanilla extract
185 g (6½ oz/1½ cups) icing (confectioners')
   sugar, sifted

1 Preheat the oven to 180°C (350°F/Gas 4). Line twelve 125 ml (4 fl oz/½ cup) muffin holes with paper cases.

2 Put the butter, sugar and vanilla extract in a bowl and beat with electric beaters for 2–3 minutes, or until thick and creamy. Add the eggs, one at a time, and beat in each until well combined.

3 Sift together the flour and baking powder. Use a metal spoon to stir in the sifted flour and baking powder in two lots. Stir in the desiccated coconut and the milk.

4 Put spoonfuls evenly into the paper cases. Bake for 18–20 minutes, or until firm and golden brown. Cool on a wire rack.

5 To make the vanilla glacé icing, spread the flaked coconut on a tray and lightly toast for 2–3 minutes in the oven. Put the butter in a small bowl and pour over 2 teaspoons of hot water to soften the butter. Add the vanilla extract. Put the icing sugar in a bowl, add the butter mixture and mix together until smooth, adding a little more water if necessary to make a spreading consistency.

6 Use a small spatula to spread the cooled cakes with the icing and dip each into the coconut flakes. Set aside to firm the icing.

PATTY CAKES

Preparation time **15 minutes**
Total cooking time **20 minutes**
Makes **24**

125 g (4½ oz) dairy-free margarine
125 g (4½ oz/½ cup) caster (superfine) sugar
2 eggs
150 g (5½ oz/1 cup) soy-free, gluten-free
   self-raising flour
90 g (3¼ oz/½ cup) rice flour
3 teaspoons gluten-free baking powder
125 ml (4 fl oz/½ cup) rice milk
icing (confectioners') sugar, to dust

1 Preheat the oven to 350°F (180°C/Gas 4).
Line two 12-hole 80 ml (2½ fl oz/⅓ cup)
muffin holes or patty pans with
paper cases.
2 Beat the margarine and sugar together in
a small bowl using electric beaters until
light and fluffy. Add the eggs, one at a
time, beating well after each addition.
3 Sift the dry ingredients into a large bowl.
Fold the dry ingredients into the margarine
mixture alternately with the rice milk.
4 Spoon the mixture evenly into the muffin
holes and bake for about 15–20 minutes, or
until just cooked.
5 Dust the cupcakes with icing sugar just
before serving..
Note If desired, they can be frozen, iced or
un-iced, in lots of six for convenience.
Thaw out at room temperature.

BUTTERFLY CUPCAKES

Preparation time **15 minutes**

Total cooking time **30 minutes**

Makes **12**

120 g (4¼ oz) unsalted butter, softened

180 g (6½ oz/¾ cup) caster (superfine) sugar

185 g (6½ oz /1½ cups) self-raising flour

125 ml (4 fl oz/½ cup) milk

2 eggs

125 ml (4 fl oz/½ cup) pouring (whipping) cream, whipped

1½ tablespoons strawberry jam

icing (confectioners') sugar, to dust

1 Preheat the oven to 180°C (350°F/Gas 4). Line a flat-bottomed 12-hole cupcake tray with paper patty cases.

2 Beat the butter, sugar, flour, milk and eggs with electric beaters on low speed. Increase the speed and beat until smooth and pale. Divide evenly among the cases and bake for 30 minutes, or until cooked and golden. Transfer to a wire rack to cool.

3 Cut shallow rounds from the centre of each cake using the point of a sharp knife, then cut in half. Spoon 2 teaspoons cream into each cavity, top with 1 teaspoon jam and position two halves of the cake tops in the jam to resemble butterfly wings. Dust with icing sugar.

Note If using foil patty cases instead of the standard paper cases as suggested, the size and number of butterfly cakes may vary.

INDIVIDUAL MILK CHOCOLATE CAKES

Preparation time **20 minutes**
Total cooking time **25 minutes**
Makes **12**

75 g (2³/4 oz) unsalted butter
75 g (2³/4 oz) milk chocolate, chopped
80 g (2³/4 oz /¹/3 cup) firmly packed brown
    sugar
2 eggs, lightly beaten
60 g (2¹/4 oz/¹/2 cup) self-raising flour, sifted

Ganache
80 g (2³/4 oz) milk chocolate, chopped
2 tablespoons thick (double) cream

1 Preheat the oven to 160°C (315°F/ Gas 2–3). Line a flat-bottomed 12-hole cupcake tray with paper patty cases.
2 Put the butter and chocolate in a heatproof bowl and place over a saucepan of simmering water—make sure the base of the bowl doesn't touch the water. Stir until melted and combined. Remove the bowl from the heat, add the sugar and egg and mix. Stir in the flour.
3 Transfer the mixture to a measuring jug and pour into the patty cases. Bake for 20–25 minutes, or until cooked. Leave in the tin for 10 minutes, then transfer to a wire rack to cool.
4 To make the ganache, place the chocolate and cream in a heatproof bowl. Place over a saucepan of simmering water—ensure the base of the bowl doesn't touch the water. Once the chocolate has almost melted, remove the bowl from the heat and stir until the remaining chocolate has melted and the mixture is smooth. Allow to cool for about 8 minutes, or until thickened slightly. Return the cakes to the cold patty tin, to keep them stable while you spread one heaped teaspoon of ganache over the top. If desired, decorate with gold cachous.

COFFEE CUPCAKES

Preparation time **15 minutes**
Total cooking time **30 minutes**
Makes **24**

195 g (7 oz) unsalted butter, softened
125 g (4½ oz/⅔ cup) soft brown sugar
2 eggs
1 tablespoon coffee and chicory extract
155 g (5½ oz/1¼ cups) self-raising flour
100 ml (3½ fl oz) buttermilk
125 g (4½ oz/1 cup) icing (confectioners')
  sugar

1 Preheat the oven to 150°C (300°F/Gas 2). Line two 50 ml (2 fl oz) 12-hole cupcake trays with paper patty cases.
2 Beat 185 g (6½ oz) of the butter and the brown sugar using electric beaters until creamy. Add the eggs one at a time, beating well after each addition. Mix in 3 teaspoons of the coffee and chicory extract.
3 Fold the flour and a pinch of salt alternately with the buttermilk into the creamed mixture until combined.
4 Spoon into the patty cases and bake for 25–30 minutes, or until just springy to the touch. Leave to cool in the tray.
5 To make the icing, combine the remaining butter, remaining extract, the icing sugar and 1½ tablespoons boiling water in a small bowl.
6 Spread a little icing over each cupcake with a palette knife until evenly covered. If desired, decorate with chocolate-coated coffee beans.

INDIVIDUAL WHITE CHOCOLATE CHIP CAKES

Preparation time **20 minutes**
Total cooking time **20 minutes**
Makes 12

125 g (4½ oz) unsalted butter, softened
185 g (6½ oz/¾ cup) caster (superfine)
   sugar
2 eggs, lightly beaten
1 teaspoon natural vanilla extract
250 g (9 oz/2 cups) self-raising flour, sifted
125 ml (4 fl oz/½ cup) buttermilk
280 g (10 oz/1⅔ cups) white chocolate chips
white chocolate, shaved, to decorate

White chocolate cream cheese icing (frosting)
100 g (3½ oz) white chocolate
60 ml (2 fl oz/¼ cup) cream
200 g (7 oz/¾ cup) cream cheese, softened
40 g (½ oz/¼ cup) icing (confectioners')
   sugar

1 Preheat the oven to 170°C (325°F/Gas 3). Lightly grease twelve 125 ml (4 fl oz/ ½ cup) muffin tins.
2 Beat the butter and sugar in a large bowl using electric beaters until pale and creamy. Gradually add the egg, beating well after each addition. Add the vanilla extract and beat. Fold in the flour alternately with the buttermilk, then fold in the chocolate chips.
3 Fill each muffin hole three-quarters full with the mixture and bake for 20 minutes, or until a skewer comes out clean when inserted into the centre of each cake. Leave in the tins for 5 minutes before turning out onto a wire rack to cool.
4 To make the icing, melt the chocolate and cream in a saucepan over low heat until smooth. Cool slightly, then add to the cream cheese and icing sugar and beat until smooth.
5 Spread the icing over the cakes and decorate with white chocolate shavings.

ORANGE CUPCAKES

Preparation time **15 minutes** +
Total cooking time **20 minutes**
Makes **12**

120 g (4¼ oz) unsalted butter, softened
145 g (5½ oz/⅔ cup) caster (superfine) sugar
185 g (6½ oz/1½ cups) self-raising flour
125 ml (4 fl oz/½ cup) orange juice
2 teaspoons natural vanilla extract
2 eggs
3 tablespoons grated orange zest
shredded orange zest, to decorate (optional)

Icing (frosting)

60 g (2¼ oz) unsalted butter, softened
90 g (3¼ oz/¾ cup) icing (confectioners')
   sugar
1 tablespoon orange juice

1 Preheat the oven to 180°C (350°F/Gas 4). Line a deep 12-hole patty pan or mini muffin tin with paper cases.
2 Place the butter, sugar, flour, orange juice, vanilla and eggs in a bowl and beat using electric beaters on low speed for 2 minutes, or until combined. Increase the speed and beat for 2 minutes, or until smooth and pale. Stir in the orange zest.
3 Divide the mixture evenly among the cases and bake for 20 minutes, or until lightly golden. Transfer to a wire rack to cool completely.
4 To make the icing, beat the butter in a bowl using electric beaters until pale. Beat in half the icing sugar, all the orange juice, then the remaining icing sugar.
5 Spread over the cakes, then decorate if desired.

LITTLE JAM-FILLED CAKES

Preparation time **20 minutes**
Total cooking time **20 minutes**
Makes **12**

280 g (10 oz/2¼ cups) self-raising flour
170 g (6 oz/¾ cup) caster (superfine) sugar
250 ml (9 fl oz/1 cup) milk
2 eggs, lightly beaten
½ teaspoon natural vanilla extract
75 g (2½ oz) unsalted butter, melted
80 g (2¾ oz/¼ cup) strawberry jam
12 small strawberries, hulled
icing (confectioners') sugar, to dust

1 Preheat the oven to 200°C (400°F/Gas 6). Grease a 12-hole standard muffin tin.

2 Sift the flour into a bowl, add the sugar and stir to combine. Make a well in the centre. Put the milk, eggs, vanilla extract and butter in a bowl, whisking to combine. Pour into the well and, using a metal spoon, gradually fold the milk mixture into the flour mixture until just combined.
3 Divide three-quarters of the cake batter between the muffin holes. Top each with 1 teaspoon of the jam and cover with the remaining cake batter. Gently press a strawberry into the centre.
4 Bake for 20 minutes, or until golden. Cool in the tin for 5 minutes, then turn out onto a wire rack. Dust with icing sugar.
Note These cakes are best served on the day they are made.

BISCUITS

It's one thing to staunchly honour the diet and refuse a whole piece of cake, but biscuits are another matter entirely. They're so little and innocent, surely one couldn't do any harm? Especially straight out of the oven. There must be some reward after the tantalising aroma of freshly baked biscuits has been following you around the house, merciless in its pursuit. Dear little jam drops with their oozy centre, the crunchy gingernut, the rich melt-in-the-mouth sweetness of Scottish shortbread. You know you can't resist—that's just the way the cookie crumbles

BISCUIT BASICS

Nothing beats the heavenly aroma of freshly baked biscuits. Biscuits are made using several methods, each giving special characteristics to the biscuits.

CREAMING METHOD

With the following recipe, you can make a basic butter biscuit and variations. To make about 30 biscuits, line two trays with baking paper or lightly grease with melted butter. Soften 125 g (4^1/2 oz) butter, then cut into cubes.

Preheat the oven to 210°C (415°F/ Gas 6–7). Cream the softened butter with 125 g (4^1/2 oz/^{1}/2 cup) caster (superfine) sugar in a bowl using electric beaters until light and fluffy. The mixture should be pale and smooth. The sugar should be almost dissolved. Add 60 ml (2 fl oz/^{1}/4 cup) milk and ^{1}/4 teaspoon natural vanilla extract and beat until combined. Add 185 g (6 oz/1^1/2 cups) self-raising flour and 60 g (2^1/4 oz/^{1}/2 cup) custard powder (instant vanilla pudding mix) and use a flat-bladed knife to bring to a soft dough. Rotate the bowl as you work and use a cutting motion to incorporate the dry ingredients. Don't overwork the dough.

Roll level teaspoonfuls into balls and place on the trays, leaving 5 cm (2 in) between each biscuit. Flatten the balls lightly with your fingertips, then press with a fork. The biscuits should be about 5 cm (2 in) in diameter. Bake for 15–18 minutes, until lightly golden. Cool on the trays for 3 minutes before transferring to a wire rack to cool completely. Store in an airtight container for up to a week.

To freeze, place in freezer bags and seal, label and date. Unfilled and un-iced cooked biscuits can be frozen for up to two months. After thawing, refresh them in a 180°C (350°F/Gas 4) oven for a few minutes, then cool and decorate, as desired, before serving. Uncooked biscuit dough freezes well. To do this, wrap it in plastic wrap, place in a plastic bag and seal. When ready to use, thaw at room temperature and bake as directed. Plain cooked biscuits can be decorated with icing (confectioners') sugar just before serving. Or they can be iced, or drizzled with melted chocolate. Below are some variations.

CITRUS

Omit the natural vanilla extract, add 2 teaspoons orange or lemon zest to the creamed butter and sugar and proceed with the recipe. When cool, combine 250 g (9 oz/2 cups) sifted icing (confectioners') sugar, 20 g (^{3}/4 oz) softened butter and 1 tablespoon lemon or orange juice in a bowl and ice the biscuits.

NUTTY

Mix 55 g (2 oz/^{1}/2 cup) finely chopped walnuts or pecans into the basic mixture before adding the flour. Press a nut onto each biscuit, instead of pressing with a fork, and bake as above.

Biscuits can also be made using the following methods:

MELT AND MIX

This quick method involves mixing the dry ingredients, then mixing in the melted butter (and any other ingredients in the recipe) with a wooden spoon until the dry ingredients are well moistened.

RUBBING IN

This involves cutting cold butter into pieces and rubbing it into the flour with your fingertips until the mixture is crumbly and resembles fine breadcrumbs. Then almost all the liquid is added and cut into the dry ingredients with a knife, adding the remaining liquid if necessary to bring the mixture together. Do not add the liquid all at once as flour varies a great deal so the full amount of liquid may not be required.

WHAT WENT WRONG?

DROP BISCUITS

Perfect The biscuit has even golden colouring on both the top and base and has even thickness.

Unevenly spread The mixture may have been placed too close together on the tray, not allowing enough room to spread. Make sure the baking tray is at room temperature before spooning the biscuits onto the tray. The mixture may have been too wet or may contain too much fat or sugar. The mixture may have needed chilling before baking.

Undercooked, sticking These biscuits are pale and the tops soft to touch. This indicates that the cooking time may have been too short, leaving the mixture undercooked and sticky. Alternatively, the oven temperature may have been too low or the oven insufficiently preheated.

Overcooked The oven temperature may have been too high or the cooking time may have been too long. Be sure to only rest the biscuits for a couple of minutes on the tray after cooking because they will continue to cook if left on the tray.

MIXTURE ROLLED OUT AND CUT INTO SHAPES

Perfect The biscuit has a light golden colouring and even thickness.

Thin, overcooked The mixture may have been rolled too thinly or the oven may have been too hot, or perhaps the biscuits cooked too long.

Too thick The mixture was rolled and cut too thickly. This biscuit, although probably too thick, would need extra baking time.

MIXTURE SHAPED BY HAND OR PIPED

Perfect The biscuit has even, golden colouring on both the top and base. It is also the correct thickness.

Undercooked The biscuit is a pale colour. The oven temperature may have been too low, the oven not preheated, or the biscuits not cooked long enough.

Overcooked and spread too much The oven may have been too hot or the biscuits cooked too long.

HINTS AND TIPS

1 Some recipes can be made using a food processor, however biscuit dough should not be overworked as this results in a tough biscuit. Only use a processor to rub the fat into the flour. When the liquid is added, pulse briefly until the mixture just comes together, then turn out onto a work surface to bring together into a soft ball, without kneading. Then cut or shape as directed.

2 Always weigh and measure wet and dry ingredients accurately.

3 Make sure your ingredients are at the right temperature. Chilled butter means butter straight out of the refrigerator. Softened butter means butter returned to room temperature—this takes about 45 minutes. Eggs also need to be at room temperature. Remove them from the refrigerator about 45 minutes before using.

4 Lightly flour the work surface and rolling pin before and during rolling if the dough starts to stick.

5 If using a pastry cutter, dip the cutting edge in extra flour to prevent sticking.

6 Don't use baking trays or tins that have high sides, otherwise the heat distribution during cooking will not be even.

7 Biscuits spread during baking. Most average-sized baking trays fit three rows of five biscuits, with the biscuit mixture spaced about 5 cm (2 in) apart.

8 Prepare baking trays as specified. Not all recipes require the tray to be greased or lined.

9 Always place biscuit dough onto a cold baking tray. If baking in batches, allow the tray to cool before adding the next batch.

10 Always preheat the oven to the required temperature and test with an oven thermometer, as ovens can vary.

11 Make sure the oven shelves are set an equal distance apart if cooking more than one tray at a time. Most biscuits are best baked in or close to the centre of the oven.

12 Biscuits can be baked on two trays at the same time, but often the tray underneath will require a longer cooking time. If you have time, cook the biscuits in batches. Alternatively, switch the trays halfway through cooking time.

13 Always bake for the minimum time given and check for doneness. Cook for only 2 minutes more and then retest (biscuits can be underdone one minute and then burnt the next).

14 Always cool biscuits on a wire cooling rack or they can become soggy. Allow biscuits to cool completely before icing or filling.

15 Some biscuit recipes call for nuts, whether whole, chopped or ground. Nuts are often toasted before being ground. To toast nuts, put them in a single layer on a baking tray and bake in a preheated 180°C (350°F/Gas 4) oven for 5–10 minutes, depending on the type of nut or whether they are ground or whole. Always time this, as nuts burn easily.

16 Most biscuits can be kept for up to a week if stored correctly. They should be allowed to cool completely after baking, then stored in an airtight container in a cool place. It is best not to store different types of biscuits in the same jar. Biscuits that are to be filled should be stored without their filling and then filled just before serving.

CLASSIC SHORTBREAD

Preparation time **30 minutes +**
Total cooking time **20 minutes**
Makes **16 wedges**

225 g (8 oz) unsalted butter
115 g (4 oz/½ cup) caster (superfine) sugar,
   plus extra to dust
225 g (8 oz/1¾ cups) plain (all-purpose) flour
115 g (4 oz/⅔ cup) rice flour

1 Preheat the oven to 190°C (375°F/Gas 5).
Lightly grease two baking trays.
2 Cream the butter and sugar in a bowl
using electric beaters until pale and fluffy.
Sift in the flour, rice flour and a pinch of
salt and, using a wooden spoon, stir into
the creamed mixture until it resembles fine
breadcrumbs. Transfer to a lightly floured
work surface and knead gently to form a
soft dough. Cover with plastic wrap and
refrigerate for 30 minutes.

3 Divide the dough in half and roll out one
half on a lightly floured work surface to
form a 20 cm (8 in) round. Carefully
transfer to a prepared tray. Using a sharp
knife, score the surface of the dough into
eight equal wedges, prick the surface
lightly with a fork and, using your fingers,
press the edges to form a fluted effect.
Repeat this process using the remaining
dough to make a second round. Lightly
dust the shortbreads with the extra sugar.
4 Bake for 18–20 minutes, or until the
shortbreads are light golden. Remove from
the oven and while still hot, follow the
score marks and cut into wedges. Cool on
the baking tray for 5 minutes, then transfer
to a wire rack.
Note The shortbread will keep, stored in
an airtight container, for up to 1 week.

   Shortbread can be made with plain flour
alone; however, the addition of rice flour
produces a lighter result.

CINNAMON CHOCOLATE SHORTBREAD

Preparation time **20 minutes** +
Total cooking time **18 minutes**
Makes **32**

200 g (7 oz/1²/₃ cups) plain (all-purpose) flour
40 g (1½ oz/⅓ cup) unsweetened cocoa
    powder
1½ teaspoons ground cinnamon
250 g (9 oz) unsalted butter
60 g (2¼ oz/½ cup) icing (confectioners')
    sugar
caster (superfine) sugar, to sprinkle

1 Preheat the oven to 160°C (315°F/ Gas 2–3). Line two baking trays with baking paper.

2 Sift together the flour, cocoa and cinnamon. Using electric beaters, beat the butter and icing sugar until light and creamy. Using a large metal spoon, fold in the sifted flour mixture. Turn the dough out onto a lightly floured surface and knead gently until smooth.

3 Roll out the dough between two sheets of baking paper until 1 cm (½ in) thick. Using a 7 cm (2³/₄ in) star cutter, cut out the biscuits. Place on the prepared trays, leaving room for spreading. Prick the dough with a fork, sprinkle the top with the caster sugar and refrigerate for 30 minutes.

4 Bake for 15–18 minutes, swapping trays halfway through cooking. Allow to cool on the trays.

CORNFLAKE COOKIES

Preparation time **15 minutes**

Total cooking time **20 minutes**

Makes **36**

125 g (4½ oz) unsalted butter, softened
165 g (5¾ oz/¾ cup) sugar
2 eggs, lightly beaten
1 teaspoon natural vanilla extract
2 tablespoons currants
135 g (4¾ oz/1½ cups) desiccated coconut
½ teaspoon bicarbonate of soda (baking soda)
½ teaspoon baking powder
250 g (9 oz/2 cups) plain (all-purpose) flour
90 g (3¼ oz/3 cups) cornflakes, crushed

1 Preheat the oven to 180°C (350°F/Gas 4). Line two baking trays with baking paper.

2 Cream the butter and sugar in a small bowl using electric beaters until light and fluffy. Gradually add the egg, beating thoroughly after each addition. Add the vanilla and beat until combined.

3 Transfer the mixture to a large bowl and stir in the currants and coconut. Fold in the sifted bicarbonate of soda, baking powder and flour with a metal spoon and stir until the mixture is almost smooth.

4 Put the cornflakes in a shallow dish, then drop level tablespoons of mixture onto the cornflakes and roll into balls. Arrange on the trays, allowing room for spreading.

5 Bake for 15–20 minutes, or until crisp and golden. Cool slightly on the tray before transferring to a wire rack to cool completely.

CHOC CHIP COOKIES

Preparation time **10 minutes**
Total cooking time **15 minutes**
Makes 16

125 g (4½ oz) unsalted butter
185 g (6½ oz/1 cup) soft brown sugar
1 teaspoon natural vanilla extract
1 egg, lightly beaten
1 tablespoon milk
215 g (7½ oz/1¾ cups) plain (all-purpose) flour
1 teaspoon baking powder
250 g (9 oz/1½ cups) dark chocolate chips

1 Preheat the oven to 180°C (350°F/Gas 4). Line a large baking tray with baking paper.

2 Cream the butter and sugar in a large bowl using electric beaters. Mix in the natural vanilla extract and gradually add the egg, beating well. Stir in the milk.
3 Sift the flour and baking powder into a large bowl, then fold into the butter and egg mixture. Stir in the dark chocolate chips.
4 Drop level tablespoons of the cookie mixture onto the baking tray, leaving about 4 cm (1½ in) between each cookie, then lightly press with a floured fork.
5 Bake for 15 minutes, or until lightly golden. Cool on a wire rack.
Note These biscuits are best eaten the same day but will keep, stored in an airtight container, for up to 4 days.

JAM DROPS

Preparation time **30 minutes**
Total cooking time **12 minutes**
Makes **about 45**

250 g (9 oz) unsalted butter, softened
140 g (5 oz) icing (confectioners') sugar
1 egg yolk, lightly beaten
90 g (3¼ oz) cream cheese, softened and
    cut into chunks
1½ teaspoons natural vanilla extract
1 teaspoon finely grated lemon zest
350 g (12 oz/2¾ cups) plain (all-purpose) flour,
    sifted
¼ teaspoon baking powder
½ teaspoon bicarbonate of soda (baking soda)
2 tablespoons each apricot, blueberry and
    raspberry jam

1 Preheat the oven to 180°C (350°F/Gas 4).
Lightly grease three baking trays.
2 Cream the butter, icing sugar and egg
yolk in a bowl using electric beaters until
pale and fluffy, then beat in the cream
cheese, vanilla extract and lemon zest until
thick and smooth.
3 Combine the flour, baking powder,
bicarbonate of soda and ¼ teaspoon salt
in a large bowl and, using a wooden spoon,
gradually stir into the creamed mixture
until a soft dough forms. Set aside for
5–10 minutes, or until the dough firms up.
4 Break off small (15 g/½ oz) pieces of
dough, shape into balls and flatten slightly
to make 4 cm (1½ in) rounds. Transfer
to the prepared trays and make an indent
in the centre of each with your thumb.
5 Spoon ¼ teaspoon of apricot jam into
one-third of the biscuits, ¼ teaspoon
of blueberry jam into one-third, and
¼ teaspoon of raspberry jam into the
remaining one-third of the biscuits.
6 Bake for 10–12 minutes, or until light
golden. Cool for a few minutes on the
trays, then transfer to a wire rack.
Note These biscuits are best eaten the
same day but will keep, stored in an
airtight container, for up to 2 days.

LEMON STARS

Preparation time **25 minutes**
Total cooking time **20 minutes**
Makes **about 22**

125 g (4½ oz) unsalted butter, cubed and
  softened
125 g (4½ oz/½ cup) caster (superfine) sugar
2 egg yolks
2 teaspoons finely grated lemon zest
155 g (5½ oz/1¼ cups) plain (all-purpose) flour
110 g (3¾ oz/¾ cup) coarse cornmeal
icing (confectioners') sugar, to dust

1 Preheat the oven to 160°C (315°F/Gas
2–3). Line a baking tray with baking paper.
2 Beat the butter and sugar until creamy.
Mix in the egg yolks, lemon zest, flour and
cornmeal until a ball of soft dough forms.
Roll out on a lightly floured surface to
1 cm (½ in) thick.
3 Cut out stars from the dough using a
3 cm (1 in) star-shaped cutter. Place on the
tray and bake for 15–20 minutes, or until
lightly golden. Cool slightly on the trays,
then transfer to a wire rack to cool
completely. Dust with the icing sugar.

PEANUT BISCUITS

Preparation time **30 minutes +**
Total cooking time **20 minutes**
Makes **about 30**

185 g (6½ oz) unsalted butter, softened
370 g (13 oz/2 cups) soft brown sugar
140 g (5 oz) smooth peanut butter
1 teaspoon natural vanilla extract
1 egg
185 g (6½ oz/1½ cups) plain (all-purpose) flour
½ teaspoon baking powder
125 g (4½ oz/1¼ cups) rolled (porridge) oats
120 g (4¼ oz/¾ cup) peanuts

1 Preheat the oven to 180°C (350°F/Gas 4). Line two baking trays with baking paper.
2 Beat the butter, sugar, peanut butter and vanilla extract in a bowl using electric beaters until light and creamy. Add the egg and beat until smooth. Transfer to a bowl and mix in the combined flour and baking powder. Fold in the oats and peanuts and mix until smooth. Chill until firm.
3 Roll heaped tablespoons of the mixture into balls and place on the trays, leaving room for spreading. Press down gently with a floured fork to make a crisscross pattern.
4 Bake for 15–20 minutes, or until golden. Cool slightly on the trays, then transfer to a wire rack to cool completely.

CHOCOLATE, RAISIN AND PEANUT CLUSTERS

Preparation time **20 minutes**

Total cooking time **15 minutes**

Makes **about 40**

200 g (7 oz) dark chocolate
60 g (2¼ oz) unsalted butter, chopped
170 g (6 oz/¾ cup) caster (superfine) sugar
1 tablespoon golden syrup or dark corn syrup
1½ teaspoons natural vanilla extract
155 g (5½ oz/1¼ cups) raisins
200 g (7 oz) peanuts, toasted and chopped
40 g (1½ oz/⅓ cup) plain (all-purpose) flour
2 tablespoons unsweetened cocoa powder

1 Preheat the oven to 170°C (325°F/Gas 3). Lightly grease two baking trays.

2 Roughly chop 80 g (2¾ oz) of the chocolate and put in a large heatproof bowl along with the butter, sugar, golden syrup and vanilla extract. Put the bowl over a saucepan of simmering water, stirring until the mixture is smooth.

3 Chop the remaining chocolate and combine with the raisins and peanuts. Sift the flour and cocoa powder over the peanut mixture and mix. Add the melted chocolate mixture and stir until combined.

4 Using a tablespoon of the mixture at a time, form into rounds, then place on the trays, about 4 cm (1½ in) apart.

5 Bake for 15 minutes, or until the biscuits are firm, swapping the trays halfway through. Leave on the trays for 5 minutes, then remove to a wire rack to cool.

GINGERBREAD

Preparation time **30 minutes +**
Total cooking time **8 minutes**
Makes **about 40 (depending on size of cutters)**

350 g (12 oz) plain (all-purpose) flour
2 teaspoons baking powder
2 teaspoons ground ginger
100 g (3½ oz) chilled unsalted butter, diced
175 g (6 oz/¾ cup) soft brown sugar
1 egg, beaten
115 g (4 oz/⅓ cup) dark treacle
silver cachous (optional)

Icing (frosting) glaze
1 egg white
3 teaspoons lemon juice
155 g (5½ oz/1¼ cups) icing (confectioners')
  sugar

Royal icing (frosting)
1 egg white
200 g (7 oz) icing (confectioners') sugar

1 Preheat the oven to 190°C (375°F/Gas 5).
Lightly grease two baking trays.
2 Sift the flour, baking powder, ground
ginger and a pinch of salt into a bowl. Rub
in the butter until the mixture resembles
fine breadcrumbs, then stir in the sugar.
Make a well in the centre, add the egg and
treacle and, using a wooden spoon, stir
until a soft dough forms. Transfer to a
clean surface and knead until smooth.
3 Divide the dough in half and roll out on
a lightly floured work surface until 5 mm
(¼ in) thick. Using various-shaped cutters
(hearts, stars or flowers), cut into desired
shapes, then transfer to the prepared trays.
4 Bake in batches for 8 minutes, or until
the biscuits are light brown. Cool on the
trays for 2–3 minutes, then transfer to a
wire rack to cool completely. (If using the
biscuits as hanging decorations, use a
skewer to make a small hole in each one
while still hot.)
5 To make the glaze, whisk the egg white
and lemon juice together until foamy, then
whisk in the icing sugar to form a smooth,
thin icing. Cover the surface with plastic
wrap until needed.
6 To make the royal icing, lightly whisk
the egg white until just foamy, then
gradually whisk in enough icing sugar to
form a soft icing. Cover the surface with
plastic wrap until needed.
7 Brush a thin layer of glaze over some
of the biscuits and leave to set. Using an
icing bag filled with royal icing, decorate
the biscuits.

GINGERBREAD PEOPLE

Preparation time **40 minutes +**
Total cooking time **10 minutes**
Makes **about 16**

125 g (4½ oz) unsalted butter, softened
60 g (2¼ oz/⅓ cup) soft brown sugar
90 g (3¼ oz/¼ cup) golden syrup or maple
   syrup
1 egg, lightly beaten
250 g (9 oz/2 cups) plain (all-purpose) flour
30 g (1 oz/¼ cup) self-raising flour
1 tablespoon ground ginger
1 teaspoon bicarbonate of soda (baking soda)
1 tablespoon currants

Icing (frosting)
1 egg white
½ teaspoon lemon juice
155 g (5½ oz/1¼ cups) icing (confectioners')
   sugar, sifted
assorted food colourings

1 Preheat the oven to 180°C (350°F/Gas 4).
Line two baking trays with baking paper.
2 Cream the butter, sugar and golden syrup
in a bowl using electric beaters until light
and fluffy. Add the egg gradually, beating
well after each addition. Transfer to a bowl.
Sift the dry ingredients onto the butter
mixture and mix with a knife until combined.
3 Combine the dough with well-floured
hands. Turn onto a well-floured surface and
knead for 1–2 minutes, or until smooth.
Roll out the dough on a chopping board,
between two sheets of baking paper, to
5 mm (¼ in) thick. Refrigerate on the
board for 15 minutes to firm.
4 Cut the dough into shapes with a 13 cm
(5 in) gingerbread person cutter. Press the
remaining dough together and re-roll. Cut
out shapes and put the biscuits on the
trays. Put currants as eyes and noses. Bake
for 10 minutes, or until lightly browned.
Cool completely on the trays.
5 To make the icing, beat the egg white
using electric beaters in a small bowl until
foamy. Gradually add the lemon juice and
icing sugar and beat until thick and creamy.
Divide the icing among several bowls. Tint
the mixture with food colourings and spoon
into small paper piping (icing) bags. Seal
the open ends, snip the tips off the bags
and pipe on faces and clothing.

MONTE CREAMS

Preparation time **30 minutes** +
Total cooking time **20 minutes**
Makes **25**

125 g (4½ oz) unsalted butter
115 g (4 oz/½ cup) caster (superfine) sugar
60 ml (2 fl oz/¼ cup) milk
185 g (6½ oz/1½ cups) self-raising flour
30 g (1 oz/¼ cup) custard powder or
    instant vanilla pudding mix
30 g (1 oz/⅓ cup) desiccated coconut
custard powder or instant vanilla pudding mix,
    extra

Filling
75 g (2¾ oz) unsalted butter, softened
85 g (3 oz/⅔ cup) icing (confectioners') sugar
2 teaspoons milk
105 g (3¾ oz/⅓ cup) strawberry jam

1 Preheat the oven to 180°C (350°F/Gas 4).
Line two baking trays with baking paper.
2 Cream the butter and sugar in a bowl
using electric beaters until light and fluffy.
Add the milk and beat until combined. Sift
the flour and custard powder and add to
the bowl with the coconut. Mix to form a
soft dough.
3 Roll 2 teaspoons of the mixture into
balls. Place on the trays and press with a
fork. Dip the fork in the extra custard
powder occasionally to prevent sticking.
4 Bake for 15–20 minutes, or until golden.
Transfer to a wire rack to cool completely.
5 To make the filling, beat the butter and
icing sugar in a bowl using electric beaters
until creamy. Beat in the milk.
6 Spread one biscuit with ½ teaspoon of
the filling and one with ½ teaspoon of
jam, then press together.

VIENNESE FINGERS

Preparation time **20 minutes** +
Total cooking time **12 minutes**
Makes **20**

100 g (3½ oz) unsalted butter, softened
40 g (1½ oz/⅓ cup) icing (confectioners')
   sugar
2 egg yolks
1½ teaspoons natural vanilla extract
125 g (4½ oz/1 cup) plain (all-purpose) flour
100 g (3½ oz) dark chocolate, chopped
30 g (1 oz) unsalted butter, extra

1 Preheat the oven to 180°C (350°F/Gas 4).
Line two baking trays with baking paper.
2 Cream the butter and icing sugar in a
small bowl using electric beaters until light
and fluffy. Gradually add the egg yolks and
vanilla and beat thoroughly. Transfer to a
large bowl, then sift in the flour. Using a
knife, mix until the ingredients are just
combined and the mixture is smooth.

3 Spoon the mixture into a piping (icing)
bag fitted with a fluted 1 cm (½ in) piping
nozzle and pipe the mixture into wavy
6 cm (2½ in) lengths on the trays.
4 Bake for 12 minutes, or until golden.
Cool slightly on the trays, then transfer to
a wire rack to cool completely.
5 Place the chocolate and extra butter in a
small heatproof bowl. Half-fill a saucepan
with water and bring to the boil, then
remove from the heat. Sit the bowl over
the pan, making sure the base of the bowl
does not touch the water. Stir occasionally
until the chocolate and butter have melted
and the mixture is smooth. Dip half of each
biscuit into the melted chocolate mixture
and leave to set on baking paper or foil.
Notes Store in an airtight container for up
to 2 days.

To make piping easier, fold down the
bag by about 5 cm (2 in) before spooning
the mixture in, then unfold. The top will be
clean and easy to twist.

LEBKUCHEN

Preparation time **25 minutes +**
Total cooking time **30 minutes**
Makes **about 35**

290 g (10¼ oz/2⅓ cups) plain (all-purpose)
  flour
60 g (2¼ oz/½ cup) cornflour (cornstarch)
2 teaspoons unsweetened cocoa powder
1 teaspoon ground mixed (pumpkin pie) spice,
  plus extra, to sprinkle
1 teaspoon ground cinnamon
½ teaspoon freshly grated nutmeg
100 g (3½ oz) unsalted butter, cubed
260 g (9¼ oz/¾ cup) golden syrup or
  dark corn syrup
2 tablespoons milk
150 g (5½ oz/1 cup) white chocolate melts
  (buttons)

1 Preheat the oven to 180°C (350°F/Gas 4).
Line two baking trays with baking paper.
2 Sift the flours, cocoa powder and spices
into a large bowl and make a well in
the centre.
3 Place the butter, golden syrup and milk
in a small saucepan, and stir over low heat
until the butter has melted and the mixture
is smooth. Remove from the heat and add
to the dry ingredients. Using a flat-bladed
knife, mix with a cutting action until the
mixture comes together in small beads.
Gather together with your hands and turn
out onto a sheet of baking paper.
4 Roll the dough out to 8 mm (³/8 in)
thick. Cut into heart shapes using a 6 cm
(2½ in) biscuit (cookie) cutter. Place on
the trays and bake for 25 minutes, or until
lightly browned. Leave on the trays to
cool slightly before transferring to a wire
rack to cool completely.
5 Place the chocolate melts in a heatproof
bowl. Bring a saucepan of water to the boil,
then remove from the heat. Sit the bowl
over the pan, making sure the base of
the bowl does not touch the water. Stir
occasionally until the chocolate has melted.
6 Dip one half of each biscuit into the
chocolate and place on a sheet of baking
paper until the chocolate has set. Sprinkle
the un-iced side of the biscuits with
mixed spice.
Note These biscuits can be stored in an
airtight container for up to 5 days.

COCONUT MACAROONS

Preparation time **20 minutes**
Total cooking time **15 minutes**
Makes **about 64**

4 egg whites, lightly beaten
450 g (1 lb/2 cups) caster (superfine) sugar
1½ tablespoons liquid glucose
1½ teaspoons natural vanilla extract
180 g (6 oz/2 cups) desiccated coconut
125 g (4½ oz/1 cup) plain (all-purpose) flour

1 Combine the egg whites, sugar and liquid glucose in a large heatproof bowl and whisk to combine. Place the bowl over a saucepan of simmering water and whisk until the mixture is just warm. Remove from the heat and add the vanilla, coconut and flour and stir to combine well. Cover the bowl with plastic wrap and refrigerate the mixture until firm.
2 Preheat the oven to 150°C (300°F/Gas 2). Line two baking trays with baking paper.
3 Take a heaped teaspoonful of the mixture and, using wet hands, form the mixture into balls. Flatten the balls slightly and place on the trays, spacing them apart.
4 Bake for 15 minutes, or until the macaroons are golden, swapping the trays halfway through cooking. Cool for 5 minutes on the tray, then transfer to a wire rack to cool completely.
Note Macaroons will keep, stored in an airtight container, for up to 1 week.

Use large baking trays, if you have them, as you will need to give the macaroons room to spread. Alternatively, cook them in two batches.

CRACKLE COOKIES

Preparation time **20 minutes +**
Total cooking time **25 minutes**
Makes **about 60**

125 g (4½ oz) unsalted butter, cubed and
softened
370 g (13 oz/2 cups) soft brown sugar
1 teaspoon natural vanilla extract
2 eggs
60 g (2¼ oz) dark chocolate, melted
80 ml (2½ fl oz/⅓ cup) milk
340 g (11¾ oz/2¾ cups) plain
(all-purpose) flour
2 tablespoons unsweetened cocoa powder
2 teaspoons baking powder
¼ teaspoon ground allspice
85 g (3 oz/⅔ cup) chopped pecan nuts
icing (confectioners') sugar, to coat

1 Lightly grease two baking trays. Beat
the butter, sugar and vanilla until light and
creamy. Beat in the eggs, one at a time.
Stir the chocolate and milk into the
butter mixture.
2 Sift the flour, cocoa, baking powder,
allspice and a pinch of salt into the butter
mixture and mix well. Stir the pecans
through. Refrigerate for at least 3 hours,
or overnight.
3 Preheat the oven to 180°C (350°F/Gas 4).
Roll tablespoons of the mixture into balls
and roll each in the icing sugar to coat.
4 Place well apart on the trays. Bake for
20–25 minutes, or until lightly browned.
Cool slightly on the trays, then transfer
to a wire rack to cool completely.
Note These biscuits will keep, stored in an
airtight container, for up to 3 days.

FLORENTINES

Preparation time **20 minutes**

Total cooking time **10 minutes**

Makes **12**

55 g (2 oz) unsalted butter

45 g (1 ½ oz/¼ cup) soft brown sugar

2 teaspoons honey

25 g (1 oz/¼ cup) flaked almonds, chopped

2 tablespoons chopped dried apricots

2 tablespoons chopped glacé cherries

2 tablespoons mixed peel (mixed candied citrus peel)

40 g (1 ½ oz/⅓ cup) plain (all-purpose) flour

120 g (4 oz) dark chocolate, chopped

1 Preheat the oven to 180°C (350°F/Gas 4). Lightly grease and line two baking trays with baking paper.

2 Melt the butter, brown sugar and honey in a saucepan until the butter is melted and all the ingredients are combined. Remove from the heat and add the almonds, apricots, glace cherries, mixed peel and the flour. Mix well.

3 Place level tablespoons of the mixture well apart on the trays. Shape and flatten the biscuits into 5 cm (2 in) rounds.

4 Bake for 10 minutes, or until lightly browned. Cool slightly on the trays, then transfer to a wire rack to cool completely.

5 To melt the chocolate, put in a heatproof bowl and set over a saucepan of simmering water. Stir until the chocolate has melted and is smooth.

6 Spread the melted chocolate on the bottom of each florentine and, using a fork, make a wavy pattern on the chocolate before it sets. Allow the chocolate to set before serving.

Note These biscuits will keep, stored in an airtight container, for up to 1 week.

CHOCOLATE FUDGE SANDWICHES

Preparation time **30 minutes +**
Total cooking time **15 minutes**
Makes **20–24**

250 g (9 oz/2 cups) plain (all-purpose) flour
30 g (1 oz/¼ cup) unsweetened cocoa powder
200 g (7 oz) unsalted butter, chilled and diced
100 g (3½ oz) icing (confectioners') sugar
2 egg yolks, lightly beaten
1 teaspoon natural vanilla extract

Filling
100 g (3½ oz/⅔ cup) chopped dark chocolate
1 tablespoon golden syrup or dark corn syrup
25 g (1 oz) unsalted butter, softened

1 Preheat the oven to 200°C (400°F/Gas 6). Lightly grease two baking trays.
2 Sift the flour and cocoa powder into a bowl and rub in the butter until the mixture resembles fine breadcrumbs. Sift in the icing sugar and stir to combine. Using a wooden spoon, gradually stir in the egg yolks and vanilla until a soft dough forms.

3 Transfer the dough to a floured work surface and shape into a 4 x 6 x 26 cm (1½ x 2½ x 10½ in) block. Wrap in plastic wrap and chill for 30 minutes, or until firm.
4 Cut the dough into 40–48 slices, about 5 mm (¼ in) wide. Place the slices, spacing them well apart, on the baking trays.
5 Bake for 10 minutes, or until firm. Cool on the trays for 5 minutes, then transfer to a wire rack to cool completely.
6 To make the filling, put the chocolate in a small heatproof bowl. Sit the bowl over a small saucepan of simmering water, stirring frequently until the chocolate has melted. Take care that the base of the bowl doesn't touch the water. Remove from the heat, stir in the golden syrup and butter and continue stirring until the mixture is smooth. Allow to cool a little, then refrigerate and chill for 10 minutes, or until the mixture is thick enough to spread. Use the chocolate filling to sandwich the biscuits together.
Note Filled biscuits are best eaten on the day they are made. Unfilled biscuits will keep, stored in an airtight container, for up to 3 days.

MELTING MOMENTS

Preparation time **40 minutes +**
Total cooking time **20 minutes**
Makes 14

250 g (9 oz) unsalted butter, softened
40 g (1½ oz/⅓ cup) icing (confectioners')
    sugar
1 teaspoon natural vanilla extract
185 g (6½ oz/1½ cups) self-raising flour
60 g (2¼ oz/½ cup) custard powder or
    instant vanilla pudding mix

Passionfruit filling
60 g (2¼ oz) unsalted butter
60 g (2¼ oz/½ cup) icing (confectioners')
    sugar
1½ tablespoons passionfruit pulp

1 Preheat the oven to 180°C (350°F/Gas 4).
Line two baking trays with baking paper.

2 Cream the butter and icing sugar in a bowl using electric beaters until light and fluffy, then beat in the vanilla extract. Sift in the flour and custard powder and mix with a flat-bladed knife, using a cutting motion, to form a soft dough.
3 Roll level tablespoons of dough into balls (you should have about 28) and place on the trays, leaving room for spreading. Flatten slightly with a floured fork.
4 Bake for 20 minutes, or until lightly golden. Cool slightly on the trays, then transfer to a wire rack to cool completely.
5 To make the passionfruit filling, beat the butter and sugar in a bowl using electric beaters until light and creamy, then beat in the passionfruit pulp. Use to sandwich the biscuits together. Leave to firm.
Note These biscuits are best eaten the same day but will keep, stored in an airtight container, for up to 2 days.

ANZAC BISCUITS

Preparation time **15 minutes**
Total cooking time **25 minutes**
Makes 26

125 g (4½ oz/1 cup) plain (all-purpose) flour
160 g (5½ oz/⅔ cup) sugar
100 g (3½ oz/1 cup) rolled oats
90 g (3 oz/1 cup) desiccated coconut
125 g (4½ oz) unsalted butter, cubed
90 g (3 oz/¼ cup) golden syrup or honey
½ teaspoon bicarbonate of soda (baking soda)

1 Preheat the oven to 180°C (350°F/Gas 4). Line two baking trays with baking paper.
2 Sift the flour into a large bowl. Add the sugar, oats and coconut and make a well in the centre.
3 Combine the butter and golden syrup in a small saucepan and stir over low heat until the butter has melted and the mixture is smooth. Remove from the heat.

4 Dissolve the bicarbonate of soda in 1 tablespoon boiling water and add immediately to the butter mixture. It will foam up instantly. Pour into the well in the dry ingredients and stir with a wooden spoon until well combined.
5 Drop level tablespoons of mixture onto the trays, allowing enough room for spreading. Gently flatten each biscuit using your fingertips.
6 Bake for 20 minutes, or until just browned. Leave on the tray to cool slightly, then transfer to a wire rack to cool completely.
Notes The biscuits will keep, stored in an airtight container, for up to 1 week.

These famous biscuits were developed at the time of the First World War and sent in food parcels to the ANZAC troops (Australia and New Zealand Army Corps). They are an economical, crisp, long-lasting biscuit made without eggs.

MAPLE AND PECAN BISCUITS

Preparation time **30 minutes +**

Total cooking time **15 minutes**

Makes **about 60**

185 g (6½ oz) unsalted butter, softened

185 g (6½ oz/1 cup) soft brown sugar

60 ml (2 fl oz/¼ cup) maple syrup

1 teaspoon natural vanilla extract

1 egg

280 g (10 oz/2¼ cups) plain (all-purpose) flour

1 teaspoon baking powder

120 g (4¼ oz/1 cup) finely chopped pecans

extra pecans, to decorate

1 Cream the butter and sugar in a small bowl using electric beaters until light and fluffy. Add the maple syrup, vanilla and egg and beat until well combined.
2 Transfer to a large bowl and add the sifted flour and baking powder. Using a flat-bladed knife, mix to a soft dough. Gather together, then divide the mixture into two portions.
3 Place one portion of the dough on a sheet of baking paper and press lightly until the dough is 30 cm (12 in) long and 4 cm (1½ in) thick. Roll into a log shape, then roll the log in the chopped pecans. Repeat the process with the other portion of dough and refrigerate for 30 minutes.
4 Preheat the oven to 180°C (350°F/Gas 4). Line two baking trays with baking paper
5 Cut the logs into slices about 1 cm (½ in) thick. Press a whole pecan into the top of each biscuit. Place on the trays, leaving 3 cm (1¼ in) between each slice.
6 Bake for 10–15 minutes, or until golden. Cool on the trays for 3 minutes, then transfer to a wire rack to cool completely.

VANILLA GLAZED RINGS

Preparation time **15 minutes**
Total cooking time **12 minutes**
Makes **40–44**

125 g (4½ oz) unsalted butter, softened
115 g (4 oz) caster (superfine) sugar
2 teaspoons natural vanilla extract
1 small egg, lightly beaten
200 g (7 oz/1⅔ cups) plain (all-purpose) flour
½ teaspoon baking powder
1 quantity icing glaze (see page 126)
yellow food colouring (optional)
1 quantity royal icing (see page 126)

1 Preheat the oven to 180°C (350°F/Gas 4). Lightly grease two baking trays.
2 Cream the butter, sugar and vanilla in a bowl using electric beaters, then add the egg, beating well. Sift in the flour, baking powder and a pinch of salt and stir with a wooden spoon to form a dough.
3 Break off small pieces of dough and roll out each piece on a lightly floured work surface to form a 10 cm (4 in) log. Curl into a ring and gently press the ends together. Transfer to the prepared trays.
4 Bake for 10–12 minutes, or until light golden. Cool briefly on the tray, then transfer to a wire rack to cool.
5 To make the icing glaze, add a little yellow food colouring (if using) to the glaze. Make the royal icing and spoon into an icing bag.
6 Using a paintbrush, brush the tops of the biscuits with the glaze and leave to set on a wire rack. Pipe the royal icing backwards and forwards across the biscuits to form a zigzag pattern and leave to set.
Note The vanilla glazed rings will keep, stored in airtight container, for up to 3 days.

MANDARIN WHIRLS

Preparation time **25 minutes** +
Total cooking time **15 minutes**
Makes **18 sandwiches**

350 g (12 oz) unsalted butter, softened
60 g (2¼ oz/½ cup) icing (confectioners')
   sugar
zest of 2 mandarins, grated
250 g (9 oz/2 cups) plain (all-purpose) flour
60 g (2¼ oz/½ cup) cornflour (cornstarch)

Icing
120 g (4¼ oz) unsalted butter, softened
250 g (9 oz/2 cups) icing (confectioners')
   sugar
2 tablespoons freshly squeezed mandarin juice

1 Preheat the oven to 180°C (350°F/Gas 4).
Line two baking trays with baking paper.
2 Cream the butter, icing sugar and zest in
a bowl using electric beaters until pale and
fluffy. Sift the flour and cornflour into the
bowl, then stir with a wooden spoon until
a soft dough forms.
3 Transfer the mixture to a piping (icing)
bag fitted with a 4 cm (1½ in) star nozzle
and pipe thirty-six 4 cm (1½ in) rounds,
spacing them well apart, on the trays.
4 Bake for 12–15 minutes, or until lightly
golden on the edges. Cool on the trays for
5 minutes, then transfer to a wire rack to
cool completely.
5 To make the icing, cream the butter,
icing sugar and mandarin juice in a large
bowl using electric beaters until pale and
soft. Use the icing to sandwich the
whirls together.
Note Filled biscuits are best eaten on the
day they are made. Unfilled biscuits will
keep, stored in an airtight container, for
up to 1 week.

GINGERNUTS

Preparation time **15 minutes**

Total cooking time **15 minutes**

Makes **50**

250 g (9 oz/2 cups) plain (all-purpose) flour

1/2 teaspoon bicarbonate of soda (baking soda)

1 tablespoon ground ginger

1/2 teaspoon ground mixed (pumpkin pie) spice

125 g (4 1/2 oz) unsalted butter, chopped

185 g (6 1/2 oz/1 cup) soft brown sugar

60 ml (2 fl oz/1/4 cup) boiling water

1 tablespoon golden syrup or dark corn syrup

1 Preheat the oven to 180°C (350°F/Gas 4). Line two baking trays with baking paper.

2 Sift the flour, bicarbonate of soda, ginger and mixed spice into a large bowl. Add the butter and sugar and rub into the flour with your fingertips until the mixture resembles fine breadcrumbs. Pour the boiling water into a small heatproof bowl, add the golden syrup and stir until dissolved. Add to the flour and mix to a soft dough with a flat-bladed knife.

3 Roll into balls using 2 heaped teaspoons of mixture at a time. Place on the trays, allowing room for spreading, and flatten out slightly with your fingertips.

4 Bake for 15 minutes, or until firm. Cool on the trays for 10 minutes, then transfer to a wire rack to cool completely. Repeat with the remaining mixture.

Notes Make icing (frosting) by combining 2–3 teaspoons lemon juice, 60 g (2 1/4 oz/ 1/2 cup) sifted icing (confectioners') sugar and 10 g (1/4 oz) melted unsalted butter in a bowl. Mix until smooth, then spread over the biscuits and allow to set.

These biscuits will keep, stored in an airtight container, for up to 4 days.

ORANGE POLENTA BISCUITS

Preparation time **25 minutes**

Total cooking time **15 minutes**

Makes **20–22**

125 g (4½ oz) unsalted butter, softened
80 g (2¾ oz/⅓ cup) caster (superfine) sugar
1 teaspoon orange flower water
finely grated zest of 1 orange
2 eggs, lightly beaten
165 g (5¾ oz/1⅓ cups) plain (all-purpose) flour
80 g (2¾ oz/½ cup) polenta (cornmeal)

1 Preheat the oven to 200°C (400°F/Gas 6). Line two baking trays with baking paper.

2 Combine the butter, sugar, orange flower water and orange zest in a food processor and process until light and creamy. Add the eggs and process until smooth. Add the flour and polenta and pulse until a sticky dough forms.

3 Transfer the mixture to a piping bag fitted with a 2 cm (³⁄₄ in) star nozzle. Pipe the mixture onto the prepared baking trays to form 7 cm (2³⁄₄ in) crescents.

4 Bake for 15 minutes, or until the biscuits are golden around the edges. Cool on the trays for 5 minutes, then transfer to a wire rack to cool completely.

Note Orange polenta biscuits will keep, stored in an airtight container, for up to 3 days.

HONEY AND CARDAMOM BISCUITS

Preparation time **15 minutes**

Total cooking time **18 minutes**

Makes **24**

200 g (7 oz) unsalted butter

150 g (5½ oz/⅔ cup) caster (superfine) sugar

3 tablespoons honey

250 g (9 oz/2 cups) plain (all-purpose) flour

1 teaspoon baking powder

80 g (2¾ oz/¾ cup) ground almonds

2 teaspoons ground cardamom

icing (confectioners') sugar, to dust

1 Preheat the oven to 170°C (325°F/Gas 3). In a small saucepan, melt the butter, sugar and honey over medium heat, stirring until the sugar dissolves.

2 In a large bowl, sift the flour and baking powder. Stir in the ground almonds and cardamom. Make a well in the centre and add the butter mixture. Stir until just combined.

3 Place tablespoons of the mixture onto baking trays lined with baking paper. Flatten slightly with the base of a glass.

4 Bake for 15–18 minutes, or until lightly golden. Rest on trays for 5 minutes before transferring to a wire rack to cool completely. Dust lightly with icing sugar.

GINGER AND PISTACHIO BISCUITS

Preparation time **25 minutes**
Total cooking time **18 minutes**
Makes 25

100 g (3½ oz) unsalted butter
125 g (4½ oz/⅔ cup) soft brown sugar
1 teaspoon natural vanilla extract
2 eggs, at room temperature
250 g (9 oz/2 cups) plain (all-purpose) flour
1½ teaspoons baking powder
2 teaspoons ground ginger
100 g (3½ oz/⅔ cup) pistachio nuts, chopped
white chocolate, for drizzling (optional)

1 Preheat the oven to 170°C (325°F/Gas 3). Line two baking trays with baking paper.

2 Beat together the butter, sugar and vanilla extract using electric beaters until light and creamy. Add the eggs, one at a time, and beat until well combined.

3 Fold through the combined sifted flour, baking powder and ginger. Stir through the pistachio nuts.

4 Using lightly floured hands, roll tablespoons of the mixture into balls. Place on the prepared trays, allowing room for spreading. Flatten the biscuits slightly with a lightly floured fork.

5 Bake for 15–18 minutes, or until crisp and golden, swapping the trays halfway through cooking. Allow to cool on the trays for 5 minutes before transferring to a wire rack to cool. Drizzle the biscuits with white chocolate, if desired.

MARZIPAN POCKETS

Preparation time **25 minutes** +
Total cooking time **15 minutes**
Makes **25**

250 g (9 oz/2 cups) plain (all-purpose) flour,
 plus 2½ teaspoons, extra
115 g (4 oz/½ cup) caster (superfine) sugar
200 g (7 oz) unsalted butter, chopped
3 eggs, separated
200 g (7 oz) good-quality marzipan, chopped
slivered almonds, to decorate

1 Combine the flour and sugar in a bowl, and rub in the butter until the mixture resembles breadcrumbs.
2 Lightly beat the egg yolks in a small bowl, then stir into the flour mixture using a fork. Knead just until a dough forms.
3 Cut the dough in half, cover with plastic wrap and refrigerate for 2 hours.
4 Meanwhile, process the marzipan in a food processor until very finely chopped.

Add the extra flour and 1½ tablespoons of egg white and process until combined. Transfer the mixture to a small bowl, cover with plastic wrap and refrigerate.
5 Preheat the oven to 180°C (350°F/Gas 4). Lightly grease and flour two baking trays.
6 Roll the dough out on a lightly floured work surface to 4 mm (¼ in) thick. Using a 6.5 cm (2½ in) pastry cutter, cut out rounds from the dough, reserving the scraps. Put 25 of the rounds on the tray, brush with egg white and place 1 teaspoon of marzipan mixture in the centre of each. Re-roll the scraps and cut out more rounds, until you have a total of 25 more rounds. Place these on top of the rounds on the trays, pressing the edges lightly to seal.
7 Brush the tops with egg white. Using a knife, make a small cut in the top of each. Scatter with slivered almonds, then bake for 12–15 minutes, or until light golden. Cool on the trays for 5 minutes, then transfer to a wire rack to cool completely.

PLUM AND CARAWAY BISCUITS

Preparation time **25 minutes +**
Total cooking time **12 minutes**
Makes **24**

80 g (2³/₄ oz) butter, softened
60 g (2¹/₄ oz) cream cheese, chopped
115 g (4 oz/¹/₂ cup) caster (superfine) sugar
1 teaspoon natural vanilla extract
2 egg yolks
1¹/₂ teaspoons caraway seeds
150 g (5¹/₂ oz/1¹/₄ cups) plain (all-purpose) flour
plum jam
icing (confectioners') sugar, to dust

1 Cream the butter, cream cheese and sugar in a bowl using electric beaters until pale and fluffy. Add the vanilla extract and 1 egg yolk and beat to combine well. Add the caraway seeds and flour and stir until a dough forms.
2 Turn the dough out onto a lightly floured work surface, form into a flat rectangle, then cover with plastic wrap and refrigerate for 2 hours, or until firm.
3 Preheat the oven to 180°C (350°F/Gas 4). Lightly grease two baking trays.
4 Combine the remaining egg yolk with 2 teaspoons water and stir to combine well.
5 Cut the dough in half, then roll out each half on a lightly floured work surface to form an 18 x 24 cm (7 x 9¹/₂ in) rectangle. Using a lightly floured sharp knife, cut the dough into 6 cm (2¹/₂ in) squares.
6 Place a scant teaspoon of jam diagonally across the centre of each square, then brush all four corners of the square with the egg mixture. Take one corner and fold it into the centre. Take the opposite corner and fold it into the centre, overlapping the first corner slightly, to partially enclose the jam.
7 Brush the tops of the biscuits with the egg mixture, then place them, seam side up, on the baking trays.
8 Bake for 10–12 minutes, or until light golden, swapping the trays halfway through cooking. Cool on the trays for 5 minutes, then transfer to a wire rack to cool completely. Dust with icing sugar.

ITALIAN ORANGE BISCUITS

Preparation time **20 minutes** +
Total cooking time **15 minutes**
Makes **about 45**

175 g (6½ oz/1½ cups) plain (all-purpose) flour
200 g (7 oz/1⅔ cups) semolina or fine polenta
100 g (3½ oz/½ cup) caster (superfine) sugar
100 g (3½ oz) unsalted butter, softened
2½ teaspoons grated orange zest
2 eggs

1 Put the flour, semolina, sugar, butter, orange zest, eggs and a pinch of salt in a food processor and mix until smooth. Chill the mixture in the fridge for 15 minutes.

2 Preheat the oven to 190°C (375°F/Gas 5). Grease a baking tray and place teaspoonfuls of the mixture on the tray.
3 Lightly moisten your fingers with a little water and press the mixture down to flatten it. Don't use too much water or it will affect the texture of the biscuits. Leave space between the biscuits as the biscuits will expand during cooking.
4 Bake for about 15 minutes, or until the edge of the biscuit is dark golden brown.
5 Remove from the oven, scoop off the tray with a spatula and cool on a wire rack.
Note If you are baking the biscuits in batches, make sure the tray is greased each time you use it.

SPICY FRUIT BISCUITS

Preparation time **30 minutes +**
Total cooking time **15 minutes**
Makes **about 60**

180 g (6½ oz) unsalted butter, softened
185 g (6½ oz/1 cup) soft brown sugar
1 teaspoon natural vanilla extract
1 egg
280 g (10 oz/2¼ cups) plain (all-purpose) flour
1 teaspoon baking powder
1 teaspoon ground mixed (pumpkin pie) spice
½ teaspoon ground ginger
95 g (3¼ oz/½ cup) fruit mince (mincemeat)

1 Cream the butter and sugar in a bowl using electric beaters until fluffy. Add the vanilla and egg and beat until combined. Transfer to a bowl and add the flour, baking powder, mixed spice and ginger. Using a flat-bladed knife, mix to a soft dough.

2 Gather together, then divide the mixture into two portions. Roll one portion out on a sheet of baking paper to a rectangle about 2 mm (¹⁄₁₆ in) thick and trim the edges. Repeat with the other portion of dough. Refrigerate until just firm.

3 Spread both portions of dough with the fruit mince and then carefully roll up Swiss-roll-style (jelly-roll-style). Refrigerate for 30 minutes, or until firm.

4 Preheat the oven to 180°C (350°F/Gas 4). Line two baking trays with baking paper. Cut the logs into slices about 1 cm (½ in) thick.

5 Place on the prepared trays, leaving 3 cm (1¼ in) between each slice. Bake for 10–15 minutes, or until golden. Cool on the trays for 3 minutes before transferring to a wire rack to cool completely.

ALMOND BREAD

Preparation time **30 minutes +**
Total cooking time **45 minutes**
Makes **50**

125 g (4½ oz) blanched almonds
3 egg whites
125 g (4½ oz/½ cup) caster (superfine) sugar
90 g (3 oz/¾ cup) plain (all-purpose) flour

1 Preheat the oven to 180°C (350°F/Gas 4). Lightly grease a 26 x 8 x 4.5 cm (10½ x 3 x 1¾ in) bar tin and line with baking paper. Make sure the paper extends up the two long sides.
2 Spread the almonds on a baking tray and toast in the oven for 2–3 minutes, then allow to cool.
3 Beat the egg whites in a clean, dry bowl and beat until stiff peaks form. Gradually add the sugar, beating constantly until the mixture is thick and glossy and all the sugar has dissolved.

4 Add the sifted flour and almonds. Using a metal spoon, gently fold the ingredients together until combined. Spread into the tin and smooth the surface.
5 Bake for 25 minutes. Remove from the oven and cool completely in the tin.
6 Reduce the oven to 160°C (315°F/ Gas 2–3). Using a serrated knife, cut the loaf into 5 mm (¼ in) slices and place on baking trays.
7 Bake for 15 minutes, turning once halfway through, or until lightly golden and crisp.
Notes Almond bread will keep for up to 1 month in an airtight container.

Blanched almonds simply means almonds with their brown skins removed. If you can't buy blanched almonds and so you need to remove the skin, place the nuts in a bowl, cover with boiling water, leave them for 5 minutes then drain and press the softened skin away from the nuts with your fingers.

ALMOND SHORTBREADS

Preparation time **30 minutes +**
Total cooking time **12 minutes**
Makes **22**

250 g (9 oz) unsalted butter
250 g (9 oz/2 cups) plain (all-purpose) flour
1 teaspoon baking powder
90 g (3¼ oz/¾ cup) icing (confectioners')
    sugar, sifted
1 egg yolk
1 teaspoon natural vanilla extract
1 tablespoon ouzo
100 g (3½ oz/¾ cup) slivered almonds,
    ground to a medium-fine texture
4 tablespoons ground almonds
60 g (2¼ oz/½ cup) icing (confectioners')
    sugar, extra, to dust

1 Melt the butter in a small heavy-based saucepan over low heat, without stirring or shaking the pan. Carefully pour the clear butter into another container, leaving the white sediment in the pan to be discarded.

Refrigerate for 1 hour.
2 Preheat the oven to 170°C (325°F/Gas 3). Line two baking trays with baking paper.
3 Sift the flour and baking powder together in a bowl. Beat the chilled butter using electric beater until light and fluffy. Gradually add the icing sugar and combine well. Add the egg yolk, vanilla and ouzo and beat until just combined. Fold in the flour, the ground slivered almonds and the ground almonds.
4 Shape heaped tablespoons of mixture into crescents. Place on the baking trays and bake for 12 minutes, or until lightly coloured. Remove from the oven and dust liberally with icing sugar. Allow to cool a little on the trays.
5 Line a baking tray with baking paper and dust the paper with icing sugar. Lift the warm biscuits onto this and dust again with icing sugar. When the biscuits are cool, dust them once again with icing sugar.
Note These biscuits will keep, stored in an airtight container, for up to 1 week.

ALMOND BISCOTTI

Preparation time **20 minutes**
Total cooking time **40 minutes**
Makes **20**

380 g (13½ oz) plain (all-purpose) flour
160 g (5¾ oz) caster (superfine) sugar
3 eggs
½ teaspoon baking powder
½ teaspoon natural vanilla extract
150 g (5½ oz) blanched almonds

1 Preheat the oven to 180°C (350°F/Gas 4). Line two baking trays with baking paper.
2 Sift the flour into a large bowl. Add the sugar, eggs, baking powder, vanilla and a pinch of salt and mix using electric beaters until you have a smooth dough. Transfer to a floured surface and knead in the almonds.
3 Divide the dough into two pieces and roll each one into a log about 20 cm (8 in) long. Put on the baking trays and press down gently along the top to flatten the logs slightly.
4 Bake for 25 minutes, or until lightly golden. Remove from the oven and leave to cool slightly. Reduce the oven temperature to 170°C (325°F/Gas 3).
5 Cut each log into 1 cm (½ in) thick diagonal slices. Place on the baking tray, well spaced, and bake for 15 minutes, or until lightly browned.
Note These biscuits will keep, stored in an airtight container, for up to 1 week.

In Italy, biscotti refers to any small biscuits, but elsewhere, it usually means those small biscuits traditionally served dipped in vin santo, a Tuscan dessert wine. Biscotto means 'twice baked', referring to the method of baking the loaf of dough, slicing it, then baking it again to produce a hard, crunchy biscuit. The most recognised versions are cantucci (or biscotti di Prato), Tuscan almond biscuits.

AMARETTI

Preparation time **20 minutes**
Total cooking time **40 minutes**
Makes **15**

125 g (4½ oz) blanched almonds
125 g (4½ oz) icing (confectioners') sugar
3 teaspoons plain (all-purpose) flour
2 egg whites
75 g (2½ oz) caster (superfine) sugar
1 teaspoon almond extract

1 Preheat the oven to 180°C (350°F/Gas 4). Line a baking tray with baking paper.
2 Put the almonds, icing sugar and flour in a pestle and mortar or food processor and grind to a fine powder (be careful not to overwork the mixture or it will become oily).
3 Whisk the egg whites in a dry glass bowl using electrc beaters until soft peaks form. Add the caster sugar 1 tablespoon at a time and beat continuously until you have a stiff shiny mixture. Fold in the almond mixture and the almond extract until just blended.
4 Spoon the mixture into a piping bag with a 1 cm (½ in) plain nozzle and pipe 3 cm (1¼ in) wide mounds, well spaced, onto a baking tray. Smooth the top of each biscuit with a damp finger.
5 Bake for 40 minutes until they are light brown. Turn off the oven, leave the door ajar and let the biscuits cool and dry out.
Notes These biscuits will keep, stored in an airtight container, for up to 1 week.

Amaretti are light, crisp Italian biscuits, similar to the macaroon, made with sweet and bitter almonds. The bitter almonds give amaretti their characteristic flavour—and their name, which means 'bitter little things'. There are many varieties of amaretti, but they are often seen wrapped in pairs and served with coffee.

CINNAMON PECAN BISCOTTI

Preparation time **20 minutes**
Total cooking time **1 hour**
Makes **30**

2 eggs, at room temperature
250 g (9 oz/1 cup) caster (superfine) sugar
280 g (10 oz/2¼ cups) plain (all-purpose) flour
½ teaspoon baking powder
2 teaspoons ground cinnamon
125 g (4½ oz/1¼ cups) pecans

1 Preheat the oven to 170°C (325°F/Gas 3). Line a baking tray with baking paper.
2 Beat the eggs and sugar using electric beaters for 2 minutes, or until pale and thick. Add the sifted flour, baking powder, cinnamon and pecans. Use a flat-bladed knife to mix to a soft dough. Turn out onto a lightly-floured surface and knead until the mixture comes together.
3 Divide the mixture into two equal portions. Shape each portion into a log about 25 cm (10 in) long and 8 cm (3¼ in) wide. Place the logs onto the prepared tray, leaving room for spreading.
4 Bake for 35–40 minutes, or until lightly coloured. Set aside to cool completely.
5 Using a serrated knife, cut the logs into 1 cm (½ in) thick slices and place in a single layer, cut side down, on the tray.
6 Bake for 15–20 minutes, or until crisp and lightly golden, turning halfway through cooking. Allow to cool completely.
Note These biscuits will keep, stored in an airtight container, for up to 1 week.

PISTACHIO BISCOTTI

Preparation time **25 minutes**
Total cooking time **50 minutes**
Makes **about 45**

250 g (9 oz/2 cups) plain (all-purpose) flour
1 teaspoon baking powder
230 g (8 oz/1 cup) caster (superfine) sugar
3 eggs
1 egg yolk
1 teaspoon natural vanilla extract
1 teaspoon grated orange zest
110 g (3³/4 oz/³/4 cup) pistachio nuts

1 Preheat the oven to 180°C (350°F/Gas 4). Line two baking trays with baking paper and lightly dust with flour.
2 Sift the flour and baking powder into a large bowl. Add the sugar and mix well. Make a well in the centre and add two whole eggs, the egg yolk, vanilla extract and orange zest. Using a large metal spoon, stir until just combined. Mix in the pistachios. Knead for 2–3 minutes on a floured surface. Sprinkle a little water onto the dough.
3 Divide the mixture into two portions and roll each into a log about 25 cm (10 in) long and 8 cm (3¹/4 in) wide. Slightly flatten the tops.
4 Place the logs on the trays, allowing room for spreading. Beat the remaining egg and brush over the logs to glaze.
5 Bake for 35 minutes, then remove from the oven. Reduce the oven to 150°C (300°F/Gas 2). Allow the logs to cool slightly and cut into 5 mm (¹/4 in) slices.
6 Place, flat side down, on the trays and bake for 8 minutes. Turn the biscuits over and cook for a further 8 minutes, or until slightly coloured and crisp and dry. Transfer to a wire rack to cool completely.

REFRIGERATOR BISCUITS

Preparation time **30 minutes +**
Total cooking time **15 minutes**
Makes **60**

180 g (6 oz) unsalted butter, softened
185 g (6½ oz/1 cup) soft brown sugar
1 teaspoon natural vanilla extract
1 egg
280 g (10 oz/2¼ cups) plain (all-purpose) flour
1 teaspoon baking powder

1 Cream the butter and sugar in a bowl using electric beaters until fluffy. Add the vanilla extract and egg. Beat until combined.
2 Transfer to a large bowl and add the sifted flour and baking powder. Using a knife, mix to a soft dough. Gather together, then divide the mixture into two portions.
3 Place one portion of the dough on a sheet of baking paper and press lightly until the dough is 30 cm (12 in) long and 4 cm (1½ in) thick. Fold the paper around the dough and roll neatly into a log shape. Twist the edges of the paper to seal. Repeat the process with the other portion. Refrigerate for 30 minutes, or until firm.
4 Preheat the oven to 180°C (350°F/Gas 4). Line two baking trays with baking paper.
5 Cut the logs into slices about 1 cm (½ in) thick. Place on the prepared trays, leaving 3 cm (1¼ in) between each slice. Bake for 10–15 minutes, or until golden. Alow to cool on the trays for 3 minutes, then transfer to a wire rack to cool completely. When cold, store in an airtight container.

VARIATIONS:

Spicy fruit Add 1 teaspoon mixed (pumpkin pie) spice and ½ teaspoon ground ginger with the sifted flour. Divide the dough into two, roll one portion out on a sheet of baking paper to a rectangle about 2 mm (⅛ in) thick and trim the edges. Refrigerate until just firm. Spread with 95 g (3 oz/½ cup) fruit mince (mincemeat), and then roll up Swiss-roll-style. Repeat the process with the other portion of dough. Refrigerate, slice and bake as directed in the original recipe.

Mocha spirals Divide the dough into two portions. Add 2 teaspoons of cocoa powder to one portion and 2 teaspoons of instant coffee powder to the other and knead each lightly. Divide both doughs in half again. Roll two of the different coloured portions separately to even rectangles about 2 mm (⅛ in) thick, and then place one layer on top of the other on a sheet of baking paper. Trim the edges and roll up Swiss-roll-style. Repeat with the remaining dough portions. Refrigerate, slice and bake as directed in the original recipe.

Maple and pecan Add 60 ml (2 fl oz/ ¼ cup) maple syrup to the creamed butter and sugar mixture. Roll the logs in 125 g (4½ oz/1 cup) finely chopped pecans before refrigerating. Press a whole nut into the top of each biscuit before baking as directed in the original recipe.

Macadamia Add 45 g (1½ oz/½ cup) desiccated coconut and 70 g (2¼ oz/ ½ cup) toasted chopped macadamia nuts with the flour. Using a ruler as a guide, shape the logs into a triangle shape. Refrigerate, slice and bake as directed in the original recipe. When the log is cut, the biscuits will be in the shape of triangles.

Marbled Replace the brown sugar with caster (superfine) sugar. Divide the creamed butter and egg mixture into three bowls. Add a few drops of red food colouring to one and 50 g (1¾ oz) melted dark chocolate, 1 tablespoon cocoa powder and 2 teaspoons milk to another. Leave one plain. Add 90 g (3 oz/¾ cup) sifted plain (all-purpose) flour and ¼ teaspoon baking powder to each bowl. Mix each to a soft dough, divide in half and roll into thin logs. Twist the 3 colours together to create a marbled effect, then shape the combined dough into 2 logs. Refrigerate, slice and bake as directed in the original recipe.

CHEESE BISCUITS

Preparation time **40 minutes**

Total cooking time **8 minutes**

Serves **4–6**

Biscuit pastry

125 g (4½ oz/1 cup) plain (all-purpose) flour
½ teaspoon baking powder
60 g (2¼ oz) butter
1 egg, lightly beaten
60 g (2¼ oz) cheddar cheese, grated
1 teaspoon snipped chives
1 teaspoon chopped flat-leaf (Italian) parsley
1 tablespoon iced water

Cheese filling

80 g (2¾ oz) cream cheese, softened
20 g (¾ oz) butter
1 tablespoon snipped chives
1 tablespoon chopped flat-leaf (Italian) parsley
¼ teaspoon lemon pepper
90 g (3¼ oz) cheddar cheese, grated

1 Preheat the oven to 190°C (375°F/Gas 5). Line two baking trays with baking paper.

2 To make the biscuit pastry, sift the flour and baking powder into a large bowl and add the chopped butter. Rub in the butter until the mixture resembles breadcrumbs.

3 Make a well in the centre and add the egg, cheese, herbs and iced water. Mix with a flat-bladed knife, using a cutting action, until the mixture comes together in beads. Gather together and lift out onto a floured surface. Press together into a ball.

4 Roll the pastry between sheets of baking paper to 3 mm (⅛ in) thick. Remove the top sheet of paper and cut the pastry into rounds, using a 5 cm (2 in) cutter. Place the rounds onto the baking trays. Re-roll the remaining pastry and repeat cutting.

5 Bake for about 8 minutes, or until lightly browned. Transfer to a wire rack to cool.

6 To make the filling, beat the cream cheese and butter in a bowl using electric beaters until light and creamy. Add the herbs, pepper and cheese and beat until smooth. Spread ½ teaspoon of filling on half of the biscuits and sandwich together with the remaining biscuits.

GRAHAM CRACKERS

Preparation time **25 minutes** +
Total cooking time **10 minutes**
Makes **12**

350 g (12 oz/2⅓ cups) wholemeal
    (whole-wheat) plain (all-purpose) flour
60 g (2¼ oz/½ cup) cornflour (cornstarch)
55 g (2 oz/¼ cup) caster (superfine) sugar
150 g (5½ oz) butter
185 ml (6 fl oz/¾ cup) pouring (whipping)
    cream

1 Sift the flours into a bowl, then stir in the sugar and ½ teaspoon salt. Rub in the butter with your fingertips until the mixture resembles breadcrumbs. Mix in the cream with a flat-bladed knife, using a cutting action, to make a pliable dough.
2 Gather the dough together and shape into a disc. Wrap in plastic wrap and refrigerate for 30 minutes.
3 Preheat the oven to 200°C (400°F/Gas 6). Line two baking trays with baking paper.
4 Roll out the dough to a rectangle measuring 24 x 30 cm (9½ x 12 in). Cut the dough into 12 rectangles with a sharp knife or pastry wheel. Place the rectangles on the baking trays, allowing a little room for spreading.
5 Bake for 7–10 minutes, or until firm and golden brown. Leave to cool on the trays for 2–3 minutes, before transferring to a wire rack to cool completely.

DIGESTIVE BISCUITS

Preparation time **15 minutes +**
Total cooking time **12 minutes**
Makes **16**

125 g (4½ oz) unsalted butter, softened
60 g (2 oz/⅓ cup) soft brown sugar
1 tablespoon malt extract
1 egg, lightly beaten
125 g (4½ oz/1 cup) plain (all-purpose) flour
150 g (5½ oz/1 cup) wholemeal plain
   (all-purpose) flour
35 g (1¼ oz/½ cup) unprocessed bran
1 teaspoon baking powder

1 Line two baking trays with baking paper. Cream the butter, sugar and malt in a small bowl with electric beaters until light and fluffy. Gradually add the egg, beating well after each addition. Transfer to a large bowl.
2 Sift the flours, bran and baking powder into a small bowl, returning the husks to the bowl. Fold the dry ingredients into the creamed mixture in three portions and mix to a firm dough. Cover and refrigerate for at least 1 hour.
3 Preheat the oven to 180°C (350°F/Gas 4). Roll out half the dough between two sheets of baking paper to 5 mm (¼ in) thick. Cut out rounds using a 7 cm (2¾ in) plain cutter and place the rounds on the trays. Repeat with the remaining dough and re-roll any scraps. Refrigerate for 20 minutes to firm.
4 Bake for 12 minutes, or until golden brown and firm. Leave on the trays to cool slightly before transferring to a wire rack to cool completely.
Notes When the biscuits are cool, store in an airtight container for up to 5 days.

Digestives can be eaten plain, buttered or served with cheese. They can also be drizzled with melted chocolate.

CRISPBREAD

Preparation time **20 minutes** +
Total cooking time **30 minutes**
Makes **24**

250 ml (9 fl oz/1 cup) lukewarm milk
1 tablespoon dried yeast
¼ teaspoon dried fennel seeds
250 g (9 oz) stoneground flour
200 g (7 oz) coarse rye meal

1 Line two baking trays with baking paper. Put the milk in a bowl, add the yeast and stir until dissolved. Leave in a warm place for 10 minutes, or until bubbles appear on the surface. The mixture should be frothy and slightly increased in volume. If your yeast doesn't foam, it is dead and you will have to discard it and start again.
2 Mix the fennel, flour, rye meal and 1 teaspoon salt in a bowl. Make a well in the centre and add the yeast mixture. Gather together and knead on a floured surface for 5 minutes, adding a little water if necessary. Divide into four portions.
3 Divide each portion into six pieces and shape each into a ball. Cover and leave in a warm place for 20 minutes, or until doubled in size.
4 Preheat the oven to 180°C (350°F/Gas 4). Roll out each ball of dough to make a circle about 13 cm (5 in) in diameter. Cut out the centre of each circle with a round 2 cm (³/4 in) cutter. Discard the centre, then prick each crispbread with a fork and put on a baking tray. Bake the crispbread, in batches, for 10 minutes, or until firm and dry and slightly coloured.
Note When completely cool, store in an airtight container.

OATCAKES

Preparation time **15 minutes**

Total cooking time **20 minutes**

Makes **30–32**

400 g (14 oz/3¼ cups) fine oatmeal
100 g (3½ oz/⅔ cup) oat bran
1 teaspoon bicarbonate of soda (baking soda)
60 g (2¼ oz) butter, melted

1 Preheat the oven to 200°C (400°F/Gas 6). Lightly grease two baking trays.
2 Combine the oatmeal, oat bran, bicarbonate of soda and 1 teaspoon salt in a bowl. Make a well in the centre and, using a wooden spoon, stir in the melted butter and 250 ml (9 fl oz/1 cup) water to form a firm, slightly sticky dough.
3 Transfer the dough to a lightly floured work surface and knead until smooth. Roll out on a floured surface to a 2 mm (¹/₁₆ in) round and, using a 7 cm (2³/₄ in) pastry cutter, cut out rounds from the dough (re-rolling the pastry scraps to press out a total of 30–32 rounds).
4 Transfer to the baking trays and bake for 18–20 minutes, or until the edges are lightly browned. Cool on trays for 5 minutes, then transfer to a wire rack to cool.

Notes Oatcakes will keep, stored in an airtight container, for up to 1 week.

Serve with cheeses, such as a blue cheese or aged cheddar.

TWO-SEED CRACKERS

Preparation time 20 minutes
Total cooking time 25 minutes
Makes 30

250 g (9 oz/2 cups) plain (all-purpose) flour
1 teaspoon baking powder
2 tablespoons poppy seeds
2 tablespoons sesame seeds
60 g (2¼ oz) butter, chilled and chopped
125 ml (4 fl oz/½ cup) iced water

1 Preheat the oven to 180°C (350°F/Gas 4). Line two baking trays with baking paper.
2 Sift the flour, baking powder and ½ teaspoon salt into a bowl. Stir in the seeds and some pepper. Rub the butter into the flour using your fingertips until the mixture resembles fine breadcrumbs.

3 Make a well in the centre and add the iced water. Mix together with a flat-bladed knife using a cutting action, adding a little extra water if necessary, until the mixture comes together in soft beads. Gather together into a rough ball. Handle the dough gently and do not knead it.
4 Divide the dough into two portions. Put one portion between two sheets of baking paper and roll out to 2 mm (⅛ in) thick. Cover the other portion with plastic wrap.
5 Using a 6 cm (2½ in) round cutter, cut rounds from the dough. Prick all over with a fork and transfer to the trays. Repeat with the remaining dough. Pile any dough trimmings together (do not knead) and gently re-roll. Cut out more rounds.
6 Bake for 20–25 minutes, or until golden. Allow to cool on a wire rack.

MARSALA AND FENNEL SEED RINGS

Preparation time **20 minutes** +
Total cooking time **40 minutes**
Makes **24**

375 g (13 oz/3 cups) plain (all-purpose) flour
55 g (2 oz/¼ cup) caster (superfine) sugar
1½ teaspoons baking powder
1 tablespoon fennel seeds
1 teaspoon sea salt flakes
80 ml (2½ fl oz/⅓ cup) sweet marsala
125 ml (4 fl oz/½ cup) extra virgin olive oil
1 egg yolk

1 Preheat the oven to 180°C (350°F/Gas 4). Lightly grease a baking tray.
2 Combine the flour, sugar, baking powder, fennel seeds and sea salt in a bowl and stir to combine well.
3 Combine the marsala, olive oil and about 80 ml (2½ fl oz/⅓ cup) water in a bowl and whisk to combine. Add to the dry ingredients, then stir until a dough forms.
4 Turn the dough out onto a work surface (the dough shouldn't stick, so there is no need to flour the surface) and divide in half. Cut each half into 12 even-sized pieces, then roll each into a 10 cm (4 in) long log. Form each log into a ring, pressing the joins firmly to seal. Place on the prepared tray.
5 To make a glaze, mix the egg yolk with 1 tablespoon water. Brush the rings with the egg yolk glaze.
6 Bake for 20 minutes. Reduce the oven to 150°C (300°F/Gas 2) and bake for a further 15–20 minutes, or until golden and crisp. Cool on a wire rack.
Notes These rings will keep, stored in an airtight container, for up to 2 weeks.
　Serve with parmesan or pecorino cheese.

CUMIN SEED WAFERS

Preparation time **25 minutes** +
Total cooking time **12 minutes**
Makes **48**

250 g (9 oz/2 cups) plain (all-purpose) flour
1 teaspoon baking powder
60 g (2¼ oz) Copha (white vegetable
   shortening), chilled
1 tablespoon cumin seeds, toasted

1 Preheat the oven to 180°C (350°F/Gas 4).
Lightly grease two baking trays.
2 Sift the flour, baking powder and
1 teaspoon salt into a bowl. Rub in the
Copha until the mixture resembles fine
breadcrumbs. Stir in the cumin seeds.
Make a well in the centre of the mixture
and gradually add 125 ml (4 fl oz/½ cup)
water, stirring with a wooden spoon until
a dough forms.
3 Knead the dough gently on a lightly
floured work surface until just smooth.
Cover with plastic wrap and refrigerate
for 30 minutes.
4 Divide the dough into quarters and roll
out each quarter on a floured work surface
until 1 mm (¹/₁₆ in) thick, then trim the
sides to form a 20 x 30 cm (8 x 12 in)
rectangle. Cut in half down the length,
then cut across the width to form 5 cm
(2 in) wide fingers. You should end up with
12 fingers from each quarter of dough.
5 Place on the baking trays and bake in
batches for 10–12 minutes, or until light
golden. Transfer to a wire rack to cool.
Note These wafers will keep, stored in an
airtight container, for up to 1 week.

SESAME AND GINGER WAFERS

Preparation time **15 minutes**

Total cooking time **4 minutes**

Makes **18**

40 g (1½ oz) unsalted butter
40 g (1½ oz) caster (superfine) sugar
2 tablespoons golden syrup or dark corn syrup
40 g (1½ oz/⅓ cup) plain (all-purpose) flour
½ teaspoon ground ginger
1 tablespoon brandy
2 teaspoons lemon juice
1 tablespoon sesame seeds, toasted

1 Preheat the oven to 190°C (375°F/Gas 5). Grease two baking trays.
2 Combine the butter, sugar and syrup in a small saucepan and heat gently until the butter has melted and the mixture is smooth. Remove from the heat. Sift the flour and ginger into a bowl. Add the melted butter mixture and the brandy, lemon juice and sesame seeds and stir to mix well.
3 Drop 2 teaspoonfuls of the mixture (1 teaspoon for each wafer) onto each of the baking trays, leaving enough room between the mixture to allow for spreading. Using a palette knife, spread each one out to form a 10 cm (4 in) round.
4 Bake for 3–4 minutes, or until the wafers begin to brown around the edges, then remove from the oven.
5 Cool for 1 minute. Using the palette knife and working quickly, carefully remove the warm biscuits from the tray, then drape them over a rolling pin to make them curl. Cool completely, then remove from pin. Repeat with the remaining mixture.
Note These wafers are best eaten on the day they are made.

FORTUNE COOKIES

Preparation time **45 minutes** +
Total cooking time **50 minutes**
Makes **30**

3 egg whites
60 g (2¼ oz/½ cup) icing (confectioners')
    sugar, sifted
45 g (1½ oz) unsalted butter, melted
60 g (2¼ oz/½ cup) plain (all-purpose) flour

1 Preheat the oven to 180°C (350°F/Gas 4).
Lightly grease a baking tray. Draw three
8 cm (3 in) circles on a sheet of baking
paper, turn over and use to line the tray.
2 Place the egg whites in a clean, dry bowl
and whisk until just frothy. Add the icing
sugar and butter and stir until smooth. Add
the flour, mix until smooth and leave for
15 minutes.
3 Using a flat-bladed knife, spread 2 level
teaspoons of mixture over each circle. Bake

for 5 minutes, or until slightly brown
around the edges.
4 Working quickly, remove from the trays
by sliding a flat-bladed knife under each
round. Place a written fortune message in
each cookie. Fold in half, then in half
again, over the edge of a bowl or a palette
knife. Keep a tea towel (dish towel) handy
to use when folding the cookies. The tray
is hot, so take care not to burn your hands.
Cool on a wire rack.
5 Repeat with the remaining mixture. Make
two or three cookies at a time, otherwise
they will harden too quickly and break
when folding.
Notes These were originated by Chinese
Americans. Each biscuit contains a
message, usually a proverb or horoscope.
The biscuits are served at the end of a
Chinese meal to wish good fortune.

These cookies keep for two days in an
airtight container.

SLICES

Crunchy, gooey, sticky, fruity, spongy, fudgy, chewy, creamy, nutty, chocolatey—whatever your culinary craving, a slice can satisfy it simply and completely. Loved by children and grown-ups alike, slices grow up with you, becoming more sophisticated as your tastes develop (or not, as the case may be!). The beauty of slices is that they can be as simple or as richly exotic as you like. Easily transportable, they can accompany you to school, to work, to a picnic, or even as far as the sitting room with a cup of coffee and a good book. Cut a piece as little or as large as you like and indulge yourself.

SLICE SECRETS

The slice has long been a favourite accompaniment for morning coffee or afternoon tea. Most are quick and easy to cook and for the beginner, slices are a dream come true: less daunting to prepare than a cake, but a lot more exciting than a batch of biscuits.

EQUIP YOURSELF

We've used an assortment of tins in our recipes to suit both the flavour and richness of each slice, giving a selection of shapes, sizes and thicknesses. Don't forget: always measure your tins across the base. Obviously we don't expect everyone to have the full array of tins in their kitchen, so if you don't have the exact size specified, use the closest you have and adjust the cooking time accordingly. If you have the choice, use a slightly larger tin—your mixture will be spread a little more thinly and so will take less time to cook. If you use a smaller tin, your mixture is likely to bubble up over the top. It may take slightly longer to cook. Using a non-stick tin means your slice will cook slightly faster and brown more—check it about 5 minutes earlier than the cooking time given in the recipe.

Basic metric cup and spoon measures and scales will help you measure your ingredients accurately and appliances such as electric beaters and food processors will help minimise preparation time.

TIN TALK

Lining the tin has a dual purpose—it prevents the slice sticking to the tin but also means you can lift your slice out of the tin after cooking. Line the tin before you start any mixing. Lightly grease the base and sides with butter or oil spray, then line the base with a piece of non-stick baking paper. The paper should fit the base of the tin neatly, without creases, but should be wide so that it overhangs the two long sides of the tin. This creates the simple handles that enable you to lift your slice out of the tin. Some recipes may only require the base to be lined. To do this, draw around the base onto paper, then cut it out. If all four sides of the tin need to be lined, simply line the base, overhanging two sides, then lay another piece of paper over the top, overhanging the other two sides.

IN THE OVEN

If the top of the slice starts to over-brown while it is cooking, cover it loosely with foil or baking paper—not tightly or the slice will become soggy. For best results cook the slice on the middle rack in the centre of the oven.

In some recipes you'll need to check if the slice is cooked by inserting a skewer into the centre. The skewer should come out clean, without sticky crumbs on it. If it doesn't, bake the slice for a further 5 minutes and retest. This doesn't apply to all slices as many have soft fillings. With many slices you will find they are soft when removed from the oven and then firm up a little as they cool. This is why the recipe will often state 'leave to cool in the tin for 5 minutes'.

Most slices can be stored in an airtight container, or in the fridge in warm weather, for between three and seven days.

CUTTING

Use the baking paper 'handles' to lift the whole slice out of the tin. It is much easier to cut the slice into neat squares, fingers or even diamonds if you use a ruler as a guide. For clean edges, wipe the blade of the knife with a damp cloth between each cut. Use a sawing action with a serrated knife for cakey slices. If you have cut the slice in the tin, remove the corner piece with a palette knife—this makes it easier to lift out the other pieces.

HINTS AND TIPS

1 Buy good quality, sturdy, non-stick baking tins. Always use the size of tin recommended in the recipe to ensure the cooking times are accurate.

2 Line trays or tins with baking paper so that the paper extends over the two long sides. This makes it easier to lift the cooled mixture out of the tin to cut into slices.

3 If you use a food processor to make the pastry, use it only to rub the fat into the flour. After adding the liquid, pulse briefly until the mixture just comes together, then turn out onto a work surface and gently shape the dough into a ball. It is really important not to overwork pastry dough or it will be tough when cooked.

4 A soft pastry dough can be rolled out between two sheets of baking paper to prevent it from sticking to the work surface.

5 If the dough is too soft to be rolled out, it may be necessary to press it into the tin. Once pressed well into the base and edges of the tin, use the back of a spoon to smooth the surface as flat and evenly as possible.

6 Use the back of a spoon to press the slice mixture evenly into the tin.

7 If you are baking 2 slices at once, swap the tins halfway through the cooking time so they brown evenly.

8 When bars and slices are made with several layers, it is important that each layer is completely cold before adding the next one.

9 If short on time, the slice can be made in two stages. After lining the tin with pastry, chill overnight, wrapped loosely in plastic wrap, ready to finish the next day.

10 Slices should only be iced when completely cooled.

11 Allow the cooked mixture to cool before slicing it, unless specified.

12 If the slice is quite sticky and difficult to cut, run the blade of the knife under hot or boiling water before cutting.

13 Cut chocolate-topped slices with a hot knife. Dip the knife in boiling water, then wipe dry before cutting.

14 Decorate slices by dusting with icing sugar or cocoa. Dust half the slice, or make decorative templates, using baking paper. You can also dip whole pieces of slice, or the corners, in melted chocolate.

15 Wrap plain, un-iced pieces of slice in plastic or foil and freeze for up to 2–3 months. Pop a frozen piece into a lunchbox to thaw out by lunch time.

16 To finely grate orange or lemon zest, place a piece of baking paper over the grater. This will prevent zest getting caught in the holes.

17 Toasting nuts and coconut before use enhances their flavour. Spread on a baking tray and toast in the oven for 5–8 minutes at 180°C (350°F/Gas 4).

VANILLA SLICE

Preparation time **15 minutes**
Total cooking time **10 minutes**
Makes **9 pieces**

500 g (1 lb 2 oz) ready-made puff pastry
250 g (9 oz/1 cup) caster (superfine) sugar
90 g (3¼ oz/¾ cup) cornflour (cornstarch)
60 g (2¼ oz/½ cup) custard powder
1 litre (35 fl oz/4 cups) pouring (whipping)
    cream
60 g (2¼ oz) unsalted butter, cubed
2 teaspoons natural vanilla extract
3 egg yolks

Icing (frosting)
185 g (6½ oz/1½ cups) icing (confectioners')
    sugar
60 g (2¼ oz/¼ cup) passionfruit pulp
15 g (½ oz) unsalted butter, melted

1 Preheat the oven to 210°C (415°F/
Gas 6–7). Lightly grease two baking trays
with oil. Line the base and sides of a
shallow 23 cm (9 in) square cake tin with
foil, leaving the foil hanging over two
opposite sides.
2 Divide the pastry in half, roll each piece
to a 25 cm (10 in) square 3 mm (¼ in)
thick. Put on a baking tray and prick all
over with a fork.
3 Bake for 8 minutes, or until golden. Trim
each pastry sheet to a 23 cm (9 in) square.
Put one sheet top side down in the tin.
4 Combine the sugar, cornflour and custard
powder in a saucepan. Add the cream,
stirring constantly over medium heat for
2 minutes, or until thick. Add the butter
and vanilla extract and stir until smooth.
Remove from the heat and whisk in the
egg yolks until combined.
5 Spread the custard over the pastry in the
tin, then cover with the other pastry sheet,
top side down. Cool completely.
6 To make the icing, combine the icing
sugar, passionfruit pulp and butter in a
bowl, and stir until smooth.
7 Lift the slice out of the tin. Ice the top
and leave to set before cutting with a
serrated knife.

PEPPERMINT AND CHOCOLATE SLICE

Preparation time **15 minutes**
Total cooking time **20 minutes**
Makes **20 pieces**

220 g (7¾ oz/1¾ cups) plain (all-purpose) flour
1 teaspoon baking powder
95 g (3¼ oz/½ cup) soft brown sugar
180 g (6 oz) unsalted butter, melted
60 g (2¼ oz) copha (white vegetable shortening)
435 g (15¼ oz/3½ cups) icing (confectioners') sugar, sifted
1 teaspoon peppermint extract
2 tablespoons milk
2 tablespoons cream
300 g (10½ oz) dark cooking chocolate
70 g (2½ oz) unsalted butter, extra

1 Preheat the oven to 180°C (350°F/Gas 4). Grease a 20 x 30 cm (8 x 12 in) baking tin and line with baking paper, leaving the paper hanging over the two long sides of the tin.
2 Sift together the flour and baking powder and add the brown sugar. Stir in the melted butter.
3 Press into the tin and bake for 20 minutes. Allow to cool.
4 Melt the copha in a saucepan over medium heat. Stir in the icing sugar, peppermint extract, milk and cream. Mix well and pour over the pastry base. Leave to set.
5 Chop the chocolate and extra butter into small even-sized pieces and place in a heatproof bowl. Bring a saucepan of water to the boil and remove from the heat. Sit the bowl over the pan, making sure the bowl doesn't touch the water. Stand, stirring occasionally, until melted and combined. Cool slightly, then spread over the icing. Chill until set, then cut into pieces.

WALNUT BROWNIES

Preparation time **20 minutes**

Total cooking time **25 minutes**

Makes **24 pieces**

85 g (3 oz/²/₃ cup) self-raising flour

85 g (3 oz/²/₃ cup) unsweetened cocoa
   powder

250 g (9 oz/1 cup) caster (superfine) sugar

330 g (11½ oz) unsalted butter, melted

4 eggs, lightly beaten

1 teaspoon natural vanilla extract

250 g (9 oz/1½ cups) dark chocolate chips

125 g (4½ oz/1 cup) walnut pieces

icing (confectioners') sugar, to dust

1 Preheat the oven to 180°C (350°F/Gas 4). Grease a 20 x 30 cm (8 x 12 in) shallow baking tin and line with baking paper, leaving it hanging over the two long sides of the tin.

2 Sift together the flour and cocoa, then add the sugar. Make a well in the centre, then add the butter, eggs and vanilla extract and beat until smooth. Fold in the chocolate chips and walnuts. Spoon into the tin and smooth the surface.

3 Bake for 25 minutes, or until a skewer comes out clean. Leave in the tin for 10 minutes, then turn onto a wire rack to cool. Dust with icing sugar.

DOUBLE CHOCOLATE BROWNIES

Preparation time **15 minutes**

Total cooking time **30 minutes**

Makes 12

80 g (2³/₄ oz) butter

40 g (1¹/₂ oz/¹/₃ cup) unsweetened cocoa powder

145 g (5 oz/²/₃ cup) caster (superfine) sugar

2 eggs

60 g (2¹/₄ oz/¹/₂ cup) plain (all-purpose) flour

¹/₂ teaspoon baking powder

100 g (3¹/₂ oz/¹/₂ cup) chocolate chips

1 Preheat the oven to 180°C (350°F/Gas 4). Grease a 20 x 30 cm (8 x 12 in) shallow baking tin and line with baking paper.

2 Melt the butter in a saucepan, then stir in the cocoa and sugar. Add the eggs, stirring to combine.

3 Sift the flour, baking powder and a pinch of salt into the saucepan, then stir to combine. Add the chocolate chips and stir to combine.

4 Pour the mixture into the tin and bake for 30 minutes, or until a skewer inserted in the centre comes out clean. Remember though, the chocolate chips may have melted and if your skewer hits one of those, it might look as if the mixture is still wet.

5 Allow to cool in the tin, then remove and cut into brownie pieces.

PASSIONFRUIT AND LEMON DELICIOUS SLICE

Preparation time **25 minutes**
Total cooking time **40 minutes**
Makes **18 pieces**

120 g (4 oz) unsalted butter, softened
60 g (2¼ oz/½ cup) icing (confectioners')
    sugar, sifted
½ teaspoon natural vanilla extract
185 g (6½ oz/1½ cups) plain (all-purpose)
    flour, sifted
1 teaspoon grated lemon zest
icing (confectioners') sugar, to dust

Filling

100 g (3½ oz/¾ cup) plain (all-purpose) flour
½ teaspoon baking powder
65 g (2¼ oz/¾ cup) desiccated coconut
3 eggs
250 g (9 oz/1 cup) caster (superfine) sugar
170 g (6 oz) tinned passionfruit pulp
2 tablespoons lemon juice
1 teaspoon grated lemon zest

1 Preheat the oven to 180°C (350°F/Gas 4). Grease an 18 x 27 cm (7 x 10½ in) baking tin and line with baking paper, leaving the paper hanging over the two long sides.
2 Cream the butter and icing sugar with electric beaters until pale and creamy, then add the vanilla extract. Fold in the flour and lemon zest with a large metal spoon.
3 Press into the tin and bake for about 20 minutes, or until lightly golden.
4 To make the filling, sift the flour and baking powder together and add the coconut. Beat the eggs and sugar in a bowl, then add the passionfruit pulp, lemon juice and zest. Add the dry ingredients and stir.
5 Pour over the base and bake for about 20 minutes, or until firm to touch. Cool in the tin. Dust with icing sugar and cut into pieces.

APPLE CUSTARD STREUSEL SLICE

Preparation time **30 minutes +**
Total cooking time **1 hour 15 minutes**
Makes **16 pieces**

155 g (5½ oz/1¼ cups) plain (all-purpose) flour
1 tablespoon caster (superfine) sugar
80 g (2¾ oz) unsalted butter, melted
1 egg yolk

Apple custard topping

3 green apples, peeled, cored and chopped
20 g (¾ oz) unsalted butter
80 g (2¾ oz/⅓ cup) caster (superfine) sugar
2 eggs
180 ml (6 fl oz) pouring (whipping) cream
1 teaspoon natural vanilla extract

Crumble topping

60 g (2¼ oz/½ cup) plain (all-purpose) flour
2 tablespoons dark brown sugar
40 g (1½ oz/⅓ cup) finely chopped walnuts
60 g (2¼ oz) unsalted butter, cubed

1 Grease an 18 x 28 cm (7 x 11 in) shallow tin and line with baking paper, leaving the paper hanging over the two long sides.
2 Sift the flour and sugar into a bowl. Add the butter, egg yolk and 2 tablespoons water and mix to form a ball. Roll out the dough between two sheets of baking paper and fit in the base of the tin. Refrigerate for 20 minutes.
3 Preheat the oven to 190°C (375°F/Gas 5). Line the pastry with baking paper, fill with baking beads or uncooked rice and bake for 15 minutes. Remove the paper and beads and reduce the oven to 180°C (350°F/Gas 4). Bake for 5 minutes, or until golden. Cool.
4 Cook the apples, butter, half the sugar and 2 tablespoons water in a saucepan, covered, over low heat for 15 minutes, or until soft. Uncover and simmer for a further 5 minutes. Allow to cool.
5 Whisk together the eggs, cream, remaining sugar and vanilla extract. Spread the apple over the pastry, then pour on the cream mixture. Bake for 20 minutes, or until the custard has half set.
6 To make the crumble, mix the flour, sugar and walnuts and rub in the butter until the mixture is crumbly. Sprinkle over the custard and bake for 15 minutes. Cool.

RUM AND RAISIN SLICE

Preparation time **15 minutes**

Total cooking time **30 minutes**

Makes **20 pieces**

60 g (2¼ oz/½ cup) raisins

80 ml (2½ fl oz/⅓ cup) dark rum

200 g (7 oz) dark chocolate

60 g (2¼ oz) unsalted butter

125 g (4½ oz/½ cup) caster (superfine) sugar

250 ml (9 fl oz/1 cup) thick (double/heavy) cream

125 g (4½ oz/1 cup) plain (all-purpose) flour

3 eggs, lightly beaten

unsweetened cocoa powder, to dust

1 Preheat the oven to 180°C (350°F/Gas 4).

Lightly grease an 18 x 28 cm (7 x 11 in) shallow baking tin and line with baking paper, hanging over on two opposite sides.

2 Combine the raisins and rum. Chop the chocolate and butter into small even-sized pieces and place in a heatproof bowl. Bring a saucepan of water to the boil and remove from the heat. Sit the bowl over the pan— ensure the bowl doesn't touch the water. Allow to stand, stirring occasionally until melted. Stir in the caster sugar and cream.

3 Sift the flour into a bowl. Add the raisins, chocolate mixture and eggs and mix well. Pour into the tin and smooth the surface.

4 Bake for 25–30 minutes, or until just set. Cool, then refrigerate overnight. Cut into pieces and sprinkle with cocoa powder.

CHOCOLATE TRUFFLE MACAROON SLICE

Preparation time **20 minutes**
Total cooking time **20 minutes**
Makes **24 pieces**

3 egg whites
185 g (6½ oz/¾ cup) caster (superfine) sugar
180 g (6½ oz/2 cups) desiccated coconut
250 g (9 oz) dark chocolate
300 ml (10½ fl oz/1¼ cups) whipping cream
1 tablespoon unsweetened cocoa powder

1 Preheat the oven to 180°C (350°F/Gas 4). Lightly grease a 20 x 30 cm (8 x 12 in) shallow baking tin and line with baking paper, leaving it hanging over the two long sides.
2 Beat the egg whites in a clean, dry bowl until soft peaks form. Slowly add the sugar, beating well after each addition until stiff and glossy. Fold in the coconut.
3 Spread into the tin and bake for about 20 minutes, or until light brown. While still warm, press down lightly but firmly with a palette knife. Cool completely.
4 Chop the chocolate into small even-sized pieces and place in a heatproof bowl. Bring a saucepan of water to the boil, then remove from the heat. Sit the bowl over the pan—ensure the bowl doesn't touch the water. Stand, stirring occasionally, until the chocolate has melted. Cool slightly.
5 Beat the cream using electric beaters until thick. Gently fold in the chocolate until well combined—do not over-mix or it will curdle.
6 Spread evenly over the base and refrigerate for 3 hours, or until set. Lift from the tin and dust with the cocoa.

RHUBARB SLICE

Preparation time **25 minutes**

Total cooking time **45 minutes**

Makes **about 25 pieces**

300 g (10½ oz) rhubarb, trimmed and cut into
    5 mm (¼ in) slices

115 g (4 oz/½ cup) caster (superfine) sugar

185 g (6½ oz) unsalted butter, chopped

230 g (8 oz/1 cup) caster (superfine) sugar

½ teaspoon natural vanilla extract

3 eggs

90 g (3¼ oz/¾ cup) plain (all-purpose) flour

¾ teaspoon baking powder

1 tablespoon sugar

icing (confectioners') sugar, for dusting

1 Combine the rhubarb and sugar in a bowl and set aside, stirring occasionally, for 1 hour, or until the rhubarb has released its juices and the sugar has dissolved. Strain well, discarding the liquid.

2 Preheat the oven to 180°C (350°F/Gas 4). Lightly grease a 20 x 30 cm (8 x 12 in) shallow baking tin with butter. Line the base with baking paper, leaving the paper hanging over on the two long sides.

3 Cream the butter, sugar and vanilla extract in a bowl using electric beaters until pale and fluffy. Add the eggs one at a time, beating well after each addition. Sift the flour and baking powder over the mixture, then stir to combine.

4 Spread the mixture over the base of the tin, then put the rhubarb over the top in a single layer. Sprinkle with the sugar.

5 Bake for 40–45 minutes, or until golden. Leave to cool slightly in the tin, then carefully lift out and cut into squares. Dust with icing sugar and serve warm as a dessert with cream, or at room temperature as a snack.

Note The rhubarb slice is best eaten on the day it is made.

BERRY AND APPLE SLICE

Preparation time **15 minutes**
Total cooking time **30 minutes**
Makes **12 pieces**

150 g (5½ oz) unsalted butter
320 g (11¼ oz/1⅓ cups) caster (superfine)
   sugar
2 eggs, lightly beaten
250 g (9 oz/2 cups) self-raising flour, sifted
160 ml (5¼ fl oz/⅔ cup) buttermilk
1 teaspoon natural vanilla extract
2 large apples
150 g (5½ oz/1 cup) blueberries
150 g (5½ oz/1¼ cups) blackberries
icing (confectioners') sugar, to dust

1 Preheat the oven to 180°C (350°F/Gas 4).
Lightly grease a 30 x 20 cm (12 x 8 in)
shallow baking tin and line with baking
paper, leaving it hanging over the two
long sides.
2 Beat the butter and sugar with electric
beaters until light and fluffy. Add the egg
gradually, beating well after each addition.
Stir in the flour and buttermilk alternately
and mix until smooth. Stir through the
vanilla extract. Spread a 5 mm (¼ in) layer
of mixture over the base of the tin.
3 Peel, quarter and core the apples.
Cut into very thin slices and arrange
on the mixture. Spoon the remaining
mixture over the apple and smooth the
surface, then scatter with the blueberries
and blackberries.
4 Bake on the middle rack for 40 minutes,
or until cooked and golden. Cool in the tin
for 30 minutes before lifting onto a wire
rack. When completely cooled, dust with
icing sugar and cut into squares.

ORANGE, PISTACHIO AND SEMOLINA SLICE

Preparation time **25 minutes** +
Total cooking time **40 minutes**
Makes **18 pieces**

100 g (3½ oz/⅔ cup) shelled pistachio nuts
200 g (7 oz) unsalted butter, chopped
160 g (5¾ oz/⅔ cup) caster (superfine) sugar
1 teaspoon natural vanilla extract
1 tablespoon finely grated orange zest
2 eggs
60 g (2¼ oz/½ cup) self-raising flour, sifted
125 ml (4 fl oz/½ cup) orange juice
185 g (6½ oz/1½ cups) fine semolina
250 g (9 oz/1 cup) caster (superfine) sugar, extra
125 ml (4 fl oz/½ cup) orange juice, extra
icing (confectioners') sugar, to dust

1 Preheat the oven to 180°C (350°F/Gas 4). Lightly grease a 20 x 30 cm (8 x 12 in) shallow baking tin and line with baking paper, leaving it hanging over on the two long sides.
2 Bake the pistachios for 8–10 minutes, or until they are toasted. Cool, then chop.
3 Beat the butter and sugar using electric beaters until light and fluffy. Add the vanilla, orange zest and eggs, and beat until combined.
4 Add the flour, orange juice, semolina and pistachio nuts, and fold in with a spatula until just combined—do not overmix. Spread into the tin.
5 Bake for 30 minutes, or until golden brown and firm when lightly touched. Cool for 10 minutes in the tin, then on a wire rack placed on a tray.
6 Mix the extra sugar and orange juice in a small saucepan. Bring to the boil over medium heat, then simmer for 1 minute. Spoon over the slice. Cool and cut into squares or diamonds. Dust with icing sugar.

LEMON SQUARES

Preparation time **15 minutes**

Total cooking time **25 minutes**

Makes **30 pieces**

125 g (4½ oz) unsalted butter
75 g (2½ oz/⅓ cup) caster (superfine) sugar
155 g (5½ oz/1¼ cups) plain (all-purpose) flour, sifted
icing (confectioners') sugar, to dust

Topping

4 eggs, lightly beaten
250 g (9 oz/1 cup) caster (superfine) sugar
60 ml (2 fl oz/¼ cup) lemon juice
1 teaspoon finely grated lemon zest
30 g (1 oz/¼ cup) plain (all-purpose) flour
½ teaspoon baking powder

1 Preheat the oven to 180°C (350°F/Gas 4). Lightly grease a 20 x 30 cm (8 x 12 in) shallow baking tin and line with baking paper, leaving the paper hanging over two opposite sides.

2 Cream the butter and sugar with electric beaters until pale and fluffy. Fold in the flour with a metal spoon. Press into the tin and bake for 20 minutes, or until golden and firm. Leave to cool.

3 Beat the eggs and sugar with electric beaters for 2 minutes, or until light and fluffy. Stir in the lemon juice and lemon zest. Sift together the flour and baking powder and gradually whisk into the egg mixture. Pour onto the base.

4 Bake for 25 minutes, or until just firm. Cool in the tin and dust with icing sugar.

APRICOT AND MACAROON SLICE

Preparation time **20 minutes** +
Total cooking time **50 minutes**
Makes **16 pieces**

100 g (3½ oz) unsalted butter, softened
90 g (3¼ oz/⅓ cup) caster (superfine) sugar
1 egg
185 g (6½ oz/1½ cups) plain (all-purpose) flour
½ teaspoon baking powder

Filling
250 g (9 oz/1⅓ cups) dried apricots,
   roughly chopped
1 tablespoon Grand Marnier
2 tablespoons caster (superfine) sugar

Topping
100 g (3½ oz) unsalted butter
90 g (3¼ oz/⅓ cup) caster (superfine) sugar
1 teaspoon natural vanilla extract
2 eggs
270 g (9¾ oz/3 cups) desiccated coconut
40 g (1½ oz/⅓ cup) plain (all-purpose) flour
½ teaspoon baking powder

1 Preheat the oven to 180°C (350°F/Gas 4). Lightly grease a 20 x 30 cm (8 x 12 in) baking tin and line with baking paper.
2 Cream the butter and sugar until light and fluffy. Add the egg and beat well. Sift flour and baking powder and fold into the butter mixture with a metal spoon.
3 Press firmly into the tin and bake for 25 minutes, or until golden brown. Allow to cool.
4 To make the filling, combine the apricots, Grand Marnier, sugar and 125 ml (4 fl oz/½ cup) boiling water in a bowl. Set aside for 30 minutes, then purée in a food processor. Spread evenly over the cooled base.
5 To make the topping, cream the butter, sugar and vanilla until light and fluffy. Gradually add the eggs, beating well after each addition. Fold in the coconut, flour and baking powder with a large metal spoon.
6 Spoon onto the apricot mixture, leaving it lumpy and loose—do not press down. Bake for about 20–25 minutes, or until lightly golden.

ORANGE AND ALMOND SLICE

Preparation time **20 minutes** +
Total cooking time **1 hour 10 minutes**
Makes **12**

30 g (1 oz) rice flour
40 g (1½ oz/⅓ cup) cornflour (cornstarch)
60 g (2¼ oz/½ cup) ground almonds
2 tablespoons icing (confectioners') sugar
60 g (2¼ oz) unsalted butter, chopped

Filling
1 small orange
1 egg, separated
55 g (2 oz/¼ cup) caster (superfine) sugar
80 g (2¾ oz/¾ cup) ground almonds
1 tablespoon caster (superfine) sugar, extra

Lemon icing (frosting)
90 g (3¼ oz/¾ cup) icing (confectioners')
   sugar
1 teaspoon unsalted butter
1–1½ tablespoons lemon juice

1 Preheat the oven to 180°C (350°F/Gas 4).
Grease the base and sides of a 35 x 11 cm
(14 x 4¼ in) loose-based rectangular
shallow tart tin.

2 Combine the rice flour, cornflour,
almonds and icing sugar in a food
processor and process to just combine. Add
the butter and process in short bursts until
a dough forms. Press the dough into the
base of the tin. Refrigerate for 30 minutes.
3 Meanwhile, to make the filling, put the
orange in a saucepan with enough water to
cover. Bring to the boil, then reduce the
heat, cover and simmer for 30 minutes, or
until soft. Drain and cool. Cut the orange
in half widthways, remove any seeds, and
process in a food processor until smooth.
4 Whisk the egg yolk and sugar in a bowl
for 5 minutes, or until thick, then fold in
the orange purée and almonds. Whisk the
egg white in a bowl until stiff peaks form.
Add the extra sugar and beat until
combined. Fold into the orange mixture.
5 Spread the filling over the base. Bake for
40 minutes. Cool in the tin.
6 To make the lemon icing, combine the
sifted icing sugar and butter in a heatproof
bowl with enough juice to form a thick
paste. Sit the bowl over a saucepan of
simmering water, stirring until the icing is
smooth, then remove from the heat. Spread
the icing evenly over the filling, then leave
to set. Cut into 2.5 cm (1 in) thick slices.

BAKEWELL SLICE

Preparation time **20 minutes** +
Total cooking time **45 minutes**
Makes **15 pieces**

125 g (4½ oz/1 cup) plain (all-purpose) flour
30 g (1 oz/¼ cup) icing (confectioners') sugar
170 g (6 oz) unsalted butter, chilled and
   chopped
1 egg yolk
125 g (4½ oz/½ cup) caster (superfine) sugar
4 eggs
125 g (4½ oz/1¼ cups) ground almonds
2 drops almond extract
160 g (5¾ oz/½ cup) raspberry jam
25 g (1 oz/¼ cup) flaked almonds

1 Preheat the oven to 180°C (350°F/Gas 4).
Lightly grease a 20 x 30 cm (8 x 12 in)
baking tin and line with baking paper,
hanging over the two long sides.
2 Sift the flour and 1 tablespoon of the
icing sugar into a bowl, add 50 g (1¾ oz)
of the butter and rub it in until the mixture
resembles breadcrumbs. Add the egg yolk
and 2 tablespoons cold water and mix
with a flat-bladed knife until the mixture
comes together in beads. Gather into a
ball, cover with plastic wrap and refrigerate
for 30 minutes.
3 Roll the dough out between two sheets
of baking paper, remove the paper and put
in the tin, pressing into the edges. Bake for
10 minutes. Allow to cool.
4 Beat the remaining butter and the caster
sugar with electric beaters until creamy.
Add the eggs and fold in the ground
almonds and almond extract.
5 Spread the jam over the pastry base and
pour over the filling. Sprinkle with flaked
almonds and bake for 30–35 minutes, or
until firm. Allow to cool.
6 Sift the remaining icing sugar into a bowl
and mix in 2 teaspoons warm water. Drizzle
over the slice in a zigzag pattern and leave
to set. Trim the edges and cut into squares.

PRINCESS FINGERS

Preparation time **35 minutes**

Total cooking time **35 minutes**

Makes **24 pieces**

125 g (4½ oz) unsalted butter, cubed and
   softened

80 g (2¾ oz/⅓ cup) caster (superfine) sugar

1 teaspoon natural vanilla extract

2 egg yolks

250 g (9 oz/2 cups) plain (all-purpose) flour

1 teaspoon baking powder

1 tablespoon milk

160 g (5¾ oz/½ cup) raspberry jam

40 g (1½ oz/⅓ cup) chopped walnuts

80 g (2¾ oz/⅓ cup) chopped red glacé
   cherries

2 egg whites

1 tablespoon grated orange zest

115 g (4 oz/½ cup) caster (superfine) sugar,
   extra

45 g (1¾ oz/½ cup) desiccated coconut

30 g (1 oz/1 cup) puffed rice cereal

1 Preheat the oven to 180°C (350°F/Gas 4). Grease a 20 x 30 cm (8 x 12 in) shallow tin and line with baking paper, leaving the paper hanging over on the two long sides.
2 Cream the butter, sugar and vanilla extract using electric beaters until light and fluffy. Add the egg yolks, one at a time, beating thoroughly after each addition.
3 Sift the flour and baking powder into a bowl, then fold into the creamed mixture with a metal spoon. Fold in the milk, then press evenly and firmly into the tin. Spread the jam over the surface and sprinkle with the chopped walnuts and glacé cherries.
4 Beat the egg whites in a dry bowl until stiff peaks form. Fold in the orange zest and extra sugar with a metal spoon, then fold in the coconut and puffed rice cereal. Spread over the slice with a metal spatula.
5 Bake for 30–35 minutes, or until firm and golden brown. Cool the slice in the tin. Lift out the slice, using the paper as handles, and cut into fingers.

FIG AND CINNAMON SLICE

Preparation time **20 minutes**

Total cooking time **55 minutes**

Makes **15 squares**

125 g (4½ oz) unsalted butter, softened

55 g (2 oz/¼ cup) soft brown sugar, firmly packed

1 teaspoon ground cinnamon

185 g (6½ oz/1½ cups) plain (all-purpose) flour

375 g (13 oz/2⅓ cups) dried figs

1 cinnamon stick

125 g (4½ oz/½ cup) caster (superfine) sugar

1 Preheat the oven to 180°C (350°F/Gas 4). Lightly grease an 18 x 27 cm (7 x 10¾ in) baking tin and line with baking paper, hanging over the two long sides.

2 Beat the butter, brown sugar and cinnamon until light and fluffy, then fold in the flour with a large metal spoon.

3 Press the mixture evenly into the tin and bake for 25 minutes. Cool slightly.

4 Put the dried figs, cinnamon stick, sugar and 375 ml (13 fl oz/1½ cups) boiling water in a saucepan, mix together and bring to the boil. Reduce the heat and simmer for 20 minutes, or until the figs have softened and the water has reduced by a third. Remove the cinnamon stick and place the mixture in a food processor. Process in short bursts until smooth.

5 Pour onto the cooked base and bake for 10 minutes, or until set. Allow to cool completely in the tin, then lift out and cut into squares.

PASSIONFRUIT AND COCONUT CHEESE SLICE

Preparation time **25 minutes** +

Total cooking time **50 minutes**

Makes **24 pieces**

100 g (3½ oz/¾ cup) slivered almonds

125 g (4½ oz/1 cup) plain (all-purpose) flour

1 teaspoon baking powder

100 g (3½ oz) unsalted butter, chopped

125 g (4½ oz/½ cup) caster (superfine) sugar

1 egg yolk

25 g (1 oz/¼ cup) desiccated coconut

750 g (1 lb 10 oz/3 cups) cream cheese

2 eggs

185 ml (6 fl oz/¾ cup) coconut milk

3 teaspoons natural vanilla extract

½ teaspoon lemon juice

185 g (6½ oz/¾ cup) caster (superfine) sugar, extra

65 g (2¼ oz/¾ cup) flaked almonds, toasted

Topping

90 g (3¼ oz/¾ cup) icing (confectioners') sugar

40 g (1½ oz) unsalted butter, softened

1 tablespoon cornflour (cornstarch)

2 tablespoons strained passionfruit juice

1 Chop the almonds in a food processor. Sift the flour and baking powder into a bowl. Rub the butter into the flour until it resembles breadcrumbs. Stir in the almonds and sugar. Make a well in the centre and add the egg yolk. Mix with a knife until the mixture comes together in beads.

2 Remove to a floured work surface and shape into a ball. Flatten slightly, cover in plastic wrap and refrigerate for 30 minutes.

3 Preheat the oven to 170°C (325°F/Gas 3). Grease a 30 x 20 x 5 cm (12 x 8 x 2 in) tin and line with baking paper, hanging over the two long sides.

4 Roll the dough out to fit the tin and press in. Sprinkle over the coconut and press it in. Bake for 10 minutes.

5 Combine the cream cheese and the eggs in the food processor. Add the coconut milk, vanilla extract, lemon juice and the extra sugar, and blend until smooth. Pour over the base. Bake for 40 minutes. Cool.

6 To make the topping, mix the icing sugar and butter until smooth. Stir in the cornflour, then the passionfruit juice. Mix until smooth, then spread over the slice. Scatter over the toasted almonds. Leave to set, then cut into squares.

GLACÉ FRUIT FINGERS

Preparation time **25 minutes** +
Total cooking time **35 minutes**
Makes **20**

60 g (2¼ oz/½ cup) plain (all-purpose) flour
2 tablespoons self-raising flour
2 tablespoons icing (confectioners') sugar
60 g (2¼ oz) unsalted butter, chopped
1 egg yolk

Topping

350 g (12 oz) assorted light-coloured glacé
   fruits (pineapple, apricots, peaches, pears)
80 ml (2½ fl oz/⅓ cup) brandy
175 g (6 oz) unsalted butter, softened
115 g (4 oz/½ cup) caster (superfine) sugar
2 tablespoons honey
1 egg
40 g (1½ oz/⅓ cup) plain (all-purpose) flour
40 g (1½ oz/⅓ cup) self-raising flour
80 g (2¾ oz/½ cup) macadamia nuts, toasted
   and chopped
icing (confectioners') sugar, to dust (optional)

1 Preheat the oven to 180°C (350°F/Gas 4). Lightly grease a 20 x 30 cm (8 x 12 in) rectangular shallow tin and line the base with baking paper, leaving the paper hanging over on the two long sides.

2 Process the flours and icing sugar in a food processor until just combined. Add the butter and, using the pulse button, process in short bursts until the mixture is crumbly. Add the egg yolk and about 1 tablespoon water and pulse just until a dough forms. Cover with plastic wrap and refrigerate for 30 minutes.

3 Roll out the pastry between two sheets of baking paper until large enough to cover the base of the tin. Transfer to the tin.

4 To make the topping, cut the fruit into 5 mm (¼ in) pieces with scissors or a sharp knife. Combine the fruit and brandy in a bowl, mix well and leave, covered, for about 1 hour, or until the fruit has absorbed the brandy.

5 Cream the butter, sugar and honey in a small bowl using electric beaters until pale and fluffy. Add the egg and beat well until combined. Sift the flours together in a bowl, then stir into the creamed mixture. Stir in the glacé fruit and macadamia nuts, then spread the mixture over the pastry.

6 Bake for 30–35 minutes, or until golden brown. The topping may be slightly soft but will firm on cooling. Allow to cool in the tin, then cut into 7.5 x 4 cm (3 x 1½ in) pieces. Dust lightly with icing sugar before serving.

RASPBERRY AND COCONUT SLICE

Preparation time **20 minutes +**
Total cooking time **1 hour 25 minutes**
Makes **30 pieces**

280 g (10 oz/2¼ cups) plain (all-purpose) flour
3 tablespoons ground almonds
500 g (1 lb 2 oz/2 cups) caster (superfine) sugar
250 g (9 oz) unsalted butter, chilled
½ teaspoon ground nutmeg
½ teaspoon baking powder
4 eggs
1 teaspoon natural vanilla extract
1 tablespoon lemon juice
300 g (10½ oz/2½ cups) fresh or thawed frozen raspberries
90 g (3¼ oz/1 cup) desiccated coconut
icing (confectioners') sugar, to dust

1 Preheat the oven to 180°C (350°F/Gas 4). Lightly grease a 20 x 30 cm (8 x 12 in) shallow tin and line with baking paper, hanging over the two long sides.
2 Sift 220 g (7¾ oz/1¾ cups) of the flour into a bowl. Add the ground almonds and 125 g (4½ oz/½ cup) of the caster sugar and stir to combine. Rub the butter into the flour with your fingertips until it resembles fine breadcrumbs.
3 Press the mixture into the tin and bake for 20–25 minutes, or until golden. Reduce the oven to 150°C (300°F/Gas 2).
4 Sift the nutmeg, baking powder and remaining flour onto a piece of baking paper. Beat the eggs, vanilla extract and remaining sugar using electric beaters for 4 minutes, or until fluffy. Fold in the flour with a metal spoon. Stir in the lemon juice, raspberries and coconut and pour over the base.
5 Bake for 1 hour, or until golden. Chill in the tin, then cut into pieces. Dust with icing sugar before serving.
Note This slice is best eaten on the day it is made.

COCONUT JAM SLICE

Preparation time **30 minutes** +
Total cooking time **45 minutes**
Makes **20 pieces**

125 g (4½ oz/1 cup) plain (all-purpose) flour
60 g (2¼ oz/½ cup) self-raising flour
60 g (2¼ oz/½ cup) icing (confectioners')
    sugar
150 g (5½ oz) unsalted butter, cubed
1 egg yolk
160 g (5¾ oz/½ cup) strawberry jam
125 g (4½ oz) caster (superfine) sugar
3 eggs
270 g (9½ oz/3 cups) desiccated coconut

1 Preheat the oven to 180°C (350°F/Gas 4).
Lightly grease a shallow 23 cm (9 in)
square tin and line with baking paper,
leaving the paper hanging over on two
opposite sides.

2 Put the flour and icing sugar in a large
bowl and rub in the butter using your
fingertips until the mixture is fine and
crumbly. Mix in the egg yolk and then
gather together.

3 Press the dough into the tin and
refrigerate for 10 minutes.

4 Bake for 15 minutes, or until golden
brown. Allow to cool, then spread the
jam evenly over the pastry.

5 Beat the caster sugar and eggs together
in a small bowl until creamy, then stir in
the coconut. Spread the mixture over the
jam, gently pressing down with the back
of a spoon.

6 Bake for 25–30 minutes, or until lightly
golden. Leave to cool in the tin, then lift
the slice out, using the paper as handles.
Cut the slice into pieces.

Note Store in an airtight container for up
to 4 days.

CHOCOLATE AND GLACÉ CHERRY SLICE

Preparation time **30 minutes** +
Total cooking time **20 minutes**
Makes **28 pieces**

125 g (4½ oz/1 cup) plain (all-purpose) flour
40 g (1½ oz/⅓ cup) unsweetened cocoa
   powder
90 g (⅓ cup) caster (superfine) sugar
125 g (4¼ oz) unsalted butter, melted
1 teaspoon natural vanilla extract
420 g (2 cups) glacé cherries, finely chopped
60 g (2¼ oz/½ cup) icing (confectioners')
   sugar
135 g (4¾ oz/1½ cups) desiccated coconut
125 ml (4 fl oz/½ cup) condensed milk
60 g (2¼ oz) unsalted butter, melted
50 g (1¾ oz) copha (white vegetable
   shortening), melted
150 g (5½ oz) dark cooking chocolate
25 g (1 oz) unsalted butter, extra

1 Preheat the oven to 180°C (350°F/Gas 4). Lightly grease an 18 x 27 cm (7 x 10½ in) shallow baking tin and line with baking paper, leaving the paper hanging over the two long sides.

2 Sift the flour, cocoa and sugar into a bowl, add the butter and vanilla, and mix to form a dough. Gather together and turn onto a well-floured surface. Press together for 1 minute, then press into the base of the tin. Chill for 20 minutes.

3 Cover with baking paper and baking beads or uncooked rice and bake for 10–15 minutes. Remove the paper and beads and bake for 5 minutes. Cool.

4 Combine the cherries, icing sugar and coconut. Stir in the condensed milk, butter and copha, then spread over the base. Chill for 30 minutes.

5 Chop the chocolate and extra butter into pieces and place in a heatproof bowl. Bring a saucepan of water to the boil and remove from the heat. Sit the bowl over the pan, making sure the bowl doesn't touch the water. Stir occasionally until melted.

6 Pour over the cooled cherry mixture, then chill until set.

CHEWY FRUIT AND SEED SLICE

Preparation time **20 minutes**

Total cooking time **25 minutes**

Makes **18 pieces**

200 g (7 oz) unsalted butter
175 g (6 oz/½ cup) golden syrup or honey
125 g (4½ oz/½ cup) crunchy peanut butter
2 teaspoons natural vanilla extract
30 g (1 oz/¼ cup) plain (all-purpose) flour
30 g (1 oz/⅓ cup) ground almonds
½ teaspoon mixed (pumpkin pie) spice
300 g (10½ oz/3 cups) quick-cooking oats
2 teaspoons finely grated orange zest
185 g (6½ oz/1 cup) soft brown sugar
45 g (1½ oz/½ cup) desiccated coconut
50 g (1¾ oz/⅓ cup) sesame seeds, toasted
90 g (3¼ oz/½ cup) pepitas (pumpkin seeds)
80 g (2¾ oz/½ cup) raisins, chopped
45 g (1½ oz/¼ cup) mixed peel (mixed candied citrus peel)

1 Preheat the oven to 170°C (325°F/Gas 3). Lightly grease a 20 x 30 cm (8 x 12 in) shallow tin and line with baking paper, leaving it hanging over the two long sides.
2 Put the butter and golden syrup in a saucepan over low heat, stirring until melted. Remove from the heat and stir in the peanut butter and vanilla extract until combined.
3 Mix together the remaining ingredients, stirring well. Make a well in the centre and add the butter and syrup mixture. Mix with a large metal spoon until combined.
4 Press evenly into the tin and bake for 25 minutes, or until golden and firm. Cool in the tin, then cut into squares.
Note Store in an airtight container for up to 5 days.

APPLE SHORTCAKE

Preparation time **25 minutes** +
Total cooking time **45 minutes**
Makes **9 pieces**

250 g (9 oz/2 cups) plain (all-purpose) flour
1 teaspoon baking powder
125 g (4½ oz) unsalted butter, chilled and
    chopped
60 g (2¼ oz/¼ cup) caster (superfine) sugar
1 egg, lightly beaten
1 tablespoon cold milk
4 small red apples, peeled, quartered and
    cored
1 teaspoon ground cinnamon
2 tablespoons caster (superfine) sugar, extra
1 tablespoon milk, extra
demerara sugar, to sprinkle

1 Preheat the oven to 180°C (350°F/Gas 4).
Lightly grease a baking tray and line with
baking paper, leaving it hanging over the
two long sides.

2 Sift the flour and baking powder into a
large bowl, add the butter and rub with
your fingers until the mixture resembles
fine breadcrumbs. Stir in the sugar.
3 Make a well in the centre and add the
combined egg and milk. Mix with a flat-
bladed knife using a cutting action until the
mixture comes together in beads.
4 Gently gather together and lift out onto
a lightly floured work surface. Press
together into a ball, flatten slightly, cover
in plastic wrap and chill for 20–30 minutes.
5 Halve the dough. Refrigerate one half
and roll the other half into a 20 cm (8 in)
square. Put on the baking tray.
6 Cut the apple quarters into thin slices
and arrange in rows, to form a double layer
of apples over the pastry. Sprinkle with the
cinnamon and extra caster sugar.
7 Roll the remaining pastry into a 20 cm
(8 in) square and put over the apple. Brush
with milk and sprinkle with demerara sugar.
Bake for 40–45 minutes, or until golden.

CHOCOLATE CARROT SLICE

Preparation time **20 minutes**

Total cooking time **30 minutes**

Makes **32 pieces**

125 g (4½ oz/1 cup) self-raising flour
1 teaspoon ground cinnamon
170 g (6 oz/¾ cup) caster (superfine) sugar
80 g (2¾ oz/½ cup) finely grated carrot
185 g (6½ oz/1 cup) mixed dried fruit
90 g (3¼ oz/ ½ cup) chocolate chips
30 g (1 oz/⅓ cup) desiccated coconut
2 eggs, beaten
90 g (3¼ oz) unsalted butter, melted
40 g (1½ oz/⅓ cup) chopped walnuts

Cream cheese frosting
125 g (4½ oz) cream cheese
30 g (1 oz) unsalted butter
185 g (6½ oz/1½ cups) icing (confectioners')
  sugar, sifted

1 Preheat the oven to 180°C (350°F/Gas 4). Lightly grease a shallow 23 cm (9 in) square cake tin and line the base and sides with baking paper.

2 Sift the flour and cinnamon into a large bowl. Add the caster sugar, grated carrot, mixed fruit, chocolate chips and coconut and stir until just combined. Add the beaten eggs and butter and then stir until combined.

3 Spread the mixture into the tin and smooth the surface.

4 Bake for 30 minutes, or until golden. Allow to cool in the tin, then turn out onto a flat surface.

5 To make the cream cheese frosting, using electric beaters, beat the cream cheese and butter in a small bowl until smooth. Add the icing sugar and beat for 2 minutes, or until the mixture is light and fluffy. Add 1 teaspoon water and beat until well combined.

6 Spread the slice with frosting using a flat-bladed knife and sprinkle with walnuts. Cut into 16 squares, then cut each square into two triangles.

CHOC FRUIT AND NUT SLICE

Preparation time **15 minutes**
Total cooking time **25 minutes**
Makes **14 pieces**

canola oil spray
150 g (5½ oz/1 cup) stoneground wholemeal
    (whole-wheat) self-raising flour
2 tablespoons unsweetened cocoa powder
50 g (1¾ oz/½ cup) rolled barley
35 g (1¼ oz/⅓ cup) ground almonds
30 g (1 oz/⅓ cup) desiccated coconut
60 g (2¼ oz/⅓ cup) soft brown sugar
60 g (2¼ oz/½ cup) fruit medley, chopped
60 g (2¼ oz/½ cup) walnuts, chopped
90 g (3¼ oz) light canola margarine,
    melted
1 tablespoon pure maple syrup
250 ml (9 fl oz/1 cup) low-fat milk
icing (confectioners') sugar, to dust

1 Preheat the oven to 180°C (350°F/Gas 4). Spray a 27 x 17 cm (10¾ x 6½ in) shallow baking tin with oil and line the base with baking paper overhanging the two long sides.
2 Sift the flour and cocoa into a large bowl, then return any husks to the bowl. Stir in the rolled barley, ground almonds, coconut, brown sugar, fruit medley and walnuts. Make a well in the centre.
3 Combine the melted margarine, maple syrup and milk in a small bowl. Add to the flour mixture and stir until well combined. Spread evenly into the prepared tin.
4 Bake for 25 minutes, or until cooked and firm. Leave in the tin to cool, then turn out onto a wire rack to cool completely.
5 Dust with icing sugar and cut into slices to serve. Serve with berries and low-fat yoghurt or berry fromage frais.

DATE AND CINNAMON SQUARES

Preparation time **25 minutes**

Total cooking time **60 minutes**

Makes **36**

600 g (1 lb 5 oz/3⅓ cups) pitted whole dried
  dates, chopped
1 teaspoon bicarbonate of soda (baking soda)
125 g (4½ oz) unsalted butter, chopped
155 g (5½ oz/⅔ cup) soft brown sugar
2 eggs
125 g (4½ oz/1 cup) plain (all-purpose) flour
60 g (2¼ oz/½ cup) self-raising flour
½ teaspoon ground cinnamon, plus
  ½ teaspoon, extra
60 g (2¼ oz/½ cup) icing (confectioners')
  sugar

1 Preheat the oven to 180°C (350°F/Gas 4).
Grease a 23 cm (9 in) square shallow tin
and line the base with baking paper.
2 Combine the dates and 500 ml (17 fl oz/
2 cups) of water in a saucepan. Bring to the
boil, then remove from the heat. Stir in the

bicarbonate of soda and mix well. Allow to
cool to room temperature.
3 Cream the butter and sugar in a large
bowl using electric beaters until pale and
fluffy. Add the eggs one at a time, beating
well after each addition. Sift the flours
and cinnamon into a bowl, then fold into
the butter mixture alternately with the
date mixture.
4 Spread into the prepared tin. Bake for
55–60 minutes, or until a skewer inserted
into the centre comes out clean. Cool in
the tin for 5 minutes, then turn out onto a
wire rack to cool completely.
5 Cut into 36 pieces and place on a sheet
of greaseproof paper. Sift the combined
icing sugar and extra cinnamon over the
cubes and toss to coat. Serve immediately
(the coating will be absorbed into the cakes
quite quickly if left to stand).
Note Date and cinnamon squares will keep
(do not coat with the icing sugar if you
intend to store them), stored in an airtight
container, for up to 4 days, or up to
3 months in the freezer.

DATE CARAMEL SHORTCAKE

Preparation time **20 minutes** +

Total cooking time **50 minutes**

Makes **12 pieces**

125 g (4½ oz) unsalted butter, softened

125 g (4½ oz/½ cup) caster (superfine) sugar

1 teaspoon natural vanilla extract

1 egg

250 g (9 oz/2 cups) plain (all-purpose) flour

1 teaspoon baking powder

175 g (6 oz/1 cup) roughly chopped pitted dates

1 tablespoon soft brown sugar

2 teaspoons unsweetened cocoa powder

10 g (¼ oz) unsalted butter, extra

icing (confectioners') sugar, to sprinkle

1 Preheat the oven to 180°C (350°F/Gas 4). Lightly grease an 18 x 27 cm (7 x 10³/4 in) shallow baking tin. Line with baking paper, leaving it hanging over the two long sides.

2 Beat the butter, sugar and vanilla extract using electric beaters until light and fluffy. Beat in the egg, then transfer to a bowl. Fold in the combined sifted flour and baking powder in batches with a spoon.

3 Press half the dough into the tin. Form the other half into a ball, cover and refrigerate for 30 minutes.

4 Put the dates, brown sugar, cocoa, extra butter and 250 ml (9 fl oz/1 cup) water in a small saucepan. Bring to the boil, stirring, then reduce the heat and simmer, stirring, for 12–15 minutes, or until the dates are soft and the water has been absorbed. Spread onto a plate and refrigerate.

5 Spread the filling over the pastry base with a metal spatula, then grate the remaining dough over the top. Bake for 35 minutes, or until light brown and crisp. Cool in the tin for 15 minutes, then lift onto a wire rack. Sprinkle with icing sugar and cut into squares.

CRUNCHY PEANUT MERINGUE SLICE

Preparation time **20 minutes +**
Total cooking time **40 minutes**
Makes **20 pieces**

125 g (4½ oz/1 cup) plain (all-purpose) flour
2 teaspoons icing (confectioners') sugar
80 g (2¾ oz) unsalted butter, cubed
1 tablespoon iced water
105 g (3¾ oz/⅓ cup) apricot jam

Nut meringue

240 g (8¾ oz/1½ cups) peanuts, roughly
    chopped
170 g (6 oz/¾ cup) caster (superfine) sugar
30 g (1 oz/⅓ cup) desiccated coconut
1 egg white

1 Preheat the oven to 180°C (350°F/Gas 4). Lightly grease a shallow tin measuring 18 x 28 cm (7 x 11¼ in) and line with baking paper, leaving the paper hanging over on the two long sides.

2 Put the flour, icing sugar and butter in a food processor and mix in short bursts until fine and crumbly. Add the iced water and process until the mixture just comes together.

3 Turn the dough out onto a floured surface, gather into a smooth ball, then press out evenly, using floured hands or the base of a floured glass, to cover the base of the tin. Prick well.

4 Bake for 15 minutes, or until golden. Cool for 10 minutes before spreading the jam evenly over the surface.

5 To make the meringue, put all the ingredients in a large saucepan and stir with a wooden spoon over low heat until just lukewarm. Spread over the slice.

6 Bake for 20 minutes, or until the topping is golden and crisp. When cool, lift out and cut into pieces.

FRUIT MINCE SLICE

Preparation time **20 minutes +**
Total cooking time **40 minutes**
Makes **15 pieces**

250 g (9 oz/2 cups) plain (all-purpose) flour
60 g (2¼ oz/½ cup) icing (confectioners')
   sugar
185 g (6½ oz) unsalted butter, cubed
1 egg
410 g (14½ oz) fruit mince (mincemeat)
150 g (5½ oz) pitted prunes, chopped
100 g (3½ oz) glacé ginger, chopped
1 egg, lightly beaten
icing (confectioners') sugar, extra, to dust

1 Preheat the oven to 190°C (375°F/Gas 5).
Lightly grease a shallow 18 x 28 cm (7 x
11¼ in) tin and line the base with baking
paper, leaving the paper hanging over the
two long sides.
2 Sift the flour and icing sugar into a bowl.
Rub in the butter with your fingertips until
the mixture resembles fine breadcrumbs.
Make a well in the centre and add the egg.
Mix with a knife, using a cutting action,
until the mixture comes together.
3 Turn onto a floured surface and press
together until smooth. Divide the dough in
half and press one portion into the tin.
4 Bake for 10 minutes, then cool. Roll the
remaining pastry out on a piece of baking
paper and refrigerate for 15 minutes.
5 Spread the fruit mince evenly over the
baked pastry, topping with the prunes and
ginger. Cut the rolled pastry into thin
strips with a sharp knife or fluted pastry
wheel. Arrange on top of the fruit in a
diagonal lattice pattern. Brush with the
beaten egg.
6 Bake for 30 minutes, or until golden.
Cool in the tin, then lift out and cut into
squares or fingers. Serve dusted with
icing sugar.

HONEY CARAMEL SLICE

Preparation time **20 minutes +**
Total cooking time **50 minutes**
Makes **20 pieces**

Base
200 g (7 oz) unsalted butter, chopped
310 g (11 oz/2½ cups) plain (all-purpose) flour
115 g (4 oz/½ cup) caster (superfine) sugar
2 egg yolks, lightly beaten

Filling
2 x 395 g (14 oz) tinned sweetened condensed
  milk
100 g (3½ oz) unsalted butter, chopped
115 g (4 oz/⅓ cup) honey

1 Preheat the oven to 180°C (350°F/Gas 4). Lightly grease a 20 x 30 cm (8 x 12 in) rectangular shallow tin with butter and line the base with baking paper, leaving the paper hanging over on the two long sides.
2 To make the base, combine all the ingredients, except the egg yolks, in a food processor and process until the mixture resembles fine breadcrumbs. Add the yolks and 1–2 tablespoons chilled water and process just until a dough forms, adding a little more water if necessary; do not overprocess. Using lightly floured hands, press half the dough over the base of the tin.
3 Bake for 12–15 minutes, or until golden and firm to the touch. Wrap the remaining dough in plastic wrap and refrigerate until firm.
4 To make the filling, put the condensed milk and butter in a heavy-based saucepan and stir over low heat until the butter has melted. Increase the heat to medium and cook for 5–8 minutes, stirring continuously, or until the mixture has thickened. Remove from the heat and stir in the honey. Allow to cool, then pour the filling over the base and spread evenly to cover.
5 Using a grater, grate the cold dough over the caramel filling to cover, then bake for 20–30 minutes, or until golden. Cool in the tray, then carefully lift out and cut into 10 x 3 cm (4 x 1¼ in) fingers.
Note This slice will keep, stored in an airtight container, for up to 3 days.

PECAN COFFEE SLICE

Preparation time 30 minutes +
Total cooking time 30 minutes
Makes 20 pieces

125 g (4½ oz/1¼ cups) pecans
175 g (6 oz) blanched almonds
2 tablespoons plain (all-purpose) flour
165 g (5¾ oz/¾ cup) sugar
7 egg whites
dark unsweetened cocoa powder, to dust

Coffee cream
200 g (7 oz) unsalted butter, cubed and
   softened
150 g (5½ oz) dark chocolate, melted and
   cooled
3–4 teaspoons instant coffee powder

1 Preheat the oven to 180°C (350°F/Gas 4). Lightly grease a shallow 23 cm (9 in) square tin and line with baking paper, leaving the paper hanging over on two opposite sides.
2 Roast the pecans and almonds on a baking tray for 5–10 minutes, or until golden. Cool slightly, then chop in a food processor until ground. Transfer to a bowl, add the flour and 110 g (3¾ oz/½ cup) of the sugar and mix well.

3 Beat the egg whites in a large dry bowl until soft peaks form. Gradually add the remaining sugar, beating until the mixture is thick and glossy and the sugar has dissolved. Gradually fold the nut mixture into the egg mixture, a third at a time.
4 Spoon the mixture into the tin and smooth the surface. Bake for 20 minutes, or until springy when touched. Leave in the tin for 5 minutes, then lift out and transfer to a wire rack to cool completely.
5 To make the coffee cream, beat the butter in a small bowl using electric beaters until light and creamy. Gradually pour in the cooled melted chocolate and beat well. Mix the coffee powder with 2 teaspoons water until dissolved, then add to the chocolate and mix well. Refrigerate for 5–10 minutes to thicken slightly.
6 Cut the slice in half horizontally with a serrated knife. Remove the top layer and spread half the coffee cream over the base. Replace the top and spread with the remaining cream. Run a palette knife backwards and forwards across the top to create a lined pattern. Refrigerate until firm.
7 Trim the edges and cut into squares or fingers. Dust with dark cocoa powder or decorate with chocolate-coated or plain coffee beans, if desired.

PASTRY

To the uncertain cook, pastry can be a scary thing, so many of us find
ourselves reaching for the frozen ready-made stuff or worse, avoiding recipes
involving pastry altogether. By doing this we really miss out—the thin, flimsy
little pies and pastries sold in supermarket freezers cannot compare to the
aromas and flavour of a home-made masterpiece. In the following pages,
we take the mystery out of pastry and talk you through the potential pitfalls
so you can proceed with confidence. You'll soon find making pastry as easy
as ... well ... pie!

SHORTCRUST PASTRY

The secret to making good shortcrust pastry is to work the dough quickly and lightly, in a cool room if possible, on a cool surface, and preferably not on a hot day.

If you don't have a marble slab, rest a tray of iced water on the work surface for a while before you start. Use real unsalted butter for pastry.

Unsweetened pastry works well with sweet fillings, giving a good contrast of flavours. To make a sweet pastry, add 2 tablespoons of caster (superfine) sugar to the flour. Some recipes contain egg yolks to enrich the pastry and give good colour.

MAKING SHORTCRUST PASTRY

To make enough to line a 23 cm (9 in) tin, use 250 g (9 oz/2 cups) plain (all-purpose) flour, 150 g (5½ oz) chilled, chopped unsalted butter and 2–4 tablespoons chilled water. This will make about 500 g (1 lb 2 oz) pastry.

1 Sift the flour into a large bowl and add the butter. Using just your fingertips, rub the butter into the flour until the mixture resembles fine breadcrumbs.
2 Make a well in the centre, then add 2–4 tablespoons water and mix with a flat-bladed knife. Use a cutting action and turn the bowl with your free hand. The mixture will come together in small beads of dough. To test if you need more water, pinch a little dough between your fingers. If it doesn't hold together, add more water.
3 Gently gather the dough together with your hand and lift out onto a sheet of baking paper or a floured work surface.
4 Press, don't knead, the dough together into a ball. Handle gently, keeping your actions light and to a minimum.
5 Press the dough into a flat disc, wrap in plastic wrap and refrigerate for 20 minutes. Roll out between two sheets of baking paper or plastic wrap, or on a lightly floured surface. Always roll from the centre outwards, rotating the dough.
6 If you used baking paper to roll out the pastry, remove the top sheet, invert the pastry over the tin, and then peel away the paper. If you rolled out on a lightly floured surface, roll the pastry back over the rolling pin so it is hanging, and ease it into the tin.
7 Once the pastry is in the tin, quickly lift up the sides so they don't break over the edges of the tin. Use a small ball of excess dough to help ease and press the pastry shell into the side of the tin. Allow the excess to hang over the side and, if using a tart tin, roll the rolling pin over the top of the tin to cut off the excess pastry. If you are using a glass or ceramic pie dish, use a small knife to cut away the excess pastry.
8 However gently you handle dough, it is bound to shrink a little, so let it sit a little above the side of the tin. If your dough has 'bunched' down the sides, press the sides of the pastry with your thumbs to flatten it a little. Refrigerate the pastry in the tin for 15 minutes. Preheat the oven.

BLIND BAKING

If pastry is to have a moist filling, it will probably require partial blind baking to prevent the base becoming soggy. If it is not cooked again after filling, it will need to be fully blind baked. This means baking the pastry without the filling, but with some weight on it to prevent it rising. Line the shell with crumpled greaseproof or baking paper. Pour in baking beads, dried beans or uncooked rice. Bake for the given time, then lift out the filled paper. Return the pastry to the oven to dry it and colour a little. When cooked, it should look dry with no greasy patches. Small pastry shells can just be pricked with a fork to prevent them rising, but only do this if specified.

Cool pastry completely before filling. Cooked filling should also be cooled before adding, to prevent soggy pastry.

WHAT WENT WRONG?

SHORTCRUST PASTRY

Perfect Pastry is even and lightly golden. The sides are cooked evenly and shrunk slightly from the sides of the tin. The base is crisp, golden and dry.

Overcooked The cooking time was too long, or the oven too hot. The pastry may have been placed either too high or too low in the oven.

Stuck to base The pastry may have had too much liquid added, or may not have been chilled before rolling.

Pastry shrunk too much The pastry was overworked or not chilled before baking. The weights may have been pressed too firmly against the sides of the pastry case.

Other problems

If there are holes in the pastry case, the pastry was rolled out too thinly or the pastry case has shrunk and split during cooking due to being overworked or not being chilled before cooking. If the fork marks are too large, this can cause holes.

If the pastry is tough, the pastry dough may have been overworked during mixing or rolling, or there was too much water added to the pastry dough.

Undercooked The cooking temperature was too low, or the cooking time not long enough. The pastry case may have been rolled out too thickly.

PUFF PASTRY

This is made by layering dough with butter and folding to create hundreds of layers. The butter melts and the dough produces steam, forcing the layers apart and making the pastry rise.

For perfect pastry which rises evenly, the edges must be cut cleanly with a sharp knife or cutter, not torn.

Egg glazes give a shine but must be applied carefully—any drips down the side may glue the layers together and stop them rising evenly.

The pastry should be chilled for at least 30 minutes before baking. Always bake puff pastry at a very high temperature—it should rise evenly so, if your oven has areas of uneven heat, turn the pastry around when it has set. If you have an oven with a bottom element, cook your pastry on the bottom shelf. When puff pastry is cooked, the top and base should be browned, with only a small amount of underbaked dough inside, and the layers should be visible. Puff pastry is not always perfect but provided you don't burn it, and it is well cooked, it will still be delicious.

MAKING PUFF PASTRY

We've given a range of butter quantity. If you've never made puff pastry before, you'll find it easier to use the lower amount. This recipe makes about 500 g (1 lb 2 oz) pastry. You will need 200–250 g (7–9 oz) unsalted butter, 250 g (9 oz/2 cups) plain (all-purpose) flour, 1/2 teaspoon salt and 170 ml (6 fl oz/2/3 cup) chilled water.
1 Melt 30 g (1 oz) of the butter in a saucepan. Sift the flour and salt onto a work surface and make a well in the centre. Add the melted butter and water to the centre and blend with your fingertips, gradually drawing in the flour. You should end up with a crumb mixture—if it seems a little dry, add extra drops of water before

bringing it all together to form a dough.
2 Cut the dough with a pastry scraper, using a downward cutting action, then turn the dough and repeat in the opposite direction. The dough should now come together to form a soft ball. Score a cross in the top to prevent shrinkage, wrap and refrigerate for 15–20 minutes.
3 Soften the remaining butter by pounding it between two sheets of baking paper with a rolling pin. Then, still between the sheets of baking paper, roll it into a 10 cm (4 in) square. The butter must be the same consistency as the dough or they will not roll out the same amount and the layers will not be even.
4 Put the pastry on a well-floured surface. Roll it out to form a cross, leaving the centre slightly thicker than the arms. Place the butter in the centre of the cross and fold over each of the arms to make a parcel. Turn the dough so that it looks like a book with the hinge side to the left. Tap and roll out the dough to form a 15 x 45 cm (6 x 18 in) rectangle. Make this as neat as possible, squaring off the corners.
5 Fold the dough like a letter, the top third down and the bottom third up, to form a square, brushing off any excess flour between the layers. Turn the dough 90° to bring the hinge side to your left and press the seam sides down with the rolling pin to seal them. Re-roll and fold as before to complete two turns and mark the dough by pressing into the corner with your fingertip for each turn. Wrap the dough in plastic wrap and chill for at least 30 minutes.
6 Re-roll and fold twice more and then chill, and then again to complete six turns. If it is a very hot day, you may need to chill for 30 minutes between each turn, rather than doing a double turn as described above. The pastry should now be an even yellow and is ready to use—if it looks a streaky, roll and fold once more. Ensure that the butter is evenly distributed throughout. Refrigerate until required.

WHAT WENT WRONG?

PUFF PASTRY

Perfect The pastry is well and evenly risen with pastry layers visible. The pastry is deep golden brown and the texture is light and flaky.

Overcooked The oven may have been too hot, or the cooking time too long, or the pastry may have been placed too high.

Unevenly risen when cooked The edges were not trimmed with a sharp knife. The glaze has dripped down the sides, gluing the layers together.

Decorative Edges

Fork pressed Press a lightly floured fork around the edge of the pie crust.

Fluted Press the pastry between your thumb and forefinger for a rippled effect.

Crimped Press the pastry between the thumb and forefinger, while indenting with the other forefinger.

Scalloped Press an upturned teaspoon on the pastry edges to mark semi-circles.

Checkerboard Make cuts in the pastry edge. Bend every second square inward.

Leaves Cut out leaf shapes with a cutter or the point of a sharp knife and mark veins using the back of a knife. Attach to the lip of the pie using water or egg glaze.

Plait Cut three long strips 5 mm (1/4 in) wide. Plait together and attach to the lip of the pie using a little water or egg.

Rope Twist two long sausages of pastry together and attach to the edge with a little water or egg.

Feathering Lift the pastry off the lip so that it stands upright and snip diagonally into the edge of the pie. Push one point inwards and one outwards.

Decorative Tops

There are endless shapes you can use to decorate pies, from stars to abstract patterns. Alternatively, you can buy small biscuit cutters in various shapes. When rolling out the pastry trimmings, don't make the shapes too thick or they won't cook through. To attach them, first brush the pie lid with an egg glaze, then arrange the decorations and glaze them as well.

You can decorate an open tart with pastry shapes, either around the edge or on top. However, if the filling is quite liquid, cook the shapes separately and arrange on the middle of the tart after it is baked and the filling has set.

CHOUX PASTRY

This is most often used to make delicious profiteroles, eclairs, gougères and croquembouche.

MAKING CHOUX PASTRY

Choux pastry is easy to make but the process is different from pastries such as shortcrust that have the butter rubbed into the flour. Instead, you melt the butter and water together, then beat the flour into the mixture and cook the mixture until it is no longer sticky. Then the mixture is cooled slightly and lightly beaten eggs are very gradually added and beaten in. The dough should be stiff enough to shape.

Before you begin, you should read the recipe and assemble all the ingredients.

1 Preheat the oven to 210°C (415°F/ Gas 6–7). Sift 185 g (6$\frac{1}{2}$ oz/1$\frac{1}{2}$ cups) plain flour and $\frac{1}{4}$ teaspoon salt onto a sheet of baking paper.

2 Place 100 g (3$\frac{1}{2}$ oz) chopped unsalted butter in a large heavy-based saucepan with 375 ml (13 fl oz/1$\frac{1}{2}$ cups) water and stir over medium heat. Once the butter has melted, increase the heat to bring the water to the boil. Remove from the heat immediately: prolonged boiling will evaporate enough water to alter the proportions of the ingredients. Add the flour and salt all at once and quickly beat it into the water using hand-held beaters or a wooden spoon. Return to the heat and continue beating until the mixture forms a ball and leaves the side of the saucepan. Transfer to a large bowl and cool slightly. Beat the mixture to release any heat.

3 Lightly beat 6 eggs in a bowl, then gradually add to the butter mixture, about 3 teaspoons at a time. Beat well after each addition. When all the egg has been added the mixture should be thick and glossy—a wooden spoon should stand up in it. If the mixture is too runny, the egg has been added too quickly. To correct this, beat for several more minutes, or until thickened.

4 The pastry is now ready to use and may be piped, spooned or shaped according to the recipe you are following. The pastry is cooked when it is golden and hollow sounding when tapped on the base. Turn off the oven and leave inside to dry out.

PROFITEROLES OR PUFFS

1 Lightly sprinkle three baking trays with water. Spoon the mixture onto the trays, leaving room for spreading. One small puff is equal to 1 heaped teaspoon of mixture.

2 Bake for 20–30 minutes or until golden. Remove from the oven and make a small hole in the base of each one. Return to the oven for 5 minutes to dry out. Cool on a wire rack. Cooked puffs can be frozen for up to 2 months. Reheat in a 180°C (350°F/Gas 4) oven for 5 minutes.

HELPFUL TIPS

Sprinkle the baking tray with water before placing the dough on it as this creates steam in the oven, helping the shapes to rise. You may need to prepare and cook them in two or more batches, especially if making a croquembouche.

MAKING GOUGÈRES

By adding a touch of cheese, such as Emmenthal or Gruyère, to choux pastry dough, you can make gougères. These delicately flavoured puffs are a great idea to have as starters. To make them, substitute half the water with the same quantity of milk and follow the procedure for choux pastry. After all the eggs have been incorporated, add 65 g (2$\frac{1}{4}$ oz/$\frac{1}{2}$ cup) grated cheese. Using a piping (icing) bag fitted with a plain tube, pipe 6 cm (2$\frac{1}{2}$ in) rounds onto a baking tray lined with baking paper. Lightly beat an egg yolk and brush over the gougères. Scatter with more grated cheese, using about 35 g (1$\frac{1}{2}$ oz/$\frac{1}{4}$ cup). Bake as for regular choux pastry. This will make 12 large or 24 small gougères.

WHAT WENT WRONG?

CHOUX PASTRY

Perfect The choux pastry is crisp and puffy, hollow inside and has a deep golden colour. To assist in drying and to release steam, make a small hole in the base of each puff with a skewer.

Poorly risen The pastry is not puffed and dense inside. Too little egg was added (the more eggs you add the more the dough will puff). Otherwise, the oven temperature was not hot enough or the oven was opened too soon during baking. Also, the cooking time may have been too short.

Notes
Spraying the inside of the oven with water, as well as sprinkling the baking tray with water, helps create steam which aids in the rising of choux pastry.

Always preheat the oven before beginning to make choux pastry because it is cooked immediately after it is shaped or piped. Likewise, prepare your equipment before you start. Lightly grease or line the baking tray with baking paper. If piping the dough, fit a large plain nozzle to the piping bag.

Add the flour to the boiling butter and water mixture in one go.

Immediately beat the mixture with a wooden spoon to prevent lumps forming. Stop beating as soon as the soft dough comes away from the side of the pan and remove from the heat.

Always allow the hot mixture to cool for 2–3 minutes before adding eggs or they can start to cook.

Beat in the eggs one at a time, making sure they are completely beaten in before adding the next egg.

The dough is ready when it is smooth and glossy. It should be piped or shaped while it is still warm. Leave about 4 cm (1 1/2 in) between the piped dough.

FILO PASTRY

This is most often used to make a variety of pies and pastries or to wrap fillings in.

ABOUT FILO PASTRY

Filo pastry is a paper-thin pastry made with flour and water. Filo means 'leaf' in Greek, and is used widely in the Middle East, Turkey, Greece and Europe for making a variety of pastries and pies such as spanokopita and baklava, or to wrap seafood or vegetable fillings. The dough for filo is simple enough to make, but stretching it until it is tissue-thin requires great skill and patience. For this reason, commercially made filo, which is available fresh or frozen, is often used.

COOKING WITH FILO PASTRY

Allow frozen filo to thaw in the packet, then take out the sheets and stack them on a cloth. Cover the sheets with a dry cloth and use them one at a time as they dry out quickly when exposed to air.

Brush each sheet with a little oil or melted butter to make them crisp when cooked.

Filled filo parcels can be frozen and then cooked when frozen.

Notes
If the filling leaks, there may be too much filling, or not enough filo layers. The oven may have been too hot or the filling too moist. Otherwise, the parcels were not shaped and secured well enough or were rolled too tightly.

WHAT WENT WRONG?

FILO PASTRY

Perfect The filo pastry is dry, crisp, flaky, puffed and golden brown.

Overcooked The pastry is unevenly coloured. The oven temperature may have been too high or the layers unevenly brushed with butter.

Undercooked The pastry is pale and soggy. The filling may be heavy and too moist or there may be too many layers of filo. The oven temperature may have been too low or the cooking time too short.

HINTS AND TIPS

1 The kitchen needs to be as cool as possible when making pastry.

2 Pastry can be made in a food processor, so you needn't worry about hot or heavy hands, but it is important not to overwork the dough or it will become tough.

3 Butter should be cold, straight from the refrigerator. Cut the butter into even-sized pieces, about 5 mm ($1/4$ in) thick.

4 Always use chilled water to bind the dough.

5 Flour should be sifted before use. This will remove any lumps and incorporate air into the flour, helping to make the dough light. For sweet shortcrust, always sift icing sugar and flour to remove any lumps and help aerate them.

6 For sweet shortcrust, stir the egg yolks with chilled water before adding them to the flour and sugar.

7 If using a food processor, take care not to overprocess the dough or it will become tough.

8 Dough needs to covered completely with plastic wrap or it will dry out.

9 Always rest dough in the refrigerator for at least 30 minutes.

10 If the dough is too cold to roll out it will crack easily, so leave at room temperature, still covered in plastic wrap, for 15 minutes to soften.

11 Roll the pastry out on a lightly floured work surface to prevent it sticking. Always roll from the middle outwards (not using a back-and-forth motion) and rotate the pastry frequently as you go to keep to the required shape. Occasionally use both hands to gently push the edges of the dough back inwards to help keep the shape.

12 If possible, use a marble slab or a cold work surface to roll dough. This helps prevent the butter from warming up.

13 If the dough feels really soft and starts to stick to the work surface, roll it out between two sheets of baking paper.

14 Never pull or stretch pastry as you roll it or the pastry will shrink during cooking.

15 When baking blind, the pastry shell is first lined with a piece of crumpled baking paper. Crumpling the paper slightly helps it to better fit the shape of the pastry.

16 Shortcrust (and sweet shortcrust) pastry keeps well once made. Cover with plastic wrap and refrigerate for up to 3 days. It also freezes for up to 3 months. The pastry can be rolled out and then frozen, either as a flat sheet on a baking tray lined with baking paper, or after it has been used to line the tin. Alternatively, freeze as a ball of dough.

OLD-FASHIONED APPLE PIE

Preparation time **30 minutes +**
Total cooking time **55 minutes**
Serves **8**

Pastry
250 g (9 oz/2 cups) self-raising flour
85 g (3 oz/²⁄₃ cup) cornflour (cornstarch)
180 g (6 oz) unsalted butter, chilled and cubed
90 g (3¼ oz/⅓ cup) caster (superfine) sugar
1 egg, lightly beaten

40 g (1½ oz) unsalted butter
6 green apples, peeled, cored and thinly sliced
1 tablespoon lemon juice
140 g (5 oz/³⁄₄ cup) soft brown sugar
1 teaspoon ground nutmeg
2 tablespoons plain (all-purpose) flour mixed
   with 60 ml (2 fl oz/¼ cup) water
25 g (1 oz/¼ cup) ground almonds
milk, to brush
sugar, to sprinkle

1 Lightly grease a 1 litre (35 fl oz/4 cup), 20 cm (8 in) metal pie dish.
2 Sift the flours into a large bowl and rub in the butter with your fingers until mixture resembles fine breadcrumbs. Stir in the sugar and a pinch of salt. Make a well, add the egg and mix with a knife, using a cutting action, until the mixture comes together in beads.
3 Put the dough on a floured surface and press into a smooth disc, cover with plastic wrap and refrigerate for 20 minutes.
4 Use two-thirds of the dough to line the base and side of the dish. Roll out the remaining dough to make a lid. Cover and refrigerate for 20 minutes.
5 Preheat the oven to 200°C (400°F/Gas 6) and heat a baking tray.
6 Melt the butter in a large frying pan, add the apple and toss. Stir in the lemon juice, sugar and nutmeg and cook for 10 minutes, or until tender. Add the flour and water mixture, then the almonds. Bring to the boil and cook, stirring, for 2–3 minutes. Pour into a bowl and cool.
7 Put the apple in the pastry case. Cover with the pastry lid and press lightly onto the rim. Trim the edges and pinch together to seal. Prick over the top, brush with milk and sprinkle with sugar. Bake on the hot tray for 40 minutes, or until golden.

LEMON MERINGUE PIE

Preparation time **30 minutes** +
Total cooking time **50 minutes**
Serves 4–6

375 g (13 oz) ready-made sweet shortcrust
   pastry
30 g (1 oz/¼ cup) plain (all-purpose) flour
30 g (1 oz/¼ cup) cornflour (cornstarch)
250 g (9 oz/1 cup) caster (superfine) sugar
185 ml (6 fl oz/¾ cup) lemon juice
1 tablespoon grated lemon zest
50 g (1¾ oz) unsalted butter, chopped
6 egg yolks

Meringue
6 egg whites
a pinch of cream of tartar
340 g (11¾ oz) caster (superfine) sugar

1 Grease a 25 x 18 x 3 cm (10 x 7 x 1¼ in)
pie plate. Roll pastry out between two
sheets of baking paper into a 30 cm (12 in)
circle. Invert the pastry into the plate. Trim
the edges. Re-roll pastry trimmings and cut
into three 10 x 2 cm (4 x ¾ in) strips.
Brush the pie rim with water, place the
pastry strips around the top and make a
decorative edge. Prick over the base with a
fork. Cover and refrigerate for 20 minutes.
2 Preheat the oven to 180°C (350°F/Gas 4).
Blind bake the pastry for 15 minutes.
Remove the beads and bake for a further
15–20 minutes. Allow to cool.
3 Increase the oven to 200°C (400°F/Gas 6).
Put the flours, sugar, lemon juice and zest
in a pan. Add 315 ml (10¾ fl oz/1¼ cups)
of water and whisk over medium heat until
smooth. Cook, stirring, for 2 minutes.
Remove from the heat and whisk in the
butter and egg yolks. Return to low heat
and stir, for 2 minutes, or until thick.
4 To make the meringue, beat the egg
whites and cream of tartar using electric
beaters until soft peaks form. Pour in the
caster sugar, beating until thick and glossy.
5 Spread the lemon filling into the pastry
base, then cover with the meringue, piling
high in the centre and making peaks. Bake
for 8–10 minutes, or until lightly browned.

APPLE TURNOVERS

Preparation time **40 minutes**

Total cooking time **25 minutes**

Makes **12 pieces**

500 g (1 lb 2 oz) block ready-made puff pastry, thawed

1 egg white, lightly beaten

caster (superfine) sugar, to sprinkle

Filling

200 g (7 oz/1 cup) tinned pie or stewed apple

1–2 tablespoons caster (superfine) sugar

30 g (1 oz/¼ cup) raisins, chopped

30 g (1 oz/¼ cup) walnut pieces, chopped

1 Preheat the oven to 210°C (415°F/ Gas 6–7). Lightly grease a baking tray.

2 Roll the pastry on a floured surface to 35 x 45 cm (14 x 17¾ in). Cut out twelve 10 cm (4 in) rounds.

3 To make the filling, combine all the ingredients in a bowl and mix well.

4 Divide the filling among the pastry rounds, then brush the edges with water. Fold in half and pinch together to seal. Use a knife to push up the pastry edge at intervals. Brush with egg white and sprinkle with caster sugar. Make two slits in the top.

5 Bake for 15 minutes, then reduce the oven to 190°C (375°F/Gas 5) and bake for 10 minutes, or until golden.

PEACH PIE

Preparation time **30 minutes** +
Total cooking time **50 minutes**
Serves **6**

500 g (1 lb 2 oz) ready-made or home-made
   sweet shortcrust pastry
1.65 kg (3 lb 10 oz) tinned peach slices,
   well-drained
125 g (4½ oz/½ cup) caster (superfine) sugar
30 g (1 oz/¼ cup) cornflour (cornstarch)
¼ teaspoon almond extract
20 g (¾ oz) unsalted butter, chopped
1 tablespoon milk
1 egg, lightly beaten
caster (superfine) sugar, to sprinkle

1 Roll out two-thirds of the dough between
two sheets of baking paper until large
enough to line a 23 x 18 x 3 cm (9 x 7 x
1¼ in) pie tin. Remove the top sheet of
paper and invert the pastry into the tin.
Use a small ball of pastry to press the
pastry into the tin. Trim any excess pastry
with a knife. Refrigerate for 20 minutes.
2 Preheat the oven to 200°C (400°F/Gas 6).
Line the pastry with crumpled baking paper
and pour in baking beads or rice.
3 Bake for 10 minutes, remove the paper
and beads and return to the oven for
5 minutes, or until the pastry base is dry
and lightly coloured. Allow to cool.
4 Mix the peaches, sugar, cornflour and
almond extract in a bowl, then spoon into
the pastry shell. Dot with butter and
moisten the edges with milk.
5 Roll out remaining dough to a 25 cm
(10 in) square. Using a fluted pastry cutter,
cut into 10 strips 2.5 cm (1 in) wide. Lay
the strips in a lattice pattern over the
filling, pressing on the edges and trim.
Brush with egg and sprinkle with sugar.
6 Bake for 10 minutes, reduce the heat to
180°C (350°F/Gas 4) and bake for about
30 minutes, or until golden. Allow to cool
before serving.

TARTE TATIN

Preparation time **30 minutes +**
Total cooking time **1 hour 15 minutes**
Serves **6–8**

215 g (7½ oz/1¾ cups) plain (all-purpose) flour
a pinch of salt
160 g (5¾ oz) unsalted butter, chilled,
  chopped
1 egg yolk
60 g (2¼ oz) unsalted butter, extra
170 g (6 oz/¾ cup) caster (superfine) sugar
1.3 kg (3 lb) of eating apples, peeled, cored
  and quartered
whipped cream, to serve (optional)

1 Sift the flour and salt into a large bowl and rub the butter in until the mixture resembles breadcrumbs.
2 Add the egg yolk and 2–3 teaspoons of ice-cold water and, using a flat-bladed knife, mix until the dough just starts to come together.
3 Turn out onto a work surface and push the dough together with your hands. Form into a disc, then wrap in plastic wrap and refrigerate for 30 minutes.
4 Combine the extra unsalted butter and the caster (superfine) sugar in a deep, 25 cm (10 in) ovenproof frying pan. Heat until the butter is melted and the sugar has dissolved. Arrange the apples over the base of the pan, placing them in rings and making sure there are no gaps. Cook over low heat for 35–40 minutes, basting often with pan juices, or until the apples are soft and pan juices are very reduced and are light caramel. Remove from heat.
5 Preheat the oven to 190°C (375°F/Gas 5). Roll out the pastry on a lightly floured board to form a 3 mm (⅛ in) thick circle slightly larger than the frying pan. Lay the pastry over the apples, pressing around the edge of the pan to enclose the apples. Trim the edge of pastry, then fold the trimmed edge back on itself to form a neat edge.
6 Bake for 25–30 minutes, or until pastry is golden and cooked through. Remove from the oven, then stand for 5 minutes before inverting the tart onto a plate. Serve the tart warm or at room temperature, with whipped cream.

PLUM AND ALMOND TART

Preparation time **30 minutes** +
Total cooking time **45 minutes**
Serves **8**

Pastry

185 g (6½ oz/1½ cups) plain (all-purpose) flour
150 g (5½ oz) unsalted butter, chilled and
   cubed
55 g (2 oz/¼ cup) caster (superfine) sugar
1 tablespoon sour cream

Filling

125 g (4½ oz) unsalted butter, softened
115 g (4 oz/½ cup) caster (superfine) sugar
2 eggs, at room temperature
100 g (3½ oz/1 cup) ground almonds
2 tablespoons plain (all-purpose) flour
8–10 plums, halved, stones removed

cream or ice cream, to serve

1 To make the pastry, put the flour, butter and sugar in a food processor and process in short bursts until the mixture resembles fine breadcrumbs. Add the sour cream and process in short bursts until the mixture comes together in a ball. Cover with plastic wrap and refrigerate for 20 minutes.

2 Preheat the oven to 200°C (400°F/Gas 6) and grease a 23 cm (9 in), 2 cm (³/4 in) deep loose-based flan (tart) tin.

3 Roll out the pastry to a thickness of 3 mm (¹/8 in) and use it to line the tin. Prick the pastry base with a fork and refrigerate for 30 minutes.

4 Line the pastry shell with a sheet of crumpled baking paper and pour in some baking beads or uncooked rice.

5 Bake for 15 minutes, remove the paper and beads and return to the oven for a further 5–7 minutes to ensure the pastry is crisp. Set aside to cool. Reduce the oven to 180°C (350°F/Gas 4).

6 To make the filling, cream the butter and sugar with electric beaters until light and fluffy. Add the eggs, one at a time, beating well after each addition. Fold in the ground almonds and flour. Spread the almond mixture over the base of the pastry and top with the plum halves, cut side down.

7 Bake for 25–30 minutes, or until the filling is set. Serve the tart warm or at room temperature with cream or ice cream.

PORTUGUESE CUSTARD TARTS

Preparation time 25 minutes +
Total cooking time 35 minutes
Makes 12

155 g (5½ oz/1¼ cups) plain (all-purpose) flour
25 g (1 oz) copha (white vegetable shortening), chopped and softened
30 g (1 oz) unsalted butter, chopped
250 g (9 oz/1 cup) sugar
500 ml (17 fl oz/2 cups) milk
3 tablespoons cornflour (cornstarch)
1 tablespoon custard powder (instant vanilla pudding mix)
4 egg yolks
1 teaspoon natural vanilla extract

1 Sift the flour into a bowl. Add 185 ml (6 fl oz/¾ cup) of water. Gather into a ball, then roll out on baking paper to form a 24 x 30 cm (9½ x 12 in) rectangle.

Spread the copha over the surface. Roll up from the short edge to form a log.
2 Roll the dough out into a rectangle again, and spread with the butter. Roll into a log and slice into 12 pieces. Working from the centre outwards, press each round out to a circle large enough to cover the base and sides of twelve 80 ml (2½ fl oz/ ⅓ cup) muffin holes. Press into the tin and refrigerate.
3 Put the sugar and 80 ml (2½ fl oz/⅓ cup) of water into a saucepan, and stir over low heat until the sugar dissolves. Mix a little milk with the cornflour and custard powder to form a smooth paste, and add to the pan with the remaining milk, egg yolks and vanilla. Stir over low heat until thickened.
4 Preheat the oven to 220°C (425°F/Gas 7). Divide the filling among the pastry bases. Bake for 30 minutes, or until the custard is set and the tops have browned. Cool in the tins, then transfer to a wire rack.

NEENISH TARTS

Preparation time **1 hour +**
Total cooking time **15 minutes**
Makes **12**

2 tablespoons plain (all-purpose) flour
70 g (2½ oz/⅔ cup) ground almonds
60 g (2¼ oz) icing (confectioners') sugar, sifted
1 egg white, lightly beaten

Creamy filling

1 tablespoon plain (all-purpose) flour
125 ml (4 fl oz/½ cup) milk
2 egg yolks
60 g (2¼ oz) unsalted butter, softened
2 tablespoons caster (superfine) sugar
¼ teaspoon natural vanilla extract

Icing (frosting)

125 g (4½ oz) icing (confectioners') sugar
2 tablespoons milk, extra
1 tablespoon unsweetened cocoa powder

1 Grease a 12-hole shallow patty pan.
2 Sift the flour into a bowl and stir in the ground almonds and icing sugar. Make a well in the centre, add the egg white and mix until the mixture forms a paste. Turn onto a floured surface and gather into a ball. Wrap in plastic wrap and refrigerate for 30 minutes, to firm.
3 Preheat the oven to 190°C (375°F/Gas 5). Roll out the dough between two sheets of baking paper to 3 mm (⅛ in) thick. Cut the pastry into 12 circles with a 7 cm (2¾ in) fluted cutter. Press the pastry circles into the patty pan and prick with a fork. Bake for 10 minutes, or until golden.
4 To make the filling, stir the flour and milk in a saucepan over medium heat for 2 minutes, or until thick. Remove from the heat, then stir in the egg yolks. Cover with plastic wrap and set aside.
5 Using electric beaters, beat the butter, sugar and vanilla in a bowl until creamy. Add the egg mixture and beat until smooth. Spoon the mixture into each pastry shell.
6 To make the icing, combine the icing sugar and milk in a heatproof bowl, place over a saucepan of simmering water, and stir until smooth. Remove, transfer half the icing to a bowl, add the cocoa and stir until smooth.
7 Spread plain icing over half of each tart. Allow to set. Reheat the chocolate icing and ice the other half of each tart.

CHERRY PIE

Preparation time **20 minutes** +
Total cooking time **1 minutes**
Serves **6**

500 g (1 lb 2 oz) ready-made or home-made
   sweet shortcrust pastry
850 g (1 lb 14 oz) tinned seedless black
   cherries, drained well
60 g (2¼ oz/⅓ cup) soft brown sugar
1½ teaspoons ground cinnamon
1 teaspoon finely grated lemon zest
1 teaspoon finely grated orange zest
1–2 drops almond extract
25 g (1 oz/¼ cup) ground almonds
1 egg, lightly beaten

1 Preheat the oven to 190°C (375°F/Gas 5). Roll out two-thirds of the dough between two sheets of baking paper to form a circle large enough to fit a 22 x 20 x 2 cm (8½ x 8 x ¾ in) pie plate. Remove the top sheet of baking paper and invert the pastry into the pie plate. Cut away the excess pastry with a small sharp knife.
2 Roll out the remaining pastry large enough to cover the pie. Refrigerate, covered in plastic wrap, for 20 minutes.
3 Place the cherries, sugar, cinnamon, lemon and orange zests, and almond extract in a bowl and mix to combine.
4 Line the pastry base with the ground almonds. Spoon in the filling, brush the pastry edges with beaten egg, and cover with the pastry lid. Use a fork to seal the pastry edges. Cut four slits in the top of the pie to allow steam to escape, then brush the pastry with beaten egg.
5 Bake for about 1 hour, or until the pastry is golden and the juices are bubbling through the slits in the pastry. Serve warm.

FREEFORM BLUEBERRY PIE

Preparation time **30 minutes +**
Total cooking time **30 minutes**
Serves **6–8**

Pastry

185 g (6½ oz/1½ cups) plain (all-purpose) flour
100 g (3½ oz) unsalted butter, chilled and
    cubed
2 teaspoons grated orange zest
1 tablespoon caster (superfine) sugar
2–3 tablespoons iced water

40 g (1½ oz/⅓ cup) crushed amaretti biscuits
    or almond bread
60 g (2¼ oz/½ cup) plain (all-purpose) flour
1 teaspoon ground cinnamon
90 g (3¼ oz/⅓ cup) caster (superfine) sugar
500 g (1 lb 2 oz/3¼ cups) fresh blueberries
milk, for brushing
2 tablespoons blueberry jam
icing (confectioners') sugar, to dust

1 Sift the flour into a large bowl and rub in
the butter with your fingertips until the
mixture resembles breadcrumbs. Stir in the
orange zest and sugar. Make a well, add
almost all the water and mix with a flat-
bladed knife, using a cutting action, until
the mixture comes together in beads. Add a
little more water if necessary to bring the
dough together.
2 Gather together and lift out onto a
lightly floured surface. Press together
into a ball and flatten it slightly into a
disc. Cover in plastic wrap and refrigerate
for 20 minutes.
3 Preheat the oven to 200°C (400°F/Gas 6).
Combine the biscuits, flour, cinnamon and
1½ tablespoons of the sugar.
4 Roll pastry out to a 36 cm (14 in) circle
and sprinkle with the biscuit mixture,
leaving a 4 cm (1½ in) border. Arrange
the blueberries over the crushed biscuits,
then bring up the edges to form a
freeform crust.
5 Brush the sides of the pie with the milk.
Sprinkle with the remaining sugar and bake
for 30 minutes, or until the sides are crisp
and brown.
6 Warm the jam in a saucepan over low
heat and brush over the berries. Cool to
room temperature, then dust the pastry
crust with sifted icing sugar.

RICOTTA AND BERRY TARTLETS

Preparation time **20 minutes** +
Total cooking time **22 minutes**
Serves **6**

Pastry

150 g (5½ oz/1¼ cups) plain (all-purpose) flour
35 g (1¼ oz/⅓ cup) ground almonds
1 tablespoon caster (superfine) sugar
85 g (3 oz) unsalted butter, chilled and cubed
1 egg yolk, at room temperature

Filling

300 g (10½ oz/2½ cups) mixed berries, such
   as raspberries, strawberries and blueberries
1 egg, at room temperature
60 g (2¼ oz/¼ cup) caster (superfine) sugar
1 tablespoon lemon juice
150 g (5½ oz/⅔ cup) smooth ricotta cheese

icing (confectioners') sugar, to dust

1 To make the pastry, put the flour,
ground almonds, sugar, butter and a pinch
of salt in a food processor. Process until the
mixture resembles breadcrumbs. Add the
egg yolk and 1 tablespoon of cold water.
Process until the mixture just forms a ball,
adding a little extra water if the pastry is
too dry. Turn the pastry out onto a work
surface. Flatten it into a disc, cover with
plastic wrap and refrigerate for 30 minutes.
2 Lightly grease six 9 cm (3½ in), 2 cm
(¾ in) deep tartlet tins.
3 Roll out the pastry on a lightly floured
surface to a thickness of 3 mm (⅛ in). Cut
out six 13 cm (5 in) circles and place in the
tins. Prick the base of the pastry with a
fork and refrigerate for 10 minutes. Preheat
the oven to 200°C (400°F/Gas 6).
4 To make the filling, hull any strawberries
and chop any larger berries. Put the egg,
caster sugar and lemon juice in a heatproof
bowl and place over a saucepan of
simmering water, making sure the base of
the bowl doesn't touch the water. Whisk
with an electric whisk for 5–6 minutes, or
until light and creamy. Stir in the ricotta.
5 Divide the berries among the tartlet cases
and spoon over the ricotta mixture.
6 Bake for 20–22 minutes, or until the
edges of the pastry are golden brown.
Serve warm, dusted with icing sugar.

MANGO AND PASSIONFRUIT PIES

Preparation time **40 minutes** +
Total cooking time **25 minutes**
Makes 6

750 g (1 lb 10 oz) ready-made or home-made
    sweet shortcrust pastry
3 mangoes (900 g/2 lb), peeled and sliced or
    400 g (14 oz) tinned mango slices, drained
60 g (2¼ oz/¼ cup) passionfruit pulp, strained
1 tablespoon custard powder (instant vanilla
    pudding mix)
90 g (3¼ oz/⅓ cup) caster (superfine) sugar
1 egg, lightly beaten
icing (confectioners') sugar, to dust

1 Preheat the oven to 190°C (375°F/Gas 5).
Grease six 10 x 8 x 3 cm (4 x 3 x 1¼ in)
fluted flan (tart) tins or round pie dishes.

2 Roll out two-thirds of the pastry between
two sheets of baking paper to a thickness
of 3 mm (¼ in). Cut out six 13 cm (5 in)
circles. Line tins with the circles and trim
the edges. Refrigerate.

3 Combine the mango, passionfruit,
custard powder and sugar in a bowl.

4 Roll out the remaining pastry between
two sheets of baking paper to 3 mm
(¼ in) thick. Cut out six 11 cm (4¼ in)
circles. Re-roll the pastry trimmings and
cut into shapes for decoration.

5 Fill the pastry cases with the mango
mixture and brush the edges with egg. Top
with the pastry circles and press the edges
to seal. Trim the edges and decorate with
the pastry shapes. Brush the tops with
beaten egg and dust with icing sugar.

6 Bake for 20–25 minutes, or until the
pastry is golden brown.

CUSTARD ROLLS

Preparation time **35 minutes**
Total cooking time **20 minutes**
Makes **18**

375 ml (13 fl oz/1½ cups) milk
115 g (4 oz/½ cup) caster (superfine) sugar
60 g (2¼ oz/½ cup) semolina
1 teaspoon grated lemon zest
1 egg, lightly beaten
12 sheets filo pastry
125 g (4½ oz) unsalted butter, melted
2 tablespoons icing (confectioners') sugar
½ teaspoon ground cinnamon

1 Put the milk, caster sugar, semolina and lemon zest in a saucepan and stir until it comes to the boil. Reduce the heat and simmer for 3 minutes. Remove from the heat and gradually whisk in the egg. Pour the custard into a bowl, cover the surface with plastic wrap and set aside to cool.
2 Preheat the oven to 180°C (350°F/Gas 4). Lightly brush two baking trays with melted butter.
3 Work with two sheets of pastry at a time. Cover the rest with a tea towel (dish towel). Brush one sheet with melted butter, then top with another. Cut lengthways into three strips. Brush the edges with melted butter.
4 Spoon about 1 tablespoon of the custard 5 cm (2 in) in from the short edge of each pastry strip. Roll the pastry over the filling, fold the ends in, then roll up. Repeat with the remaining pastry and custard. Arrange on the trays 2 cm (³/4 in) apart. Brush with the remaining butter.
5 Bake for 12–15 minutes, or until crisp and golden. Cool on a wire rack. Dust with a little of the combined icing sugar and cinnamon.

CHOC-HAZELNUT PUFF PASTRY ROLLS

Preparation time **15 minutes** +
Total cooking time **15 minutes**
Serves **4**

80 g (2³/₄ oz) choc-hazelnut spread
80 g (2³/₄ oz) icing (confectioners') sugar
2 sheets puff pastry, thawed
1 egg, lightly beaten
icing (confectioners') sugar, to dust

1 Preheat the oven to 200°C (400°F/Gas 6). Combine the choc-hazelnut spread and icing sugar and roll into a 20 cm (8 in) long roll. Wrap the roll in plastic wrap and twist the ends to enclose. Refrigerate for 30 minutes. When firm, cut the roll into eight even pieces. Roll each of the pieces in icing sugar.

2 Cut each sheet of puff pastry into four squares. Place a piece of the choc-hazelnut mixture roll onto each square of pastry and roll up to enclose. Pinch the ends and brush lightly with egg.

3 Bake for 15 minutes, or until the pastry is golden. Dust with icing sugar just before serving.

APPLE GALETTE

Preparation time **25 minutes**

Total cooking time **35 minutes**

Serves **6**

1 sheet frozen puff pastry, thawed
80 g (2³/₄ oz/¹/₄ cup) apricot jam
1 granny smith apple
2 teaspoons demerara sugar

1 Preheat the oven to 210°C (415°F/ Gas 6–7). Lightly grease a baking tray and place in the oven to heat.
2 Trim the corners from the pastry to make a neat circle (use a large plate as a guide).

3 Place the jam in a small saucepan and stir over low heat to warm through and thin. Strain through a sieve to remove any chunks of fruit. Brush over the puff pastry, leaving a 1.5 cm (¹/₂ in) border.
4 Peel, halve and core the apple, and cut into 2 mm (¹/₈ in) thick slices. Arrange over the pastry in an overlapping circular pattern, leaving a 1.5 cm (¹/₂ in) border around the edge. Sprinkle evenly with the sugar.
5 Place the galette on the prepared baking tray and bake for 35 minutes, or until the edge of the pastry is well browned and puffed.

PITHIVIERS

Preparation time **30 minutes +**
Total cooking time **30 minutes**
Serves **6**

140 g (5 oz) softened unsalted butter
140 g (5 oz) caster (superfine) sugar
2 eggs, beaten
2 tablespoons dark rum
finely grated zest of 1 small orange
140 g (5 oz) ground almonds
20 g (^{3}/4 oz) plain (all-purpose) flour
500 g (1 lb 2 oz) puff pastry
1 egg, extra, beaten
icing (confectioners') sugar, to dust

1 To make the filling, beat the butter and caster sugar until creamy. Mix in the 2 beaten eggs, rum and zest. Fold in the almonds and flour.

2 On a floured surface, roll out one half of the pastry. Cut out a 28 cm (11^1/4 in) circle and place on a baking tray lined with baking paper. Spread the filling over the pastry, leaving a 2 cm (^{3}/4 in) border around edges. Brush the borders with beaten egg.

3 Roll out the remaining pastry and cut out a 28 cm (11^1/4 in) circle. Lay the circle on top of the filling and press the edges of the pastry together. Cover and refrigerate for 1 hour.

4 Preheat the oven to 220°C (425°F/Gas 7). Brush the extra egg over the pithivier, then score the top in a spiral pattern.

5 Bake for 25–30 minutes, or until risen and golden brown. Dust with the icing sugar and cool. Cut into slices to serve.

MILLE FEUILLE

Preparation time **30 minutes**
Total cooking time **1 hour 30 minutes**
Serves **6–8**

600 g (1 lb 5 oz) ready-made puff pastry or
   3 sheets ready-rolled, thawed
625 ml (21½ fl oz/2½ cups) thick
   (double/heavy) cream
500 g (1 lb 2 oz) small strawberries, halved
70 g (2½ oz) blueberries (optional)

1 Preheat the oven to 220°C (425°F/Gas 7). Line a baking tray with baking paper.
2 If using a block of puff pastry, cut the pastry into three and roll out to 25 cm (10 in) squares. Place one sheet of puff pastry on the tray, prick all over and top with another piece of baking paper and another baking tray and bake for about 15 minutes. Turn the trays over and bake on the other side for 10–15 minutes, or until golden brown. Allow to cool and repeat with the remaining pastry.
3 Trim the edges of each pastry sheet and cut each one in half.
4 Pour the cream into a large bowl and whisk to firm peaks. Place two of the pastry pieces on a serving dish and spoon some of the cream on top. Carefully arrange some of the strawberries and blueberries over the cream, pressing them well down. Top each one with another pastry sheet and repeat with the cream, strawberries and blueberries. Top with a final layer of pastry and dust with icing sugar.

SUMMER BERRY TART

Preparation time **35 minutes** +
Total cooking time **35 minutes**
Serves 4–6

Pastry

125 g (4½ oz/1 cup) plain (all-purpose) flour
90 g (3¼ oz) chilled unsalted butter, cubed
2 tablespoons icing (confectioners') sugar
1–2 tablespoons iced water

Filling

3 egg yolks
2 tablespoons caster (superfine) sugar
2 tablespoons cornflour (cornstarch)
250 ml (9 fl oz/1 cup) milk
1 teaspoon natural vanilla extract
250 g (9 oz/1⅔ cups) strawberries, halved
125 g (4½ oz) blueberries
125 g (4½ oz/1 cup) raspberries
1–2 tablespoons baby apple gel

1 Preheat the oven to 180°C (350°F/Gas 4).
Lightly grease a 20 cm (8 in) round, loose-based, fluted flan (tart) tin.
2 To make the pastry, sift the flour into a bowl. Using your fingertips, rub in the butter until the mixture resembles fine breadcrumbs. Mix in the sugar. Make a well in the centre and add almost all the water. Mix with a flat-bladed knife, using a cutting action, until the mixture comes together in beads. Add more water if the dough is too dry.
3 Roll out the pastry between two sheets of baking paper to fit the base and side of the tin. Line the tin with the pastry and trim away excess. Refrigerate for 20 minutes.
4 Line the tin with baking paper and spread a layer of baking beads or uncooked rice evenly over the paper.
5 Bake for 15 minutes, remove the paper and beads and bake for a further 15 minutes, or until golden.
6 To make the filling, put the egg yolks, sugar and cornflour in a bowl and whisk until pale. Heat the milk in a small saucepan until almost boiling, then remove from the heat and add gradually to the egg mixture, beating constantly. Strain into the pan. Stir over low heat for 3 minutes, or until the mixture boils and thickens. Remove from the heat and add the vanilla extract. Transfer to a bowl, cover with plastic wrap and set aside to cool.
7 Spread the filling in the pastry shell and top with the berries.
8 Heat the apple gel in a heatproof bowl in a saucepan of simmering water, or in the microwave, until it liquefies. Brush over the fruit with a pastry brush. Allow to set before cutting.

RHUBARB PIE

Preparation time **30 minutes +**
Total cooking time **40 minutes**
Serves **6**

Pastry

250 g (9 oz/2 cups) plain (all-purpose) flour
30 g (1 oz) unsalted butter, chilled and cubed
70 g (2½ oz) copha (white vegetable
   shortening)
2 tablespoons icing (confectioners') sugar
160 ml (5¼ fl oz/⅔ cup) iced water

1.5 kg (3 lb 5 oz) rhubarb, trimmed and
   cut into 2 cm (¾ in) pieces
250 g (9 oz/1 cup) caster (superfine) sugar
½ teaspoon ground cinnamon
2½ tablespoons cornflour (cornstarch), mixed
   with 60 ml (2 fl oz/¼ cup) water
30 g (1 oz) unsalted butter, cubed
1 egg, lightly beaten
icing (confectioners') sugar, to dust

1 Lightly grease a 25 x 20 x 4 cm (10 x 8 x 1½ in) ceramic pie dish.
2 Sift the flour and ½ teaspoon salt into a bowl and rub in the butter and copha until the mixture looks like breadcrumbs. Stir in the icing sugar. Make a well, add most of the water and mix until it comes together in beads.
3 Gather dough together and put on a floured surface. Press into a ball, flatten a little and cover in plastic wrap. Refrigerate for 30 minutes.
4 Put the rhubarb, sugar, cinnamon and 2 tablespoons of water in a saucepan and stir over low heat until the sugar dissolves. Simmer, covered, for 5–8 minutes, or until the rhubarb is tender. Add the cornflour and water mixture. Bring to the boil, stirring until thickened. Cool.
5 Preheat the oven to 180°C (350°F/Gas 4) and heat a baking tray.
6 Roll out two-thirds of the dough to a 30 cm (12 in) circle and put into the pie dish. Spoon in the rhubarb and dot with butter. Roll out remaining pastry for a lid. Brush the pie rim with egg and press the top in place. Trim the edges and make a slit in the top. Decorate with pastry scraps and brush with egg.
7 Bake on the hot tray for 35 minutes, or until golden. Dust with icing sugar.

BLACKBERRY PIE

Preparation time **30 minutes** +
Total cooking time **40 minutes**
Serves **6**

500 g (1 lb 2 oz) ready-made or home-made
   sweet shortcrust pastry
500 g (1 lb 2 oz/4 cups) blackberries
160 g (5¾ oz/⅔ cup) caster (superfine) sugar
2 tablespoons cornflour (cornstarch)
milk, to brush
1 egg, lightly beaten
caster (superfine) sugar, extra, to sprinkle

1 Preheat the oven to 200°C (400°F/Gas 6).
Grease a 26 x 20.5 x 4.5 cm (10¼ x 8 x
1¾ in) ceramic pie dish.
2 Roll out two-thirds of the pastry between
two sheets of baking paper until large
enough to line the base and side of the pie
dish. Remove the top paper, invert the
pastry into the dish and press into place,
leaving the excess overhanging the edges.
3 Toss the blackberries (if frozen, thaw and
drain well), sugar and cornflour together in
a bowl until well mixed, then transfer to
the pie dish.
4 Roll out the remaining pastry between
two sheets of baking paper until large
enough to cover the pie. Moisten the rim
of the pie base with milk and press the
pastry lid firmly into place. Trim and crimp
the edges. Brush with egg and sprinkle with
the extra sugar. Pierce the top of the pie
with a knife.
5 Bake on the bottom shelf of the oven
for 10 minutes. Reduce the oven to 180°C
(350°F/Gas 4) and move the pie to the
centre shelf. Bake for a further 30 minutes,
or until golden on top. Cool before serving.

CHOCOLATE ÉCLAIRS

Preparation time **30 minutes**
Total cooking time **40 minutes**
Makes **18**

125 g (4½ oz) unsalted butter
125 g (4½ oz/1 cup) plain (all-purpose) flour, sifted
4 eggs, lightly beaten
300 ml (10½ fl oz) whipped cream
150 g (5½ oz) dark chocolate, chopped

1 Preheat the oven to 210°C (415°F/ Gas 6–7). Lightly grease two baking trays.
2 Combine the butter and 250 ml (9 fl oz/ 1 cup) of water in a large heavy-based saucepan. Stir over medium heat until the butter melts. Increase the heat, bring to the boil, then remove from the heat.
3 Add the flour to the saucepan all at once and quickly beat into the water with a wooden spoon. Return to the heat and continue beating until the mixture leaves the side of the pan and forms a ball. Transfer to a large bowl and cool slightly. Beat the mixture to release any remaining heat. Add the egg gradually, 3 teaspoons at a time. Beat thoroughly after each addition until all the egg has been added and the mixture is glossy.
4 Spoon the mixture into a piping (icing) bag fitted with a 1.5 cm (⁵/8 in) plain nozzle. Sprinkle the baking trays lightly with water. Pipe 15 cm (6 in) lengths onto the trays, leaving room for expansion.
5 Bake for 10–15 minutes. Reduce the heat to 180°C (350°F/Gas 4). Bake for 15 minutes, or until golden and firm. Cool on a wire rack.
6 Split each éclair, removing any uncooked dough. Fill the puffs with cream.
7 Put the chocolate in a heatproof bowl. Bring a saucepan of water to the boil and remove the pan from the heat. Sit the bowl over the pan, making sure the base of the bowl does not touch the water. Allow to stand, stirring, until the chocolate has melted. Spread over the tops of the éclairs.

PROFITEROLES WITH COFFEE MASCARPONE AND DARK CHOCOLATE SAUCE

Preparation time **30 minutes** +
Total cooking time **40 minutes**
Makes **16**

125 g (4½ oz/1 cup) plain (all-purpose) flour
70 g (2½ oz) unsalted butter, cubed
½ teaspoon salt
4 eggs, at room temperature

Filling
2 tablespoons instant coffee granules
1 tablespoon boiling water
225 g (8 oz/1 cup) mascarpone cheese
2 tablespoons icing (confectioners') sugar

Dark chocolate sauce
100 g (3½ oz/⅔ cup) chopped dark chocolate
20 g (¾ oz) unsalted butter
80 ml (2½ fl oz/⅓ cup) cream (whipping)

1 Preheat the oven to 200°C (400°F/Gas 6). Lightly grease two baking trays.
2 Sift the flour onto a large piece of baking paper. Put the butter, salt and 250 ml (9 fl oz/1 cup) of water into a saucepan and bring to the boil, stirring occasionally. Using the baking paper as a funnel, pour the flour into the boiling mixture. Reduce the heat to low, then beat until the mixture leaves the side of the pan and forms a ball.
3 Transfer the mixture to a bowl and set aside to cool until it is lukewarm. Using electric beaters, beat in the eggs, one at a time, until the mixture is thick and glossy.
4 Using two spoons, drop 16 balls of the mixture about 3 cm (1¼ in) in diameter and 3 cm (1¼ in) apart onto the trays. Bake for 20 minutes, or until puffed. Reduce the oven to 180°C (350°F/Gas 4). Bake for a further 10 minutes, or until golden brown.
5 Using a knife, slit the puffs to allow the steam to escape, then return them to the oven for 10 minutes, or until the insides are dry. Set aside to cool to room temperature.
6 Meanwhile, to make the filling, dissolve the instant coffee in the boiling water. Set aside to cool. Beat the coffee, mascarpone and icing sugar until just combined.
7 To make the dark chocolate sauce, put the chocolate, butter and cream in a heatproof bowl over a saucepan of simmering water, making sure the base of the bowl doesn't touch the water. Stir until combined. Set aside to cool slightly.
8 Just before serving, slit the profiteroles in half and sandwich together with the filling. Drizzle with the dark chocolate sauce.

APPLE STRUDEL

Preparation time **20 minutes**

Total cooking time **30 minutes**

Makes **2**

---

30 g (1 oz) unsalted butter

4 green cooking apples, peeled, cored and
  thinly sliced

2 tablespoons orange juice

1 tablespoon honey

55 g (2 oz/¼ cup) sugar

60 g (2¼ oz/½ cup) sultanas (golden raisins)

2 sheets ready-rolled puff pastry, thawed

25 g (1 oz/¼ cup) ground almonds

1 egg, lightly beaten

2 tablespoons soft brown sugar

1 teaspoon ground cinnamon

1 Preheat the oven to 220°C (425°F/Gas 7). Lightly grease two baking trays.

2 Heat the butter in a saucepan. Add the apple slices and cook for 2 minutes, or until lightly golden. Add the orange juice, honey, sugar and sultanas. Stir over medium heat until the sugar dissolves and the apple is just tender. Transfer the mixture to a bowl and leave until cool.

3 Place one sheet of pastry on a flat work surface. Fold it in half and make small cuts in the folded edge of the pastry at 2 cm (³/4 in) intervals. Open out the pastry and sprinkle with half of the ground almonds. Drain away the liquid from the apple and place half of the mixture in the centre of the pastry. Brush the edges with some of the lightly beaten egg, and fold together, pressing firmly to seal.

4 Place the strudel on a tray, seam side down. Brush the top with egg and sprinkle with half of the combined brown sugar and cinnamon. Repeat the process with the other sheet of pastry, remaining filling and the rest of the brown sugar and cinnamon.

5 Bake for 20–25 minutes, or until the pastry is golden and crisp. Serve hot with cream or ice cream, or at room temperature as a teatime treat.

Note Many types of fresh or tinned fruit, such as pears, cherries or apricots, can be used to make strudel. Just make sure that the fruit is well drained before using, or the pastry base will become soggy.

BLACKBERRY AND PEAR STRUDEL

Preparation time **30 minutes** +
Total cooking time **50 minutes**
Serves 6–8

120 g (4¼ oz) unsalted butter
½ teaspoon natural vanilla extract
4 pears, peeled, cored and chopped
1 teaspoon finely grated orange zest
½ lemon, juiced
5 sheets filo pastry
120 g (4¼ oz/1½ cups) fresh breadcrumbs
200 g (7 oz/1½ cups) blackberries
50 g (13/4 oz/½ cup) toasted flaked almonds
60 g (2¼ oz/½ cup) sultanas
105 g (3¾ oz/¾ cup) caster (superfine) sugar
icing (confectioners') sugar, to dust
custard or vanilla ice cream, to serve

1 Preheat the oven to 180°C (350°F/Gas 4). Lightly grease a baking tray.
2 Melt 100 g (3½ oz) of the butter with the vanilla.

3 Melt the remaining butter in a frying pan and sauté the pears over low heat for 5 minutes, or until tender. Transfer to a large bowl and add the orange zest and lemon juice. Toss lightly to combine.
4 Lay a sheet of filo pastry on a flat surface. Brush the melted butter over the pastry and sprinkle lightly with ⅕ of the breadcrumbs. Cover with another sheet of pastry and another ⅕ of the breadcrumbs and repeat the process until you have used all the pastry. Sprinkle the top of the pastry with the remaining breadcrumbs.
5 Add the blackberries, almonds, sultanas and caster sugar to the pear mixture and toss gently to combine.
6 Shape the filling into a log along one long edge of the pastry, leaving a 5 cm (2 in) border. Fold in the sides, then roll up and place, seam side down, on the tray. Brush with the remaining melted butter.
7 Bake for 40 minutes, or until golden brown. Dust with icing sugar and serve with custard or vanilla ice cream.

PUMPKIN PIE

Preparation time **30 minutes +**
Total cooking time **1 hour 20 minutes**
Serves **6–8**

Pastry

155 g (5½ oz/1¼ cups) plain (all-purpose) flour
100 g (3½ oz) unsalted butter, chilled and
   cubed
2 teaspoons caster (superfine) sugar
4 tablespoons iced water

750 g (1 lb 10 oz) butternut pumpkin, cubed,
   boiled, mashed and strained, then cooled
2 eggs, lightly beaten
185 g (6½ oz/1 cup) soft brown sugar
80 ml (2½ fl oz/⅓ cup) thick (double/heavy)
   cream
1 tablespoon sweet sherry or brandy
½ teaspoon ground ginger
½ teaspoon ground nutmeg
1 teaspoon ground cinnamon

1 Sift the flour into a bowl and rub in
the butter with your fingertips until the
mixture resembles breadcrumbs. Mix in
the caster sugar. Make a well in the centre,
add almost all the water and mix with a
flat-bladed knife, using a cutting action,
until the mixture comes together in beads.
2 Gather the dough and put on a floured
surface. Press into a ball and flatten. Cover
in plastic wrap. Refrigerate for 20 minutes.
3 Roll out the pastry between two sheets of
baking paper large enough to cover the
base and side of a 23 x 18 x 3 cm (9 x 7 x
1¼ in) pie dish. Line the dish with pastry,
trim the excess and crimp the edges
with a fork. Cover with plastic wrap and
refrigerate for 20 minutes.
4 Preheat the oven to 180°C (350°F/Gas 4).
Line the pastry shell with crumpled
baking paper.
5 Pour in baking beads and bake for
10 minutes, then remove the paper and
beads. Bake for a further 10 minutes, or
until lightly golden. Cool.
6 Whisk the eggs and sugar in a bowl. Stir
in the cooled pumpkin, cream, sherry and
the spices. Pour into the pastry shell and
bake for 1 hour, or until set—cover the
edges with foil if overbrowning. Cool.

TREACLE TART

Preparation time **30 minutes** +
Total cooking time **35 minutes**
Serves **4–6**

Shortcrust pastry

150 g (5½ oz/1¼ cups) plain (all-purpose) flour
90 g (3¼ oz) chilled unsalted butter, chopped
2–3 tablespoons iced water
1 egg, lightly beaten, to glaze

Filling

350 g (12 oz/1 cup) golden syrup or
    dark corn syrup
25 g (1 oz) unsalted butter
½ teaspoon ground ginger
140 g (5 oz/1¾ cups) fresh white breadcrumbs

icing (confectioners') sugar, to dust (optional)

1 To make the pastry, sift the flour into a large bowl. Using your fingertips, rub in the butter until the mixture resembles fine breadcrumbs. Add almost all the iced water and mix to a firm dough, with a flat-bladed knife, using a cutting action. Add more water if the dough is too dry. Turn onto a lightly floured work surface and gather together into a ball. Cover with plastic wrap and refrigerate for 20 minutes.

2 Brush a 20 cm (8 in) diameter flan (tart) tin with melted butter or oil. Roll out the pastry large enough to fit the base and side of the tin, allowing a 4 cm (1½ in) overhang. Ease the pastry into the tin and trim by running a rolling pin firmly across the top of the tin.

3 Re-roll the trimmed pastry to a rectangle 10 x 20 cm (4 x 8 in). Using a sharp knife or fluted pastry wheel, cut into long 1 cm (½ inch) strips. Cover the pastry-lined tin and strips with plastic wrap and refrigerate for 20 minutes.

4 Preheat the oven to 180°C (350°F/Gas 4). To make the filling, combine the golden syrup, butter and ginger in a saucepan and stir over low heat until the butter melts. Stir in the breadcrumbs until combined. Pour the mixture into the pastry case.

5 Lay half the pastry strips over the tart, starting at the centre and working outwards. Lay the remaining strips over the tart to form a lattice pattern. Brush the lattice with beaten egg.

6 Bake for 30 minutes, or until the pastry is lightly golden. Serve warm or at room temperature. Dust the top with icing sugar and serve with ice cream or cream.

BAKLAVA

Preparation time **20 minutes +**
Total cooking time **1 hour**
Makes **18 pieces**

560 g (1 lb 4 oz/2¼ cups) caster (superfine)
   sugar
1½ teaspoons lemon zest
90 g (3¼ oz/¼ cup) honey
60 ml (2 fl oz/¼ cup) lemon juice
2 tablespoons orange blossom water
200 g (7 oz/2 cups) walnuts, finely chopped
200 g (7 oz/1⅓ cups) shelled pistachio nuts,
   finely chopped
200 g (7 oz/1⅓ cups) almonds, finely chopped
2 tablespoons caster (superfine) sugar, extra
2 teaspoons ground cinnamon
375 g (13 oz) filo pastry
200 g (7 oz) unsalted butter, melted

1 Put the sugar, lemon zest and 375 ml
(13 fl oz/1½ cups) water in a pan and stir
over high heat until the sugar dissolves,
then boil for 5 minutes. Reduce the heat
and simmer for 5 minutes. Add the honey,
lemon juice and orange blossom water and
cook for 2 minutes. Remove from the heat
and refrigerate.
2 Preheat the oven to 170°C (325°F/
Gas 3). Grease a 30 x 27 cm (12 x 10½ in)
baking dish.
3 Cover the base with a single layer of
filo pastry and brush with melted butter,
folding in any overhanging edges. Layer
10 more sheets of filo. Store the remaining
filo under a damp tea towel (dish towel).
4 Combine the nuts, extra sugar and
cinnamon. Sprinkle half the nuts over the
pastry and pat down. Repeat the layering
and buttering of five more filo sheets,
sprinkle with the rest of the nuts, then
layer and butter the remaining filo,
brushing the top with butter and pat down.
Score into large diamonds. Pour any
remaining butter over the top.
5 Bake for 30 minutes, then reduce the
heat to 150°C (300°F/Gas 2) and cook for
30 minutes. Cut through the original
diamond markings, then strain the syrup
over the top. Refrigerate before serving.

YOGHURT TART WITH FIGS AND HAZELNUTS

Preparation time **1 hour +**
Total cooking time **15 minutes**
Makes 12

Pastry

150 g (5½ oz/1¼ cups) plain (all-purpose) flour
80 g (2¾ oz/¾ cup) ground hazelnuts
90 g (3¼ oz) unsalted butter, cubed
1 egg yolk, at room temperature

Filling

3 eggs, at room temperature
2 egg yolks, at room temperature
125 g (4½ oz/½ cup) caster (superfine) sugar
2 vanilla beans, split lengthway
200 g (7 oz/¾ cup) Greek-style yoghurt
30 g (1 oz/¼ cup) cornflour (cornstarch)
30 g (1 oz/¼ cup) plain (all-purpose) flour
7 figs, sliced
100 g (3½ oz) roasted hazelnuts, chopped
whipped cream, to serve

1 To make the pastry, put the flour, ground hazelnuts, butter and a pinch of salt in a food processor and process until the mixture resembles breadcrumbs. Add the egg yolk and 1 tablespoon of cold water. Process until the mixture just forms a ball. Turn out onto a work surface and flatten into a disc. Cover with plastic wrap and refrigerate for 30 minutes.

2 Preheat the oven to 180°C (350°F/Gas 4). Grease a 23 cm (9 in) shallow tart tin. Roll out the pastry on a lightly floured surface until 3 mm (⅛ in) thick. Transfer the pastry into the tin, prick the base with a fork and refrigerate for 10 minutes. Roll a rolling pin across the top of the tart tin to remove any excess pastry.

3 To make the filling, beat the eggs, egg yolks and sugar in a bowl until the sugar has dissolved. Scrape the seeds from the vanilla beans into the egg mixture and stir in the yoghurt. Combine the cornflour and plain flour and fold through the yoghurt mixture. Pour into the pastry case and top with the figs and hazelnuts.

4 Bake for 18–20 minutes, or until just set. Leave to cool in the tin, then remove and serve with whipped cream.

BAKED CUSTARD TARTS WITH RHUBARB

Preparation time **30 minutes +**
Total cooking time **1 hour 25 minutes**
Makes **8**

800 g (1 lb 12 oz) sweet shortcrust pastry
1/2 vanilla bean or 1/2 teaspoon natural vanilla
    extract
250 ml (9 fl oz/1 cup) milk
250 ml (9 fl oz/1 cup) pouring (whipping) cream
4 eggs
145 g (5 1/2 oz/2/3 cup) caster (superfine) sugar
400 g (14 oz) rhubarb, trimmed, then cut into
    2 cm (3/4 in) pieces
80 g (2 3/4 oz/1/3 cup) soft brown sugar
1/2 teaspoon ground cinnamon
1 teaspoon lemon juice

1 Preheat the oven to 200°C (400°F/Gas 6). Lightly grease eight loose-based tartlet tins, 10 cm (4 in) in diameter and 3 cm (1 1/4 in) deep.
2 Roll out the pastry on a lightly floured work surface to 3 mm (1/8 in) thick. Cut the pastry into rounds to fit the base and sides of the tins. Gently press in the sides to fit, trim the edges, then cover with plastic wrap and refrigerate for 30 minutes.
3 Line each of the pastry shells with a crumpled piece of baking paper and fill with baking beads or uncooked rice.
4 Bake for 15 minutes, then remove the paper and beads and bake for a further 7–8 minutes, or until golden. Reduce the oven to 160°C (315°F/Gas 2–3).
5 If using the vanilla bean, split it down the middle and scrape out the seeds. Combine the milk, cream, vanilla bean and seeds (or vanilla extract) in a saucepan, then bring just to the boil. Whisk the eggs and sugar in a bowl until thick and pale. Pour the milk mixture onto the egg mixture, whisking to combine well. Cool the custard, then strain into a bowl.
6 Pour the custard into the tartlet shells and bake for 25–30 minutes, or until the filling has just set. Remove from the oven.
7 Increase the oven to 180°C (350°F/Gas 4). Put the rhubarb, brown sugar, cinnamon, lemon juice and 2 teaspoons water in a small baking dish, toss to combine, then cover with foil and bake for 30 minutes. Remove the tartlets from the tins and just before serving spoon on the rhubarb and juices. Serve warm or at room temperature.

FRUIT MINCE PIES

Preparation time **30 minutes**
Total cooking time **25 minutes**
Makes **24**

Fruit mince

40 g (1 1/2 oz/1/3 cup) raisins, chopped
60 g (2 1/4 oz/1/3 cup) soft brown sugar
30 g (1 oz/1/4 cup) sultanas (golden raisins)
50 g (1 3/4 oz/1/4 cup) mixed peel (mixed
    candied citrus peel)
1 tablespoon currants
1 tablespoon chopped almonds
1 small apple, grated
1 teaspoon lemon juice
1/2 teaspoon finely grated orange zest
1/2 teaspoon finely grated lemon zest
1/2 teaspoon mixed (pumpkin pie) spice
pinch freshly grated nutmeg
25 g (1 oz) unsalted butter, melted
1 tablespoon brandy

Pastry

250 g (9 oz/2 cups) plain (all-purpose) flour
150 g (5 1/2 oz) chilled unsalted butter, cubed
85 g (3 oz/2/3 cup) icing (confectioners')
    sugar
2–3 tablespoons iced water

icing (confectioners') sugar, extra, to dust

1 To make the fruit mince, combine all the ingredients, spoon into a sterilised jar and seal. You can use it straightaway but the flavours develop if kept for a while.
2 Preheat the oven to 180°C (350°F/Gas 4). Lightly grease two 12-hole shallow patty pans or mini muffin tins.
3 To make the pastry, sift the flour into a bowl. Rub in the butter until the mixture resembles fine breadcrumbs. Stir in the icing sugar and make a well in the centre. Add almost all the water and mix with a flat-bladed knife, using a cutting action, until the mixture comes together in beads. Add the remaining water if the dough is too dry. Turn out onto a floured work surface and gather into a ball. Roll out two-thirds of the pastry and cut out 24 rounds, larger than the holes in the patty pans, with a round fluted cutter. Fit into the tins.
4 Divide the mince among the pastry cases. Roll out the remaining pastry, thinner than before, and cut 12 rounds with the same cutter. Using a smaller fluted cutter, cut 12 more rounds. Place the large circles on top of half the pies and press the edges. Place the smaller circles on the remainder.
5 Bake for 25 minutes, or until golden. Leave in the tins for 5 minutes, then lift out cool on wire racks. Dust with icing sugar.

PECAN PIE

Preparation time **30 minutes**
Total cooking time **1 hour 15 minutes**
Serves **6**

Shortcrust pastry
185 g (6½ oz/1½ cups) plain (all-purpose) flour
125 g (4½ oz) chilled unsalted butter, chopped
2–3 tablespoons chilled water

Filling
200 g (7 oz/2 cups) pecans
3 eggs, lightly beaten
50 g (1¾ oz) unsalted butter, melted and
    cooled
140 g (5 oz/¾ cup) soft brown sugar
170 ml (5½ fl oz/⅔ cup) light corn syrup
1 teaspoon natural vanilla extract

1 Preheat the oven to 180°C (350°F/Gas 4).
2 Sift the flour into a large bowl. Using your fingertips, rub in the butter until the mixture resembles fine breadcrumbs. Add almost all the water and mix with a flat-bladed knife, using a cutting action, until the mixture comes together in beads. Add more water if the dough is too dry. Turn out onto a lightly floured work surface and gather together into a ball.

3 Roll out the pastry to a 35 cm (14 in) round. Line a 23 cm (9 in) flan (tart) tin with the pastry. Trim the edges and refrigerate for 20 minutes.

4 Pile the pastry trimmings together, roll out on baking paper to a rectangle about 2 mm (1/16 in) thick, then refrigerate.

5 Line the pastry-lined tin with a sheet of baking paper and spread a layer of baking beads or uncooked rice over the paper.

6 Bake for 15 minutes, remove the paper and beads and bake for another 15 minutes, or until lightly golden. Cool completely.

7 Spread the pecans over the pastry base. Whisk together the eggs, butter, sugar, corn syrup, vanilla extract and a pinch of salt until combined, then pour over the nuts.

8 Using a fluted pastry wheel or small sharp knife, cut narrow strips from half of the pastry trimmings. Cut out small stars with a biscuit (cookie) cutter from the remaining trimmings. Arrange decoratively over the filling. Bake the pie for 45 minutes, or until firm. Allow to cool completely and serve at room temperature.

PEACH AND CUSTARD TART

Preparation time **30 minutes** +
Total cooking time **55 minutes**
Serves 6

185 g (6½ oz/1½ cups) plain (all-purpose) flour
2 tablespoons icing (confectioners') sugar
90 g (3¼ oz) unsalted butter, chilled, cut into
  cubes
2 large peaches
2 eggs, lightly whisked
2 tablespoons caster (superfine) sugar
160 ml (5¼ fl oz) thickened (whipping) cream
3/4 teaspoon ground nutmeg

1 Put the flour, icing sugar and butter in a food processor and process until the mixture resembles fine breadcrumbs. Add 3–4 tablespoons of iced water and pulse until the mixture comes together and forms a dough. Turn out onto a lightly floured surface and bring together in a ball. Cover with plastic wrap and place in the fridge for 20 minutes to rest.

2 Preheat the oven to 190°C (375°F/Gas 5). Lightly grease a 24 cm (9½ in) loose-bottomed fluted flan (tart) tin with melted butter, then place on a baking tray.
3 Roll out the pastry between two sheets of baking paper and line the prepared tin, trimming the edges. Line the pastry shell with a piece of crumpled baking paper, and pour in rice or beans to cover the base.
4 Bake in the oven for 15 minutes, then remove the paper and rice and bake for a further 10 minutes, or until the pastry is cooked and lightly golden in colour. Allow the pastry to cool.
5 Reduce the oven temperature to 170°C (325°F/Gas 3). Cut the peaches in half and remove the seeds. Finely slice the peaches and arrange in a circular pattern over the pastry base. Whisk together the eggs, sugar, cream and nutmeg. Carefully pour the mixture over the peaches.
6 Bake in the oven for 25–30 minutes, or until the mixture is just set. Allow to cool completely before serving.

LINZERTORTE

Preparation time **30 minutes** +
Total cooking time **30 minutes**
Serves **6–8**

100 g (3½ oz/⅔ cup) blanched almonds
185 g (6½ oz/1½ cups) plain (all-purpose) flour
½ teaspoon ground cinnamon
90 g (3¼ oz) chilled unsalted butter, cubed
55 g (2 oz/¼ cup) caster (superfine) sugar
1 egg yolk
2–3 tablespoons lemon juice or water
320 g (11¼ oz/1 cup) raspberry jam
1 egg yolk, extra, to glaze
80 g (2¾ oz/¼ cup) apricot jam

1 Grind the almonds in a food processor until they are the consistency of medium coarse meal.
2 Put the flour and cinnamon in a large bowl. Using your fingertips, rub in the butter until the mixture resembles fine breadcrumbs. Stir in the caster sugar and almonds. Make a well in the centre and add the egg yolk and lemon juice. Mix with a flat-bladed knife, using a cutting action, until the mixture comes together in beads.
3 Turn onto a lightly floured work surface and knead briefly until smooth. Wrap in plastic wrap and refrigerate for at least 20 minutes to firm.

4 Roll two-thirds of the pastry out between two sheets of baking paper into a circle to fit a 20 cm (8 in) round, loose-based, fluted flan (tart) tin. Press into the tin and trim away any excess pastry. Spread the raspberry jam over the base.
5 Roll out the remaining pastry, including any scraps, to a thickness of 3 mm (⅛ in). Cut it into 2 cm (¾ in) strips with a fluted cutter. Lay half the strips on a sheet of baking paper, leaving a 1 cm (½ in) gap between each strip. Interweave the remaining strips to form a lattice pattern. Invert the lattice on top of the tart, remove the paper and trim the edge with a sharp knife. Cover with plastic wrap and refrigerate for 20 minutes.
6 Preheat the oven to 180°C (350°F/Gas 4). Place a baking tray in the oven to heat.
7 Combine the extra egg yolk with 1 teaspoon water and brush over the tart. Place the tin on the heated tray and bake for 25–30 minutes, or until the pastry is golden brown.
8 Heat the apricot jam with 1 tablespoon of water, then strain the jam and brush over the tart while hot. Leave to cool in the tin, then remove and cut into wedges.
Note Fluted cutters or special lattice cutters are available from speciality kitchenware stores.

BAKEWELL TART

Preparation time **25 minutes** +
Total cooking time **55 minutes**
Serves **6**

125 g (4½ oz/1 cup) plain (all-purpose) flour
90 g (3¼ oz) unsalted butter, chilled and cubed
2 teaspoons caster (superfine) sugar
2 tablespoons iced water

Filling
90 g (3¼ oz) unsalted butter
80 g (2¾ oz/⅓ cup) caster (superfine) sugar
2 eggs, lightly beaten
3 drops natural almond extract
70 g (2½ oz/⅔ cup) ground almonds
40 g (1½ oz/⅓ cup) self-raising flour, sifted
160 g (5¾ oz/½ cup) raspberry jam
icing (confectioners') sugar, to dust

1 Preheat the oven to 180°C (350°F/Gas 4). Lightly grease a 20 cm (8 in) round, loose-based, fluted flan (tart) tin.
2 Sift the flour into a large bowl and rub in the butter, using your fingertips, until the mixture resembles fine breadcrumbs. Stir in the sugar. Make a well in the centre, then add almost all the water and mix with a flat-bladed knife, using a cutting action, until the mixture comes together in beads, adding more water if the dough is too dry.
2 Gather the dough together and roll out between two sheets of baking paper to cover the base and side of the tin. Line the tin with the pastry, trim the edges and refrigerate for 20 minutes.
3 Line the pastry with baking paper and spread a layer of baking beads or uncooked rice evenly over the paper.
4 Bake for 10 minutes, remove the paper and beads, then bake the pastry for a further 7 minutes, or until golden. Cool.
5 Beat the butter and sugar in a bowl using electric beaters until light and creamy. Add the egg gradually, beating after each addition. Add the almond extract and beat until combined. Transfer to a large bowl and fold in the almonds and flour.
6 Spread the jam over the pastry, then spoon the almond mixture on top. Bake for 35 minutes, or until risen and golden. Dust with icing sugar.

KEY LIME PIE

Preparation time **30 minutes +**
Total cooking time **40 minutes**
Serves **6–8**

375 g (13 oz) ready-made or home-made
   sweet shortcrust pastry
4 egg yolks
395 g (14 oz) tinned condensed milk
125 ml (4 fl oz/½ cup) lime juice
2 teaspoons grated lime zest
lime slices, to garnish
icing (confectioners') sugar, to dust
whipped cream, to serve

1 Preheat the oven to 180°C (350°F/Gas 4).
Grease a 23 cm (9 in) loose-bottomed
flan (tart) tin.
2 Roll the dough out between two sheets
of baking paper until it is large enough to
fit into the pie tin. Remove the top sheet of
paper and invert the pastry into the tin.
Use a small ball of pastry to help press the
pastry into the tin, allowing any excess to
hang over the sides. Use a small sharp knife
to trim away any extra pastry.
3 Line the pastry shell with a piece of
crumpled baking paper that is large enough
to cover the base and side of the tin and
pour in some baking beads or rice.
4 Bake for 10 minutes, remove the paper
and beads and return the pastry to the oven
for another 4–5 minutes, or until the base is
dry. Leave to cool.
5 Beat the egg yolks, condensed milk, lime
juice and zest in a large bowl using electric
beaters for 2 minutes, or until well
combined. Pour into the pie shell and
smooth the surface.
6 Bake for 20–25 minutes, or until set.
Allow the pie to cool, then refrigerate for
2 hours, or until well chilled. Garnish with
lime slices, dust with sifted icing sugar and
serve with whipped cream.

TARTE AU CITRON

Preparation time **30 minutes** +
Total cooking time **55 minutes**
Serves **8**

Pastry
350 g (2¾ cups) plain (all-purpose) flour
small pinch of salt
150 g (5½ oz) unsalted butter
100 g (3½ oz/¾ cup) icing (confectioners')
   sugar
2 eggs, beaten

Filling
4 eggs
2 egg yolks
275 g (9¾ oz/1¼ cups) caster (superfine)
   sugar
190 ml (6½ fl oz/¾ cup) thick (double) cream
250 ml (9 fl oz/1 cup) lemon juice
finely grated zest of 3 lemons

1 To make the pastry, sift the flour and salt onto a work surface and make a well. Put the butter into the well and work, using a pecking action with your fingertips and thumb, until it is very soft. Add the sugar to the butter and mix. Add the eggs to the butter and mix. Gradually incorporate the flour, flicking it onto the mixture, then chop through it until you have a rough dough. Bring together, knead a few times to make a smooth dough, then roll into a ball. Cover with plastic wrap and refrigerate for at least 1 hour.

2 Preheat the oven to 190°C (375°F/Gas 5). Roll out the pastry to line a 23 cm (9 in) round loose-based fluted flan (tart) tin. Chill for 20 minutes.

3 To make the filling, whisk together the eggs, egg yolks and sugar. Add the cream, whisking all the time, then the lemon juice and zest.

4 Blind bake the pastry for 10 minutes, then remove the paper and bake for a further 3–5 minutes, or until the pastry is just cooked. Remove from the oven and reduce the oven to 150°C (300°F/Gas 2). Put the tin on a baking tray and carefully pour the filling into the pastry case. Return to the oven for 35–40 minutes, or until set. Cool before serving.

PEAR AND ALMOND FLAN

Preparation time **30 minutes +**
Total cooking time **1 hour 10 minutes**
Serves **8**

155 g (5½ oz/1¼ cups) plain (all-purpose) flour
90 g (3¼ oz) unsalted butter, chilled and chopped
60 g (2¼ oz/¼ cup) caster (superfine) sugar
2 egg yolks

Filling
165 g (6 oz) unsalted butter, softened
160 g (5¾ oz/⅔ cup) caster (superfine) sugar
3 eggs
230 g (8½ oz/2¼ cups) ground almonds
1½ tablespoons plain (all-purpose) flour
2 ripe pears, peeled, halved lengthways with cores removed

1 Grease a shallow 24 cm (9½ in) round flan (tart) tin with a removable base.
2 Put the flour, butter and caster sugar in a food processor and process until the mixture resembles breadcrumbs. Add the egg yolks and about 1 tablespoon of water until the mixture just comes together. Turn out onto a floured surface and gather into a ball. Cover in plastic wrap and refrigerate for 30 minutes. Preheat the oven to 180°C (350°F/Gas 4).
3 Roll the pastry between baking paper dusted with flour and line the tin with the pastry. Trim off any excess. Prick the base a few times. Blind bake the pastry for 10 minutes. Remove the paper and beads and bake for 10 minutes.
4 To make the filling, mix the butter and sugar with electric beaters for 30 seconds. Add the eggs one at a time, beating after each addition. Fold in the ground almonds and flour and spread the filling over the cooled base.
5 Cut the pears crossways into 3 mm (¼ in) slices, separate them slightly, then place on top of the tart to form a cross.
6 Bake for 50 minutes, or until the filling has set (the middle may still be a little soft). Cool in the tin, then refrigerate for 2 hours before serving.

MASCARPONE TART WITH BLUEBERRIES

Preparation time **25 minutes** +
Total cooking time **50 minutes**
Serves 4–6

Pastry

185 g (6½ oz/1½ cups) plain (all-purpose) flour
2 tablespoons caster (superfine) sugar
1 teaspoon finely grated lemon zest
90 g (3¼ oz/⅓ cup) sour cream
2–3 tablespoons light olive oil

250 g (9 oz/1¼ cups) mascarpone cheese
60 g (2¼ oz/¼ cup) sour cream
165 g (5¾ oz/¾ cup) caster (superfine) sugar
½ teaspoon finely grated lemon zest
1 teaspoon natural vanilla extract
2 tablespoons cornflour (cornstarch)
4 egg yolks
100 g (3½ oz/⅔ cup) blueberries
icing (confectioners') sugar, to serve

1 To make the pastry, put the flour, sugar, lemon zest, sour cream and a large pinch of salt in a small food processor. Blend for 8–10 seconds, or until combined. With the motor running, gradually add the olive oil, until the mixture resembles wet breadcrumbs. Remove from the processor and knead briefly to form a smooth ball. Cover with plastic wrap and chill for 30 minutes.

2 Preheat the oven to 190°C (375°F/Gas 5). Grease an 18 cm (7 in) loose-based flan (tart) tin. Roll out the pastry between two sheets of baking paper to a circle large enough to fit the prepared tin. Use the pastry to line the tin, then trim the edges. Line the pastry with a piece of crumpled baking paper and pour in baking beads or uncooked rice.

3 Bake for 12 minutes, then remove the paper and beads and bake for a further 8 minutes, or until golden. Set aside to cool for 10 minutes.

4 Meanwhile, put the mascarpone, sour cream and sugar in the processor. Process for 15–20 seconds, or until smooth. Add the lemon zest, vanilla, cornflour and egg yolks and process for 12–15 seconds.

5 Transfer the mixture to a metal bowl set over a saucepan of simmering water. Cook, stirring, for 30 minutes, or until the mixture is thickened. Spoon into the pastry case and level the surface. Sprinkle over the blueberries, pressing in gently. Set aside to cool. Serve dusted with icing sugar.

TARTLETS

These delicious tartlets can be made with either home-made or bought puff pastry. They can be made as four individual servings or shaped into two rectangles to serve 4 people as a light meal.

You will need 500 g (1 lb 2 oz) of home-made or purchased puff pastry. The pastry should be divided into two and each portion rolled between two sheets of baking paper.

If making four tartlets, cut out two 12 cm (5 in) circles of pastry from each portion, or for two long tartlets roll each portion of pastry into a rectangle 12 x 25 cm (5 x 10 in).

The topping variations are placed on the pastry shapes, leaving a 1.5 cm ($^1/2$ in) border. The tartlets are then baked in the top half of a preheated 200°C (400°F/ Gas 6) oven.

These tartlets are best served warm or hot. Serve with green salad leaves. They are best eaten on the day they are made.

TOPPINGS

Tapenade and anchovy

Spread 125 g (4$^1/2$ oz/$^1/2$ cup) tapenade evenly over the pastry, leaving a 1.5 cm ($^1/2$ in) border. Drain 45 g (1$^1/2$ oz) of tinned anchovies, cut into thin strips and arrange over the top of the tapenade.

Sprinkle 35 g (1$^1/4$ oz/$^1/3$ cup) grated parmesan cheese and 75 g (2$^1/2$ oz/$^1/2$ cup) grated mozzarella cheese over the top and bake for 10 minutes, or until risen and golden.

Mushroom, asparagus and feta

Heat 2 tablespoons oil in a frying pan, add 400 g (14 oz) sliced, small button mushrooms and 100 g (3$^1/2$ oz) thin asparagus spears and stir until softened. Remove from the heat, add 2 tablespoons chopped flat-leaf (Italian) parsley and 200 g (7 oz) chopped feta cheese. Stir and season. Spoon onto the pastry bases, leaving a 1.5 cm ($^1/2$ in) border. Bake for 10–15 minutes, until risen and brown.

Fried green tomato

Thinly slice 2 green tomatoes. Heat
1 tablespoon oil in a frying pan, add
$^{1}/_{2}$ teaspoon cumin and 1 crushed garlic
clove and cook for 1 minute. Add the
tomatoes in two batches and cook for
2–3 minutes each batch, adding more oil
and garlic if needed, until slightly softened.
Drain on paper towels.

Combine 90 g (3$^{1}/_{4}$ oz/$^{1}/_{3}$ cup) sour
cream, 2 tablespoons chopped basil and
2 tablespoons chopped flat-leaf (Italian)
parsley and set aside. Sprinkle 120 g (4 oz/
1 cup) grated cheddar cheese over the
centre of the pastry bases, leaving a 1.5 cm
($^{1}/_{2}$ in) border. Arrange the tomato over
the cheese and bake for 10 minutes. Place a
dollop of cream mixture in the middle and
sprinkle the tarts with another tablespoon
of shredded basil.

Italian summer

Heat 2 tablespoons olive oil in a saucepan
over low heat, add 2 sliced red onions and
cook, stirring occasionally, for 10 minutes.
Add 1 tablespoon each of balsamic vinegar
and soft brown sugar and cook for
10 minutes, or until soft and browned.
Remove from the heat, stir in 1 tablespoon
chopped thyme, then leave to cool. Spread
evenly over the pastry, leaving a 1.5 cm
($^{1}/_{2}$ in) border. Bake for 10 minutes. Drain
a 170 g (5$^{1}/_{2}$ oz) jar of quartered,
marinated artichokes and arrange over the
onion. Fill the spaces with 24 pitted black
olives and 6 quartered slices of lightly
rolled prosciutto. Drizzle with extra virgin
olive oil and garnish with thyme.

Cherry tomato and pesto

Spread 125 g (4$^{1}/_{2}$ oz/$^{1}/_{2}$ cup) pesto over
the pastry shapes, leaving a 1.5 cm ($^{1}/_{2}$ in)
border. Top with cherry tomatoes (you
will need about 375 g/12 oz) and 2 finely
sliced spring onions (scallions). Season and
bake for 10 minutes, or until golden.
Drizzle with extra virgin olive oil and
garnish with sliced spring onion.

QUICHES

Sift 215 g (7 oz/1³/4 cups) plain (all-purpose) flour into a bowl and add 100 g (3½ oz) chopped chilled butter. Rub the butter into the flour with your fingertips until it resembles fine breadcrumbs. Make a well in the centre and add 2 tablespoons iced water. Mix with a flat-bladed knife, using a cutting action, until the mixture comes together in beads. Add a little more water if the dough is too dry.

Turn out onto a lightly floured surface and gather into a ball. Cover with plastic wrap and refrigerate for 20 minutes.

Preheat the oven to 190°C (375°F/Gas 5). Roll out the pastry between two sheets of baking paper to fit a shallow loose-based 25 cm (10 in) flan (tart) tin. Lift the pastry into the tin and press it well into the sides. Trim off any excess by rolling a rolling pin across the top of the tin. Refrigerate the pastry for 20 minutes. Cover the shell with baking paper, fill evenly with baking beads or uncooked rice and bake for 15 minutes, or until the pastry is dried out and golden.

Cool slightly before filling with one of these fillings. For all these quiches, bake the pastry, then reduce the oven temperature to 180°C (350°F/Gas 4).

FILLINGS
Quiche Lorraine

Melt 30 g (1 oz) butter in a frying pan and cook 1 finely chopped onion and 3 finely chopped bacon slices over medium heat for 10 minutes. Cool, then spread over the cooled pastry.

Whisk together 3 eggs, 185 ml (6 fl oz/³/4 cup) pouring (whipping) cream and 40 g (1¼ oz) grated Gruyère cheese. Season. Pour over the onion and sprinkle with 40 g (1¼ oz) grated Gruyère and ¼ teaspoon nutmeg. Bake for 30 minutes, or until just firm.

Salmon

Drain and flake a 415 g (14³/4 oz) tinned red salmon and spread over the cooled pastry. Mix 4 lightly beaten eggs, 60 g (2¹/4 oz/¹/2 cup) grated cheddar cheese, 125 ml (4 fl oz/¹/2 cup) each of milk and pouring (whipping) cream, 4 sliced spring onions (scallions) and 4 tablespoons chopped flat-leaf (Italian) parsley. Pour over the salmon. Bake for 30 minutes or until set.

Crab

Make the pastry using the basic pastry recipe, then line two greased 12 cm (5 in) round, 4 cm (1¹/2 in) deep flan (tart) tins with the dough. Bake the pastry as directed in the basic recipe, then set aside to cool. Heat 20 g (³/4 oz) of butter in a frying pan and cook 1 thinly sliced onion until just soft. Remove from the pan and drain. Drain 200 g (7 oz) tinned crab meat and squeeze out any excess moisture. Spread the onion and crab over the cooled pastry. Mix 3 eggs, 185 ml (6 fl oz/³/4 cup) pouring (whipping) cream and 90 g (3¹/4 oz/³/4 cup) grated cheddar cheese in a bowl. Pour into the pastry case. Bake for 40 minutes, or until lightly golden and set.

Asparagus and artichoke

Trim 155 g (5¹/2 oz) asparagus, cut into bite-sized pieces and blanch the pieces in a saucepan of boiling salted water. Drain, then refresh in ice-cold water. Lightly beat together 3 eggs, 125 ml (4 fl oz/¹/2 cup) pouring (whipping) cream and 40 g (1¹/2 oz/ ¹/3 cup) grated Gruyère cheese, then season. Cut 140 g (5 oz) marinated artichoke hearts into quarters and spread over the cooled pastry, along with the asparagus. Pour on the egg and cream mixture and sprinkle with 60 g (2¹/4 oz/¹/2 cup) grated cheddar cheese. Bake for 25 minutes, or until the filling is set and golden.

VOL-AU-VENTS

Preparation time **20 minutes** +
Total cooking time **30 minutes**
Makes 4

250 g (9 oz) block ready-made puff pastry,
   thawed
1 egg, lightly beaten

Sauce and filling

40 g (1½ oz) butter
2 spring onions (scallions), finely chopped
2 tablespoons plain (all-purpose) flour
375 ml (13 fl oz/1½ cups) milk
your choice of filling (see Notes)

1 Preheat the oven to 220°C (425°F/Gas 7).
Line a baking tray with baking paper.
2 Roll out the pastry to a 20 cm (8 in)
square. Cut four circles of pastry with a
10 cm (4 in) cutter. Place the rounds onto
the tray and cut 6 cm (2½ in) circles into
the centre of the rounds with a cutter.
Place the baking tray in the refrigerator
for 15 minutes.
3 Using a floured knife blade, 'knock up'
the sides of each pastry round by making
even indentations about 1 cm (½ in) apart
around the circumference. This should
allow even rising of the pastry as it cooks.

The cases can be made ahead of time up to
this stage and frozen until needed.
Carefully brush the pastry with the egg,
avoiding the 'knocked up' edge.
4 Bake for 15–20 minutes, or until the
pastry has risen and is golden brown and
crisp. Cool on a wire rack.
5 Remove the centre from each pastry
circle and pull out and discard any partially
cooked pastry from the centre. The pastry
can be returned to the oven for 2 minutes
to dry out if the centre is undercooked.
The pastry cases are now ready to be filled
with a hot filling before serving.
6 To make the sauce, melt the butter in a
saucepan, add the spring onion and stir
over low heat for 2 minutes, or until soft.
Add the flour and stir for 2 minutes, or
until lightly golden. Gradually add the
milk, stirring until smooth. Stir constantly
over medium heat for 4 minutes, or until
the mixture boils and thickens. Season well.
Remove and stir in your choice of filling.
Note Add 350 g (12 oz) of any of the
following to your white sauce: sliced,
cooked mushrooms; peeled, deveined and
cooked prawns; chopped, cooked chicken
breast; poached, flaked salmon; cooked and
dressed crabmeat; oysters; and steamed
asparagus spears.

SPINACH PIE DIAMONDS

Preparation time **50 minutes** +
Total cooking time **50 minutes**
Makes 15

250 g (9 oz/2 cups) plain (all-purpose) flour
30 g (1 oz) butter, chopped
60 ml (2 fl oz/¼ cup) olive oil
125 ml (4 fl oz/½ cup) warm water
olive oil, extra, for brushing

Filling
420 g (15 oz) English spinach
1 leek, white part only, halved lengthways and
   thinly sliced
¼ teaspoon freshly grated nutmeg
2 teaspoons chopped dill
200 g (7 oz) feta cheese, crumbled
1 tablespoon dry breadcrumbs
3 eggs, lightly beaten
2 tablespoons olive oil

1 Grease a 3 cm (1¼ in) deep baking tin
with a base measuring 17 x 26 cm (6½ x
10½ in).
2 Sift the flour and ½ teaspoon salt into a
bowl. Rub the butter into the flour until it
resembles fine breadcrumbs. Pour in the oil
and rub it in. Make a well in the centre and
add enough water to form a supple dough.
Knead to bring the dough together. Cover

with plastic wrap and chill for 1 hour.
3 Trim away the bottom quarter from the
spinach stalks. Wash and shred the
remaining leaves and stalks. Pile the spinach
onto a tea towel (dish towel), twist and
squeeze out moisture. Put into a bowl with
the leek, nutmeg, dill, feta, breadcrumbs
and ½ teaspoon cracked black pepper.
4 Preheat the oven to 220°C (425°F/Gas 7).
Roll out just over half the dough on a
floured surface until large enough to line the
base and sides of the tin. Lift the dough into
the tin, pressing over the base and sides.
5 Add the eggs and oil to the spinach
mixture. Mix with your hand, but do not
overmix. Spoon into the pastry-lined tin.
6 Roll out the remaining pastry on a floured
surface until large enough to cover the tin.
Lift onto the tin and press the two pastry
edges together to seal. Trim the excess
pastry, then brush the top with a little extra
olive oil. Using a knife, mark into three
strips lengthways and then diagonally into
diamonds. Make two or three slits through
the top layer of pastry to allow the steam to
escape during cooking.
7 Bake the pie on the centre shelf for
45–50 minutes, or until well browned. Turn
out onto a wire rack to cool for 10 minutes,
then transfer to a cutting board or back into
the tin to cut into diamonds.

SAVOURY POTATO EMPANADAS

Preparation time **1 hour**
Total cooking time **40 minutes**
Makes **32**

60 ml (2 fl oz/¼ cup) olive oil
1 small onion, finely diced
2 spring onions (scallions), thinly sliced
1 garlic clove, crushed
100 g (3½ oz) minced (ground) beef
1 teaspoon ground cumin
1 teaspoon dried oregano
125 g (4½ oz) all-purpose potatoes, cubed
4 sheets frozen puff pastry, thawed
50 g (1¾ oz) black olives, pitted and quartered
1 hard-boiled egg, finely chopped
1 egg, separated
pinch paprika
pinch sugar

1 Heat 1 tablespoon of the oil in a heavy-based frying pan over medium heat. Add the onion and spring onion and stir for 5 minutes. Stir in the garlic and cook for 3 minutes. Remove and set aside.

2 Heat another tablespoon of oil in the pan, add the beef and stir until browned. Add the onion mixture and stir well.
3 Add the cumin, oregano, and season. Stir for a further 2 minutes. Transfer to a bowl.
4 Heat another tablespoon of oil in the pan, add the potato and stir over high heat for 1 minute. Reduce the heat to low and stir for 5 minutes, or until tender. Cool slightly and then mix into the beef mixture.
5 Preheat the oven to 200°C (400°F/Gas 6). Cut rounds from the pastry with an 8 cm (3 in) cutter. Grease two baking trays.
6 Spoon heaped teaspoons of the beef mixture onto one side of each pastry round, leaving a border wide enough for the pastry to be folded over. Put a few olive quarters and some chopped egg on top of the beef mixture. Brush the border with egg white. Fold the pastry over to make a half moon shape, pressing to seal. Press the edges with a floured fork, to decorate, and then transfer to the baking trays. Stir the egg yolk, paprika and sugar together and brush over the empanadas. Bake for 15 minutes, or until golden and puffed.

OLIVE AND ALMOND PALMIERS

Preparation time 30 minutes +
Total cooking time 20 minutes
Makes 24

75 g (2½ oz) black olives, pitted and chopped
95 g (3¼ oz/1 cup) ground almonds
25 g (1 oz) parmesan cheese, grated
2 tablespoons chopped basil
60 ml (2 fl oz/¼ cup) olive oil
2 teaspoons wholegrain mustard
2 sheets frozen puff pastry, thawed
60 ml (2 fl oz/¼ cup) milk

1 Preheat the oven to 200°C (400°F/Gas 6). Line two baking trays with baking paper.
2 In a food processor, process the olives, almonds, parmesan, basil, oil, mustard, ¼ teaspoon salt and ½ teaspoon cracked black pepper until they form a paste.
3 Lay out one sheet of pastry and cover evenly with half the olive-almond paste. Fold two opposite ends into the centre to meet. Fold the same way again.
4 Brush the pastry with the milk. Repeat the process with the remaining pastry and filling. Cut into 1.5 cm (⁵/₈ in) thick slices. Shape the slices into a V-shape, with the two sides curving out slightly. Place on the trays, leaving enough room for spreading.
5 Bake for 15–20 minutes, or until puffed and golden. Allow to cool on a wire rack. Serve at room temperature.
Notes Palmiers can be cooked up to 6 hours ahead and stored in an airtight container.
   You can also use ready-made olive paste.

ONION TART

Preparation time **40 minutes +**
Total cooking time **1 hour 30 minutes**
Serves **4–6**

Shortcrust pastry
150 g (5½ oz/1¼ cups) plain (all-purpose) flour
90 g (3¼ oz) chilled butter, cubed
2–3 tablespoons iced water

Filling
25 g (1 oz) butter
7 onions, sliced
1 tablespoon dijon mustard
3 eggs, lightly beaten
125 g (4½ oz/½ cup) sour cream
25 g (1 oz/¼ cup) freshly grated parmesan
   cheese

1 Lightly grease a round 23 cm (9 in) fluted flan (tart) tin.
2 Sift the flour into a bowl. Using your fingertips, rub in the butter until the mixture resembles fine breadcrumbs. Make a well in the centre, add almost all the water and mix with a flat-bladed knife, using a cutting action, until the mixture comes together in beads. Add more water if the dough is too dry.
3 Gather the dough together and lift out onto a lightly floured work surface. Press together until smooth, cover with plastic wrap and refrigerate for 20 minutes.
4 Roll out between two sheets of baking paper large enough to cover the base and side of the tart tin. Place the pastry in the tin and trim the edge. Cover with plastic wrap and refrigerate for 20 minutes.
5 Preheat the oven to 180°C (350°F/Gas 4). Line the pastry shell with a piece of baking paper and pour in some baking beads or uncooked rice. Bake for 10 minutes, remove the paper and beads and bake for another 10 minutes, or until lightly golden. Cool completely.
6 To make the filling, melt the butter in a heavy-based frying pan. Add the onion, cover and cook over medium heat for 25 minutes. Uncover and cook for a further 10 minutes, stirring, until golden. Cool.
7 Spread the mustard over the base of the pastry, then spread the onion over the mustard. Whisk together the eggs and sour cream and pour over the onion. Sprinkle with parmesan and bake for 35 minutes, or until set and golden.

TOMATO AND BOCCONCINI FLAN

Preparation time **30 minutes +**
Total cooking time **50 minutes**
Serves **6**

185 g (6½ oz/1½ cups) plain (all-purpose) flour
100 g (3½ oz) butter, chopped
1 egg
2 tablespoons cold water
5–6 roma (plum) tomatoes
salt, to sprinkle
1 tablespoon olive oil
8 bocconcini (fresh baby mozzarella cheese) (about 220 g/7¾ oz), sliced
6 spring onions (scallions), chopped
2 tablespoons chopped rosemary

1 Combine the flour and butter in a food processor. Process for 10 seconds, or until fine and crumbly. Combine the egg and water in a small bowl. With the motor constantly running, gradually add to the flour mixture and process until the mixture just comes together.
2 Turn out onto a lightly floured surface and knead to form a smooth dough. Refrigerate, covered with plastic wrap, for 20 minutes.
3 Preheat the oven to 210°C (415°F/ Gas 6–7). On a floured board, roll the pastry to fit a 23 cm (9 in) round, loose-based flan (tart) tin. Ease the pastry into the tin and trim the edges. Cut a sheet of baking paper to cover the pastry-lined tin. Place over the pastry then spread a layer of baking beads or uncooked rice over the paper.
4 Bake for 15 minutes, then remove the paper and beads and bake for a further 10 minutes, or until the pastry case is lightly golden, then cool. Reduce the oven to 180°C (350°F/Gas 4).
5 Cut the tomatoes in half, sprinkle with salt and drizzle with the oil. Place in an ovenproof dish, cut side up and bake for 15 minutes.
6 Arrange the tomatoes, cut side up, over the pastry. Place the bocconcini slices and spring onion between the tomatoes. Scatter with rosemary and season. Bake for 10 minutes. Remove from the oven and cool for 10 minutes before serving.

BOREK

Preparation time **1 hour**
Total cooking time **20 minutes**
Makes **24**

400 g (14 oz) feta cheese
2 eggs, beaten
2 large handfuls flat-leaf (Italian) parsley,
   chopped
375 g (13 oz) filo pastry
80 ml (2½ fl oz/⅓ cup) olive oil

1 Preheat the oven to 180°C (350°F/Gas 4).
Lightly grease a baking tray.
2 Crumble the feta into a large bowl
using your fingers. Mix in the eggs and
parsley and season with freshly ground
black pepper.
3 Cover the filo pastry with a damp tea
towel (dish towel) so it doesn't dry out.
Remove one sheet at a time. Brushing each
sheet lightly with olive oil, layer four
sheets on top of one another. Cut the
pastry into four 7 cm (2¾ in) strips.
4 Put 2 rounded teaspoons of the feta
mixture in one corner of each strip and fold
diagonally, creating a triangle pillow.
5 Put on the baking tray, seam side down,
and brush with olive oil. Repeat with the
remaining pastry and filling to make
24 parcels. Bake for 20 minutes, or
until golden.

VEGETABLE STRUDEL

Preparation time **30 minutes**

Total cooking time **35 minutes**

Serves **4–6**

12 English spinach leaves

2 tablespoons olive oil

1 onion, finely sliced

1 red capsicum (pepper), seeded, membrane
    removed and cut into strips

1 green capsicum (pepper), seeded, membrane
    removed and cut into strips

2 zucchinis (courgettes), sliced

2 slender eggplants (aubergines), sliced

6 sheets filo pastry

40 g (1½ oz) butter, melted

20 g (¾ oz) finely sliced basil leaves

60 g (2¼ oz/½ cup) grated cheddar cheese

2 tablespoons sesame seeds

1 Preheat the oven to 210°C (415°F/ Gas 6–7). Brush an oven tray with melted butter or oil.

2 Wash the spinach leaves thoroughly and steam or microwave them until they are just softened. Squeeze out any excess moisture and spread the leaves out to dry.

3 Heat the oil in a frying pan, add the onion and cook over medium heat for 3 minutes. Add the capsicum, zucchini and eggplant and cook, stirring, for 5 minutes, or until the vegetables have softened. Season and then set aside to cool.

4 Brush one sheet of filo pastry with melted butter and top with a second sheet. Repeat with the remaining pastry, brushing with butter between each layer. Place the spinach, cooled vegetable mixture, basil and cheese along one long side of the pastry, about 5 cm (2 in) in from the edge. Fold the sides over the filling, fold the short end over and roll up tightly.

5 Place the strudel, seam side down, on the prepared tray. Brush with the remaining melted butter and sprinkle with the sesame seeds. Bake for 25 minutes, or until golden brown and crisp.

Note This dish is best made just before serving. Serve sliced as a first course, or with a green salad as a main meal.

CORNISH PASTIES

Preparation time **35 minutes** +
Total cooking time **45 minutes**
Makes **6**

Shortcrust pastry

310 g (11 oz/2½ cups) plain (all-purpose) flour
125 g (4½ oz) chilled butter, cubed
80–100 ml (2½–3½ fl oz) iced water

165 g (5¾ oz) round steak, finely chopped
1 small potato, finely chopped
1 small onion, finely chopped
1 small carrot, finely chopped
1–2 teaspoons worcestershire sauce
2 tablespoons beef stock
1 egg, lightly beaten

1 Lightly grease a baking tray. Sift the flour and a pinch of salt into a large bowl. Using your fingertips, rub in the butter until the mixture resembles fine breadcrumbs. Make a well in the centre and add almost all the water. Mix together with a flat-bladed knife, using a cutting action, until the mixture comes together in beads. Add more water if the dough is too dry. Turn out onto a lightly floured work surface and form into a ball. Cover with plastic wrap and refrigerate for 20 minutes.

2 Preheat the oven to 210°C (415°F/ Gas 6–7). Mix together the steak, potato, onion, carrot, worcestershire sauce and stock in a bowl and season well.

3 Divide the dough into six portions. Roll out each portion to 3 mm (⅛ in) thick. Using a 16 cm (6¼ in) diameter plate as a guide, cut six circles. Divide the filling among the circles.

4 Brush the edges with beaten egg and bring the pastry together to form a semi-circle. Pinch the edges into a frill and place on the tray. Brush the pastry with beaten egg and bake for 15 minutes. Reduce the oven to 180°C (350°F/Gas 4) and cook for 25–30 minutes, or until golden.

CORN AND RED CAPSICUM TARTLETS

Preparation time **20 minutes**
Total cooking time **25 minutes**
Makes **about 36**

3 sheets frozen puff pastry, thawed
310 g (11 oz) tinned corn kernels, drained
150 g (5½ oz) red leicester cheese, grated
1 small red capsicum (pepper), finely chopped
2 eggs, lightly beaten
60 ml (2 fl oz/¼ cup) buttermilk
170 ml (5½ fl oz/⅔ cup) thick (double/heavy) cream
1 teaspoon dijon mustard
dash Tabasco sauce
snipped chives, to garnish

1 Preheat the oven to 200°C (400°F/Gas 6). Lightly grease three 12-hole round-based patty pans or mini muffin tins.

2 Using a 6 cm (2½ in) round pastry cutter, cut circles from the pastry sheets. Press the circles into the prepared tins and prick the bases all over with a fork.

3 Combine the corn, cheese and capsicum in a large bowl and season. Whisk the eggs, buttermilk, cream, mustard and Tabasco sauce in a measuring cup with a pouring lip.

4 Spoon some of the vegetable mixture into the pastry cases, then pour the egg mixture over the top until the cases are almost full.

5 Bake for 20–25 minutes, or until well risen and set. Serve cold. Garnish with snipped chives.

Note The tarts can be made up to a day ahead and refrigerated, covered, in an airtight container.

SILVERBEET PIE

Preparation time **40 minutes** +
Total cooking time **50 minutes**
Serves 6–8

Pastry

250 g (9 oz/2 cups) plain (all-purpose) flour
80 g (2¾ oz/½ cup) wholemeal (whole-wheat)
    plain (all-purpose) flour
125 g (4½ oz) butter, chopped
80 ml (2½ fl oz/⅓ cup) iced water

Filling

800 g (1 lb 12 oz) silverbeet (Swiss chard)
70 g (2½ oz/½ cup) chopped pistachio nuts
40 g (1½ oz/⅓ cup) chopped raisins
35 g (1¼ oz/⅓ cup) grated parmesan cheese
60 g (2¼ oz/½ cup) grated cheddar cheese
3 eggs
170 ml (5½ fl oz) pouring (whipping) cream
¼ teaspoon freshly grated nutmeg

1 egg, extra, lightly beaten, to glaze

1 To make the pastry, sift the flours into a bowl. Rub in the butter for 2 minutes, or until the mixture resembles breadcrumbs. Add almost all the water and mix with a flat-bladed knife, using a cutting action, until the mixture forms a firm dough.
2 Turn the dough onto a lightly floured work surface and press together until smooth. Roll out two-thirds of the pastry and line a greased 23 cm (9 in) pie dish. Wrap the remaining pastry in plastic wrap and refrigerate both for 20 minutes. Preheat the oven to 180°C (350°F/Gas 4).
3 To make the filling, remove the stems from the silverbeet and wash the leaves. Shred finely. Steam or microwave for 3 minutes, or until tender. Cool, squeeze thoroughly to remove any excess moisture and spread out to dry in separate strands.
4 Sprinkle the pistachios onto the pastry base. Combine the silverbeet, raisins and cheeses and spread over the pistachios.
5 Whisk the eggs with the cream and nutmeg. Pour over the silverbeet mixture.
6 Roll out the remaining pastry to cover the top of the pie and trim the edges with a sharp knife. Press the edges together to seal. Brush the pie top with the beaten egg and decorate with pastry trimmings.
7 Bake for 45 minutes, or until golden.

COUNTRY VEGETABLE PIES

Preparation time **50 minutes** +
Total cooking time **45 minutes**
Makes 6

Pastry

250 g (9 oz/2 cups) plain (all-purpose) flour
125 g (4½ oz) butter, chilled and cubed
2 egg yolks
2–3 tablespoons iced water

Filling

2 new potatoes, cubed
350 g (12 oz) butternut pumpkin (squash),
   cubed
100 g (3½ oz) broccoli, cut into small florets
100 g (3½ oz) cauliflower, cut into small florets
1 zucchini (courgette), grated
1 carrot, grated
3 spring onions (scallions), chopped
90 g (3¼ oz/¾ cup) grated cheddar cheese
125 g (4½ oz/½ cup) ricotta cheese
50 g (1¾ oz/½ cup) grated parmesan cheese
3 tablespoons chopped flat-leaf (Italian) parsley
1 egg, lightly beaten

1 To make the pastry, sift the flour into a bowl. Rub in the butter until the mixture resembles fine breadcrumbs. Make a well in the centre, add the egg yolks and the iced water and mix with a flat-bladed knife, using a cutting action, until the mixture comes together in beads.

2 Gently gather the dough together and lift out onto a lightly floured work surface. Press into a ball, cover with plastic wrap and refrigerate for at least 15 minutes.

3 To make the filling, steam or boil the potato and pumpkin for 10–15 minutes, or until just tender. Drain and cool. Combine with the broccoli, cauliflower, zucchini, carrot, spring onion, cheddar, ricotta, parmesan, parsley and beaten egg. Season.

4 Preheat the oven to 190°C (375°F/Gas 5). Grease six 10 cm (4 in) pie tins. Divide the pastry into six and roll each portion into a rough 20 cm (8 in) circle. Place the pastry in the tins, leaving the excess overhanging.

5 Divide the filling evenly among the pastry cases. Fold over the overhanging pastry, folding or pleating as you go. Place on a baking tray, cover and refrigerate for 15 minutes. Bake for 25–30 minutes, or until the pastry is golden brown. Serve hot.

GOAT'S CHEESE GALETTE

Preparation time **20 minutes +**
Total cooking time **1 hour 15 minutes**
Serves **6**

Pastry
125 g (4½ oz/1 cup) plain (all-purpose) flour
60 ml (2 fl oz/¼ cup) olive oil

Filling
1 tablespoon olive oil
2 onions, thinly sliced
1 teaspoon thyme
125 g (4½ oz) ricotta cheese
100 g (3½ oz) goat's cheese
2 tablespoons pitted niçoise olives
1 egg, beaten
60 ml (2 fl oz/¼ cup) pouring (whipping) cream

1 To make the pastry, sift the flour and a pinch of salt into a bowl and make a well in the centre. Add the olive oil and mix with a flat-bladed knife until crumbly. Gradually add 60–80 ml (2–2½ fl oz/¼–⅓ cup) water until the mixture comes together. Remove and pat together to form a disc. Refrigerate for 30 minutes.

2 Meanwhile, to make the filling, heat the oil in a frying pan. Add the onion, cover and cook for 30 minutes. Season and stir in half the thyme. Cool.

3 Preheat the oven to 180°C (350°F/Gas 4). Lightly flour the workbench and roll out the pastry to a 30 cm (12 in) circle. Put on a heated baking tray.

4 Spread the onion over the pastry, leaving a 2 cm (¾ in) border. Sprinkle the ricotta and goat's cheese evenly over the onion. Put the olives over the cheeses, then sprinkle with the remaining thyme. Fold the pastry border in to the edge of the filling, pleating as you go.

5 Combine the egg and cream, then pour over the filling. Bake in the lower half of the oven for 45 minutes, or until the pastry is golden.

RATATOUILLE TARTS

Preparation time **40 minutes**
Total cooking time **1 hour 10 minutes**
Makes **12**

Pastry

375 g (13 oz/3 cups) plain (all-purpose) flour
175 g (6 oz) chilled butter, chopped
125 ml (4 fl oz/^{1}/2 cup) iced water

Filling

1 eggplant (aubergine) (about 500 g/1 lb 2 oz)
60 ml (2 fl oz/^{1}/4 cup) oil
1 onion, chopped
2 garlic cloves, crushed
2 zucchini (courgettes), sliced
1 red capsicum (pepper), seeded, membrane
  removed and chopped
1 green capsicum (pepper), seeded, membrane
  removed and chopped
250 g (9 oz) cherry tomatoes, halved
1 tablespoon balsamic vinegar
125 g (4^1/2 oz/1 cup) grated cheddar cheese

1 Sift the flour into a bowl. Rub in the butter. Make a well in the centre and add the iced water. Mix until the dough just comes together. Gather into a ball and divide into 12 portions.

2 Grease 12 loose-based fluted flan (tart) tins measuring 8 cm (3^1/4 in) across the base and 3 cm (1^1/4 in) deep. Roll each portion of dough out on a sheet of baking paper to a circle a little larger than the tins. Lift into the tins and press into the sides. Refrigerate for 30 minutes. Preheat the oven to 200°C (400°F/Gas 6).

3 Put the tins on baking trays, prick the bases all over with a fork and bake for 20–25 minutes, or until golden. Cool.

4 Meanwhile, to make the filling, cut the eggplant into 2 cm (^{3}/4 in) cubes, put into a colander and sprinkle with salt. After 20 minutes, rinse, drain and pat dry.

5 Heat 2 tablespoons of the oil in a frying pan. Cook batches of the eggplant for 8–10 minutes, or until browned. Drain.

6 Heat the remaining oil, add the onion and cook until soft. Add the garlic and cook for 1 minute. Add the zucchini and capsicum and cook for 10 minutes, or until softened. Add the eggplant and tomatoes. Cook for 2 minutes. Transfer to a bowl, stir in the vinegar, then cover and cool.

7 Reduce the oven to 180°C (350°F/Gas 4). Divide the mixture among the pastry shells. Sprinkle with the cheddar and cook for 10–15 minutes.

SAUSAGE ROLLS

Preparation time **30 minutes**

Total cooking time **30 minutes**

Makes **36**

3 sheets frozen puff pastry, thawed

2 eggs, beaten

750 g (1 lb 10 oz) minced (ground) sausage
    meat

1 onion, finely chopped

1 garlic clove, crushed

80 g (2¾ oz/1 cup) fresh breadcrumbs

3 tablespoons chopped flat-leaf (Italian) parsley

3 tablespoons chopped thyme

½ teaspoon ground sage

½ teaspoon freshly grated nutmeg

½ teaspoon ground cloves

1 Preheat the oven to 200°C (400°F/Gas 6).
Lightly grease two baking trays.

2 Cut the pastry sheets in half and brush the edges with some of the beaten egg.

3 Mix half the remaining egg with the remaining ingredients in a large bowl, then divide into six even portions.

4 Pipe or spoon the filling down the centre of each piece of pastry, then brush the edges with some of the egg. Fold the pastry over the filling, overlapping the edges and placing the join underneath. Brush the rolls with more egg, then cut each into six short pieces. Cut two small slashes on top of each roll and put on the baking trays.

5 Bake for 15 minutes, then reduce the oven temperature to 180°C (350°F/Gas 4) and bake for a further 15 minutes, or until puffed and golden.

CHICKEN AND LEEK PIES

Preparation time **20 minutes**

Total cooking time **1 hour 10 minutes**

Serves 4

60 g (2¼ oz) butter
1 leek, thinly sliced
4 chicken breasts (about 200 g/7 oz each)
50 g (1¾ oz) plain (all-purpose) flour
250 ml (9 fl oz/1 cup) chicken and herb stock
300 ml (10½ fl oz) cream
155 g (5½ oz/1 cup) fresh or frozen peas, blanched
1 sheet ready-rolled puff pastry, thawed

1 Melt the butter in a large saucepan over medium heat and cook the leek for 2 minutes, or until soft. Add the chicken and cook for 45 minutes, or until cooked. Add the flour and cook, stirring, until it starts to bubble. Add the stock and cook until the mixture starts to thicken. Add the cream, reserving 1 tablespoon to glaze the pastry. Cook until the mixture just starts to boil. Stir in the peas. Season. Remove from the heat.

2 Preheat the oven to 200°C (400°F/Gas 6).

3 Divide the filling among four individual pie dishes or ramekins. Top with a circle of pastry, cut just bigger than the top of the dish, then press around the edges to seal. Brush the surface with the cream. Make a slit in the top to allow steam to escape.

4 Place the dishes on a metal tray and bake for 20–25 minutes, or until the pastry is golden.

BEEF PIE

Preparation time **35 minutes +**
Total cooking time **2 hours 45 minutes**
Serves 6

Filling
2 tablespoons oil
1 kg (2 lb 4 oz) trimmed chuck steak, cubed
1 large onion, chopped
1 large carrot, finely chopped
2 garlic cloves, crushed
250 ml (9 fl oz/1 cup) beef stock
2 tablespoons plain (all-purpose) flour
2 teaspoons thyme
1 tablespoon worcestershire sauce

Pastry
250 g (9 oz/2 cups) plain (all-purpose) flour
150 g (5½ oz) chilled butter, cubed
1 egg yolk
2–3 tablespoons iced water

1 egg yolk, to glaze
1 tablespoon milk, to glaze

1 Lightly grease a 23 cm (9 in) pie dish.
2 To make the filling, heat half of the oil in a frying pan and brown the meat in batches. Remove from the pan. Heat the remaining oil, add the onion, carrot and garlic and brown over medium heat.
3 Return the meat to the pan and stir in the flour. Cook for 1 minute, then remove from the heat and stir in the stock and flour. Add the thyme and worcestershire sauce and bring to the boil. Season to taste.
4 Reduce the heat to low, cover and simmer for 1½–2 hours, or until the meat is tender. During the last 15 minutes of cooking, remove the lid and allow the liquid to reduce so that the sauce is very thick and suitable for filling a pie. Cool.
5 To make the pastry, sift the flour into a bowl. Rub in the butter until it resembles fine breadcrumbs. Add the egg yolk and 2 tablespoons of the water and mix until the mixture comes together in beads. Turn out onto a floured work surface and gather together to form a smooth dough. Wrap in plastic wrap and refrigerate for 30 minutes.
6 Preheat the oven to 200°C (400°F/Gas 6). Divide the pastry in half and roll out one piece between two sheets of baking paper until large enough to line the pie dish. Line the dish with the pastry, fill with the cold filling and roll out the remaining pastry to cover the dish. Brush the pastry edges with water. Lay the pastry over the pie and press to seal. Trim any excess pastry. Re-roll the scraps to make shapes and press on the pie.
7 Cut steam holes in the top of the pastry. Beat together the egg yolk and milk and brush over the top of the pie. Bake for 20–30 minutes, or until golden.

STEAK AND KIDNEY PIE

Preparation time **20 minutes**
Total cooking time **1 hour 50 minutes**
Serves **6**

750 g (1 lb 10 oz) round steak, trimmed of
    excess fat and sinew
4 lamb kidneys
2 tablespoons plain (all-purpose) flour
1 tablespoon oil
1 onion, chopped
30 g (1 oz) butter
1 tablespoon worcestershire sauce
1 tablespoon tomato paste (concentrated
    purée)
125 ml (4 fl oz/1/2 cup) red wine
250 ml (9 fl oz/1 cup) beef stock
125 g (41/2 oz) button mushrooms, sliced
1/2 teaspoon dried thyme
4 tablespoons chopped flat-leaf (Italian) parsley
500 g (1 lb 2 oz) block ready-made puff pastry,
    thawed
1 egg, lightly beaten

1 Cut the steak into 2 cm (3/4 in) cubes.
Peel the skin from the kidneys, quarter
them and trim away any fat or sinew. Put
the flour in a plastic bag with the meat
and kidneys and toss gently.
2 Heat the oil in a frying pan, add the
onion and fry for 5 minutes, or until soft.
Remove from the pan with a slotted spoon.
Add the butter to the pan, brown the steak
and kidneys in batches and then return the
steak, kidneys and onion to the pan.
3 Add the worcestershire sauce, tomato
paste, wine, stock, mushrooms and herbs to
the pan. Bring to the boil, reduce the heat
and simmer, covered, for 1 hour, or until
the meat is tender. Season and allow to
cool. Spoon into a 1.5 litre (52 fl oz/
6-cup) pie dish.
4 Preheat the oven to 210°C (415°F/Gas
6–7). Roll the pastry between two sheets
of baking paper, to a size 4 cm (11/2 in)
larger than the pie dish. Cut thin strips
from the edge of the pastry and press onto
the rim of the dish, sealing the joins. Place
the pastry on the pie, trim the edges and
cut two steam holes in the pastry. Decorate
the pie with leftover pastry and brush the
top with egg.
5 Bake for 35–40 minutes, or until the
pastry is golden.

LAMB AND FILO PIE

Preparation time **20 minutes**

Total cooking time **55 minutes**

Serves **6**

2 tablespoons oil

2 onions, chopped

1 garlic clove, chopped

1 teaspoon ground cumin

1 teaspoon ground coriander

½ teaspoon ground cinnamon

1 kg (2 lb 4 oz) minced (ground) lamb

3 tablespoons chopped flat-leaf (Italian) parsley

2 tablespoons chopped mint

1 tablespoon tomato paste (concentrated purée)

10 sheets filo pastry

250 g (9 oz) butter, melted

1 Heat the oil in a large frying pan. Add the onion and garlic and cook for about 3 minutes, or until just soft. Add the cumin, coriander and cinnamon to the pan and cook, stirring continuously, for 1 minute. Add the lamb to the pan and cook over medium heat for 10 minutes, or until the meat is brown and all the liquid has evaporated. Use a fork to break up any lumps of meat. Add the herbs, tomato paste and ¼ teaspoon salt and mix well. Cool.

2 Preheat the oven to 180°C (350°F/Gas 4). Lightly grease a 23 x 33 cm (9 x 13 in) ovenproof dish.

3 Remove three sheets of filo. Cover the remainder with a damp tea towel (dish towel) to prevent them drying out. Brush the top sheet of filo with melted butter. Cover with another two sheets of filo and brush the top one with butter. Line the ovenproof dish with these sheets, leaving the excess overhanging the dish.

4 Spread the lamb mixture over the pastry and fold the overhanging pastry over the filling. Butter two sheets of filo, place one on top of the other and fold in half. Place over the top of the filling and tuck in the edges. Butter the remaining sheets of filo, cut into squares and then scrunch over the top of the pie.

5 Bake for 40 minutes, or until golden.

POTATO PIES

Preparation time **25 minutes**

Total cooking time **1 hour 5 minutes**

Makes **6**

1 kg (2 lb 4 oz) all-purpose potatoes, chopped

1 tablespoon oil

1 onion, finely chopped

1 garlic clove, crushed

500 g (1 lb 2 oz) minced (ground) beef

2 tablespoons plain (all-purpose) flour

500 ml (17 fl oz/2 cups) beef stock

2 tablespoons tomato paste (concentrated
    purée)

1 tablespoon worcestershire sauce

500 g (1 lb 2 oz) shortcrust (pie) pastry

50 g (1$^{3}/_{4}$ oz) butter, softened

60 ml (2 fl oz/$^{1}/_{4}$ cup) milk

1 Boil the potatoes for about 10 minutes, or until tender. Drain, then mash.

2 Preheat the oven to 210°C (415°F/ Gas 6–7). Grease six 11 cm (4$^{1}/_{4}$ in) pie tins.

3 Heat the oil in a frying pan, add the onion and cook for 5 minutes, or until soft. Add the garlic and cook for 1 minute. Add the beef and cook over medium heat for 5 minutes, or until browned, breaking up any lumps with a fork.

4 Sprinkle the flour over the meat and stir to combine. Add the stock, tomato paste, worcestershire sauce and some salt and pepper to the pan and stir for 2 minutes. Bring to the boil, then reduce the heat slightly and simmer for 5 minutes, or until the mixture has reduced and thickened. Allow to cool completely.

5 Roll out the pastry between two sheets of baking paper and, using a plate as a guide, cut the pastry into 15 cm (6 in) circles and line the pie tins. Cut baking paper to cover each tin, spread baking beads or uncooked rice over the paper and bake for 7 minutes. Remove the paper and beads and cook the pastry for a further 5 minutes. Cool.

6 Divide the meat filling among the pastry cases. Stir the butter and milk into the mashed potato and pipe or spread all over the top of the meat filling. Bake for 20 minutes, or until lightly golden.

BAKED DESSERTS

Baked desserts are the stuff of childhood dreams ... reminiscences of chilly afternoons and the hot rush of spicy-sweet air when the oven door is opened. The majority of the recipes in this chapter are real old-fashioned favourites—crumbles and cobblers, soufflés and puddings. Comfort food to warm and nurture; often an irresistible combination of autumn fruits and buttery doughs. But that's not to say this is strictly a cold-weather chapter ... the truly dedicated can enjoy their baked desserts all year round.

ABOUT BAKED DESSERTS

Dessert is a luxury, a sweet indulgence that signals the end of a meal. However, desserts, or puddings, weren't always the sweet dishes we enjoy today.

In the Middle Ages puddings made from a mixture of grain and dried fruit were assembled in a thick cloth (or animal gut) and cooked in large pans of boiling water. The blancmange of medieval England was a thick gruel made with almonds, milk, rice and chicken, and has evolved to become a sweet custard thickened with gelatine and set in moulds.

Although cane syrup, honey and fruit have been used as sweeteners for thousands of years, sugar only reached the Western world in the 14th century. Then, sugar was called white gold as it was very expensive. It was used in medicines, to cover the bitter taste, and was the domain of only the very wealthy, who sprinkled it on just about everything. By the 18th century, sugar became more plentiful, prices dropped, and sugar became readily available to all—and so the sweet dessert was born.

Today there are hundreds of different types of desserts and these dishes are often made using a traditional baking method—whisking eggs for a soufflé, creaming butter and sugar for a sponge pudding, or making pastry for a cheesecake crust.

Desserts are enjoyed the world over—different cultures have their own versions yet it is surprising how similar they can be. Such as sweet rice pudding, which comes in many forms, from India, Greece and Italy, to the sticky black rice puddings eaten in Thailand.

There's something quite decadent about finishing off a delicious meal with a rich baked dessert. It brings a lovingly prepared meal to a close with a fanfare, not a whimper. Desserts are an exquisite indulgence and should be enjoyed often.

MORE ABOUT BAKED DESSERTS

Bread and butter pudding
Bread and butter pudding can be made with all sorts of bread or cake leftovers. Croissants, Danish pastries, panettone, brioche and any kind of fruit loaf and buns make luscious bread and butter puddings.

Clafoutis
A clafoutis (pronounced 'clafootee') is a classic French batter pudding, a speciality of the Limousin region. Clafoutis comes from Clafir, a dialect verb meaning 'to fill'. It is traditionally made with cherries. Other berries such as blueberries, blackberries, raspberries, or strawberries may be used.

Cobbler
These are simple fruit desserts, with a topping, that are served straight from the oven. Cobblers are topped with a scone-type dough, in shapes like cobbles.

Crumbles
Crumbles are topped with a rubbed-in mixture of flour, butter and sugar. Additions such as nuts and oats vary the flavour and texture. They can also be topped with biscuit crumbs, muesli and breadcrumbs.

Rice pudding
Short-grain rice is traditionally used for rice pudding, as the starch in the grains breaks down to thicken the pudding and give it a creamy quality. Short-grain rice is also much more absorbent.

Soufflé
A soufflé is a light and fluffy dish made with either a sweet or savoury base into which beaten egg whites are gently folded. A sweet soufflé is based on a custard-type base or fruit purée and may include liqueur, melted chocolate, nuts and fruit.

Crème brûlée
A thick, rich egg custard baked in individual ramekins. The top is sprinkled with sugar and heated to form a caramel topping.

Crème caramel
A smooth, rich egg custard made in individual moulds or ramekins, coated in hot caramel and filled with custard.

HINTS AND TIPS

1 Always read the recipe through before you start cooking and make sure you have all the ingredients ready and the correct equipment necessary. Preheat the oven.

2 Have the baking dish, or dishes, greased and lined (as necessary) before you start.

3 Measure a dish using its liquid capacity.

4 If using butter to grease a baking dish, first melt in a small saucepan over a low heat or in the microwave on medium for 30 seconds. Use a pastry brush to brush thoroughly and evenly over the inside of the dish.

5 If using ready-made frozen pastry, allow it to thaw completely before use.

6 If whisking egg whites, make sure you use clean beaters and a clean, dry bowl or the whites will not whisk to their full volume.

7 When a recipe requires a dish to be baked in a roasting tin filled with boiling water, make sure the kettle is filled, boiled and ready to pour as soon as it is needed. You may prefer to fill the dish with boiling water once the roasting tin is sitting on the oven tray. This will prevent you from having to carefully carry a tray filled with boiling water to the oven.

8 Always use oven gloves when you transfer a tin filled with boiling water: the tin may not be hot but the water is.

9 Always use oven gloves when you are unmoulding a hot pudding.

10 Before cooking your soufflé, run your thumb or a knife around the inside rim of the dish, between the dish and the mixture. This ridge helps the soufflé to rise evenly.

11 Once your soufflé is poured into the dish, it should be baked immediately in a preheated oven on a preheated baking tray so that the egg white will puff and set on cooking. Once cooked, serve the soufflé straightaway before it collapses.

12 When baking a soufflé, never open the oven door until the cooking time is reached.

13 When making bread and butter pudding, it is very important that you use good-quality bread. Ordinary sliced white bread will tend to go a bit claggy when it soaks up the milk.

14 When making a clafoutis, use a shallow pie plate or the top will not turn a lovely golden brown.

15 When making bread and butter pudding, a sprinkling of demerara sugar or crushed sugar cubes will give a crunchy topping. For a shiny top, glaze the hot pudding with apricot jam.

16 To get that perfect smooth, creamy texture when making crème caramel is ensuring that the water in the bain-marie does not bubble, causing the custard to bubble.

BREAD AND BUTTER PUDDING

Preparation time **30 minutes**

Total cooking time **35 minutes**

Serves **4**

50 g (1³/₄ oz) unsalted butter

8 thick slices day-old white bread

1 teaspoon ground cinnamon

2 tablespoons sultanas

3 eggs

1 egg yolk

3 tablespoons caster (superfine) sugar

250 ml (9 fl oz/1 cup) milk

500 ml (17 fl oz/2 cups) pouring (whipping) cream

¹/₂ teaspoon natural vanilla extract

1 tablespoon demerara sugar

1 Preheat the oven to 180°C (350°F/Gas 4). Melt 10 g (¹/₄ oz) of the butter and grease a 1.5 litre (52 fl oz/6-cup) ovenproof dish.
2 Spread the bread very lightly with the remaining butter and cut each slice in half diagonally. Layer the bread in the prepared dish, sprinkling the cinnamon and sultanas between each layer.
3 Lightly whisk together the eggs, egg yolk and caster sugar in a large bowl.
4 Heat the milk with the cream until just warm and stir in the vanilla extract.
5 Whisk the cream mixture into the egg mixture. Strain the custard over the layered bread, then leave for 5 minutes. Sprinkle with the demerara sugar.
6 Bake for 30 minutes, or until the custard has set and the bread is golden brown.

APPLE CRUMBLE

Preparation time **25 minutes**
Total cooking time **1 hour 15 minutes**
Serves **4**

8 apples
90 g (3¼ oz/⅓ cup) caster (superfine) sugar
zest of 1 lemon
120 g (4 oz) butter
125 g (4½ oz/1 cup) plain (all-purpose)
    flour
1 teaspoon ground cinnamon
thick (double/heavy) cream, to serve

1 Preheat the oven to 180°C (350°/Gas 4).
2 Peel and core the apples, then cut into chunks. Put the apple, 2 tablespoons of the sugar and the lemon zest in a small baking dish and mix to combine. Dot 40 g (1½ oz) of butter over the top.
3 Rub the remaining butter into the flour until you have a texture that resembles coarse breadcrumbs.
4 Stir in the rest of the sugar and the cinnamon. Add 1–2 tablespoons of water and stir the crumbs together so they form bigger clumps. Sprinkle the crumble mixture over the apple.
5 Bake for 1 hour 15 minutes, or until the top is browned and the juice is bubbling up through the crumble. Serve warm with thick cream.

PASSIONFRUIT SOUFFLÉ

Preparation time **30 minutes**
Total cooking time **30 minutes**
Serves 4

caster (superfine) sugar, for lining
40 g (1½ oz) unsalted butter
2 tablespoons plain (all-purpose) flour
185 ml (6 fl oz/¾ cup) milk
125 g (4½ oz/½ cup) caster (superfine) sugar
250 ml (9 fl oz/1 cup) fresh passionfruit pulp
   (about 7 large passionfruit)
6 egg whites
icing (confectioners') sugar, to dust

1 Preheat the oven to 180°C (350°F/Gas 4). Put a baking tray in the oven to heat. Lightly grease four 300 ml (10½ fl oz) ovenproof ramekins with oil and sprinkle the base and side with caster sugar, shaking out any excess.
2 Melt the butter in a saucepan over medium heat, add the flour and stir for 1 minute, or until foaming. Remove from the heat and gradually add the milk. Return to the heat and stir for 5–6 minutes, or until the sauce boils and thickens. Reduce the heat and simmer, stirring, for 2 minutes. Transfer to a bowl and stir in the sugar and passionfruit pulp.
3 Beat the egg whites in a clean, dry bowl using electric beaters until firm peaks form.
4 Using a metal spoon, fold a large dollop of the beaten egg white into the passionfruit mixture, then gently fold in the remaining egg white. Make sure you fold the mixture quickly and lightly to incorporate all of the egg white, without losing volume.
5 Spoon the mixture into the ramekins. Place on the baking tray and bake for 18–20 minutes, or until golden and well risen but still a bit wobbly. Dust with icing sugar and serve immediately.

CHOCOLATE SOUFFLÉ

Preparation time **25 minutes**
Total cooking time **20 minutes**
Makes 6

melted butter, to grease
caster (superfine) sugar, to dust
175 g (6 oz/1¼ cups) chopped good-quality
   dark chocolate
5 egg yolks, lightly beaten
60 g (2¼ oz/¼ cup) caster (superfine) sugar
7 egg whites
icing (confectioners') sugar, to dust

1 Preheat the oven to 200°C (400°F/Gas 6). Put a baking tray in the oven to heat. Wrap a double layer of baking paper around 6 x 250 ml (9 fl oz/1 cup) ramekins to come 3 cm (1¼ in) above the rim and secure with string. Brush the ramekins with melted butter and sprinkle the base and side with caster sugar, shaking out any excess.
2 Put the chocolate in a large heatproof bowl. Place over a saucepan of simmering water, making sure the base of the bowl doesn't touch the water. Stir until the chocolate is melted and smooth, then remove the bowl from the saucepan.
3 Stir the egg yolks and caster sugar into the chocolate.
4 Beat the egg whites until firm peaks form. Gently fold one-third of the egg whites into the chocolate mixture to loosen it. Then, using a metal spoon, fold in the remaining egg whites until just combined.
5 Spoon the mixture into the prepared ramekins and run your thumb or a blunt knife around the inside rim of the dish and the edge of the mixture.
6 Place the ramekins on the preheated baking tray and bake for 12–15 minutes, or until well risen and just set. Do not open the oven door while the soufflés are baking. Cut the string and remove the paper collars. Dust with icing sugar and serve immediately.

SPICED QUINCE CHARLOTTE

Preparation time **30 minutes** +
Total cooking time **30 minutes**
Serves **4–6**

460 g (1 lb/2 cups) caster (superfine) sugar
1 vanilla bean
1 cinnamon stick
1 teaspoon ground allspice
1.5 kg (3 lb 5 oz) quinces, peeled, quartered
　and cored
unsalted butter
2 loaves thinly sliced brioche
crème anglaise, to serve (optional)

1 Preheat the oven to 180°C (350°F/Gas 4).
2 Combine 1 litre (35 fl oz/4 cups) water
and the sugar in a saucepan and stir over
medium heat until the sugar dissolves.
3 Split the vanilla bean down the middle
and scrape out the seeds. Put the bean and
its seeds in the saucepan with the cinnamon
and allspice. Remove from the heat.
4 Place the quinces in a roasting tin or
baking dish and pour over the syrup. Cover

with foil and bake for 2 hours, or until the
fruit is very tender. Drain the quinces.
5 Butter the slices of brioche. Cut out a
circle from two slices of brioche (cut a half-
circle from each slice), large enough to fit
the base of a 2 litre (70 fl oz/8 cup)
capacity charlotte mould or ovenproof
bowl. Reserving 4 slices of brioche for the
top, cut the remaining brioche into 2 cm
($^3/_4$ in) wide fingers, and long enough to fit
the height of the mould. Press the brioche
vertically around the side of the dish,
overlapping the strips slightly.
6 Put the quinces in the brioche-lined
mould and cover with the reserved slices
of brioche.
7 Sit the mould on a baking tray and bake
for 25–30 minutes. Allow to cool for
10 minutes, then unmould onto a serving
plate. Serve with crème anglaise, if desired.
Note Brioche is a rich, buttery bread that
has an almost cake-like texture. It is
available from most bakeries. If preferred,
substitute with 1 loaf of sliced white bread
(crusts removed).

QUEEN OF PUDDINGS

Preparation time **30 minutes +**
Total cooking time **50 minutes**
Serves **6**

500 ml (17 fl oz/2 cups) milk
50 g (1³/₄ oz) unsalted butter
140 g (5 oz/1³/₄ cups) fresh breadcrumbs
115 g (4 oz/½ cup) caster (superfine) sugar,
   plus 1 tablespoon extra
finely grated zest of 1 orange
5 eggs, separated
210 g (7½ oz/²/₃ cup) orange marmalade
1 teaspoon honey
whipped cream, to serve

1 Preheat the oven to 180°C (350°F/Gas 4).
Lightly grease a 1.25 litre (44 fl oz/5 cup)
rectangular ovenproof dish.
2 Combine the milk and butter in a small
saucepan and heat over low heat until the
butter has melted. Put the breadcrumbs,
the extra sugar and orange zest in a large
bowl. Stir in the milk mixture and set aside
for 10 minutes.
3 Lightly whisk the egg yolks, then stir
them into the breadcrumb mixture.
4 Spoon into the prepared dish, then bake
for 25–30 minutes, or until firm to touch.
5 Combine the marmalade and honey in a
saucepan and heat over low heat until
melted. Pour evenly over the pudding.
6 Whisk the egg whites in a clean, dry
bowl until stiff peaks form. Gradually add
the sugar, whisking well, until the mixture
is glossy and the sugar has dissolved.
7 Spoon the meringue evenly over the top
of the pudding. Bake for 12–15 minutes, or
until the meringue is golden. Serve the
pudding warm with whipped cream.

RHUBARB AND BERRY CRUMBLE

Preparation time **25 minutes** +

Total cooking time **35 minutes**

Serves 4

850 g (1 lb 14 oz) rhubarb, cut into 2.5 cm
(1 in) lengths
150 g (5½ oz/1¼ cups) blackberries
1 teaspoon grated orange zest
250 g (9 oz/1 cup) caster (superfine) sugar
125 g (4½ oz/1 cup) plain (all-purpose) flour
115 g (4 oz/1 cup) ground almonds
½ teaspoon ground ginger
150 g (5½ oz) chilled unsalted butter, cubed
thick (double/heavy) cream or ice cream,
to serve (optional)

1 Preheat the oven to 180°C (350°F/Gas 4). Lightly grease a deep 1.5 litre (52 fl oz/ 6-cup) ovenproof dish.

2 Bring a saucepan of water to the boil over high heat, add the rhubarb, and cook for 2 minutes, or until just tender. Drain well and combine with the berries, orange zest and 90 g (3¼ oz/⅓ cup) of the caster sugar. Taste and add more sugar if needed. Spoon the fruit mixture into the prepared dish.

3 To make the topping, combine the flour, ground almonds, ginger and the remaining sugar. Rub the butter into the flour mixture with your fingertips until it resembles coarse breadcrumbs. Sprinkle the crumble mix over the fruit, pressing lightly. Don't press it down too firmly, or it will become flat and dense.

4 Put the dish on a baking tray. Bake for 25–30 minutes, or until the topping is golden and the fruit is bubbling. Leave for 5 minutes. Serve warm with thick cream or ice cream, if desired.

APPLE SAGO PUDDING

Preparation time **20 minutes**
Total cooking time **55 minutes**
Serves 4

90 g (3¼ oz/⅓ cup) caster (superfine) sugar
100 g (3½ oz/½ cup) sago
600 ml (21 fl oz/2½ cups) milk
55 g (2 oz/½ cup) sultanas
1 teaspoon natural vanilla extract
pinch ground nutmeg
¼ teaspoon ground cinnamon
2 eggs, lightly beaten
3 small ripe apples, peeled, cored and sliced
1 tablespoon soft brown sugar

1 Preheat the oven to 180°C (350°F/Gas 4). Grease a 1.5 litre (52 fl oz/6-cup) ceramic soufflé dish.
2 Heat the sugar, sago, milk, sultanas and ¼ teaspoon salt in a saucepan over medium heat, stirring often. Bring to the boil, then reduce the heat and simmer for 5 minutes.
3 Stir in the natural vanilla extract, nutmeg, cinnamon, egg and the apple slices.
4 Pour into the prepared dish. Sprinkle with the brown sugar and bake for 45 minutes, or until set and golden brown. Serve warm with thick cream or ice cream, if desired.

CHOCOLATE CROISSANT PUDDING

Preparation time **20 minutes**
Total cooking time **1 hour**
Serves **6–8**

4 croissants, torn into pieces
125 g (4½ oz) dark chocolate, chopped
4 eggs
5 tablespoons caster (superfine) sugar
250 ml (9 fl oz/1 cup) milk
250 ml (9 fl oz/1 cup) cream
3 teaspoons orange liqueur
3 teaspoons grated orange zest
4 tablespoons orange juice
2 tablespoons roughly chopped hazelnuts
thick (double/heavy) cream, to serve

1 Preheat the oven to 180°C (350°F/Gas 4). Grease the base and side of a 20 cm (8 in) deep-sided cake tin and line the bottom of the tin with baking paper.

2 Put the croissant pieces into the tin, then scatter over 100 g (3½ oz) of the chocolate pieces.

3 Beat the eggs and sugar together until pale and creamy.

4 Heat the milk, cream and liqueur and remaining chocolate pieces in a large saucepan over medium heat until almost boiling. Stir to melt the chocolate, then remove the pan from the heat. Gradually add to the egg mixture, stirring constantly. Stir in the orange zest and juice. Slowly pour the mixture over the croissants, allowing the liquid to be fully absorbed before adding more.

5 Sprinkle the hazelnuts over the top and bake for 50 minutes, or until a skewer comes out clean when inserted into the centre. Cool for 10 minutes.

6 Turn the pudding out and invert onto a serving plate. Slice into wedges and serve warm with a dollop of cream.

BAKED CHOCOLATE PUDDINGS WITH RICH CHOCOLATE SAUCE

Preparation time **20 minutes**
Total cooking time **15 minutes**
Serves 6

1 1/2 tablespoons unsweetened cocoa powder
120 g (4 1/4 oz) good-quality dark chocolate, chopped
120 g (4 1/4 oz) unsalted butter, softened
3 eggs, at room temperature
2 egg yolks, at room temperature
55 g (2 oz/1/4 cup) caster (superfine) sugar
90 g (3 1/4 oz/3/4 cup) plain (all-purpose) flour

Chocolate sauce
80 g (2 3/4 oz/1/2 cup) good-quality dark chocolate, chopped
125 ml (4 fl oz/1/2 cup) pouring (whipping) cream

1 Preheat the oven to 180°C (350°F/Gas 4) and grease 6 x 125 ml (4 fl oz/1/2 cup) metal dariole moulds. Dust the moulds with the cocoa powder.

2 Put the chocolate in a small heatproof bowl over a small saucepan of simmering water, making sure the base of the bowl doesn't touch the water. Allow the chocolate to melt, then add the butter. When the butter has melted, stir to combine, then remove from the heat.
3 Beat the eggs, egg yolks and sugar in a large bowl using electric beaters until thick, creamy and pale in colour. Gently fold in the chocolate mixture. Sift in the flour and gently fold through.
4 Spoon the mixture into the prepared moulds, leaving about 1 cm (1/2 in) at the top of the moulds to allow the puddings to rise. Bake for 10 minutes, or until the top is firm and risen.
5 Meanwhile, to make the chocolate sauce, put the chocolate and cream in a heatproof bowl and melt over a small saucepan of simmering water, making sure the base of the bowl doesn't touch the water. Stir well.
6 To serve, run a knife around the moulds to loosen the puddings, then carefully turn out onto serving plates. Drizzle with the sauce and serve immediately.

STICKY DATE PUDDINGS

Preparation time **30 minutes**

Total cooking time **45 minutes**

Serves **6**

180 g (6½ oz/1 cup) dates, pitted and roughly
  chopped
1 teaspoon bicarbonate of soda (baking soda)
75 g (2½ oz) unsalted butter, softened
155 g (5½ oz/⅔ cup) soft brown sugar
1 teaspoon natural vanilla extract
2 eggs
185 g (6½ oz/1½ cups) self-raising flour, sifted
100 g (3½ oz/1 cup) walnut halves, roughly
  chopped

Caramel sauce
155 g (5½ oz/⅔ cup) soft brown sugar
60 g (2¼ oz) unsalted butter
250 ml (9 fl oz/1 cup) pouring (whipping) cream

1 Preheat the oven to 180°C (350°F/Gas 4).
Lightly brush six 250 ml (9 fl oz/1 cup)
moulds with melted butter and line the
bases with circles of baking paper.

2 Put the dates and bicarbonate of soda in
a saucepan and pour in 250 ml (9 fl oz/
1 cup) of water. Bring to the boil, remove
from the heat and set aside to cool.
3 Beat the butter, sugar and vanilla with
electric beaters until light and creamy.
Add 1 egg, beat well and fold through
1 tablespoon of the flour. Add the other
egg and repeat the process.
4 Fold through the remaining flour, walnuts
and date mixture, and mix well.
5 Divide the mixture among the moulds,
filling them three-quarters full. Bake for
30–35 minutes, or until slightly risen and
firm to the touch.
6 To make the caramel sauce, put the
brown sugar, butter and cream in a pan
and simmer for 5 minutes.
7 Prick a few holes in each pudding using a
skewer. Drizzle with some of the caramel
sauce and return to the oven for about
5 minutes.
8 Loosen the side of each pudding with
a small knife, turn out, remove the baking
paper and serve with the remaining sauce.

BUTTERSCOTCH PUDDINGS

Preparation time **20 minutes**

Total cooking time **45 minutes**

Serves **4–6**

butter, for greasing
150 g (5½ oz/1 cup) self-raising flour
80 g (2¾ oz/⅓ cup) soft brown sugar
125 ml (4 fl oz/½ cup) milk
60 g (2¼ oz) butter, melted, cooled
1 egg
1 tablespoon golden syrup or honey
115 g (4 oz/½ cup) soft brown sugar, extra
2 tablespoons golden syrup, extra
325 ml (11 fl oz/1¼ cups) boiling water

1 Preheat the oven to 170°C (325°F/Gas 3). Lightly grease a 1.25 litre (44 fl oz/5-cup) ovenproof dish.

2 Sift the flour into a large bowl. Add the sugar.

3 In a separate bowl, whisk the milk, butter, egg and golden syrup together. Pour into the flour mixture and whisk until a smooth batter forms. Pour into the prepared dish. Place the dish on a baking tray.

4 Sprinkle the extra brown sugar over the batter. Combine the extra golden syrup and the boiling water and carefully pour over the batter.

5 Bake the pudding for 35–45 minutes, or until a skewer inserted halfway into the pudding comes out clean.

6 Set the pudding aside for 5–10 minutes to allow the sauce to thicken slightly before serving.

CHOCOLATE MINT SELF-SAUCING PUDDING

Preparation time **20 minutes**

Total cooking time **45 minutes**

Serves **6–8**

185 ml (6 fl oz/¾ cup) milk

115 g (4 oz/½ cup) caster (superfine) sugar

60 g (2¼ oz) unsalted butter, melted

1 egg

125 g (4½ oz/1 cup) self-raising flour

40 g (1½ oz/⅓ cup) unsweetened cocoa
  powder

125 g (4½ oz) dark mint-flavoured chocolate,
  roughly chopped

230 g (8 oz/1 cup) soft brown sugar

ice cream, to serve

1 Preheat the oven to 180°C (350°F/Gas 4). Grease a 1.5 litre (52 fl oz/6-cup) capacity ovenproof dish.

2 Whisk together the milk, sugar, butter and egg in a bowl.

3 Sift the flour and half the cocoa powder onto the milk mixture, add the chocolate and stir to mix well.

4 Pour the mixture into the prepared dish. Put the brown sugar and remaining cocoa powder into a bowl and stir in 250 ml (9 fl oz/1 cup) of boiling water. Carefully pour this over the pudding mixture.

5 Bake for 40–45 minutes, or until the pudding is cooked and is firm to the touch. Spoon over the sauce and serve hot or warm with ice cream.

HAZELNUT CRACKLE LOG

Preparation time **25 minutes** +
Total cooking time **25 minutes**
Serves **6–8**

70 g (2½ oz/½ cup) roasted skinned hazelnuts
4 egg whites, at room temperature
150 g (5½ oz/⅔ cup) caster (superfine) sugar
1 teaspoon cornflour (cornstarch)
1 teaspoon natural vanilla extract
1 teaspoon white wine vinegar

Filling
2 teaspoons instant coffee granules
2 teaspoons hot water
225 g (8 oz/1 cup) mascarpone cheese
2 tablespoons icing (confectioners') sugar,
  sifted

1 Preheat the oven to 150°C (300°F/Gas 2).
Draw a 20 x 35 cm (8 x 14 in) rectangle on
a sheet of baking paper. Put the sheet,
pencil side down, on a baking tray.
2 Put the hazelnuts in a food processor and
process until the nuts are coarsely ground.
3 Whisk the egg whites in a large bowl
until soft peaks form. Gradually add the
sugar, 1 tablespoon at a time, and whisk
until stiff and glossy. Gently fold in the
hazelnuts, then the cornflour, vanilla
and vinegar.
4 Spoon onto the baking tray and spread
evenly inside the marked rectangle. Bake
for 25 minutes, or until the meringue is set
and lightly golden.
5 Lay a large sheet of baking paper on
a work surface and invert the cooked
meringue on top. Peel off the baking paper
and set aside to cool for 15 minutes.
6 To make the filling, dissolve the instant
coffee in the hot water. Put the coffee,
mascarpone and icing sugar in a bowl and
mix well.
7 Spread the filling evenly over the
meringue. Starting at one short end and
using the baking paper as a lever, gently
roll up the meringue. Serve immediately,
cut into slices.

BAKED RICE PUDDING

Preparation time **20 minutes**

Total cooking time **55 minutes**

Serves **4–6**

20 g (³/₄ oz) unsalted butter, melted

3 tablespoons short-grain rice

3 eggs

60 g (2 fl oz/¼ cup) caster (superfine) sugar

440 ml (15¼ fl oz/1³/₄ cups) milk

125 ml (4 fl oz/½ cup) pouring (whipping) cream

1 teaspoon natural vanilla extract

¼ teaspoon ground nutmeg

1 Preheat the oven to 160°C (315°F/ Gas 2–3) and brush a 1.5 litre (52 fl oz) ovenproof dish with the melted butter.

2 Cook the rice in a large saucepan of boiling water for 12 minutes, or until tender, then drain well.

3 Place the eggs in a bowl and beat lightly. Add the sugar, milk, cream and natural vanilla extract, and whisk until well combined. Stir in the cooked rice, pour into the prepared dish and sprinkle with nutmeg.

4 Place the dish in a deep roasting tin and pour enough hot water into the tin to come halfway up the side of the pudding dish.

5 Bake for 45 minutes, or until the custard is lightly set and a knife inserted into the centre comes out clean. Remove the pudding dish from the roasting tin and leave for 5 minutes before serving. Serve the pudding with poached or stewed fruit.

Variation Add 2 tablespoons of sultanas or chopped, dried apricots to the custard mixture before baking.

BAKED CUSTARD

Preparation time **20 minutes +**
Total cooking time **30 minutes**
Serves 4

10 g (¼ oz) unsalted butter, melted
3 eggs
90 g (3¼ oz/⅓ cup) caster (superfine) sugar
500 ml (17 fl oz/2 cups) milk
125 ml (4 fl oz/½ cup) cream
1½ teaspoons natural vanilla extract
ground nutmeg

1 Preheat the oven to 160°C (315°F/ Gas 2–3). Brush four 250 ml (9 fl oz/1 cup) ramekins or a 1.5 litre (52 fl oz/6 cup) ovenproof dish with the melted butter.
2 Whisk together the eggs and sugar in a large bowl until they are combined.

3 Place the milk and cream in a small saucepan and stir over medium heat for 3–4 minutes, or until the mixture is warmed through, then stir into the egg mixture with the natural vanilla extract. Strain into the prepared dishes and sprinkle with the ground nutmeg.
4 Place the dishes in a deep roasting tin and add enough hot water to come halfway up the side of the dishes.
5 Bake for 25 minutes for the individual custards, or 30 minutes for the large custard, or until it is set and a knife inserted into the centre comes out clean.
6 Remove the custards from the roasting tin and leave for 10 minutes before serving.
Variation Omit the vanilla and add 1½ tablespoons of Amaretto or Grand Marnier liqueur before baking.

PETIT POTS DE CRÈME

Preparation time **15 minutes**
Total cooking time **35 minutes**
Serves **4**

400 ml (14 fl oz) milk
1 vanilla bean
3 egg yolks
1 egg
80 g (2¾ oz/⅓ cup) caster (superfine) sugar

1 Preheat the oven to 140°C (275°F/Gas 1).
2 Put the milk in a saucepan. Split the vanilla bean in two, scrape out the seeds and add the whole lot to the milk. Bring the milk just to the boil.
3 Meanwhile, mix together the egg yolks, egg and sugar. Strain the boiling milk over the egg mixture and stir well. Skim off the surface to remove any foam.
4 Ladle into four 25 ml (1 fl oz) ramekins and place in a roasting tin. Pour enough hot water into the tin to come halfway up the sides of the ramekins.
5 Bake for 30 minutes, or until the custards are firm to the touch. Leave the ramekins on a wire rack to cool, then refrigerate until ready to serve.

CHERRY CLAFOUTIS

Preparation time **25 minutes**

Total cooking time **40 minutes**

Serves **6**

200 ml (7 fl oz) thick (double/heavy)
  cream
1 vanilla bean
100 ml (3½ fl oz) milk
3 eggs
50 g (1¾ oz) caster (superfine) sugar
70 g (2½ oz) plain (all-purpose) flour
1 tablespoon kirsch
450 g (1 lb) black cherries
icing (confectioners') sugar, to dust

1 Preheat the oven to 180°C (350°F/Gas 4).
2 Put the cream in a small saucepan. Split
the vanilla bean in two, scrape out the
seeds and add the scraped seeds and bean
to the cream. Heat gently for a few
minutes, then remove from the heat, add
the milk and cool. Strain the mixture,
discarding the vanilla bean.
3 Whisk the eggs with the sugar and flour,
then stir into the cream mixture. Add the
kirsch and cherries and stir well.
4 Pour into a 23 cm (9 in) round baking
dish and bake for 30–35 minutes, or until
golden on top. Dust with icing sugar
and serve.

PLUM COBBLER

Preparation time **30 minutes**
Total cooking time **40 minutes**
Serves 4

825 g (1 lb 13 oz) tinned dark plums, pitted
1 tablespoon honey
2 ripe pears, peeled, cored and cut into eighths

Topping

250 g (9 oz/1 cup) self-raising flour
1 tablespoon caster (superfine) sugar
1/4 teaspoon ground cardamom or ground
   cinnamon
40 g (1 1/2 oz) unsalted butter, chilled and
   chopped
60 ml (2 fl oz/1/4 cup) milk
extra milk, for brushing
1 tablespoon caster (superfine) sugar, extra
1/4 teaspoon ground cardamom or ground
   cinnamon, extra

1 Preheat the oven to 200°C (400°F/Gas 6).
Grease an 18 cm (7 in) round 1.5 litre
(52 fl oz/6 cup) ovenproof dish.
2 Drain the plums, reserving 185 ml
(6 fl oz/3/4 cup) of the syrup.
3 Put the syrup, honey and pear in a large
wide saucepan and bring to the boil.
Reduce the heat and simmer for 8 minutes,
or until the pear is tender. Add the plums.
4To make the topping, sift the flour, sugar,
cardamom and a pinch of salt into a large
bowl. Rub in the butter with your fingers
until it resembles fine breadcrumbs. Stir in
the milk using a flat-bladed knife, mixing
lightly to form a soft dough—add a little
more milk if necessary.
5 Turn onto a floured surface and form
into a smooth ball. Roll out to a 1 cm (1/2
in) thickness and cut into rounds with a 4
cm (1 1/2 in) cutter.
6 Spoon the hot fruit into the dish,
then arrange the circles of dough in an
overlapping pattern over the fruit, on the
inside edge of the dish only—leave the fruit
in the centre exposed. Brush the dough
with the extra milk. Mix the extra sugar and
cardamom and sprinkle over the dough.
7 Place the dish on a baking tray and bake
for 30 minutes, or until the topping is
golden and cooked.

BAKED CHOCOLATE CUSTARDS

Preparation time **20 minutes**

Total cooking time **45 minutes**

Serves **10**

30 g (1 oz) unsalted butter, melted

55 g (2 oz/¼ cup) caster (superfine) sugar, to dust

300 ml (10½ fl oz) pouring (whipping) cream

200 ml (7 fl oz) milk

200 g (7 oz) dark chocolate, roughly chopped

grated zest of 1 orange

6 eggs

115 g (4 oz/½ cup) caster (superfine) sugar, extra

raspberries, to serve

icing (confectioners') sugar, to dust

1 Preheat the oven to 160°C (315°F/ Gas 2–3). Grease ten 125 ml (4 fl oz/ ½ cup) ramekins or ovenproof moulds with butter and dust the inside of each with caster sugar.

2 Put the cream and milk in a saucepan over low heat and bring almost to the boil. Add the chocolate and stir over low heat until the chocolate has melted and is well combined. Stir in the orange zest.

3 Whisk the eggs and sugar in a large bowl for 5 minutes, or until thick. Whisk a little of the hot chocolate cream into the eggs, then pour the egg mixture onto the remaining chocolate cream, whisking.

4 Divide the mixture among the ramekins. Put the custards in a roasting tin and pour in enough hot water to come halfway up the sides of the ramekins.

5 Cover the tin with foil and bake for 30–35 minutes, or until the custards are set. Remove the ramekins from the water bath. Set aside to cool.

6 Turn out onto a serving dish, top with the raspberries and dust with icing sugar.

PEAR DUMPLINGS

Preparation time **30 minutes**
Total cooking time **40 minutes**
Serves 6

6 firm, ripe pears
100 g (3½ oz) goat's cheese, crumbled
55 g (2 oz/½ cup) ground almonds
½ teaspoon ground nutmeg
½ teaspoon grated lemon zest
55 g (2 oz/¼ cup) caster (superfine) sugar
400 g (14 oz) sweet shortcrust pastry
1 egg, lightly beaten
icing (confectioners') sugar, to dust
crème anglaise, to serve (optional)

1 Preheat the oven to 180°C (350°F/Gas 4). Grease a large roasting tin.
2 Leaving the pears whole and unpeeled, core the pears using an apple corer.
3 Combine the goat's cheese, almonds, nutmeg, lemon zest and 2 tablespoons of the sugar. Using a teaspoon, fill the pear cavities with the goat's cheese mixture.
4 Roll out the pastry to 3 mm (⅛ in) thick and cut into six 15 cm (6 in) squares. Lightly brush the squares with egg and sprinkle with the remaining sugar. Place a pear in the centre of each piece of pastry and bring the corners of the pastry up and around the pear to enclose it. Press the edges together to seal, trimming where necessary, and reserving the pastry scraps.
5 Using a small knife, cut 12 leaf shapes from the pastry scraps. Brush the dumplings with the remaining egg and attach two pastry leaves to the top of each, pressing firmly to secure.
6 Transfer to the roasting tin and bake for 35–40 minutes, or until the pastry is golden. Dust with icing sugar and serve immediately with crème anglaise.

APPLE AND PASSIONFRUIT CRUMBLE

Preparation time **20 minutes**

Total cooking time **30 minutes**

Serves **4–6**

4 passionfruit

4 green apples

55 g (2 oz/¼ cup) caster (superfine) sugar, plus 80 g (2¾ oz/⅓ cup) extra

60 g (2¼ oz/1 cup) shredded coconut

90 g (3¼ oz/¾ cup) plain (all-purpose) flour

80 g (2¾ oz) unsalted butter, softened

1 Preheat the oven to 180°C (350°F/Gas 4). Lightly grease a 1 litre (35 fl oz/4 cup) ovenproof dish.

2 Sieve the passionfruit, discarding the pulp, and place the juice in a bowl.

3 Peel, core and thinly slice the apples and add to the passionfruit juice, along with the 55 g (2 oz/¼ cup) of sugar. Mix well, then transfer the mixture to the prepared dish.

4 Combine the shredded coconut, flour, extra sugar and butter in a bowl and rub together until the mixture has a crumbly texture. Pile on top of the apple mixture.

5 Bake the crumble for 25–30 minutes, or until the topping is crisp and golden.

LEMON DELICIOUS

Preparation time **30 minutes**

Total cooking time **55 minutes**

Serves 4–6

70 g (2½ oz) unsalted butter, at room
  temperature
185 g (6½ oz/¾ cup) sugar
2 teaspoons finely grated lemon zest
3 eggs, separated
30 g (1 oz/¼ cup) self-raising flour
185 ml (6 fl oz/¾ cup) milk
80 ml (2½ fl oz/⅓ cup) lemon juice
icing (confectioners') sugar, to dust
thick (double/heavy) cream, to serve

1 Preheat the oven to 180°C (350°F/Gas 4). Melt 10 g (¼ oz) of the butter and use to lightly grease a 1.25 litre (44 fl oz/5 cup) ovenproof ceramic dish.

2 Using an electric beater, beat the remaining butter, the sugar and grated zest together in a bowl until the mixture is light and creamy. Gradually add the egg yolks, beating well after each addition. Fold in the flour and milk alternately to make a smooth but runny batter. Stir in the lemon juice.

3 Whisk the egg whites in a dry bowl until firm peaks form and, with a large metal spoon, fold a third of the whites into the batter. Gently fold in the remaining egg whites, being careful not to overmix.

4 Pour the batter into the prepared dish and place in a large roasting tin. Pour enough hot water into the tin to come one-third of the way up the side of the dish and bake for 55 minutes, or until the top of the pudding is golden, risen and firm to the touch. Leave for 5 minutes before serving. Dust with icing sugar and serve with cream.

MIXED BERRY SPONGE PUDDINGS

Preparation time **30 minutes**
Total cooking time **40 minutes**
Serves **6**

20 g ($^3/_4$ oz) unsalted butter, melted
125 g ($4^1/_2$ oz) unsalted butter, softened
115 g (4 oz/$^1/_2$ cup) caster (superfine) sugar,
   plus 6 teaspoons extra
2 eggs
165 g ($5^3/_4$ oz/$1^1/_3$ cups) self-raising flour, sifted
60 ml (2 fl oz/$^1/_4$ cup) milk
200 g (7 oz) mixed berries, fresh or frozen

1 Preheat the oven to 180°C (350°F/Gas 4). Grease six 125 ml (4 fl oz/$^1/_2$ cup) pudding or dariole moulds with melted butter.
2 Cream the butter and sugar in a bowl using electric beaters until pale and fluffy. Add the eggs one at a time, beating well after each addition. Gently fold in the flour alternately with the milk.
3 Divide the berries between the moulds and top each with a teaspoon of the extra caster sugar. Top the berries with the pudding mixture, dividing the mixture evenly between the moulds.
4 Put the puddings in a large roasting tin and pour in enough hot water to come halfway up the sides of the moulds. Cover the baking tin with a sheet of baking paper, then cover with foil, pleating two sheets of foil together if necessary. Fold the foil tightly around the edges of the tin to seal.
5 Bake the puddings for 35–40 minutes, or until the pudding springs back when touched. Remove the puddings from the water bath, leave to cool in the moulds for 5 minutes, then run a small knife around the inside of the mould and turn out onto plates. Serve with custard or ice cream.

CRÈME BRÛLÉE

Preparation time **15 minutes**
Total cooking time **1 hour 30 minutes**
Serves **6**

500 ml (17 fl oz/2 cups) pouring (whipping)
   cream
200 ml (7 fl oz) milk
125 g (4½ oz) caster (superfine) sugar
1 vanilla bean
5 egg yolks
1 egg white
1 tablespoon orange flower water
100 g (3½ oz) raw (demerara) sugar

1 Preheat the oven to 120°C (250°F/
Gas ½). Put the cream, milk and half the
caster sugar in a saucepan with the vanilla
bean and bring just to the boil.
2 Meanwhile, mix together the remaining
caster sugar, egg yolks and egg white.
Strain the milk mixture over the egg
mixture, whisking well. Stir in the orange
flower water.
3 Pour into eight 125 ml (4 fl oz/½ cup)
ramekins and place in a roasting tin. Pour
enough hot water into the tin to come
halfway up the sides of the ramekins.
4 Cook for 1½ hours, or until set in the
centre. Allow to cool, then refrigerate until
ready to serve.
5 Just before serving, sprinkle the tops with
raw sugar and caramelise under a hot grill
(broiler) or with a chef's blowtorch.

CRÈME CARAMEL

Preparation time **20 minutes**
Total cooking time **35 minutes**
Serves **6**

250 ml (9 fl oz/1 cup) milk
250 ml (9 fl oz/1 cup) pouring (whipping) cream
375 g (13 oz/1½ cups) caster (superfine) sugar
1 teaspoon natural vanilla extract
4 eggs, lightly beaten
90 g (3¼ oz/⅓ cup) caster (superfine) sugar,
   extra

1 Preheat the oven to 200°C (400°F/Gas 6).
Put the milk and cream in a saucepan and
gradually bring to boiling point.
2 Put the sugar in a frying pan and cook
over medium heat for 8–10 minutes. Stir
occasionally as the sugar melts to form a
golden toffee. The sugar may clump
together—break up any lumps with a
wooden spoon. Pour the toffee into the
base of six 125 ml (4 fl oz/½ cup) ramekins
or ovenproof dishes.
3 Combine the vanilla, eggs and extra
sugar in a bowl. Remove the milk and
cream from the heat and gradually add to
the egg mixture, whisking well. Pour the
custard mixture evenly over the toffee.
4 Place the ramekins in a baking dish and
pour in boiling water until it comes halfway
up the sides of the dishes.
5 Bake for 20 minutes, or until set. Use a
flat-bladed knife to run around the edges of
the dishes and carefully turn out the crème
caramel onto a serving plate, toffee-side-up.
Note When making toffee, watch it
carefully as it will take a little while to
start melting, but once it starts it will
happen very quickly. Stir occasionally to
make sure it melts evenly and doesn't stick
to the saucepan.

MERINGUES

Just two ingredients are all that you require to make a basic mixture for meringues. When egg white and sugar are beaten together, then baked, they miraculously turn into crunchy, delicate delights.

BASIC MERINGUE RECIPE

Preheat the oven to 150°C (300°F/Gas 2) and line two biscuit or baking trays with baking paper. Beat 2 egg whites into stiff peaks in a small dry bowl with electric beaters. Add 125 g (4½ oz/½ cup) caster (superfine) sugar, 1 tablespoon at a time, beating well after each addition. Beat until the mixture is thick and glossy and the sugar has dissolved (this will take up to 10 minutes). Spoon into a piping (icing) bag and pipe small shapes onto the trays.

Bake for 20–25 minutes, or until pale and dry. Turn off the oven, leave the door ajar and cool the meringues in the oven. When cold, store in an airtight jar. **Makes 30.**

CUSTARD DISCS

Prepare the basic meringue mixture until it is thick and glossy, then beat in 1 tablespoon custard powder. Spoon the mixture into a piping bag with a plain 5 mm (¼ in) or 1 cm (½ in) nozzle. Pipe spirals onto trays and bake as above. Dust with icing (confectioners') sugar. **Makes 40.**

COFFEE KISSES

Prepare the basic meringue mixture until it is thick and glossy, then beat in 2–3 teaspoons instant coffee powder. Spoon the mixture into a piping bag fitted with a small star nozzle and pipe onto the trays. Bake as for the basic recipe. Coffee

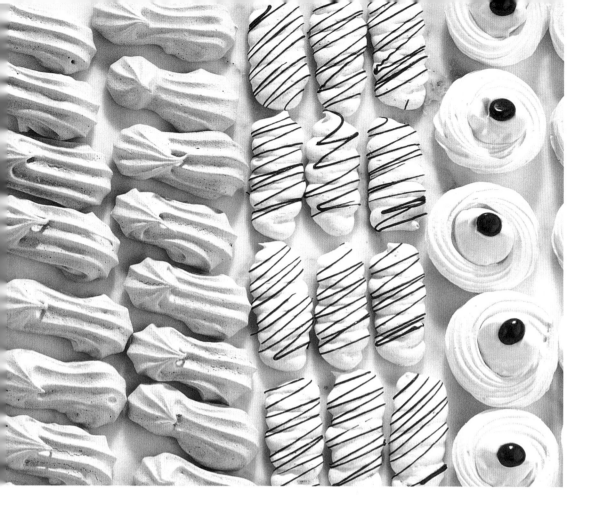

kisses are delicious if served as is or sandwiched together with 60 g (2¼ oz) melted chocolate. **Makes 30.**

CHOCOLATE FINGERS

Prepare the basic meringue mixture until it is thick and glossy, then beat in 1 tablespoon sifted cocoa powder. Spoon the mixture into a piping bag fitted with a plain round nozzle and pipe fine 8 cm (3 in) lengths onto lined trays, allowing room for spreading. Bake as for the basic recipe and serve as they are, or drizzled with melted chocolate or lightly dusted with dark cocoa powder combined with a little icing (confectioners') sugar. **Makes 40.**

HAZELNUT SNAILS

Prepare the basic meringue mixture until it is thick and glossy. Gently beat in 2 tablespoons ground hazelnuts. Spoon the mixture into a piping bag fitted with a plain 1 cm (½ in) nozzle and pipe in fine short zigzag lengths onto the trays. Bake as for the basic recipe. These can be served lightly dusted with a mixture of icing (confectioners') sugar and ground cinnamon, or drizzled with melted chocolate. **Makes 30.**

MERINGUE NESTS

Prepare the basic meringue mixture until it is thick and glossy. Spoon into a piping bag fitted with a star nozzle and pipe into nests on the trays. Bake as for the basic recipe. Meringue nests are delicious if filled with whipped cream flavoured with coffee or chocolate liqueur, topped with a chocolate-coated coffee bean. They can also be filled with a chocolate truffle mixture and topped with a slice of strawberry. **Makes 40.**

MINI PAVLOVAS

Preparation time **50 minutes**
Total cooking time **30 minutes**
Makes **35–40**

3 egg whites
125 g (4½ oz/1 cup) icing (confectioners')
    sugar
150 g (5½ oz) dark chocolate, melted
250 ml (9 fl oz/1 cup) thick (double/heavy)
    cream
1 tablespoon icing (confectioners') sugar, extra
1 teaspoon finely grated orange zest
assorted fresh fruit, to garnish, such as straw-
    berries, cut into thin wedges, sliced pawpaw
    and kiwi fruit, and passionfruit pulp

1 Preheat the oven to 150°C (300°F/Gas 2).
Beat the egg whites in a large bowl until
stiff peaks form. Add the icing sugar to the
egg whites while continuing to beat. At
this stage it is best to use electric beaters
as you must now beat the meringue until
thick and very solid.
2 Using a cutter as a guide, draw about
forty 4 cm (1½ in) circles onto two sheets
of baking paper, then invert these sheets
onto baking trays (so the pencil won't
come off on the base of the pavlovas).
3 Spread a little of the meringue mixture
over each round—this will be the base of
each pavlova.
4 Spoon the remaining meringue into
a piping (icing) bag fitted with a 5 mm
(¼ in) plain piping nozzle. Pipe three
small circles on top of each other on the
outer edge of each base, leaving a small
hole in the centre.
5 Bake for 30 minutes, or until firm to
touch. Leave to cool in the oven with the
door slightly ajar.
6 When cold, dip the bases of the
meringues into the melted chocolate to
come about 2 mm (⅛ in) up the sides of
the meringues, then place on trays covered
with baking paper and allow to set.
7 Combine the cream, extra icing sugar
and orange zest, stirring until just thick.
If necessary, beat slightly. Spoon into a
piping bag fitted with a small plain nozzle
and pipe into the meringues. Top with fruit
and passionfruit pulp.

ROSEWATER MERINGUES WITH RASPBERRY CREAM

Preparation time 30 minutes +
Total cooking time 1 hour
Makes 30

4 egg whites
235 g (8½ oz/1 cup) caster (superfine) sugar
1 tablespoon rosewater
a few drops of pink food colouring (optional)
icing (confectioners') sugar, to dust

sugared rose petals (optional)
2–3 unsprayed pink or red roses
1 egg white, lightly beaten
115 g (4 oz/½ cup) caster (superfine) sugar

Raspberry cream
300 ml (10½ fl oz) thick (double/heavy) cream
1 tablespoon icing (confectioners') sugar, sifted
100 g (3⅓ oz) fresh raspberries, or frozen
   raspberries, thawed

1 Preheat the oven to 120°C (235°F/ Gas ½). Line two baking trays with baking paper. Mark out sixty 3 cm (1¼ in) rounds.
2 Whisk the egg whites in a dry bowl until stiff peaks form. Add the sugar gradually, whisking well after each addition. Whisk until the mixture is glossy and the sugar has dissolved. Add the rosewater and food colouring, if using, to tint the meringue.
3 Transfer the mixture to a piping bag fitted with a 1 cm (½ in) plain nozzle. Following the marked rounds as a guide, pipe sixty 3 cm (1¼ in) rounds, each about 2 cm (¾ in) high, onto the paper.
4 Bake for 1 hour, then turn off the oven and leave the meringues to cool in the oven with the door slightly ajar.
5 To make sugared rose petals, if using, remove the petals from the roses. Working on one petal at a time, use a paintbrush to brush the egg white over both sides of the petal. Toss lightly in the sugar and set aside to dry. Repeat with the remaining petals.
6 To make the raspberry cream, beat the cream and icing sugar until thick, then fold in the raspberries. Spread the raspberry cream over the bases of half the meringues and then join together with the remaining meringues to make a 'sandwich'. Decorate with the sugared rose petals, if using, and dust lightly with icing sugar.

BREADS & SCONES

The smell of freshly baked bread can drive you mad with a craving for still-warm bread with a slathering of butter or a drizzle of extra virgin olive oil. Once you've mastered the basics, you'll quickly see how easy it is. But remember, as tempting as it may seem, man cannot live by bread alone.

ALL ABOUT BREAD

When you master the techniques described here, in no time you will be delighted by the wonderful aroma of freshly baked bread all over the house.

PLAIN BREAD

Once you have an understanding of some of the important elements of bread making, such as working with yeast, and kneading techniques, you will find that delicious bread is simple to make.

Make sure you read the recipe thoroughly, carefully weigh all the ingredients and assemble the equipment you need.

MYSTERIES OF YEAST SOLVED

Working with yeast, probably the most important ingredient in bread, is not as difficult as you may think. Yeast is available dried or fresh. Dried yeast, available at supermarkets, generally comes in a box containing 7 g (¼ oz) sachets, one of which is enough for a standard loaf. Fresh yeast, sometimes harder to obtain, is available at some health food shops and bakeries. It has quite a short storage life. About 15 g (½ oz) of fresh yeast is equivalent to a 7 g (¼ oz) sachet of dried. We used dried yeast in our recipes as it is readily available, can be stored in the pantry and carries a use-by date.

TYPES OF FLOUR

The type and quality of flour you use is vital. The correct flour makes a big difference to the quality of bread. Many of the recipes call for the use of flour that is labelled as bread flour. This is high in protein and will form gluten, which helps the bread rise well and bake into a light airy loaf with a good crust. For most breads, if you use a regular flour the loaf will not rise well, gluten will not form and the loaf will be heavy and dense.

TO MAKE YOUR LOAF

Put a 7 g (¼ oz) sachet of dried yeast, 125 ml (4 fl oz/½ cup) warm water and 1 teaspoon caster (superfine) sugar in a bowl and stir to combine. Leave in a warm, draught-free place for 10 minutes, or until bubbles appear on the surface. The mixture should be frothy and slightly increased in volume. If it isn't, discard it and start again. Sift 500 g (1 lb 2 oz/4 cups) white bread flour, 1 teaspoon salt, 2 tablespoons dried whole milk powder and 1 tablespoon caster sugar into a large bowl. Make a well in the centre, add the yeast mixture, 60 ml (2 fl oz/¼ cup) vegetable oil and 250 ml (9 fl oz/1 cup) warm water. Mix to a soft dough using a large metal spoon. The moisture content of flour can vary greatly between brands and even between batches so add extra water or flour, 1 tablespoon at a time, if the dough is too dry or sticky. Do not add too much flour because the dough will absorb more flour during kneading.

Kneading the dough

The dough is then formed into a ball on a lightly floured surface and kneaded. Don't be tempted to cut short the kneading time as it affects the texture of the finished bread. Kneading distributes the yeast evenly throughout the dough and allows the flour's protein to develop into gluten. Gluten gives the dough elasticity, strength and the ability to expand, as it traps the carbon dioxide gas created by the yeast and this allows the bread to rise.

The kneading action is simple and it is quite easy to get into a rhythm. Hold one end of the dough down with one hand, and stretch it away from you with the other hand. Fold the dough back together, make a quarter turn and repeat the action. Knead for 10 minutes, or until smooth and elastic. When you have finished, gather the dough into a ball, then follow the instructions on the next page to complete the bread-making process.

PREPARING TO BAKE

PROVING THE BREAD

After kneading, put the dough into a lightly greased bowl. Cover loosely with plastic wrap or a damp cloth. Leave the bowl in a warm place (around 30°C is ideal) to allow the dough to rise—this stage is called proving. When the dough is ready it should be doubled in volume and not spring back when touched with a fingertip. This will take about an hour. Lightly grease a bread tin that measures 22 x 9 x 9 cm (9 x 3½ x 3½ in) with melted butter or oil.

PUNCHING DOWN

After proving, punch down the dough to expel the air, and knead again for 1 minute, or until smooth. The dough is now ready for shaping. Shape the loaf to fit into the prepared tin, placing it in with any seam at the base. Cover with plastic wrap or a damp tea towel and place the tin in a warm, draught-free place until the dough is well risen and doubled in size. This will take about 45–60 minutes. This is the final rise for the dough.

BAKING

Preheat the oven to 210°C (415°F/ Gas 6–7). To glaze, beat 1 egg with 1 tablespoon milk and brush over the top of the dough with a pastry brush. Place the bread in the middle of the hot oven and bake for 10 minutes. Don't open the oven during the first 10 minutes of baking as intense heat is needed during this time. Reduce the oven temperature to 180°C (350°F/Gas 4) and bake for a further 30–40 minutes. At the end of the cooking time, test for doneness by turning the loaf out of the tin and tapping the base. The bread will sound hollow when cooked. If it is not cooked, return it to the tin and bake for a further 5–10 minutes. Remove from the tin and cool on a wire rack.

OTHER SHAPES

Bread dough can be made into many shapes and does not have to be baked in a bread or loaf tin.

Bloomer At the shaping stage, roll out the dough on a lightly floured surface to a rectangle about 2.5 cm (1 in) thick. Starting from the short end, roll up the dough like you would a swiss roll. Roll firmly to make a short, rather thick loaf. Place with the seam underneath on the baking tray. Cover the dough with a cloth and leave in a warm, draught-free place for an hour, or until doubled in size. Using a sharp knife, make 6 evenly spaced slashes across the top of the dough. Spray the loaf with water and place in a hot 220°C (425°F/Gas 7) oven for 10 minutes. Reduce to 200°C (400°F/Gas 6) and bake for 30 minutes, or until the loaf is golden brown and sounds hollow when tapped underneath. Cool on a wire rack.

Plaited loaf After knocking back, divide the dough into three. Roll each portion into a 30 cm (12 in) sausage, then transfer to a greased baking tray. Arrange next to one another on the tray, then join the strands at one end and start plaiting them together. Pinch and tuck under at both ends to seal the plait. Cover with a tea towel and set aside in a warm, draught-free place for 1 hour, or until doubled in size. Brush with milk and bake in a 220°C (425°F/Gas 7) oven for 10 minutes. Reduce the oven to 200°C (400°F/Gas 6) and cook for 30 minutes, or until the loaf is golden brown and sounds hollow when tapped underneath. Cool on a wire rack.

STORAGE

Home-baked bread is best eaten on the day of baking. Because it has no preservatives it doesn't keep as long as commercial bread, but it can be wrapped and frozen for up to 3 months. When required, thaw at room temperature, then refresh in a 180°C (350°F/Gas 4) oven for 10 minutes.

WHAT WENT WRONG?

YEAST

Perfect The mixture above looks frothy and has doubled in size.

Dead If your yeast mixture has not risen and is not frothy, the yeast is dead. If this happens, you will have to throw away the mixture and start again. Take care when measuring the yeast. The temperature of the water should be tepid, not too warm, or you may kill the yeast. If using dry yeast, check the expiry date on the back of the packet before you start.

OTHER PROBLEMS

Strong smell and taste of yeast If there is a strong smell and taste of yeast, the bread was undercooked or there was too much yeast used in proportion to the amount of flour.

Loaf didn't rise or rose poorly If the loaf didn't rise or rose poorly, the yeast was old or dead. The liquid may have been too hot and killed the yeast. The yeast may have worked itself out too early by being placed to rise in a spot that was too warm. It may have been left too long to prove.

Loaf over-risen and puffy If there are large holes in the loaf and it has risen too much and is puffy, the dough may have been insufficiently kneaded during the first kneading stage. The rising time for the dough may have too long, or the dough may not have been correctly knocked backed before shaping the loaf.

Loaf crust and crumb separate If the crumb and crust separate from one another, the bread dough was not properly knocked back before shaping the loaf.

Loaf rose unevenly If the loaf rises unevenly, or is cracked along one side, the oven temperature was uneven or the bread was not placed in the centre of the oven or was too close to the oven heating elements. The baking tin used may have been too small.

Loaf has uneven colour If the bread is unevenly coloured, the oven temperature was uneven, too high or the bread was placed too low in the oven. A hard crust forms if the dough is not covered during the rising stage, allowing the surface to dry out and thus form a crust.

WHAT WENT WRONG?

BREAD

Perfect The bread has a good even crumb and the loaf has risen evenly and well. It has even spring on the sides and sounds hollow when tapped. The crust is coloured to a golden brown.

Undercooked The crumb is damp and sticky and the crust soft and pale. If very under-baked, the loaf may not hold its shape and may be wet or have wet holes. If the loaf does not sound hollow when tapped, bake it for another 10 minutes. Check that the oven is the correct temperature before putting the dough in the oven.

Overcooked The crust is too dark and is cracked on top. The crumb is dry. The oven may have been too hot or the cooking time too long or there may have been too much sugar. The bread may have been placed too high in the oven.

WHAT WENT WRONG?

FOCACCIA

Perfect The bread is evenly and well risen and has coloured to a golden brown. The crust is crisp but not hard.

Soggy, under-baked The crust is soft and pale and the crumb is dense and wet. The bread may not have been cooked long enough, or the oven temperature may have been too low.

Uneven rising, puffy The dough was not rolled evenly. Also the dough may not have been sufficiently kneaded. The rising time for the dough may have been too long or too much yeast was used.

PIZZA

Perfect The dough is well risen and lightly browned. It is crisp but not tough. The topping is evenly spread and light golden brown.

Risen too much The dough is unevenly risen and may be dry with a yeasty taste. Too much yeast may have been used or the dough allowed to prove too quickly (too warm) or for too long.

Uneven rising, puffy The dough is not evenly rolled and the topping not even. The oven heat may have been uneven or the shelf placed too low or too high.

HINTS AND TIPS

1 When adding water to yeast (or a yeast and flour mixture), warm it first until tepid or hand hot. Do not use water that is too hot to touch or it will kill the yeast.

2 If dissolving yeast first, leave it in a warm place for at least 10 minutes, or until a good foam appears on the surface. If it does not foam, the yeast is dead and you will have to start again with a new batch.

3 If mixing dough by hand use a wooden spoon to bring the ingredients together. The dough should feel sticky when it first comes together. If it feels dry, add a little more water, a tablespoon at a time.

4 If using an electric stand mixer always use the dough attachment, unless otherwise specified. Stand the mixer well away from the edge of the work surface because it may move as it is mixing the dough.

5 Always start with the electric mixer on its lowest setting to first mix the ingredients, then increase the speed to medium to knead the dough.

6 When leaving dough to rise, use a large bowl at least twice the size of the dough so it has plenty of room to expand.

7 Lightly oil both the bowl and the surface of the dough before leaving the dough to rise. The dough should be covered with plastic wrap to prevent it forming a skin, which prevents it rising properly.

8 To test if a dough has risen sufficiently, press a finger into the surface. The fingerprint should remain indented and should not spring back.

9 Draughts can cause dough to deflate, so make sure the room is draught-free.

10 Doughs will rise too fast if the room is overly hot, which will give an unpleasant smell and flavour to the bread. If this happens, deflate the dough and leave to rise again in a cool place (for at least 1 hour to develop flavour).

11 If leaving bread dough overnight in the refrigerator, allow time for it to return to room temperature so it can begin to rise. This should take 45–60 minutes.

12 Always grease the tin with spray oil or melted butter. Baking trays should be lightly greased or dusted with flour.

13 When pressing dough into a tin it should reach to 1.5 cm ($\frac{1}{2}$ in) below the top of the tin. After rising, the centre of the dough should protrude about 2.5 cm (1 in) above the top of the tin. The dough is then ready to be baked.

14 Never open the oven door during the first half of the total baking time or the bread can collapse. If you do need to turn the bread to get even browning, do this after the halfway point.

15 To test if a bread is cooked, gently remove it from the tray or tin and tap it on the bottom—it should sound hollow. If it doesn't, return it to the oven for a further 5 minutes, then test again.

16 Store bread in a paper or cloth bag for up to 24 hours in a cool place. Do not refrigerate bread as this makes it become stale more quickly. If keeping bread longer, store in a plastic bag or a zip lock bag.

17 To freeze bread, wrap it in plastic wrap and then place inside a freezer bag. Defrost to room temperature before use. Bread that is allowed to defrost slowly, at room temperature, will retain its freshness for longer.

SIMPLE WHITE BREAD

Preparation time **30 minutes +**
Total cooking time **40 minutes**
Makes **1 loaf**

2½ teaspoons (7 g) instant dried yeast
1 teaspoon caster (superfine) sugar
450 g (1 lb/3⅔ cups) white strong flour

1 Sprinkle the yeast and sugar over 150 ml (5 fl oz) warm water in a small bowl. Stir to dissolve the sugar, then leave in a draught-free place for 10 minutes, or until the yeast is foamy.

2 Combine the flour and 2 teaspoons salt in the bowl of an electric mixer with a dough hook attachment and make a well in the centre. Add another 150 ml (5 fl oz) warm water to the yeast mixture, then pour the mixture into the well. With the mixer set to the lowest speed, mix for 2 minutes, or until a dough forms. Increase the speed to medium and knead the dough for another 10 minutes, or until it is smooth and elastic. Alternatively, mix the dough by hand using a wooden spoon, then turn out onto a floured work surface and knead the dough for 10 minutes, or until smooth and elastic.

3 Grease a large bowl with oil, then transfer the dough to the bowl, turning the dough to coat in the oil. Cover with plastic wrap and leave to rise in a draught-free place for 1–1½ hours, or until the dough has doubled in size.

4 Knock back the dough by punching it gently, then turn out onto a lightly floured work surface. Shape into a rounded oval and transfer to a greased baking tray. Cover loosely with a damp cloth and leave for 30 minutes, or until doubled in size. Meanwhile, preheat the oven to 190°C (375°F/Gas 5).

5 Using a sharp knife, make three diagonal slashes, about 4 cm (1½ in) apart, on the top of the loaf. Bake for 40 minutes, or until it sounds hollow when tapped on the base. Transfer to a wire rack to cool.

SOY AND LINSEED LOAF

Preparation time **30 minutes +**
Total cooking time **50 minutes**
Makes **1 loaf**

110 g (3³/4 oz/¹/2 cup) pearl barley
2 teaspoons dried yeast
1 teaspoon caster (superfine) sugar
1 tablespoon linseeds (flax seeds)
2 tablespoons soy flour
2 tablespoons gluten flour
150 g (5¹/2 oz/1 cup) wholemeal (whole-wheat)
   strong flour
310 g (11 oz/2¹/2 cups) white strong flour
2 tablespoons olive oil

1 Brush a 10 x 26 cm (4 x 10¹/2 in) bread tin with oil. Put the barley in a saucepan with 500 ml (17 fl oz/2 cups) water, bring to the boil and boil for 20 minutes, or until softened. Drain.

2 Put the yeast, sugar and 150 ml (5 fl oz) warm water in a small bowl and mix well. Leave in a warm, draught-free place for 10 minutes, or until bubbles appear on the surface. The mixture should be frothy and slightly increased in volume. If your yeast doesn't foam, it is dead, so you will have to discard it and start again.

3 Put the barley, linseeds, soy and gluten flours, wholemeal flour, 250 g (9 oz/2 cups) of the white flour and 1 teaspoon salt in a large bowl. Make a well in the centre and add the yeast mixture, oil and 150 ml (5 fl oz) warm water. Mix with a wooden spoon to a soft dough. Turn out onto a floured surface and knead for 10 minutes, or until smooth and elastic. Incorporate enough of the remaining flour until the dough is no longer sticky.

4 Place in an oiled bowl and brush the dough with oil. Cover with plastic wrap or a damp tea towel (dish towel) and leave in a warm, draught-free place for 45 minutes, or until doubled in size. Punch down and knead for 2–3 minutes.

5 Pat the dough into a 20 x 24 cm (8 x 9¹/2 in) rectangle. Roll up firmly from the long side and place, seam side down, in the bread tin. Cover with plastic wrap or a damp tea towel and set aside in a warm, draught-free place for 1 hour, or until risen to the top of the tin. Preheat the oven to 200°C (400°F/Gas 6).

6 Brush the dough with water and make two slits on top. Bake for 30 minutes, or until golden. Remove from the tin and cool on a wire rack.

SOURDOUGH BREAD

Preparation time **30 minutes** +
Total cooking time **40 minutes**
Makes **2 loaves**

Starter
125 g (4½ oz/1 cup) white strong flour
2 teaspoons fresh yeast

Sponge
125 g (4½ oz/1 cup) white strong flour

Dough
375 g (13 oz/3 cups) white strong flour
2 teaspoons fresh yeast

1 To make the starter, sift the flour into a bowl and make a well in the centre. Cream the yeast and 250 ml (9 fl oz/1 cup) warm water together, pour into the flour and gradually draw the flour into the centre to form a thick smooth paste. Cover with plastic wrap or a damp tea towel (dish towel) and leave at room temperature for 24 hours. The starter will begin to ferment and bubble.

2 To make the sponge, stir the flour into the starter mixture and gradually whisk in 125 ml (4 fl oz/½ cup) warm water to form a smooth mixture. Cover with plastic wrap and leave for 24 hours.

3 To make the dough, sift the flour and 1 teaspoon salt into a large bowl and make a well in the centre. Cream the yeast and 80 ml (2½ fl oz/⅓ cup) warm water together and add to the dry ingredients with the starter and sponge mixture. Gradually incorporate the flour into the well. Turn the dough onto a lightly floured surface and knead for 10 minutes, or until smooth and elastic, incorporating extra flour if needed.

4 Place the dough in a lightly oiled bowl, cover with plastic wrap or a damp tea towel and place in a warm place for 1 hour, or until doubled in size. Lightly grease two baking trays and dust lightly with flour. Punch the dough down and turn onto the work surface. Knead for 1 minute, or until smooth. Divide into two equal portions and shape each into a 20 cm (8 in) round. Using a sharp knife, score diagonal cuts 1 cm (½ in) deep along the loaves.

5 Place the loaves on the trays and cover with plastic wrap or a damp tea towel. Leave in a warm place for 45 minutes, or until doubled in size. Preheat the oven to 190°C (375°F/Gas 5). Bake for 35–40 minutes, changing the breads around halfway through. Bake until the bread is golden and crusty and sounds hollow when tapped. Cool on a wire rack before cutting.

POTATO BREAD

Preparation time 45 minutes +
Total cooking time 35 minutes
Makes 1 loaf

2 teaspoons dried yeast
500 g (1 lb 2 oz/4 cups) unbleached plain
    (all-purpose) flour
2 tablespoons full-cream milk powder
235 g (8½ oz/1 cup) warm cooked mashed
    potato
25 g (1 oz) snipped chives
1 egg white, to glaze
2 teaspoons cold water
sunflower seeds and pepitas (pumpkin seeds),
    to sprinkle

1 Lightly grease a 25 cm (10 in) round
cake tin and line the base with baking
paper. Put the yeast and 60 ml (2 fl oz/
¼ cup) warm water in a small bowl and stir
well. Leave in a warm, draught-free place
for 10 minutes, or until bubbles appear on
the surface. The mixture should be frothy
and slightly increased in volume.
2 Sift 440 g (15½ oz/3½ cups) of the
flour, the milk powder and 1 teaspoon salt
into a large bowl. Using a fork, mix the
potato and chives through the dry
ingredients. Add the yeast mixture and
250 ml (9 fl oz/1 cup) warm water and mix
until combined. Add enough of the
remaining flour to make a soft dough.
3 Turn the dough onto a lightly floured
surface. Knead for 10 minutes, or until the
dough is smooth and elastic. Place in an
oiled bowl, then brush the surface with oil.
Cover with plastic wrap and leave in a
warm place for 1 hour, or until well risen.
4 Punch down the dough, then knead for
1 minute. Divide into 12 equal pieces and
form each piece into a smooth ball. Place
evenly spaced balls in a daisy pattern in the
tin, piling two balls in the centre. Cover
with plastic wrap and leave to rise for
45 minutes, or until the dough has risen to
the top of the tin. Preheat the oven to
210°C (415°F/Gas 6–7).
5 Brush the top with the combined egg
white and water and sprinkle the sunflower
seeds and pepitas over the top. Bake for
15 minutes. Reduce the oven to 180°C
(350°F/Gas 4) and bake for a further
20 minutes, or until a skewer inserted into
the centre comes out clean. Leave for
10 minutes, then turn out onto a wire rack.

DAMPER

Preparation time **20 minutes**
Total cooking time **25 minutes**
Makes **1 damper**

375 g (13 oz/3 cups) self-raising flour
90 g (3¼ oz) butter, melted
125 ml (4 fl oz/½ cup) milk
milk, extra, to glaze
flour, extra, to dust

1 Preheat the oven to 210°C (415°F/
Gas 6–7). Grease a baking tray.
Sift the flour and 1–2 teaspoons salt into a
bowl and make a well in the centre.
2 Combine the butter, milk and 125 ml
(4 fl oz/½ cup) water and pour into the
well. Stir with a knife until just combined.
Turn the dough onto a lightly floured
surface and knead for 20 seconds, or until
smooth. Place the dough on the baking
tray and press out to a 20 cm (8 in) circle.
3 Using a sharp pointed knife, score the
dough into eight sections about 1 cm
(½ in) deep. Brush with milk, then dust
with flour. Bake for 10 minutes. Reduce the
oven to 180°C (350°F/Gas 4) and bake the
damper for a further 15 minutes, or until
the crust is golden and the damper sounds
hollow when the surface is tapped. Serve
warm with butter.
Note Damper is the Australian version of
soda bread. It is traditionally served warm
with slatherings of golden syrup. If you
prefer, you can make four rounds instead of
one large damper and slightly reduce the
cooking time. Cut two slashes in the form
of a cross on the top.

RYE BREAD

Preparation time **40 minutes +**
Total cooking time **45 minutes**
Makes **1 loaf**

7 g (1/4 oz) sachet dried yeast
1 teaspoon sugar
185 ml (6 fl oz/3/4 cup) warm milk
200 g (7 oz/2 cups) rye flour
165 g (5 1/2 oz/1 1/3 cups) white bread flour
1 teaspoon salt
rye flour, extra, to dust

1 Place the yeast, sugar and milk in a small bowl and mix well. Leave in a warm place for 10 minutes, or until bubbles appear on the surface. The mixture should be frothy and slightly increased in volume. If your yeast doesn't foam it is dead, so you will have to discard it and start again.

2 Sift the flours and salt into a large bowl and make a well in the centre. Add the yeast mixture and 185 ml (6 fl oz/3/4 cup) warm water and, using your fingers, incorporate the flour to form a dough.

3 Turn the dough onto a lightly floured surface and knead for 10 minutes, or until smooth and elastic. Place the dough in a large lightly oiled bowl and cover with plastic wrap or a damp cloth. Leave in a warm place for up to 1 1/2 hours, until doubled in size.

4 Lightly grease a baking tray and dust lightly with flour. Punch down the dough and turn onto a lightly floured surface. Knead for 1 minute, or until smooth. Shape into an 18 cm (7 in) circle and, using a sharp knife, score a shallow criss-cross pattern on top of the loaf. Lightly dust the top with the extra rye flour.

5 Cover the dough with plastic wrap or a damp tea towel and leave in a warm place for 1 hour, or until doubled in size.

6 Preheat the oven to 180°C (350°F/Gas 4) and bake the bread for 40–45 minutes, or until golden brown and the bread sounds hollow when tapped. Transfer to a wire rack to cool completely before cutting.

PUMPERNICKEL

Preparation time **1 hour +**
Total cooking time **50 minutes**
Makes **2 loaves**

1 tablespoon dried yeast
1 teaspoon caster (superfine) sugar
90 g (3¼ oz/¼ cup) molasses
60 ml (2 fl oz/¼ cup) cider vinegar
90 g (3¼ oz) butter
30 g (1 oz) dark chocolate, chopped
1 tablespoon instant coffee powder
560 g (1 lb 4 oz/4½ cups) unbleached
    plain (all-purpose) flour
300 g (10½ oz/3 cups) rye flour
75 g (2¾ oz/1 cup) bran
1 tablespoon caraway seeds
2 teaspoons fennel seeds
1 egg white
caraway seeds, extra, to sprinkle

1 Grease a 20 cm (8 in) round cake tin and a 12 x 28 cm (4½ x 11¼ in) loaf (bar) or bread tin. Line the base of each tin with baking paper.
2 Put 125 ml (4 fl oz/½ cup) warm water, the yeast and sugar in a bowl and stir. Leave in a warm, draught-free place for 10 minutes, or until bubbles appear on the surface. The mixture should be frothy.
3 Put the molasses, vinegar, butter,

chocolate, coffee powder and 500 ml (17 fl oz/2 cups) cold water into a saucepan and stir over low heat until smooth.
4 Put 440 g (15½ oz/3½ cups) of the plain flour, the rye flour, bran, caraway and fennel seeds and 1 teaspoon salt in a large bowl. Make a well in the centre and add the yeast and chocolate mixtures. Mix until the dough leaves the side of the bowl and forms a firm, sticky ball.
5 Turn out onto a floured surface and knead for 10 minutes. Incorporate enough of the remaining plain flour to make a dense but smooth dough. Divide in half and place in oiled bowls. Brush the surface of the dough with oil. Cover with plastic wrap and leave in a warm, draught-free place for 1¼ hours, or until well risen.
6 Punch down the dough and knead each portion for 1 minute. Shape each portion to fit a tin and place one in each tin. Cover with lightly oiled plastic wrap and leave in a warm place for 1 hour, or until well risen.
7 Preheat the oven to 180°C (350°F/Gas 4). Glaze the dough with combined egg white and 1 tablespoon water and sprinkle with caraway seeds.
8 Bake for 50 minutes, or until browned. During the last 15 minutes, cover with foil. Leave in the tins for 15 minutes before turning out onto a wire rack to cool.

WALNUT BREAD

Preparation time **45 minutes +**
Total cooking time **50 minutes**
Makes **1 loaf**

2¹/₂ teaspoons dried yeast
90 g (3¹/₄ oz/¹/₄ cup) liquid malt
2 tablespoons olive oil
300 g (10¹/₂ oz/3 cups) walnut halves,
   lightly toasted
540 g (1 lb 3 oz/4¹/₃ cups) white strong flour
1 egg, lightly beaten

1 Grease a baking tray. Put the yeast, liquid malt and 330 ml (11¹/₄ fl oz/1¹/₃ cups) warm water in a small bowl and stir well. Leave in a warm, draught-free place for 10 minutes, or until bubbles appear on the surface. The mixture should be frothy and slightly increased in volume. Stir in the oil.
2 Process 200 g (7 oz/2 cups) of the walnuts in a food processor until they resemble coarse meal. Combine 500 g (1 lb 2 oz/4 cups) of the flour with 1¹/₂ teaspoons salt in a large bowl and stir in the walnut meal. Make a well and add the yeast mixture. Mix with a large metal spoon until just combined. Turn out onto a lightly floured surface and knead for 10 minutes, or until smooth, incorporating enough of the remaining flour to keep the dough from sticking—it should be soft and moist, but it won't become very springy. Shape the dough into a ball. Place in a lightly oiled bowl, cover with plastic wrap or a damp tea towel (dish towel) and leave in a warm place for up to 1¹/₂ hours, or until doubled in size.
3 Punch down the dough and turn out onto a lightly floured surface. With very little kneading, shape the dough into a flattened 20 x 25 cm (8 x 10 in) rectangle. Spread with the remaining walnuts and roll up firmly from the short end. Place the loaf on the baking tray, cover with plastic wrap or a damp tea towel and leave to rise for 1 hour, or until doubled in size.
4 Preheat the oven to 190°C (375°F/Gas 5). Glaze the loaf with the egg and bake for 45–50 minutes, or until golden and hollow sounding when tapped. Transfer to a wire rack to cool.

PUMPKIN BREAD

Preparation time **35 minutes +**
Total cooking time **50 minutes**
Makes **1 round loaf**

300 g (10½ oz) pumpkin, chopped
7 g (¼ oz) sachet dried yeast
1 teaspoon salt
560 g (1 lb 2 oz/4½ cups) white bread flour
1 egg, beaten
pumpkin seeds (pepitas), to decorate

1 Boil the pumpkin for 10 minutes, or until tender. Drain thoroughly, then mash.
2 Grease a 20 cm (8 in) cake tin and line the base with baking paper.
3 Place the yeast and 60 ml (2 fl oz/¼ cup) warm water in a small bowl and stir well. Leave in a warm, draught-free place for 10 minutes. The mixture should be frothy. If your yeast doesn't foam it is dead, so you will have to discard it and start again.
4 Sift the salt and 500 g (1 lb 2 oz/4 cups) of the flour into a large bowl. Add the pumpkin, yeast mixture and 60 ml (2 fl oz/ ¼ cup) warm water. Mix until combined.
5 Turn onto a floured surface. Knead for 10 minutes, or until the dough is smooth and elastic. Incorporate enough of the remaining flour to form a smooth dough. Place the dough in a lightly oiled bowl and brush the dough with oil. Cover with plastic wrap and leave in a warm place for 1 hour, or until well risen.
6 Punch down the dough, knead for 1 minute, then pull away a golf ball-sized piece of dough. Shape the remaining dough into a smooth ball and place in the tin. Roll the smaller ball into a rope 35 cm (14 in) long. Tie into a loose knot and place across the top of the dough, then seal with water to hold in place. Cover with plastic wrap and leave in a warm place for 1 hour, or until risen to the top of the tin.
7 Preheat the oven to hot 210°C (415°F/Gas 6–7). Beat 2 teaspoons water into the egg and brush over the dough.

Sprinkle with the pumpkin seeds and bake for 20 minutes. Reduce the oven to 180°C (350°F/Gas 4), then bake for a further 20 minutes, or until cooked. Transfer to a wire rack to cool.

FOUGASSE

Preparation time **30 minutes +**
Total cooking time **35 minutes**
Makes **4**

7 g (¼ oz) sachet dried yeast
1 teaspoon sugar
500 g (1 lb 2 oz/4 cups) white bread flour
2 teaspoons salt
60 ml (2 fl oz/¼ cup) olive oil

1 Place the yeast, sugar and 125 ml (4 fl oz/ ½ cup) warm water in a small bowl and stir until dissolved. Leave in a warm, draught-free place for 10 minutes, or until bubbles appear on the surface. The mixture should be frothy. If your yeast doesn't foam it is dead, so you will have to discard it.
2 Sift the flour and salt into a bowl and make a well in the centre. Add 185 ml (6 fl oz/¾ cup) warm water, the yeast mixture and oil. Mix to a soft dough and gather into a ball with floured hands. Turn out onto a floured surface and knead for 10 minutes, or until smooth.
3 Place in a lightly oiled bowl, cover loosely with plastic wrap or a damp cloth and leave in a warm place for 1 hour, or until doubled in size.
4 Punch down the dough and knead for 1 minute. Divide the mixture into four equal portions. Press each portion into an oval shape 1 cm (½ in) thick and make several cuts on either side of all of them. Lay on floured baking trays, cover with plastic wrap and leave to rise for 20 minutes.
5 Preheat the oven to 210°C (415°F/ Gas 6–7). Bake the fougasse for 35 minutes, or until crisp. After 15 minutes, spray the oven with water to make the crust crispy.

COTTAGE LOAF

Preparation time **30 minutes** +
Total cooking time **40 minutes**
Makes **1 large loaf**

2 teaspoons dried yeast
1 tablespoon soft brown sugar
250 g (9 oz/2 cups) white strong flour
300 g (10½ oz/2 cups) wholemeal
  (whole-wheat) strong flour
1 tablespoon vegetable oil

1 Put the yeast, 1 teaspoon of the sugar and 125 ml (4 fl oz/½ cup) warm water in a small bowl and mix well. Leave in a warm, draught-free place for 10 minutes, or until bubbles appear on the surface. The mixture should be frothy and slightly increased in volume.

2 Put the flours and 1 teaspoon salt in a large bowl. Make a well in the centre and add the yeast mixture, oil, the remaining sugar and 250 ml (9 fl oz/1 cup) warm water. Mix with a wooden spoon then turn out onto a lightly floured surface. Knead for 10 minutes, or until smooth and elastic.

Incorporate a little extra flour into the dough as you knead, to stop the dough from sticking.

3 Place the dough in an oiled bowl and lightly brush oil over the dough. Cover with plastic wrap or a damp tea towel (dish towel) and leave in a warm place for 45 minutes, or until doubled in size.

4 Punch down the dough then turn out onto a lightly floured surface and knead the dough for 3–4 minutes. Pull away one-third of the dough and knead both portions into a smooth ball. Place the large ball on a large floured baking tray and brush the top with water. Sit the smaller ball on top and, using two fingers, press down into the centre of the dough to join the two balls together. Cover with plastic wrap or a damp tea towel and set aside in a warm place for 40 minutes, or until well risen.

5 Preheat the oven to 190°C (375°F/Gas 5). Sift some white flour over the top of the loaf and bake for 40 minutes, or until golden brown and cooked. Leave on the tray for 2–3 minutes to cool slightly, then turn out onto a wire rack to cool.

BEER BREAD

Preparation time **15 minutes**

Total cooking time **20 minutes**

Makes 4

405 g (14¼ oz/3¼ cups) plain (all-purpose) flour

3 teaspoons baking powder

1 tablespoon sugar

50 g (1¾ oz) butter, chopped

375 ml (13 fl oz/1½ cups) beer

1 Process the flour, baking powder, sugar, butter and 1 teaspoon salt in a food processor until crumbly. Add the beer and process in bursts to form a soft dough.

2 Preheat the oven to 210°C (415°F/ Gas 6–7). Turn the dough out onto a well-floured surface and knead until smooth, adding extra flour if needed.

3 Divide the dough into four balls, place on greased oven trays and flatten slightly. Brush with a little water and slash the tops with a knife.

4 Bake for 10 minutes. Reduce the oven to 180°C (350°F/Gas 4) and bake for about 10 minutes, or until cooked. Cool on a wire rack. Serve with butter.

WALNUT AND CHEDDAR SODA BREAD

Preparation time **30 minutes +**
Total cooking time **40 minutes**
Makes **1 loaf**

250 g (9 oz/2 cups) plain (all-purpose) flour
225 g (8 oz/1 1/2 cups) wholemeal
   (whole-wheat) flour
1 tablespoon baking powder
1 teaspoon bicarbonate of soda (baking soda)
1 tablespoon soft brown sugar
60 g (2 1/4 oz/1/2 cup) walnut pieces, chopped
175 g (6 oz/1 1/2 cups) grated mature cheddar
   cheese
40 g (1 1/2 oz) butter, melted and cooled
2 eggs, lightly beaten
250 ml (9 fl oz/1 cup) buttermilk

1 Preheat the oven to 180°C (350°F/Gas 4).
Line a baking tray with baking paper.
2 Sift the flours, baking powder and
bicarbonate of soda into a large bowl (tip
any husks from the wholemeal flour left
in the sieve back into the mixture). Stir
in the sugar, walnuts and cheese. Make a
well in the centre. Combine the butter,
eggs and buttermilk in a bowl and pour
into the well. Stir with a wooden spoon
until a soft dough forms, then turn out
onto a lightly floured work surface. Using
lightly floured hands, knead briefly just
until smooth, then shape the dough into
a 20 cm (8 in) round. Transfer to the
baking tray.
3 Using a sharp, lightly floured knife, cut
a 1 cm (1/2 in) deep cross into the top
of the loaf. Bake for 30–40 minutes, or
until golden.
Note For a variation, replace the cheddar
cheese with 100 g (3 1/2 oz/1/2 cup)
chopped dried pear and 1 teaspoon
aniseed. Bake as above and serve warm,
with cheese.

GREEK LEMON, DILL AND FETA BREAD

Preparation time 30 minutes +
Total cooking time 30 minutes
Makes 2 loaves

375 g (13 oz/3 cups) white strong flour
125 g (4½ oz/1 cup) semolina
1 tablespoon (12 g) instant dried yeast
1 teaspoon caster (superfine) sugar
2 tablespoons olive oil
60 g (2¼ oz/1 bunch) dill, finely chopped
grated zest of 1 lemon
200 g (7 oz/1⅓ cups) coarsely crumbled feta
   cheese, well drained

1 Combine the flour, semolina, yeast, sugar and 1½ teaspoons salt in the bowl of an electric mixer with a dough hook attachment and make a well in the centre. Pour 250 ml (9 fl oz/1 cup) warm water and the oil into the well. With the mixer set to the lowest speed, mix for 3 minutes, or until a dough forms. Increase the speed to medium, add the dill and lemon zest and knead for another 8 minutes, or until the dough is smooth and elastic. Add the feta and knead for 2 minutes, or until the feta is incorporated into the dough.
2 Alternatively, mix the dough by hand using a wooden spoon, then turn out onto a floured work surface, sprinkle over the dill and lemon zest and knead for 8 minutes or until the dill and zest are incorporated and the dough is smooth and elastic. Pat the dough into a rectangle approximately 20 x 10 cm (8 x 4 in) and sprinkle over the feta. Fold the dough over several times, then knead for 2 minutes, or until the feta is incorporated.
3 Grease a large bowl with oil, then transfer the dough to the bowl, turning the dough to coat in the oil. Cover with plastic wrap and leave to rise in a draught-free place for 1½–2 hours, or until the dough has doubled in size.
4 Knock back the dough by punching it, then turn out onto a floured work surface. Divide the dough in half and form each into a loaf shape and place, seam side down, into two greased 20 x 10 cm (8 x 4 in) loaf tins. Cover with a damp cloth and leave for 30 minutes, or until doubled in size.
5 Meanwhile, preheat the oven to 200°C (400°F/Gas 6). Bake the bread for 10 minutes, then reduce the oven to 180°C (350°F/Gas 4) and bake for a further 20 minutes, or until golden and hollow sounding when tapped on the base. Transfer to a wire rack to cool.

CHEESE AND HERB PULL-APART

Preparation time **30 minutes +**
Total cooking time **30 minutes**
Makes **1 loaf**

2 teaspoons dried yeast
1 teaspoon sugar
500 g (1 lb 2 oz/4 cups) plain (all-purpose) flour
2 tablespoons chopped flat-leaf (Italian) parsley
2 tablespoons snipped chives
1 tablespoon chopped thyme
60 g (2¼ oz) cheddar cheese, grated
milk, to glaze

1 Put the yeast, sugar and 125 ml (4 fl oz/ ½ cup) warm water in a small bowl and stir well. Leave in a warm place for 10 minutes, or until bubbles appear on the surface. The mixture should be frothy.

2 Sift the flour and 1½ teaspoons salt in a large bowl. Make a well in the centre and add the yeast mixture and 250 ml (9 fl oz/ 1 cup) warm water. Mix to a soft dough.

Turn onto a lightly floured surface and knead for 10 minutes, or until smooth. Place the dough in an oiled bowl, cover with plastic wrap or a damp tea towel (dish towel) and leave for 1 hour, or until doubled in size.

3 Punch down the dough and knead for 1 minute. Divide the dough in half and shape each half into 10 flat discs, 6 cm (2½ in) in diameter. Mix the herbs with the cheddar and put 2 teaspoons of the mixture on one of the discs. Press another disc on top, then repeat with the remaining discs and herb mixture.

4 Grease a 6 x 10.5 x 21 cm (2½ x 4¼ x 8¼ in) loaf (bar) tin. Stand the filled discs upright in the prepared tin, squashing them together. Cover the tin with plastic wrap or a damp tea towel and leave in a warm place for 30 minutes, or until the dough is well risen.

5 Preheat the oven to 210°C (415°F/ Gas 6–7). Lightly brush the loaf with a little milk and bake for 30 minutes, or until the bread is brown and crusty and sounds hollow when tapped on the base.

TRADITIONAL CORN BREAD

Preparation time **15 minutes**
Total cooking time **25 minutes**
Makes **1 loaf**

150 g (5½ oz/1 cup) polenta
2 tablespoons caster (superfine) sugar
125 g (4½ oz/1 cup) plain (all-purpose) flour
2 teaspoons baking powder
½ teaspoon bicarbonate of soda (baking soda)
1 egg, lightly beaten
250 ml (9 fl oz/1 cup) buttermilk
60 g (2¼ oz) butter, melted

1 Preheat the oven to 210°C (415°F/ Gas 6–7). Brush a 20 cm (8 in) square cake tin with oil or melted butter, and line the base with baking paper.

2 Put the polenta and sugar in a large bowl. Add the sifted flour, baking powder, soda and ½ teaspoon salt and mix thoroughly.
3 Combine the beaten egg, buttermilk and melted butter. Stir the mixture quickly into the dry ingredients. Stir only until the ingredients are moistened.
4 Pour the mixture into the prepared tin and smooth the surface. Bake for 20–25 minutes, or until a skewer inserted in the centre of the bread comes out clean. Place on a wire rack and leave to cool for 10 minutes before turning out. Cut into squares and serve warm.
Note This bread is best eaten on day of baking. For successful results, use fine to medium cornmeal, available from most health food stores.

OLIVE BREAD

Preparation time **30 minutes +**
Total cooking time **35 minutes**
Makes **1 loaf**

375 g (13 oz/3 cups) plain (all-purpose)
 flour
2 teaspoons dry yeast
2 teaspoons sugar
2 tablespoons olive oil
110 g (3¾ oz/⅔ cup) pitted and halved
 Kalamata olives
2 teaspoons plain (all-purpose) flour,
 extra, to coat
1 small oregano sprig, leaves removed and
 torn into small pieces (optional)
olive oil, to glaze

1 Put one-third of the flour in a large bowl
and stir in 1 teaspoon salt. Put the yeast,
sugar and 250 ml (9 fl oz/1 cup) warm
water in a small bowl and stir well. Leave in
a warm, draught-free place for 10 minutes,
or until bubbles appear on the surface.
The mixture should be frothy. If your yeast
doesn't foam, it is dead.
2 Add the yeast mixture to the flour
mixture and stir to make a thin, lumpy
paste. Cover with a tea towel (dish towel)
and set aside in a warm, draught-free place
for 45 minutes, or until doubled in size.

3 Stir in the remaining flour and the oil
and 125 ml (4 fl oz/½ cup) warm water.
Mix with a wooden spoon until a rough
dough forms. Transfer to a lightly floured
work surface and knead for 10–12 minutes,
incorporating as little extra flour as possible
to keep the dough soft and moist, but not
sticky. Form into a ball. Oil a large bowl
and roll the dough around in it to coat in
the oil. Cut a cross on top, cover the bowl
with a tea towel and set aside in a warm
place for 1 hour, or until doubled in size.
4 Lightly grease a baking tray and dust
with flour. Punch down the dough on a
floured surface. Roll out to 1 x 25 x 30 cm
(½ x 10 x 12 in). Squeeze any excess liquid
from the olives and toss to coat in the extra
flour. Scatter over the dough and top with
the oregano. Roll up lengthways, pressing
to expel any air pockets as you roll. Press
the ends together to form an oval loaf
25 cm (10 in) long. Transfer to the tray,
join side down. Make three shallow
diagonal slashes across the top. Slide the
tray into a plastic bag and leave in a warm
place for 45 minutes.
5 Preheat the oven to 220°C (425°F/Gas 7).
Brush the top of the loaf with olive oil and
bake for 30 minutes. Reduce the heat to
180°C (350°F/Gas 4) and bake for a further
5 minutes. Cool on a wire rack.

HAM, CHEESE & ONION QUICKBREAD

Preparation time **25 minutes**
Total cooking time **1 hour 5 minutes**
Makes **1 loaf**

1 tablespoon oil
3 onions, thinly sliced into rings
2 teaspoons soft brown sugar
200 g (7 oz) sliced ham, finely chopped
375 g (13 oz/3 cups) self-raising flour
100 g (3½ oz) chilled butter
90 g (3¼ oz/¾ cup) grated cheddar cheese
125 ml (4 fl oz/½ cup) milk

1 Heat half of the oil in a large, heavy-based frying pan. Add the onion and cook over medium heat for 10 minutes, stirring occasionally. Add the sugar and continue to cook for 10–15 minutes, or until the onion is golden brown. Set aside to cool.
2 Heat the remaining oil in a small frying pan, add the ham and cook over moderately high heat until golden brown. Drain on crumpled paper towel and add to the onion. Allow to cool slightly.

3 Preheat the oven to 210°C (415°F/ Gas 6–7). Lightly grease a baking tray. Sift the flour into a large bowl and rub in the butter with your fingertips until the mixture resembles fine breadcrumbs.
4 Add three-quarters of the onion mixture and 60 g (2¼ oz/½ cup) of the cheddar to the flour and mix well. Make a well in the centre and add the milk and about 125 ml (4 fl oz/½ cup) of water (add enough water to bring the dough together). Mix with a flat-bladed knife, using a cutting action, until the mixture forms a soft dough. Gently gather together into a ball.
5 Lay the dough on the tray and press out to form a 22 cm (8½ in) circle. Using a sharp knife, mark the dough into quarters, cutting two-thirds of the way through. Sprinkle with the rest of the onion mixture and the remaining cheddar. Bake for 15 minutes, then reduce the oven to 180°C (350°F/Gas 4). Cover the top loosely with foil if it starts getting too brown. Bake for another 20 minutes, or until the base sounds hollow when tapped.

CIABATTA

Preparation time **30 minutes +**
Total cooking time **30 minutes**
Makes **1 loaf**

2 teaspoons dried yeast
1 teaspoon sugar
375 g (13 oz/3 cups) white strong flour
50 ml (1³/4 fl oz) olive oil
extra flour, to sprinkle

1 Put the yeast, sugar and 80 ml (2¹/2 fl oz/ ¹/3 cup) warm water in a small bowl and stir well. Leave in a warm, draught-free place for 10 minutes, or until bubbles appear on the surface. The mixture should be frothy and slightly increased in volume.

2 Put 250 g (9 oz/2 cups) of the flour in a large bowl with 2 teaspoons salt and make a well in the centre. Add the yeast mixture, oil and 230 ml (7³/4 fl oz) water to the bowl and stir to combine. Use a cupped hand to knead the wet dough, lifting and stirring for 5 minutes. The dough will be quite wet at this stage. Shape the dough into a ball and put in a clean bowl. Cover with plastic wrap or a damp tea towel (dish towel) and leave in a warm place for 4 hours, or until doubled in size.

3 Stir in the remaining flour, using a cupped hand, and mix until the flour has been incorporated. Scrape down the side of the bowl. Cover with plastic wrap or a clean tea towel and leave in a warm place for 1–1¹/4 hours.

4 Liberally sprinkle a large baking tray with flour. Do not punch down the dough but carefully tip it out onto the tray. Use floured hands to spread the dough into an oval about 12 x 30 cm (4¹/2 x 12 in). Use heavily floured hands to spread evenly and tuck under the dough edges to plump up the dough. Sprinkle liberally with flour. Cover with plastic wrap and leave for 30 minutes.

5 Preheat the oven to 210°C (415°F/ Gas 6–7). Place a heatproof container of ice on the base of the oven. Bake the ciabatta for 30 minutes, or until puffed and golden. Remove the melted ice after about 20 minutes. The loaf is cooked when it sounds hollow when tapped.

BRIOCHE

Preparation time **1 hour +**
Total cooking time **50 minutes**
Makes **6 small and 1 medium brioche**

2 teaspoons dried yeast
1 teaspoon caster (superfine) sugar
125 ml (4 fl oz/½ cup) warm milk
540 g (1 lb 3 oz/4¼ cups) (all-purpose) flour
2 tablespoons caster (superfine) sugar, extra
4 eggs, at room temperature, lightly beaten
175 g (6 oz) butter, softened
1 egg yolk, to glaze
1 tablespoon pouring (whipping) cream

1 Grease six small brioche moulds and a 11 x 21 cm (4¼ x 8¼ in) bread or loaf (bar) tin. Put the yeast, sugar and warm milk in a bowl and stir well. Leave in a warm, draught-free place for 10 minutes, or until bubbles appear on the surface.
2 Sift 500 g (1 lb 2 oz/4 cups) of the flour, 1 teaspoon salt and the extra sugar into a bowl. Make a well in the centre and pour in the yeast mixture and beaten egg. Beat until combined and the mixture forms a ball. Turn out onto a floured surface and knead for 5 minutes, or until the dough is smooth. Incorporate small amounts of the butter into the dough. This will take about 10 minutes and the dough will be sticky.
3 Knead the dough for 10 minutes, or until smooth and elastic. Place in a buttered bowl and brush the surface with oil. Cover with plastic wrap and leave in a warm place for 1½–2 hours, or until well risen.
4 Punch down the dough and divide in half. Cover one half with plastic wrap and set aside. Divide the other half into six even-sized pieces. Remove a quarter of the dough from each piece. Mould the larger pieces into even rounds and place into the brioche moulds. Brush the surface with the combined egg yolk and cream glaze. Shape the small pieces into small even-sized balls and place on top of each roll. Push a floured wooden skewer through the centre of the top ball to the base of the roll, then remove. Brush again with the glaze, cover and leave in a warm place for 45 minutes, or until well risen.
5 Meanwhile, place the remaining dough in the bread tin and brush with glaze. Cover and set aside for 1 hour, or until risen.
6 Preheat the oven to 210°C (415°F/ Gas 6–7). Bake the small brioche for 10 minutes then reduce the oven to 180°C (350°F/Gas 4). Bake for 10 minutes, or until golden. Turn out onto a wire rack to cool.
7 Increase the oven to 210°C (415°F/ Gas 6–7). Bake the medium loaf for 15 minutes. Reduce the oven to 180°C (350°F/Gas 4). Bake for 15 minutes, or until golden. Turn out onto a wire rack to cool.

FOCACCIA

Preparation time **50 minutes +**
Total cooking time **25 minutes**
Makes **1 flat loaf**

2 teaspoons dried yeast
1 teaspoon caster (superfine) sugar
2 tablespoons olive oil
405 g (14¼ oz/3¼ cups) white strong flour
1 tablespoon full-cream milk powder

Topping

1 tablespoon olive oil
1–2 garlic cloves, crushed
black olives
rosemary sprigs or leaves
1 teaspoon dried oregano
1–2 teaspoons coarse sea salt

1 Grease a 18 x 28 cm (7 x 11¼ in) baking tin. Put the yeast, sugar and 250 ml (9 fl oz/ 1 cup) warm water in a bowl and stir well. Leave in a warm, draught-free place for 10 minutes, or until bubbles appear on the surface. The mixture should be frothy.
2 Sift 375 g (13 oz/3 cups) of the flour, the milk powder and ½ teaspoon salt into a bowl. Make a well in the centre and add the yeast mixture. Beat until the mixture is combined. Add enough of the remaining flour to form a soft dough, and then turn onto a lightly floured surface.
3 Knead for 10 minutes, or until the dough is smooth. Place in an oiled bowl. Brush the surface with oil. Cover with plastic wrap and leave in a warm place for 1 hour.
4 Punch down the dough and knead for 1 minute. Roll into a rectangle, 18 x 28 cm (7 x 11¼ in) and place in the tin. Cover with plastic wrap and leave to rise in a warm place for 20 minutes. Using the handle of a wooden spoon, form indents 1 cm (½ in) deep all over the dough at regular intervals. Cover with plastic wrap and set aside for 30 minutes. Preheat the oven to 180°C (350°F/Gas 4).
5 To make the topping, brush the olive oil and garlic over the surface of the dough. Top with the olives and rosemary sprigs, then sprinkle with the oregano and salt.
6 Bake for 20–25 minutes, or until golden and crisp. Cut into squares and serve warm.

UNLEAVENED LAVASH

Preparation time **40 minutes +**
Total cooking time **35 minutes**
Makes 4

125 g (4½ oz/1 cup) plain (all-purpose)
  flour
½ teaspoon sugar
20 g (¾ oz) chilled butter, chopped
80 ml (2½ fl oz/⅓ cup) milk
sesame and poppy seeds, to sprinkle

1 Put the flour, sugar, butter and
½ teaspoon salt in a food processor.
Process in short bursts until the butter is
incorporated. With the machine running,
pour in the milk and process until the
dough comes together—you may need to
add an extra 1 tablespoon milk. Turn out
onto a floured surface and knead until
smooth. Wrap in plastic wrap and
refrigerate for 1 hour.
2 Preheat the oven to 190°C (375°F/Gas 5).
Lightly grease a baking tray.
3 Cut the dough into four pieces. Working
with one piece at a time, roll until very
thin, into a rough square shape measuring
about 20 cm (8 in) along the sides. Place
the dough shapes on the tray, brush the
tops lightly with water and sprinkle with
the seeds. Roll a rolling pin lightly over the
surface of the dough to press in the seeds.
4 Bake for 6–8 minutes, or until golden
brown. Transfer to a wire rack until cool
and crisp. Break into large pieces. Repeat
the process with the remaining dough.

TURKISH BREAD

Preparation time **30 minutes +**
Total cooking time **30 minutes**
Makes **3 loaves**

1 tablespoon dried yeast
1/2 teaspoon sugar
60 g (21/4 oz/1/2 cup) plain (all-purpose) flour
440 g (151/2 oz/31/2 cups) white strong flour
80 ml (21/2 fl oz/1/3 cup) olive oil
1 egg, lightly beaten with 2 teaspoons water
nigella or sesame seeds, to sprinkle

1 Put the yeast, sugar and 125 ml (4 fl oz/ 1/2 cup) warm water in a small bowl and stir well. Add a little of the plain flour and mix to a paste. Leave in a warm, draught-free place for 10 minutes, or until bubbles appear on the surface. The mixture should be frothy and slightly increased in volume. If your yeast doesn't foam, it is dead, so you will have to discard it and start again.
2 Put the remaining flours and 11/2 teaspoons salt in a large bowl and make a well in the centre. Add the yeast mixture, olive oil and 250 ml (9 fl oz/ 1 cup) warm water. Mix to a rough dough, then turn out onto a floured surface and knead for about 5 minutes. Add minimal flour as the dough should remain damp and springy.
3 Shape the dough into a ball and place in a large oiled bowl. Cover with plastic wrap or a damp tea towel (dish towel) and leave in a warm place for 1 hour to triple in size. Punch down and divide into three. Knead each portion for 2 minutes and shape each into a ball. Cover with plastic wrap or a damp tea towel and leave for 10 minutes.
4 Roll each portion of dough into a rectangle 15 x 35 cm (6 x 14 in). Cover with damp tea towels and leave in a warm place for 20 minutes. Indent all over the surface with your fingers, brush with the egg glaze and sprinkle with the seeds. Preheat the oven to 220°C (425°F/Gas 7).
5 For the best results, bake each loaf separately. Place a baking tray in the oven for a couple of minutes until hot, remove and sprinkle lightly with flour. Place one portion of dough on the hot tray and bake for 10–12 minutes, or until puffed and golden brown. Wrap in a clean tea towel to soften the crust and set aside to cool. Meanwhile, repeat baking the remaining portions of dough.

FLATBREAD WITH ZA'ATAR

Preparation time **35 minutes** +
Total cooking time **15 minutes**
Makes **10**

1 tablespoon dried yeast
1 teaspoon sugar
405 g (14¼ oz/3¼ cups) plain (all-purpose)
   flour
125 ml (4 fl oz/½ cup) olive oil
20 g (¾ oz/⅓ cup) za'atar (see Note)
1 tablespoon sea salt flakes

1 Put the yeast and sugar in a small bowl
with 60 ml (2 fl oz/¼ cup) warm water and
stir until dissolved. Leave in a warm,
draught-free place for 10 minutes, or until
bubbles appear on the surface. The mixture
should be frothy and slightly increased in
volume. If your yeast doesn't foam, it is
dead, so you will have to discard it and
start again.
2 Sift the flour and ½ teaspoon salt into
a large bowl. Make a well in the centre
and pour in the yeast mixture and 310 ml
(10¾ fl oz/1¼ cups) warm water.

Gradually combine to form a dough,
then knead on a floured surface for
10–15 minutes until smooth and elastic,
gradually adding 1 tablespoon olive oil as
you knead, until all the oil has been used.
Cover and set aside in a warm place for
1 hour, or until risen.
3 Punch down the dough with your fist
and then knead again. Set aside and leave
to rise for 30 minutes. Knead briefly and
divide into 10 portions.
4 Roll each portion to a smooth circle
about 5 mm (¼ in) thick. Set aside covered
with a tea towel (dish towel) for a further
20 minutes.
5 Preheat the oven to 220°C (425°F/Gas 7).
Grease two baking trays. Place the rolls on
the trays and gently press the surface with
your fingers to create a dimpled effect.
Brush with the remaining oil and sprinkle
with za'atar and sea salt flakes. Bake for
12–15 minutes. Serve warm.
Note Za'atar mix is a Middle Eastern spice
blend of toasted sesame seeds, dried thyme,
dried majoram and sumac. It is available
from speciality food stores.

PARMESAN GRISSINI

Preparation time **25 minutes +**
Total cooking time **20 minutes**
Makes **32**

1 teaspoon (3 g) instant dried yeast
a pinch of caster (superfine) sugar
1 tablespoon extra virgin olive oil
250 g (9 oz/2 cups) white strong flour
60 g (2¼ oz/⅔ cup) grated parmesan cheese

1 Sprinkle the yeast and sugar over 170 ml (5½ fl oz/⅔ cup) warm water in a bowl. Stir to dissolve the sugar, then leave in a draught-free place for 10 minutes, or until the yeast is foamy. Stir in the olive oil.
2 Put the flour in a large bowl, add the parmesan and 1 teaspoon salt and stir to combine well. Pour in the yeast mixture and stir until a dough forms. Turn the dough out onto a lightly floured work surface and knead for 5 minutes, or until the dough is smooth and elastic.
3 Grease a large bowl with oil, then transfer the dough to the bowl, turning the dough to coat in the oil. Cover with plastic wrap and leave to rise in a draught-free place for 1 hour, or until the dough has doubled in size.
4 Preheat the oven to 200°C (400°F/Gas 6). Lightly grease two baking trays. Knock back the dough by punching it gently, then turn out onto a floured work surface and cut in half. Roll out one piece of dough to form a 20 x 16 cm (8 x 6¼ in) rectangle, then cut into sixteen 1 cm (½ in) wide strips. Using your hands, gently roll each strip to form a 22–24 cm (8½–9½ in) long stick, then place on the baking tray. Repeat for the second piece of dough. Bake for 17–20 minutes, or until golden and crisp, swapping the trays halfway through to ensure even cooking. Transfer to a wire rack to cool.
Note Grissini will keep, stored in an airtight container, for up to 7 days. Re-crisp in a 180°C (350°F/Gas 4) oven for 5 minutes if they become soft.

PRETZELS

Preparation time **50 minutes +**
Total cooking time **15 minutes**
Makes 12

1 teaspoon dried yeast
1/4 teaspoon sugar
150 ml (5 fl oz) warm milk
185 g (6 1/2 oz/1 1/2 cups) white strong flour
30 g (1 oz) butter, melted
1 egg yolk, lightly beaten
coarse sea salt, to sprinkle

1 Put the yeast, sugar and warm milk in a small bowl and stir well. Leave in a warm, draught-free place for 10 minutes, or until bubbles appear on the surface. The mixture should be frothy and slightly increased in volume.

2 Put the flour and 1/4 teaspoon salt in a large bowl and make a well in the centre. Add the yeast mixture and butter and mix to a rough dough with a wooden spoon. Turn out onto a floured surface and knead for 10 minutes until smooth and elastic.

3 Place into an oiled bowl, oil the surface of the dough, cover with plastic wrap or a clean tea towel (dish towel) and set aside in a warm place for 1 hour until doubled in size.

4 Preheat the oven to 190°C (375°F/Gas 5). Line a large baking tray with baking paper. Punch down the dough and knead again for 2–3 minutes. Divide into 12 pieces. Cover the dough while working with each piece. Roll each piece into a long rope 40 cm (16 in) long. Circle and knot into a pretzel shape. Place well spaced on the tray. Cover with a tea towel. Leave to rise in a warm, draught-free place for 20–30 minutes.

5 Lightly brush the pretzels with the beaten egg yolk and sprinkle with sea salt. Place the pretzels in the oven and spray them twice with water before baking for 12–15 minutes, or until crisp and golden brown. Transfer to a wire rack to cool.

BREAD ROLLS

Create your own selection of delicious rolls using plain or wholemeal bread dough and the following toppings and glazes.

SPIRAL ROLLS

Divide the dough into 16–24 even pieces. Roll each piece into a 30 cm (12 in) long rope. Shape the dough into tight spirals, tuck under the ends, then seal. Place 5 cm (2 in) apart on lightly oiled baking trays. Cover with plastic wrap and leave in a warm place for about 20 minutes, or until well risen. Brush with a glaze or topping. Bake in a 180°C (350°F/Gas 4) oven for about 15–20 minutes, or until risen and golden.

KNOT ROLLS

Divide the dough into 16–24 even pieces. Roll into 30 cm (12 in) long ropes. Tie each rope into a loose knot. Place 5 cm (2 in) apart on lightly oiled baking trays. Proceed as for spiral rolls.

CLOVER LEAF ROLLS

Divide the dough into 16–24 even pieces. Divide each piece into 3 even-sized balls. Place the trio of balls from each piece close together on lightly oiled baking trays and 5 cm (2 in) apart. Proceed as for spiral rolls.

OVAL ROLLS

Divide the dough into 16–24 even pieces, and then shape into ovals. Leave plain or slash the tops once lengthways, or twice diagonally. Place 5 cm (2 in) apart on lightly oiled baking trays. Proceed as for spiral rolls.

TOPPINGS AND GLAZES

Glazing dough and adding toppings will change the appearance as well as the taste of the bread. Glazing affects the result of the crust and is done before or after baking, depending on the result you are after. The high oven temperature used for baking bread may cause some toppings to brown too quickly. If you notice this happening, lower the oven

temperature slightly or place a sheet of foil or double thickness of baking paper on top of the rolls to prevent them from burning.

TOPPINGS

Lightly sprinkle the dough with a topping such as flour, rolled oats, crushed rock salt, cracked wheat or grated cheddar cheese. You can also try seeds such as poppy, sesame, caraway, pumpkin, dill, fennel or sunflower. Cereals such as polenta, barley flakes, cracked wheat and rye flakes also make interesting toppings and add a different flavour.

GLAZES

Use a wide pastry brush to brush one of these glazes over the dough, choosing the appropriate glaze for your desired result.

After baking

Soft crust Brush the cooked, hot bread with melted butter and return to the oven for 2 minutes. Remove, brush again with melted butter and leave to cool.

Glossy crust Whisk 1 egg white with 1 tablespoon water. Brush the cooked, hot bread with the glaze, then return to the oven for 5 minutes. Cool.

Sweet glossy crust Combine 1 tablespoon sugar with 2 tablespoons milk and brush over the hot bread. Return to the oven for 5 minutes. Cool.

Sugar glaze Dissolve 60 g (2 oz/¼ cup) sugar in 2 tablespoons water over low heat. Boil for 2 minutes, or until the mixture is syrupy. Brush on the hot bread.

Before baking

Deep colour in the crust Beat 1 whole egg with 1 teaspoon water. For a very deep colour, beat 1 egg yolk with 1 teaspoon water.

Rich, dark gleam on savoury breads Beat 1 egg with 1 teaspoon oil and some salt and pepper.

Crisp crust Whisk together 1 egg white with 1 teaspoon water.

Light sheen Brush with milk, cream or melted butter.

GLUTEN-FREE MINI LOAVES

Preparation time **40 minutes +**

Total cooking time **35 minutes**

Makes **8 individual loaves**

canola oil, for greasing

4 teaspoons (2 x 7 g packages) dried yeast

1 tablespoon soft brown sugar

500 ml (17 fl oz/2 cups) warm water

2 teaspoons guar gum (from health food stores)

300 g (10½ oz/2 cups) soy-free, gluten-free plain (all-purpose) flour

130 g (4¾ oz/¾ cup) rice flour

2 teaspoons ground sea salt

45 g (½ cup) rice bran

60 g (2¼ oz) dairy-free margarine, melted and cooled

2 tablespoons poppy seeds (optional)

canola oil, for brushing

1 Preheat the oven to 400°F (200°C/Gas 6). Lightly grease eight 4 x 2¼ x 1½ in (10 x 5.5 x 3.5 cm) individual loaf tins.

2 Combine the yeast, sugar and warm water in a bowl, then stir to dissolve the yeast. Stand the bowl in a warm place for about 10 minutes, or until the mixture is frothy.

3 Sift the guar gum and flours into a large bowl. Add the salt and rice bran. Make a well in the centre and add the yeast mixture and cooled margarine. Mix well to form a soft dough. Divide into eight equal portions, then gently shape with floured hands into an oval shape. Place in the prepared tins. Sprinkle with poppy seeds, if using.

4 Cover loosely and leave in a warm place for 45–60 minutes, or until the mixture comes to the top of the tins.

5 Bake for 25–30 minutes, or until cooked through. Brush the loaves with oil during cooking at least twice to help promote browning. Remove from the tins and allow to cool on a wire rack.

Note The loaves are best eaten on the day they are made, or they can be frozen until required.

ROSETTAS

Preparation time **40 minutes** +
Total cooking time **25 minutes**
Makes 10

7 g (¼ oz) dried yeast
1 teaspoon sugar
560 g (1 lb 4 oz/4½ cups) unbleached plain
   (all-purpose) flour, sifted
50 g (1¾ oz) butter, softened
60 ml (2 fl oz/¼ cup) olive oil
55 g (2 oz/¼ cup) caster (superfine) sugar
milk, to glaze
plain (all-purpose) flour, extra, to dust

1 Grease two baking trays. Put the yeast, sugar and 125 ml (4 fl oz/½ cup) warm water in a bowl and stir well. Leave in a warm, draught-free place for 10 minutes, or until bubbles appear on the surface. The mixture should be frothy and increased in volume. If your yeast doesn't foam it is dead, so you will have to discard it.
2 Set aside 30 g (1 oz/¼ cup) of the flour and put the rest in a bowl with 1 teaspoon salt. Make a well in the centre. Add the yeast mixture, butter, oil, sugar and 315 ml (10¾ fl oz/1¼ cups) warm water. Stir with a wooden spoon until the dough leaves the side of the bowl and forms a rough, sticky ball. Turn out onto a floured surface. Knead for 10 minutes, or until the dough is smooth and elastic. Add enough of the reserved flour, if necessary, to make a smooth dough. Put in a lightly oiled bowl and brush the surface with melted butter or oil. Cover with plastic wrap and leave in a warm place for 1 hour, or until well risen.
3 Punch down the dough, then knead for 1 minute. Divide into ten portions and shape each into a smooth ball. Place the balls 5 cm (2 in) apart on the trays. Using a 3 cm (1¼ in) round cutter, press a 1 cm (½ in) deep indent into the centre of each ball. With a sharp knife, score five evenly spaced, 1 cm (½ in) deep cuts down the side of each roll. Cover with plastic wrap and leave in a warm place for 1 hour.
4 Preheat the oven to 180°C (350°F/Gas 4). Brush the rolls with milk and sift a fine layer of the extra flour over them. Bake for 25 minutes, or until golden. Rotate the trays in the oven if one tray is browning faster than the other. Cool on a wire rack.

MINI WHOLEMEAL LOAVES

Preparation time **40 minutes** +
Total cooking time **45 minutes**
Makes **4 small loaves**

2 teaspoons dried yeast
1 tablespoon caster (superfine) sugar
125 ml (4 fl oz/½ cup) warm milk
600 g (1 lb 5 oz/4 cups) wholemeal
   (whole-wheat) strong flour
60 ml (2 fl oz/¼ cup) oil
1 egg, lightly beaten

1 Grease four 13 x 6½ x 5 cm (5 x 2¾ x 2 in) baking tins. Put the yeast, sugar and milk in a small bowl and mix well. Leave in a warm, draught-free place for 10 minutes, or until bubbles appear on the surface. The mixture should be frothy and slightly increased in volume.
2 Put the flour and 1 teaspoon salt in a large bowl, make a well in the centre and add the yeast mixture, oil and 250 ml (9 fl oz/1 cup) warm water. Mix to a soft dough and gather into a ball. Turn out onto a floured surface and knead for 10 minutes. Add extra flour if the dough is too sticky.
3 Place the dough in a large oiled bowl, cover loosely with plastic wrap or a damp tea towel (dish towel) and leave in a warm place for 1 hour, or until well risen.
4 Punch down the dough, turn out onto a floured surface and knead for 1 minute, or until smooth. Divide into four portions, knead into shape and put in the tins. Cover with plastic wrap and leave in a warm place for 45 minutes, or until risen.
5 Preheat the oven to 210°C (415°F/Gas 6–7). Brush the loaf tops with the beaten egg. Bake for 10 minutes, then reduce the oven temperature to 180°C (350°F/Gas 4). Bake for a further 30–35 minutes, or until the base sounds hollow when tapped. Cover with foil if the tops become too brown.

MINI BAGUETTES

Preparation time **25 minutes** +
Total cooking time **30 minutes**
Makes **3 loaves**

2 teaspoons dried yeast
1 teaspoon sugar
90 g (3¼ oz/¾ cup) plain (all-purpose) flour
375 g (13 oz/3 cups) white strong flour
2 tablespoons polenta, to sprinkle

1 Put the yeast, sugar and about 310 ml (10³/4 fl oz/1¼ cups) warm water in a small bowl and mix well. Leave in a warm, draught-free place for 10 minutes, or until bubbles appear on the surface.
2 Mix together the flours and ½ teaspoon salt and transfer half the dry ingredients to a large bowl. Make a well in the centre and add the yeast mixture. Fold the flour into the yeast mixture. This should form a soft dough. Cover the bowl with plastic wrap and set aside for 30–35 minutes, or until frothy and risen by about one third of its original size.
3 Mix in the remaining dry ingredients and add up to 60 ml (2 fl oz/¼ cup) warm water, enough to form a soft, but slightly sticky dough. Knead the dough on a floured surface for about 10 minutes, or until smooth and elastic. If the dough sticks to the work surface while kneading, flour the surface sparingly, but try to avoid adding too much flour. Shape the dough into a ball and place in a lightly greased bowl. Cover with a damp cloth or plastic wrap and leave in a warm place for about 1 hour, until the dough has doubled in size.

4 Lightly grease two large baking trays and sprinkle with polenta. Punch down the dough and knead for 2–3 minutes. Divide the dough into three portions and press or roll each into a rectangle about 20 x 40 cm (8 x 16 in). Roll each up firmly into a long sausage shape and place, seam side down, well spaced on the prepared trays. Cover loosely with a damp tea towel or plastic wrap and set aside in a warm place for 40 minutes, or until doubled in size.
5 Preheat the oven to 220°C (425°F/Gas 7). Lightly brush the loaves with water and make diagonal slashes across the top at 6 cm (2½ in) intervals. Place the trays in the oven and spray the oven with water.
6 Bake the bread for 20 minutes, spraying inside the oven with water twice during this time. Lower the temperature to 180°C (350°F/Gas 4) and bake for a further 5–10 minutes, or until the crust is golden and firm and the base sounds hollow when tapped underneath. Cool on a wire rack.
Note Baguettes are best eaten within a few hours of baking.

SCOTTISH BAPS

Preparation time **40 minutes** +
Total cooking time **30 minutes**
Makes **12**

2 teaspoons dried yeast
1 teaspoon caster (superfine) sugar
440 g (15½ oz/3½ cups) white strong flour
250 ml (9 fl oz/1 cup) lukewarm milk
50 g (1¾ oz) butter, melted
1 tablespoon plain (all-purpose) flour

1 Lightly dust two baking trays with flour. Put the yeast, sugar and 2 tablespoons of the strong flour in a small bowl. Gradually add the milk, blending until smooth and dissolved. Leave in a warm, draught-free place for 10 minutes, or until bubbles appear on the surface. The mixture should be frothy.

2 Sift the remaining flour and about 1½ teaspoons salt into a large bowl. Make a well in the centre and add the yeast mixture and butter. Using a flat-bladed knife, mix to form a soft dough. Turn the dough onto a lightly floured surface and knead for 3 minutes, or until smooth. Shape into a ball and place in a large oiled bowl. Cover with plastic wrap or a damp tea towel (dish towel) and leave in a warm place for 1 hour, or until well risen.

3 Preheat the oven to 210°C (415°F/ Gas 6–7). Punch down the dough with your fist. Knead the dough again for 2 minutes, or until smooth. Divide into 12 pieces. Knead one portion at a time on a lightly floured surface for 1 minute, roll into a ball and shape into a flat oval. Repeat with the remaining dough.

4 Place the baps on the trays and dust with the plain flour. Cover with plastic wrap and leave in a warm place for 15 minutes, or until well risen. Make an indent in the centre of each bap with your finger. Bake for 30 minutes until browned and cooked through. Serve warm.

BAGELS

Preparation time **35 minutes +**
Total cooking time **16 minutes**
Makes **8**

2 teaspoons dried yeast
1 teaspoon sugar
1 tablespoon barley malt syrup or honey
500 g (1 lb 2 oz/4 cups) white strong flour
2 teaspoons salt
coarse polenta, to dust

1 Put the yeast, sugar and 375 ml (13 fl oz/ 1 1/2 cups) warm water in a small bowl and stir until dissolved. Leave in a warm place for 10 minutes, or until bubbles appear on the surface. The mixture should be frothy and slightly increased in volume.

2 Put 250 g (9 oz/2 cups) of the flour in a large bowl, make a well in the centre and add the yeast mixture and salt. Stir with a wooden spoon, adding flour as necessary to make a firm dough. Turn out onto a floured work surface and knead for 10–12 minutes, or until smooth and stiff. Add more flour if necessary, to make the dough quite stiff, then divide into eight portions and roll them into smooth balls. Cover with plastic wrap or a clean tea towel (dish towel) and leave for 5 minutes.

3 Roll each ball under your palms to form a rope 28 cm (11 1/4 in) long. Do not taper the ends of the rope. Dampen the ends slightly, overlap by 4 cm (1 1/2 in) and pinch firmly together. Place one at a time around the base of your fingers and, with the overlap under your palm, roll the rope several times. Apply firm pressure to seal the seam. Place all the balls on polenta-dusted baking trays, cover with plastic wrap and refrigerate for 12 hours.

4 Preheat the oven to 240°C (475°F/Gas 8). Line two baking trays with baking paper. Remove the bagels from the fridge 20 minutes before baking. Bring a saucepan of water to the boil and drop the bagels, in batches of three or four, into the water for 30 seconds. Remove and drain, base-down, on a wire rack.

5 Place the bagels on the baking trays and bake for 15 minutes, or until deep golden brown and crisp. Cool on a wire rack.

CARAWAY SEED ROLLS

Preparation time **30 minutes +**
Total cooking time **20 minutes**
Makes **12**

3 teaspoons dried yeast
1 teaspoon caster (superfine) sugar
500 g (1 lb 2 oz/4 cups) strong flour
1 tablespoon caraway seeds
250 g (9 oz/1²/₃ cups) wholemeal (whole-
   wheat) flour
2 teaspoons salt
2 tablespoons milk

1 Stir the yeast, sugar, 50 g (1³/₄ oz/¹/₃ cup) of the strong flour and 125 ml (4 fl oz/ ¹/₂ cup) of warm water together until smooth and place in a warm place for 10 minutes, or until frothy.

2 Lightly pound the caraway seeds using a mortar and pestle to help release their aroma. Sift the remaining strong flour and wholemeal flour into a large bowl. Stir in the salt and work in the frothed yeast mixture, caraway seeds and 250 ml (9 fl oz/ 1 cup) of warm water to form a soft dough. Knead for 10 minutes.

3 Shape into a round and place in an oiled bowl. Cover with a tea towel (dish towel) and leave to rise in a warm place for 45 minutes, or until doubled in size.

4 Preheat the oven to 220°C (425°F/Gas 7). Knock back the dough on a floured surface, divide into 12 pieces and roll each one out to a 25 x 2.5 cm (10 x 1 in) log. Form a horseshoe shape and then loop one end over and through the horseshoe to form a knot. Place on two oiled baking trays, cover with oiled plastic wrap and leave to rise for a further 30 minutes.

5 Brush the rolls with milk and bake for 15–20 minutes, or until risen and hollow sounding when tapped underneath. Cool on a wire rack.

ENGLISH MUFFINS

Preparation time **20 minutes +**
Total cooking time **15 minutes**
Makes **15**

2 teaspoons dried yeast
1/2 teaspoon sugar
530 g (1 lb 3 oz/4 1/4 cups) plain
    (all-purpose) flour
350 ml (12 fl oz) lukewarm milk
1 egg, lightly beaten
40 g (1 1/2 oz) butter, melted

1 Lightly dust two 28 x 32 cm (11 1/4 x 12 3/4 in) baking trays with flour.
2 Put the yeast, sugar, 1 teaspoon of the flour and 60 ml (2 fl oz/1/4 cup) warm water in a small bowl and mix well. Leave in a warm, draught-free place for about 10 minutes, or until bubbles appear on the surface. The mixture should be frothy. If your yeast doesn't foam, it is dead.
3 Sift the remaining flour and 1 teaspoon salt into a large bowl. Make a well in the centre and add the milk, egg, butter and yeast mixture all at once. Using a flat-bladed knife, mix to a soft dough.
4 Turn the dough onto a lightly floured surface and knead lightly for 2 minutes, or until smooth. Shape the dough into a ball and place in a large, lightly oiled bowl. Cover with plastic wrap or a damp tea towel (dish towel) and leave in a warm place for 1 1/2 hours, or until well risen.
5 Preheat the oven to 210°C (415°F/ Gas 6–7). Punch the dough down and knead again for 2 minutes, or until smooth. Roll to 1 cm (1/2 in) thick, then cut into rounds with a lightly floured plain 8 cm (3 1/4 in) cutter and place on the trays. Cover with plastic wrap or a damp tea towel and leave in a warm, draught-free place for 10 minutes.
6 Bake for 15 minutes, turning once halfway through cooking. Transfer to a wire rack to cool. Serve warm or cold.

PISSALADIÈRE

Preparation time **30 minutes +**
Total cooking time **1 hour 5 minutes**
Serves **6**

Bread dough

2 teaspoons dried yeast
250 g (9 oz/2 cups) plain (all-purpose) flour
½ teaspoon salt
3 tablespoons olive oil

40 g (1½ oz) butter
1 tablespoon olive oil
1.5 kg (3 lb 5 oz) onions, thinly sliced
2 tablespoons thyme
1 tablespoon olive oil
16 anchovy fillets, halved lengthways
24 black olives, pitted

1 To make the bread dough, mix the yeast with 120 ml (4 fl oz) of warm water. Leave for 10 minutes in a warm place until the yeast becomes frothy.
2 Sift the flour into a bowl and add the salt, olive oil and the yeast mixture. Mix until the dough forms a ball. Turn out onto a floured work surface. Knead the dough until you have a soft dough. Knead for a further 10 minutes, or until smooth.
3 Rub the inside of a bowl with olive oil. Roll the ball of dough around in the bowl to coat it with oil, then cut a shallow cross on the top of the ball with a knife. Leave the dough in the bowl, cover with a tea towel (dish towel) and leave in a draught-free place for 1–1½ hours.
4 Knock back the dough by punching it several times to expel the air and then knead it again for a couple of minutes. Leave in a warm place until doubled in size.
5 Melt the butter with the olive oil in a saucepan and add the onion and half the thyme. Cover the saucepan and cook over low heat for 45 minutes, stirring, until the onion is softened. Season and cool. Preheat the oven to 200°C (400°F/Gas 6).
6 Roll out the bread dough to roughly fit a greased 34 x 26 cm (13½ x 10½ in) shallow baking tray. Brush with the olive oil, then spread with the onion.
7 Lay the anchovies in a lattice pattern over the onion and arrange the olives in the lattice diamonds. Bake for 20 minutes, or until the dough is lightly browned. Sprinkle with the remaining thyme leaves and cut into squares. Serve hot or warm.

TURKISH PIZZA

Preparation time **25 minutes +**
Total cooking time **45 minutes**
Makes **8**

1 teaspoon dried yeast
1/2 teaspoon sugar
225 g (8 oz) plain (all-purpose) flour
80 ml (2 1/2 fl oz/1/3 cup) olive oil
250 g (9 oz) onions, finely chopped
500 g (1 lb 2 oz) minced (ground) lamb
2 garlic cloves
1 teaspoon ground cinnamon
1 1/2 teaspoons ground cumin
1/2 teaspoon cayenne pepper
60 g (2 1/4 oz/1/4 cup tomato paste
   (concentrated purée)
400 g (14 oz) tinned crushed tomatoes
50 g (1 3/4 oz/1/3 cup) pine nuts
3 tablespoons chopped coriander (cilantro)
Greek-style yoghurt, to serve

1 Mix the yeast, sugar and 60 ml (2 fl oz/1/4 cup) warm water in a bowl. Leave in a warm, draught-free place for 10 minutes.
2 Sift the flour and 1 teaspoon salt into a large bowl, stir in the yeast mixture, 1 tablespoon of the oil and about 100 ml (3 1/2 fl oz) warm water. Mix to form a soft dough, then turn onto a floured board and knead for 10 minutes, or until smooth. Place in an oiled bowl, cover and leave in a warm place for 1 hour.
3 Heat 2 tablespoons of the oil in a frying pan over low heat and cook the onion for 5 minutes, or until soft but not golden. Add the lamb and cook for 10 minutes, or until brown. Add the garlic and spices, tomato paste and tomatoes. Cook for 15 minutes. Add half the pine nuts and 2 tablespoons of the coriander. Season, then leave to cool.
4 Preheat the oven to 210°C (415°F/ Gas 6–7). Grease two baking trays.
5 Knock down the dough, then turn out onto a floured surface. Form into eight portions and roll each into an 12 x 18 cm (4 1/2 x 7 in) oval. Place on the trays. Divide the lamb mixture evenly among them and spread, leaving a small border. Sprinkle with the remaining pine nuts. Brush the edges with oil. Roll the uncovered dough over to cover the outer edges of the filling. Pinch the sides together at each end. Brush with oil. Bake for 15 minutes, or until golden. Sprinkle with coriander and serve with yoghurt.

POTATO AND ROSEMARY PIZZETTAS

Preparation time 25 minutes +
Total cooking time 15 minutes
Makes 48

1 teaspoon dried yeast
1/2 teaspoon sugar
310 g (11 oz/2 1/2 cups) plain (all-purpose)
    flour
80 ml (2 1/2 fl oz/1/3 cup) olive oil
400 g (14 oz) all-purpose potatoes,
    unpeeled
2 tablespoons olive oil, extra
1 tablespoon rosemary leaves
sea salt, to sprinkle

1 Place the yeast, sugar and 80 ml (2 1/2 fl oz/ 1/3 cup) water in a small bowl. Cover and leave in a warm, draught-free place for 10 minutes, or until bubbles appear on the surface. The mixture should be frothy and slightly increased in volume. If your yeast doesn't foam, it is dead, so you will have to discard it and start again.

2 Sift the flour and 1/4 teaspoon salt into a large bowl. Make a well in the centre and stir in the yeast mixture, the oil and 80 ml (2 1/2 fl oz/1/3 cup) water. Mix to a soft dough. Turn out onto a lightly floured surface and knead for 5 minutes, or until the dough is smooth and elastic. Place the dough in an oiled bowl, cover and leave in a warm place for about 1 hour, or until the dough has doubled in size.

3 Preheat the oven to 220°C (425°F/Gas 7). Punch down the dough to expel the air. Turn out and knead for 1 minute, or until smooth. Divide into 48 portions and roll each portion to a 5 cm (2 in) round. Place on lightly greased baking trays.

4 Cut the potatoes into slices. Cover each dough round with a slice of potato, leaving a 1 cm (1/2 in) border. Brush the pizzettas with the extra olive oil and sprinkle with rosemary leaves and sea salt. Bake on the highest shelf in the oven for 15 minutes, or until the pastry is crisp. Serve immediately.

HAM AND PINEAPPLE PIZZA WHEELS

Preparation time **25 minutes** +
Total cooking time **20 minutes**
Makes **16**

250 g (9 oz/2 cups) self-raising flour
40 g (1½ oz) butter, chopped
125 ml (4 fl oz/½ cup) milk
90 g (3¼ oz/⅓ cup tomato paste
    (concentrated purée)
2 small onions, finely chopped
4 pineapple slices, finely chopped
200 g (7 oz) sliced ham, shredded
80 g (2¾ oz) cheddar cheese, grated
2 tablespoons finely chopped flat-leaf
    (Italian) parsley

1 Preheat the oven to 180°C (350°F/Gas 4). Brush two baking trays with oil. Sift the flour into a bowl. Using your fingertips, rub in the butter until the mixture resembles fine breadcrumbs. Make a well in the centre and add almost all the milk. Mix with a flat-bladed knife, using a cutting action, until the mixture comes together in beads. Gather into a ball and turn out onto a lightly floured work surface.

2 Divide the dough in half. Roll out each half on baking paper to a 20 x 30 cm (8 x 12 in) rectangle, about 5 mm (¼ in) thick. Spread the tomato paste over each rectangle, leaving a 1 cm (½ in) border.

3 Mix the onion, pineapple, ham, cheddar and parsley. Spread over the tomato paste, leaving a 2 cm (¾ in) border. Roll up the dough from the long side.

4 Cut each roll into eight even slices. Place the slices on the trays and bake for 20 minutes, or until golden. Serve warm.

PIZZA MARGHERITA

Preparation time **40 minutes** +
Total cooking time **40 minutes**
Serves **4–6**

225 g (8 oz) white strong flour
1 teaspoon sugar
2 teaspoons dried yeast
1 tablespoon olive oil
90 ml (3 fl oz) milk

Topping
1 tablespoon olive oil
1 garlic clove, crushed
425 g (15 oz) tinned crushed tomatoes
1 bay leaf
1 teaspoon chopped thyme
6 chopped basil leaves
polenta, to sprinkle
150 g (51/2 oz) bocconcini cheese (fresh baby
   mozzarella cheese), thinly sliced
olive oil, extra, to drizzle

1 To make the base, put the flour, sugar, yeast and $^1/_2$ teaspoon salt in a large bowl. Stir the olive oil with the milk and 80 ml ($2^1/_2$ fl oz/$^1/_3$ cup) warm water and add to the bowl. Stir with a wooden spoon.
2 Place on a lightly floured work surface and knead for 5 minutes, or until soft and smooth. Lightly oil a bowl, add the dough and turn to coat in the oil. Leave in a warm place for 1 hour, or until doubled in size. Preheat the oven to 210°C (415°F/Gas 6–7).
3 To make the topping, heat the oil in a saucepan over medium heat, add the garlic and stir for 30 seconds. Add the tomatoes, bay leaf, thyme and basil and simmer, stirring occasionally, for 20–25 minutes, or until thick. Cool, then remove the bay leaf.
4 Place the dough on a floured work surface, punch down to expel the air and knead for 5 minutes. Shape into a ball and roll to 28–30 cm ($11^1/_4$–12 in) diameter.
5 Oil a pizza tray the size of the dough. Sprinkle the tray with polenta and place the dough on top. Spread the sauce over the dough, leaving a 3 cm ($1^1/_4$ in) border. Arrange the bocconcini over the top and drizzle with olive oil. Bake for 15 minutes, or until crisp and bubbling.

SPANISH PIZZA

Preparation time **30 minutes** +
Total cooking time **45 minutes**
Serves 4–6

Base

2 teaspoons dried yeast
1 teaspoon caster (superfine) sugar
280 g (10 oz/2¼ cups) plain (all-purpose) flour

Topping

10 English spinach leaves, shredded
1 tablespoon olive oil
2 garlic cloves, crushed
2 onions, chopped
440 g (15½ oz) tinned tomatoes, drained
   and crushed
12 pitted black olives, chopped

1 Preheat the oven to 210°C (415°F/Gas 6–7). Brush a 25 x 30 cm (10 x 12 in) Swiss roll tin (jelly roll tin) with oil.
2 To make the base, combine the yeast, sugar and flour in a large bowl. Gradually add 250 ml (9 fl oz/1 cup) warm water and blend until smooth. Knead the dough on a lightly floured surface until smooth and elastic. Place in a lightly oiled bowl, cover with a tea towel (dish towel) and leave to rise in a warm position for 15 minutes, or until the dough has almost doubled in size.
3 To make the topping, put the spinach in a large saucepan, cover and cook on low heat for 3 minutes. Drain the spinach and cool. Squeeze out the excess moisture with your hands and set the spinach aside. Heat the oil in a frying pan and add the garlic and onions. Cook over low heat for 5–6 minutes. Add the tomatoes and ¼ teaspoon ground pepper and simmer gently for 5 minutes.
4 Punch the dough down, remove from the bowl and knead on a lightly floured board for 2–3 minutes. Roll the dough out and fit it in the tin. Spread with spinach, top with the tomato mixture and sprinkle the olives on top.
5 Bake for 25–30 minutes. Cut into small squares or fingers. The pizza can be served hot or cold.

LIGHT FRUIT BREAD

Preparation time **25 minutes** +
Total cooking time **35 minutes**
Serves **8–10**

125 g (4½ oz/1 cup) raisins
1 tablespoon sherry
1 tablespoon grated orange zest
2 teaspoons dried yeast
250 ml (9 fl oz/1 cup) milk, warmed
55 g (2 oz/¼ cup) caster (superfine) sugar
375 g (13 oz/3 cups) white strong flour
30 g (1 oz) butter, cubed

Glaze
1 egg yolk
2 tablespoons pouring (whipping) cream

1 Combine the raisins, sherry and zest in a small bowl and set aside.
2 Place the yeast, milk and 1 teaspoon of the sugar in a small bowl and mix well. Leave in a warm, draught-free place for 10 minutes, or until bubbles appear on the surface. The mixture should be frothy and slightly increased in volume. If your yeast doesn't foam, it is dead, so you will have to discard it and start again.

3 Place 340 g (11¾ oz/2¾ cups) of the strong flour and ½ teaspoon salt in a large bowl. Rub in the butter and remaining sugar with your fingertips. Make a well in the centre, add the yeast mixture and mix to a soft dough. Turn out onto a floured surface and knead for 10 minutes, or until smooth and elastic, incorporating the remaining flour as necessary.
4 Place the dough in an oiled bowl and brush with oil. Cover with plastic wrap and leave for 1 hour, or until well risen. Punch down, knead for 2 minutes, then roll to a rectangle, 20 x 40 cm (8 x 16 in). Scatter with the raisins and roll up from the long end.
5 Grease a loaf (bar) tin with a base measuring 8 x 21 cm (3¼ x 8¼ in) and line the base with baking paper. Place the dough in the tin, cover with plastic wrap or a damp cloth and leave for 30 minutes, or until well risen. Preheat the oven to 180°C (350°F/Gas 4).
6 To make the glaze, combine the egg yolk and cream and brush a little over the loaf. Bake for 30 minutes, or until cooked and golden. Glaze again, bake for 5 minutes then glaze again. Cool on a wire rack.

DENSE FRUIT BREAD

Preparation time **25 minutes +**
Total cooking time **50 minutes**
Makes **1 large loaf**

2 teaspoons dried yeast
¼ teaspoon sugar
450 g (1 lb oz) white strong flour
25 g (1 oz) butter
½ teaspoon ground ginger
¼ teaspoon freshly grated nutmeg
80 g (2¾ oz/⅓ cup) caster (superfine) sugar
250 g (9 oz/2 cups) sultanas (golden raisins)
185 g (6½ oz/1¼ cups) currants
50 g (1¾ oz/¼ cup) mixed peel
   (mixed candied citrus peel)

1 Put the yeast, sugar and 310 ml (10¾ fl oz/1¼ cups) warm water in a small bowl and mix well. Leave in a warm, draught-free place for 10 minutes, or until bubbles appear on the surface. The mixture should be frothy and slightly increased in volume. If your yeast doesn't foam, it is dead, so you will have to discard it and start again.
2 Put the flour and ¼ teaspoon salt in a large bowl. Using your fingertips, rub in the butter until the mixture resembles coarse breadcrumbs. Stir in the spices and three-quarters of the caster sugar. Make a well in the centre and stir in the yeast mixture. Mix well until the dough comes together and leaves the side of the bowl clean. Turn onto a lightly floured surface and knead for 10 minutes, or until elastic and smooth. Place in a clean bowl, cover with plastic wrap or a damp tea towel (dish towel) and leave in a warm, draught-free place for 1 hour, or until doubled in size.
3 Turn the dough onto a lightly floured surface, add the fruit and knead for a couple of minutes, or until the fruit is incorporated. Shape the dough into a large round and place on a greased baking tray. Cover with plastic wrap or a damp tea towel and leave in a warm, draught-free place for 30–40 minutes.
4 Preheat the oven to 200°C (400°F/Gas 6). Bake on the middle shelf for 40 minutes, or until the loaf has browned and sounds hollow when tapped on the base. Transfer to a wire rack to cool slightly.
5 Dissolve the remaining caster sugar in 1 tablespoon hot water and brush over the loaf. Bake for 2–3 minutes, then cool on a wire rack.

CHELSEA BUNS

Preparation time **30 minutes +**
Total cooking time **25 minutes**
Makes **8**

2 teaspoons dried yeast
1 teaspoon sugar
310 g (11 oz/2½ cups) plain (all-purpose) flour
125 ml (4 fl oz/½ cup) milk, warmed
185 g (6½ oz) unsalted butter, cubed
1 tablespoon sugar, extra
2 teaspoons grated lemon zest
1 teaspoon ground mixed (pumpkin pie) spice
1 egg, lightly beaten
45 g (1¾ oz/¼ cup) soft brown sugar
185 g (6½ oz/1 cup) mixed dried fruit
1 tablespoon milk, extra, to glaze
2 tablespoons sugar, extra, to glaze

Glacé icing (frosting)
60 g (2¼ oz) icing (confectioners') sugar
1–2 tablespoons milk

1 Combine the yeast, sugar and about 1 tablespoon of the flour in a bowl. Add the milk and mix until smooth. Leave in a warm, draught-free place for 10 minutes.
2 Place the remaining flour in a large bowl and rub in 125 g (4½ oz) of the butter. Stir in the extra sugar, lemon zest and half the mixed spice. Make a well in the centre, add the yeast mixture and egg and mix. Gather together and turn out onto a floured surface.
3 Knead for 2 minutes, or until smooth, then shape into a ball. Place in a large, lightly oiled bowl, cover with plastic wrap and set aside in a warm place for 1 hour. Punch down and knead for 2 minutes.
4 Preheat the oven to 210°C (415°F/ Gas 6–7). Grease a baking tray. Beat the remaining butter with the brown sugar in a bowl until creamy. Roll the dough out to a 25 x 40 cm (10 x 16 in) rectangle. Spread the butter mixture all over the dough to within 2 cm (³/4 in) of the edge of one of the longer sides. Spread with the combined fruit and remaining spice. Roll the dough from the long side to enclose the fruit. Use a knife to cut the roll into eight slices about 5 cm (2 in) wide. Arrange the slices, close together and with the seams inwards, on the tray. Flatten slightly.
5 Set aside, covered with plastic wrap, in a warm place for 30 minutes, or until risen. Bake for 20 minutes, or until brown. When almost ready, stir the extra milk and sugar for glazing in a saucepan over low heat until the sugar dissolves and the mixture is almost boiling. Brush over the hot buns. Cool.
6 To make the icing, mix the icing sugar and milk, stir until smooth, then drizzle over the buns.

ITALIAN DRIED FRUIT BUNS

Preparation time **30 minutes** +
Total cooking time **15 minutes**
Makes 12

90 g (3¼ oz/¾ cup) raisins
3 teaspoons (9 g) instant dried yeast
80 g (2¾ oz/⅓ cup) caster (superfine) sugar
400 g (14 oz/3¼ cups) white bread (strong) flour
1 teaspoon almond extract
1 tablespoon olive oil
finely grated zest of 1 orange
40 g (1½ oz/¼ cup) mixed peel (mixed candied citrus peel)
40 g (1½ oz/¼ cup) pine nuts
1 egg, lightly beaten
115 g (4 oz/½ cup) caster (superfine) sugar, extra

1 Cover the raisins with 250 ml (9 fl oz/ 1 cup) boiling water in a bowl and set aside for 20 minutes. Drain, reserving the liquid. Put half the liquid into a bowl, add the yeast, a pinch of the sugar and 30 g (1 oz/ ¼ cup) of the flour. Stir to combine, then leave in a draught-free place for 10 minutes.
2 Sift the remaining flour, sugar and 1 teaspoon salt into the bowl of an electric mixer with a dough hook attachment and make a well in the centre. Combine the remaining raisin water with the almond essence and oil, then pour it, along with the yeast mixture, into the well. Add the raisins, orange zest, mixed peel and pine nuts. With the mixer set to the lowest speed, mix until a dough forms. Increase the speed to medium and knead the dough for 5 minutes, or until it is smooth and elastic; add a little more flour if necessary. Alternatively, mix the dough by hand using a wooden spoon, then turn out onto a floured work surface and knead for 5 minutes, or until smooth and elastic.
3 Grease a bowl with oil, then transfer the dough to the bowl, turning the dough to coat in the oil. Cover with plastic wrap and leave to rise in a draught-free place for 2 hours, or until doubled in size.
4 Knock back the dough by punching it, then turn out onto a floured work surface. Divide the dough into 12 equal portions and shape each piece into an oval. To glaze the rolls, coat in egg, then roll in the extra sugar to coat. Transfer the rolls to a greased baking tray and leave for 30–40 minutes, or until risen a little. Meanwhile, preheat the oven to 200°C (400°F/Gas 6).
5 Bake the rolls for 15 minutes, or until golden, then transfer to a wire rack to cool.

CHOCOLATE BREAD

Preparation time **30 minutes +**
Total cooking time **50 minutes**
Makes **2 loaves**

2½ teaspoons (7 g) instant dried yeast
55 g (2 oz/¼ cup) caster (superfine) sugar
90 g (3¼ oz) dark chocolate, roughly chopped
50 g (1¾ oz) unsalted butter
375 g (13 oz/3 cups) white strong flour
30 g (1 oz/¼ cup) unsweetened cocoa powder
1 egg, lightly beaten
½ teaspoon natural vanilla extract
90 g (3¼ oz/½ cup) dark chocolate chips

1 Sprinkle the yeast and a pinch of the sugar over 185 ml (6 fl oz/¾ cup) warm water in a small bowl. Stir to dissolve the sugar, then leave in a draught-free place for 10 minutes, or until the yeast is foamy.
2 Put the chocolate and butter in a heatproof bowl. Sit the bowl over a saucepan of simmering water, stirring frequently until the chocolate and butter have melted. Take care that the base of the bowl doesn't touch the water.
3 Combine the flour, cocoa powder, ¼ teaspoon salt and the remaining sugar in the bowl of an electric mixer with a dough hook attachment. Combine the egg and vanilla with the chocolate and butter, then pour the chocolate and yeast mixtures into the flour mixture. With the mixer set to the lowest speed, mix for 1–2 minutes, or until a dough forms. Increase the speed to medium and knead the dough for another 10 minutes, or until the dough is smooth and elastic.
4 Grease a large bowl with oil, then transfer the dough to the bowl, turning the dough to coat in the oil. Cover with plastic wrap and leave to rise in a draught-free place for 1½–2 hours, or until the dough has doubled in size.
5 Knock back the dough by punching it gently, then turn out onto a floured work surface. Divide the dough in half. Gently press out each half until 1 cm (½ in) thick, then scatter the chocolate chips over each. Roll up each piece of dough to form a log. Transfer to a greased baking tray. Cover with a damp cloth and leave for 1 hour, or until doubled in size. Meanwhile, preheat the oven to 180°C (350°F/Gas 4).
6 Bake for 45–50 minutes, or until the bread is light brown and sounds hollow when tapped on the base. Transfer to a wire rack to cool.

HOT CROSS BUNS

Preparation time **30 minutes** +
Total cooking time **20 minutes**
Makes **16**

1 tablespoon (12 g) instant dried yeast
80 g (2³/4 oz/¹/3 cup) caster (superfine) sugar
625 g (1 lb 6 oz) white strong flour
1¹/2 teaspoons mixed (pumpkin pie) spice
1 teaspoon ground cinnamon
1 teaspoon ground nutmeg
250 ml (9 fl oz/1 cup) warm milk
100 g (3¹/2 oz) unsalted butter, melted
2 eggs, lightly beaten
200 g (7 oz/1¹/3 cups) currants
70 g (2¹/2 oz/¹/3 cup) mixed peel

Glaze
2 tablespoons caster (superfine) sugar

Cross dough
60 g (2¹/4 oz/¹/2 cup) plain (all-purpose) flour

1 Sprinkle the yeast and a pinch of sugar over 125 ml (4 fl oz/¹/2 cup) warm water in a bowl. Stir to dissolve the sugar. Leave in a draught-free place for 10 minutes.
2 Combine the flour, spices and ¹/2 teaspoon salt in a bowl and set aside.
3 Combine the milk, butter, remaining sugar, eggs and 125 g (4¹/2 oz/1 cup) of the flour mixture in the bowl of an electric mixer with a dough hook attachment. Mix for 1 minute, or until smooth. Add the yeast mixture, currants and mixed peel and stir. Add the flour and knead for 5 minutes.
4 Transfer the dough to a bowl and coat in oil. Cover with plastic wrap. Leave to rise in a draught-free place for 1¹/2–2 hours.
5 Knock back the dough by punching it, then turn out onto a floured work surface. Divide the dough into 16 equal portions. Roll each portion into a ball, then place on baking trays, spacing the rolls about 4 cm (1¹/2 in) apart. Cover with a damp cloth and leave for 30 minutes.
6 Preheat the oven to 180°C (350°F/Gas 4). To make the glaze, combine the sugar with 2 tablespoons water in a saucepan. Bring to the boil over high heat.
7 To prepare the cross dough, put the flour in a bowl and add 60 ml (2 fl oz/¹/4 cup) water, stirring to form a dough. Roll out the dough on a floured work surface to a 2 mm (¹/16 in) thickness. Cut into 5 mm (¹/4 in) wide strips, about 12 cm (4¹/2 in) long. Brush with water and place two strips over each bun to form a cross. Bake the buns for 15–20 minutes, or until golden brown. Brush the hot buns with the glaze.

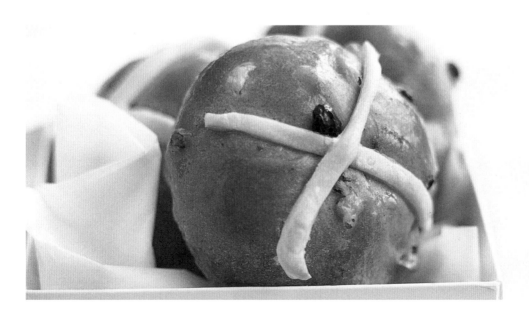

FINGER BUNS

Preparation time **45 minutes +**
Total cooking time **15 minutes**
Makes 12

500 g (1 lb 2 oz/4 cups) plain (all-purpose) flour
35 g (1¼ oz/⅓ cup) milk powder
1 tablespoon dried yeast
115 g (4 oz/½ cup) caster (superfine) sugar
60 g (2¼ oz/½ cup) sultanas (golden raisins)
60 g (2¼ oz) unsalted butter, melted
1 egg, lightly beaten
1 egg yolk, extra, to glaze

Glacé icing (frosting)
155 g (5½ oz/1¼ cups) icing (confectioners')
   sugar
20 g (¾ oz) unsalted butter, melted
pink food colouring

1 Mix 375 g (13 oz/3 cups) of the flour
with the milk powder, yeast, sugar, sultanas
and ½ teaspoon salt in a large bowl. Make
a well in the centre. Combine the butter,
egg and 250 ml (9 fl oz/1 cup) warm water
and add all at once to the flour. Stir for
2 minutes, or until well combined. Add
enough of the remaining flour to make a
soft dough.

2 Turn out onto a lightly floured surface.
Knead for 10 minutes, or until the dough is
smooth and elastic, adding more flour if
necessary. Place in a large lightly oiled
bowl and brush with oil. Cover with plastic
wrap and leave in a warm place for 1 hour,
or until well risen.

3 Lightly grease two large baking trays.
Preheat the oven to 180°C (350°F/Gas 4).
Punch down the dough and knead for 1
minute. Divide into 12 pieces. Shape each
into a 15 cm (6 in) long oval. Put on the
trays 5 cm (2 in) apart. Cover with plastic
wrap and set aside in a warm place for
20–25 minutes, or until well risen.

4 Mix the extra egg yolk with about
1½ teaspoons water and brush over the
dough. Bake for 12–15 minutes, or until
golden. Transfer to a wire rack to cool.

5 To make the icing, stir the icing sugar,
2–3 teaspoons water and the melted butter
together in a bowl until smooth. Mix
in the food colouring and spread over
the tops of the buns. Finger buns are
delicious buttered.

CREAM BUNS

Preparation time **40 minutes** +
Total cooking time **20 minutes**
Makes **12**

2 teaspoons dried yeast
2 tablespoons sugar
350 ml (12 fl oz) milk, warmed
435 g (15½ oz/3½ cups) plain (all-purpose)
  flour
60 g (2¼ oz) unsalted butter, melted
160 g (5¾ oz/½ cup) strawberry jam
310 ml (10¾ fl oz/1¼ cups) pouring (whipping)
  cream
1 tablespoon icing (confectioners') sugar
2 tablespoons icing (confectioners') sugar,
  extra, to dust

1 Put the yeast, 1 teaspoon of the sugar and the milk in a small bowl. Leave in a warm, draught-free place for 10 minutes, or until bubbles appear on the surface. The mixture should be frothy and slightly increased in volume.

2 Sift the flour into a large bowl, stir in ½ teaspoon salt and the remaining sugar. Make a well in the centre and add the milk mixture and butter and mix to a dough, first with a wooden spoon, then with your hands. Turn onto a lightly floured surface and knead for 10 minutes, or until smooth and elastic. Place in a lightly oiled bowl, cover with plastic wrap, and leave in a warm place for 1 hour, or until well risen.

3 Punch down the dough and turn onto a lightly floured surface, then knead for 2 minutes or until smooth. Divide into 12 pieces. Knead one portion at a time for 30 seconds on a lightly floured surface and then shape into a ball.

4 Preheat the oven to 210°C (415°F/ Gas 6–7). Lightly grease two baking trays, dust lightly with flour and shake off any excess. Place balls of dough, evenly spaced, on the trays. Set aside, covered with plastic wrap, in a warm place for 15 minutes, or until well risen.

5 Bake for 20 minutes or until well browned and cooked. Set aside for 5 minutes before transferring to a wire rack to cool completely. Using a serrated knife, make a slanted cut into the centre of each bun, to a depth of 5 cm (2 in), from the top towards the base.

6 Spread jam over the cut base of each bun. Using electric beaters, beat the cream and icing sugar in a small bowl until firm peaks form. Spoon into a piping (icing) bag and pipe the whipped cream into the buns. Dust the tops with the extra icing sugar.

STOLLEN

Preparation time **30 minutes +**
Total cooking time **40 minutes**
Makes **1**

80 ml (2³/4 fl oz/¹/3 cup) lukewarm milk
2 teaspoons sugar
7 g (¹/4 oz) dried yeast
125 g (4¹/2 oz) butter, softened
90 g (3 oz/¹/3 cup) caster (superfine) sugar
1 egg
2 teaspoons natural vanilla extract
¹/2 teaspoon ground cinnamon
375 g (12 oz/3 cups) white flour
80 g (2³/4 oz/¹/2 cup) raisins
75 g (2¹/2 oz/¹/2 cup) currants
95 g (3 oz/¹/2 cup) mixed peel
60 g (2 oz/¹/2 cup) slivered almonds
30 g (1 oz) butter, melted
icing sugar, for dusting

1 Put the milk, sugar and yeast with 80 ml (2³/4 fl oz/¹/3 cup) warm water in a small bowl and mix well. Leave in a warm, draught-free place for 10 minutes, or until bubbles appear on the surface. The mixture should be frothy and slightly increased in volume. If your yeast doesn't foam it is dead, so you will have to discard it and start again.
2 Beat the butter and sugar with electric beaters until light and creamy, then beat in the egg and vanilla. Add the yeast mixture, cinnamon and almost all the flour and mix to a soft dough, adding more flour if necessary.
3 Turn out onto a lightly floured surface and knead for 10 minutes, or until the dough is smooth and elastic. Place in a lightly oiled bowl, cover with plastic wrap or a damp tea towel and leave in a warm, draught-free place for 1 hour 45 minutes or until doubled in volume.
4 Knock back the dough by punching it to expel the air. Press it out to a thickness of about 1.5 cm (⁵/8 in). Sprinkle the fruit and nuts over the dough, then gather up and knead for a few minutes to mix the fruit and nuts evenly through the dough.
5 Shape the dough into an oval about 18 cm (7 in) wide and 30 cm (12 in) long. Fold in half lengthways, then press down to flatten slightly, with the fold slightly off centre on top of the loaf. Place on the tray, cover with plastic wrap and leave in a warm place for 1 hour, or until doubled in size. Preheat the oven to 180°C (350°F/Gas 4). Lightly grease a baking tray.
6 Bake the dough for 40 minutes, or until golden. As soon as it comes out of the oven, brush with the melted butter, allowing each brushing to be absorbed until you have used all the butter. Cool on a wire rack. Dust with icing sugar.

CHRISTOPSOMO

Preparation time 30 minutes +
Total cooking time 45 minutes
Makes 1

1 tablespoon sesame seeds
7 g (¼ oz) sachet dry yeast
2 teaspoons sugar
310 g (11 oz/2½ cups) plain (all-purpose) flour
2 teaspoons whole aniseeds
2 tablespoons unsalted butter, melted
125 ml (4 fl oz/½ cup) milk, warmed
1 tablespoon ouzo
1 egg, lightly beaten
2 tablespoons chopped walnuts
1 tablespoon whole blanched almonds,
    chopped
4 dried figs, chopped
1 teaspoon sesame seeds, extra
2 tablespoons honey

1 Grease a 20 cm (8 in) round cake tin lightly with oil. Sprinkle the sesame seeds over the base and side of the tin.
2 Place the yeast, sugar and 90 ml (3 fl oz) warm water in a bowl and leave in a warm place until foamy.
3 Sift the flour into a bowl, add the aniseeds and stir. Make a well in the centre and add the yeast mixture and combined butter, milk and ouzo. Mix together to form a soft dough, then turn out onto a floured surface and knead for 10 minutes.
4 Place the dough in a greased bowl. Cover and leave in a warm place for 60 minutes, or until doubled. Turn out the dough onto a floured surface and knead until smooth. Break off a small portion of dough about the size of a lime and reserve. This portion will be used for decorating the bread.
5 Shape the larger piece of dough into a round to fit in the cake tin. Brush lightly all over with some of the beaten egg. Roll the reserved ball of dough into two thin sausage shapes and form an equal-armed cross on the top of the dough, brushing with a little more beaten egg. Arrange the nuts and figs on top of the dough and sprinkle with extra sesame seeds. Cover and leave in a warm place for 45 minutes, or until the dough has doubled in size.
6 Preheat the oven to 190°C (375°F/Gas 5). Bake the bread for 45 minutes, or until it is golden brown and sounds hollow when tapped on the base. Cover loosely with foil if the top is over-browning. Turn onto a wire cake rack and brush with honey while still hot.

SCONE SECRETS

Scones are so easy—they can be mixed and baked in no time at all. For perfect scones, handle them quickly and lightly and cook in a hot oven.

LIGHT AND EASY

All scones are made according to the same principles: add the wet ingredients to the dry and mix the dough as briefly and lightly as possible. Because the moisture content of flour varies, you may not need all the liquid stated in your recipe. The amount of liquid the flour absorbs can also change according to the room temperature and even the altitude. Although our recipe uses self-raising flour, some people prefer to use plain flour and add more raising agents such as baking powder. Salt is added to enhance the flavour of all scones, even sweet ones, and the taste is not noticeable.

MAKING PERFECT SCONES

Follow these simple directions to achieve a good batch of high, light and golden scones. Remember that unlike bread, which requires vigorous kneading, scone dough just needs quick light handling.

To make 10–12 scones, you will need 310 g (11 oz/2 1/2 cups) self-raising flour, 1 teaspoon baking powder, a pinch of salt, 40 g (1 1/2 oz) chilled unsalted butter, cut into small cubes, and 250 ml (9 fl oz/1 cup) milk. Assemble all the ingredients as well as a large bowl, a flat-bladed metal spatula or knife, a round scone or biscuit cutter, a pastry brush and a baking tray. You will also need a cloth to wrap the scones.

Before you begin mixing, preheat the oven to 220°C (425°F/Gas 7) and lightly grease the baking tray or line it with baking paper. Sift the flour, baking powder and salt into a bowl. Sifting aerates the dry ingredients and helps achieve lighter scones. Many bakers sift the flour twice. Rub in the butter briefly with your fingertips until the mixture is crumbly and resembles fine breadcrumbs. Mixing in 1 tablespoon of sugar at this stage will lessen any floury taste. Make a well in the centre.

Pour in almost all the milk and mix with a flat-bladed knife, using a cutting action, until the dough comes together in clumps. Rotate the bowl as you work. Use the remaining milk if the mixture seems dry. Handle the mixture with care and a light hand. If you are heavy-handed and mix too much, your scones will be tough. The dough should feel slightly wet and sticky.

With floured hands, gently gather the dough together, lift onto a lightly floured surface and pat into a smooth ball. Do not knead. Pat or lightly roll the dough out to 2 cm (3/4 in) thick. Using a floured 6 cm (2 1/2 in) cutter, cut into rounds. Don't pat out too thinly or the scones will not be a good height. Gather the scraps together and, without handling too much, press out as before and cut out more rounds. Place close together on the baking tray and lightly brush the tops with milk. Bake in the top half of the oven for 12–15 minutes, or until risen and golden. It is important to cook scones at a high temperature, otherwise the raising agents will not work. If you aren't sure they are cooked, break one open. If still doughy in the centre, cook for a few more minutes. For soft scones, wrap them in a dry tea towel while hot. For scones with a crisp top, transfer to a wire rack to cool slightly before wrapping. Serve warm, or at room temperature, with butter or jam and whipped or clotted cream. As scones contain little fat, they dry out quickly so are best eaten soon after baking. They freeze successfully.

FRUIT SCONES

To make fruit scones, add 75 g (2 1/2 oz/ 1/2 cup) currants or 95 g (3 oz) chopped pitted dates to the mixture after you've rubbed in the butter. Mix well to distribute the fruit, then proceed with the recipe.

WHAT WENT WRONG?

SCONES

Perfect The scone is evenly risen, has a soft crust and soft inside texture and is light golden.

Overcooked The scone has a dark crust and a dry texture. Either the cooking time was too long or the oven temperature was too hot.

Poorly risen If the scone texture feels heavy and dense, the dough may have been either too dry or too wet, or the dough may have been mixed too much.

Undercooked The scone is pale, sticky in the centre and has a dense texture. The cooking time was too short or the oven temperature too low.

More about scones

Originating in Scotland, the scone is a flat cake, soft and light on the inside and golden and crisp on the outside. Scones are at their best when served fresh and warm from the oven, most famously with butter or jam and cream. Originally scones were made from oat flour, oatmeal or barley meal, but today the basic scone is usually made with flour, a raising agent and an acid ingredient such as soured milk or buttermilk. Sweet additions to a scone dough can include sugar, spices and dried fruits such as chopped pitted dates, raisins and mixed peel. Savoury flavours can include a variety of herbs, ham, pumpkin or cheese. Scone doughs can be cut into individual rounds or into one large flat dough and marked into wedges before baking.

Devonshire Tea, known all over the world, consists of scones with jam and cream served with a pot of tea. The name originally came from the thick rich cream of Devon, called clotted cream.

CURRANT CREAM SCONES

Preparation time **20 minutes**
Total cooking time **12 minutes**
Makes **12**

375 g (13 oz/3 cups) plain (all-purpose) flour
1½ teaspoons bicarbonate of soda
   (baking soda)
3 teaspoons cream of tartar
1 teaspoon mixed (pumpkin pie) spice
2 teaspoons caster (superfine) sugar,
   plus extra for sprinkling
50 g (1¾ oz) unsalted butter, chilled and diced
150 ml (5 fl oz) pouring cream
150 ml (5 fl oz) milk, plus extra for brushing
125 g (4½ oz/¾ cup) currants
jam and thick (double/heavy) cream, to serve

1 Preheat the oven to 220°C (425°F/Gas 7). Grease a baking tray or line the tray with baking paper.
2 Sift the flour, bicarbonate of soda, cream of tartar, mixed spice and sugar into a large bowl. Using your fingertips, rub in the butter until the mixture resembles breadcrumbs. Add the cream, milk and currants and mix with a flat-bladed knife to form a soft dough, adding a little extra flour if the mixture is too sticky.
3 Using floured hands, gently gather the dough together and lift out onto a lightly floured work surface. Pat into a smooth ball, then press out to about a 2 cm (³/4 in) thickness.
4 Using a 6 cm (2¹/2 in) pastry cutter, cut the dough into rounds, or use a knife dipped in flour to cut 4 cm (1¹/2 in) squares.
5 Place the scones on the baking tray, brush the tops lightly with milk and sprinkle with the extra sugar. Bake for 10–12 minutes, or until golden. Transfer to a wire rack lined with a tea towel (dish towel). Serve the scones warm with marmalade or jam and thick cream.
Tip When making scones, handle the mixture with care. Don't be too heavy-handed when mixing the dough or the scones will be tough.

SULTANA SCONES

Preparation time **10 minutes**
Total cooking time **15 minutes**
Makes **12**

250 g (9 oz/2 cups) self-raising flour
1 teaspoon baking powder
30 g (1 oz) unsalted butter, chilled and cubed
60 g (2¼ oz/½ cup) sultanas (golden raisins)
250 ml (9 fl oz/1 cup) milk
milk, extra, to glaze

1 Preheat the oven to 220°C (425°F/Gas 7). Lightly grease a baking tray or line with baking paper. Sift the flour, baking powder and a pinch of salt into a bowl. Using your fingertips, rub in the butter until it resembles fine breadcrumbs. Stir in the sultanas. Make a well in the centre.

2 Add almost all the milk and mix with a flat-bladed knife, using a cutting action, until the dough comes together in clumps. Use the remaining milk if necessary. With floured hands, gently gather the dough together, lift out onto a lightly floured surface and pat into a smooth ball. Do not knead or the scones will be tough.

3 Pat the dough out to 2 cm (³/4 in) thick. Using a floured 5 cm (2 in) cutter, cut into rounds. Gather the trimmings and without over-handling, press out as before and cut more rounds. Place close together on the tray and brush with the extra milk. Bake for 12–15 minutes, or until risen and golden brown. Serve warm or at room temperature.

CHEESE SCONES

Preparation time **15 minutes**
Total cooking time **15 minutes**
Makes 12

250 g (9 oz/2 cups) self-raising flour
1 teaspoon baking powder
½ teaspoon dry mustard
30 g (1 oz) butter, chilled and cubed
25 g (1 oz/¼ cup) freshly grated
   parmesan cheese
90 g (3¼ oz/¾ cup) finely grated cheddar
   cheese
250 ml (9 fl oz/1 cup) milk

1 Preheat the oven to 220°C (425°F/Gas 7). Lightly grease a baking tray or line with baking paper.
2 Sift the flour, baking powder, mustard and a pinch of salt into a bowl. Using your fingertips, rub in the butter until the mixture resembles fine breadcrumbs. Stir in the parmesan and 60 g (2¼ oz/½ cup) of the cheddar cheese, making sure they don't clump together. Make a well in the centre.
3 Add almost all the milk and mix with a flat-bladed knife, using a cutting action, until the dough comes together in clumps. Use the remaining milk if necessary.
4 With floured hands, gently gather the dough together, lift out onto a lightly floured surface and pat into a smooth ball. Do not knead or the scones will be tough.
5 Pat the dough out to 2 cm (¾ in) thick. Using a floured 5 cm (2 in) biscuit (cookie) cutter, cut into rounds. Gather the trimmings and, without over-handling, press out as before and cut more rounds.
6 Place the rounds close together on the tray and sprinkle with the remaining cheese. Bake for 12–15 minutes, or until risen and golden brown. Serve warm or at room temperature.

PUMPKIN AND SAGE SCONES

Preparation time **10 minutes**

Total cooking time **20 minutes**

Makes **8**

250 g (9 oz/2 cups) self-raising flour

250 g (9 oz/1 cup) cooked and puréed
   pumpkin (winter squash)

20 g ($^3/_4$ oz) butter

1 tablespoon chopped sage

1–2 tablespoons milk

1 Preheat the oven to 180°C (350°F/Gas 4).

Lightly grease a baking tray or line with baking paper. Sift the self-raising flour into a bowl with a pinch of salt. Using your fingertips, rub the pumpkin and butter into the flour and then add the sage.

2 Bring the mixture together with a little milk and turn it out onto the tray. Shape the mixture into a round and roll it out to about 3 cm (1 $^1/_4$ in) thick.

3 Gently mark or cut the scone into eight segments and bake for 15–20 minutes, or until lightly browned and cooked through. Serve warm.

INDEX

C

Published in 2010 by Murdoch Books Pty Limited.

Murdoch Books Australia
Pier 8/9, 23 Hickson Road, Millers Point NSW 2000
Phone: +61 (0)2 8220 2000 Fax: +61 (0)2 8220 2558
www.murdochbooks.com.au

Murdoch Books UK Limited
Erico House, 6th Floor North, 93–99 Upper Richmond Road
Putney, London SW15 2TG
Phone: + 44 (0) 20 8785 5995 Fax: + 44 (0) 20 8785 5985
www.murdochbooks.co.uk

Chief Executive: Juliet Rogers

Publisher: Lynn Lewis
Senior Designer: Heather Menzies
Designer: Michelle Cutler
Cover Designer: Heather Menzies
Editorial Coordinator: Liz Malcolm
Production: Alexandra Gonzalez

National Library of Australia Cataloguing-in-Publication Data:
Title: Commonsense Baking.
ISBN: 978-1-74196-942-9 (pbk.)
Series: Commonsense guide. Notes: Includes index.
Subjects: Baking. Confectionery. Cooking.
641.815

Printed by 1010 Printing International Limited. PRINTED IN CHINA.

CONVERSION GUIDE: You may find cooking times vary depending on the oven you are using. For
fan-forced ovens, as a general rule, set the oven temperature to 20°C (35°F) lower than indicated in the
recipe. We have used 20 ml (4 teaspoon) tablespoon measures. If you are using a 15 ml (3 teaspoon)
tablespoon, for most recipes the difference will not be noticeable. However, for recipes using baking
powder, gelatine, bicarbonate of soda (baking soda), small amounts of flour and cornflour (cornstarch),
add an extra teaspoon for each tablespoon specified.